Implementing Microsoft Dynamics 365 for Finance and Operations Apps
Second Edition

Learn best practices, architecture, tools, techniques, and more

JJ Yadav
Sandeep Shukla
Rahul Mohta
Yogesh Kasat

BIRMINGHAM - MUMBAI

Implementing Microsoft Dynamics 365 for Finance and Operations Apps
Second Edition

Commissioning Editor: Kunal Chaudhari
Acquisition Editor: Denim Pinto
Content Development Editor: Digvijay Bagul
Technical Editor: Gaurav Gala
Copy Editor: Safis Editing
Senior Editor: Rohit Singh
Project Coordinator: Francy Puthiry
Proofreader: Safis Editing
Indexer: Pratik Shirodkar
Production Coordinator: Alishon Mendonca

First published: September 2017
Second edition: March 2020

Production reference: 1060320

Published by Packt Publishing Ltd.
Livery Place
35 Livery Street
Birmingham
B3 2PB, UK.

ISBN 978-1-78995-084-7

www.packtpub.com

This book is my mother's blessings.

- Rahul Mohta

I dedicate this book to my beautiful wife, Khushboo, my son, Hrehaan, and daughter, Mira.

- JJ Yadav

To my wife, Ruchi, and my children, Ishanvi and Itash, without whom this wouldn't have been possible.

- Sandeep Shukla

This book is dedicated to my mom, my loving wife, Ashwini, and my wonderful kids, Neel and Brinda.

- Yogesh Kasat

Packt.com

Subscribe to our online digital library for full access to over 7,000 books and videos, as well as industry leading tools to help you plan your personal development and advance your career. For more information, please visit our website.

Why subscribe?

- Spend less time learning and more time coding with practical eBooks and Videos from over 4,000 industry professionals

- Improve your learning with Skill Plans built especially for you

- Get a free eBook or video every month

- Fully searchable for easy access to vital information

- Copy and paste, print, and bookmark content

Did you know that Packt offers eBook versions of every book published, with PDF and ePub files available? You can upgrade to the eBook version at www.packt.com and as a print book customer, you are entitled to a discount on the eBook copy. Get in touch with us at customercare@packtpub.com for more details.

At www.packt.com, you can also read a collection of free technical articles, sign up for a range of free newsletters, and receive exclusive discounts and offers on Packt books and eBooks.

Contributors

About the authors

JJ Yadav has 16 years of consulting experience working on ERP systems and implementations, and has been working since Axapta 3.0. He has worked with Microsoft Dynamics 365 for Finance and Operations in multiple roles as a solutions architect, project manager, technical lead, and developer. JJ is currently in the Microsoft FastTrack elite team, helping customers in their Dynamics 365 journey and making them successful.

I would like to thank my family, my parents, colleagues, and friends who continuously motivated and supported me on my journey. I would like to thank my co-authors and the Packt Publishing team for making this book possible.

Sandeep Shukla is a founding partner of Real Dynamics and has over 16 years of consulting experience, working on ERP systems and implementations. He has worked on many successful Microsoft Dynamics AX/365 implementations for multiple customers and has experience of working in multiple domains, including multi-channel retail, supply chains, distribution, manufacturing, and warehousing. He has played key roles including project manager, solution/technical architect, technical lead, and developer, and has great experience in requirement gathering, integration to third-party applications, creating detailed functional and technical design documents, data migration, development, go-live planning/execution, post go-live support, and end user training.

It has been a privilege and a rewarding experience working on this book. I would like to thank my dear family, colleagues, and friends for motivating me to finish this book. I would like to thank my co-authors (Rahul, JJ, and Yogesh) and the Packt Publishing team for giving me the opportunity to join them to write this book.

Rahul Mohta is a founding partner of Real Dynamics and has more than 16 years of expertise in ERP consulting, implementation, and pre-sales, focusing on Microsoft Dynamics 365 for Finance and Operations. Rahul has a diverse and rich experience working with customers and partners globally, enabling them to realize the full value of their future Dynamics platform. As a trusted advisor, he works in different roles across functional and technical domains.

Rahul's experience spans multiple regions and multiple domains (such as financials, supply chains, distribution, manufacturing, warehousing, retail, professional services, and more). He is also a worldwide trainer for Microsoft, imparting training to partners.

I would like to thank Yogesh for inspiring me to write this book, and my co-authors (JJ, Sandeep, and Yogesh), my mentors, and Packt. I would also like to thank Mehul, Krutika, Mahika, Mannan, Saket, Jason, Laxmi; my colleagues, customers, friends, as well as critics who supported me in making this book a reality.

Yogesh Kasat is a founding partner of Real Dynamics and has led more than 20 full-cycle ERP implementations and upgrade projects, working closely with several CFOs to design solutions for better visibility into inventory levels, costs, and aging, as well as improving collection processes and reducing open accounts receivables. His experience with company splits and mergers enables him to design straightforward solutions with better support for shared services, budget planning, and financial reporting. Yogesh is also a Microsoft-recognized Fasttrack Solutions Architect.

I would like to thank my co-authors (Rahul, JJ, and Sandeep), my mentors, and Packt. I would also like to thank our customers, colleagues, friends, and family who supported me in making this book a reality. Special thanks to James Phillips, Muhammad Alam, and Swamy Narayana of Microsoft for great leadership and commitment to Dynamics 365 customers.

About the reviewer

Deepak Agarwal is a **Microsoft Certified Solution Expert** (**MCSE**) and has been working professionally on Dynamics AX since 2011. He has had a wide range of development, consulting, and leading roles, while always maintaining a significant role as a business application developer.

He has been awarded as a **Microsoft's Most Valuable Professional** (**MVP**) on business solutions six times in a row, and he has held this title since 2013.

> *I would like to thank the authors and the Packt team for their support and effort during the project.*

> *I would like to dedicate this work to my lovely daughter, Maahi Agarwal, with loads of love.*

Packt is searching for authors like you

If you're interested in becoming an author for Packt, please visit `authors.packtpub.com` and apply today. We have worked with thousands of developers and tech professionals, just like you, to help them share their insight with the global tech community. You can make a general application, apply for a specific hot topic that we are recruiting an author for, or submit your own idea.

Table of Contents

Preface

Microsoft Dynamics 365 is a cloud-based business application platform consisting of purpose-built intelligent applications that unifies ERP and **Customer Relationship Management (CRM)**. Part of Dynamics 365, Finance and Operations is a modern cloud-based ERP platform that helps you manage financials, manufacturing, and supply chain operations in a medium to large organization.

This book is written from the perspective of the ERP implementation team, encompassing everything required to achieve a successful implementation of Finance and Operations apps. You will deep dive into various aspects of Finance and Operations implementation and learn about best practices, architecture, tools, life cycle management, deployment, support, and maintenance.

This second edition is updated with the latest developments in Finance and Operations applications and technology. The book starts with an overview of Finance and Operations applications, life cycle services, implementation methodologies, application architecture, and deployment choices.

As you progress, you'll learn about requirement and process analysis, integration planning techniques, configuration and data management, as well as custom solution design and customization. This book demonstrates analytics and financial reporting capabilities and integration with Power BI and Azure Data Lake.

Toward the end of this journey, you'll understand the importance of testing and training and go-live planning. Managing predictable and continuous updates through One Version is the final takeaway from this book.

Who this book is for

This book is for consultants, technical managers, project managers, or solution architects who are looking to implement Microsoft Dynamics Finance and Operations Apps in their business. A basic understanding of the ERP implementation process and software life cycle is expected.

What this book covers

Chapter 1, *Introduction to Dynamics 365 Finance and Operations*, introduces you to Microsoft Dynamics 365 and shares details of various applications. This chapter also describes Finance and Operations basics, core capabilities, deployment options. It describes using AppSource which is one of Microsoft portals to find ISV independent software vendor solutions as well list of partners who could help customers implement Dynamics 365. It also describes how to sign up for a free trial and the ERP implementation team structure.

Chapter 2, *Methodology and Initiation*, shares information on various implementation methodologies, such as CRP, Agile, and Waterfall for selection, implementation, and maintenance of Finance and Operations.

Chapter 3, *Life Cycle Services (LCS) and Tools*, introduces **Life Cycle Services** (**LCS**) and tools and how they are used to manage your application life cycle from project on-boarding to the implementation and operation of the project.

Chapter 4, *Architecture, Deployment, and Environments*, explains the Finance and Operations application components and architecture, as well as deployment choices such as cloud and on-premises deployment. It also covers cloud deployment and various aspects of environment planning.

Chapter 5, *Requirements and Process Analysis*, explains the need for capturing requirements well in **SMART** (short for **Specific, Measurable, Achievable, Realistic, Time-bound**) format. This chapter also covers requirements, processes, solution blueprints, and emphasizing the needs of business process and various other aspects of managing the scope of the project.

Chapter 6, *Configuration and Data Management*, helps you explore configuration management and data migration, data management tools, data management frameworks, data management scenarios, and best practices in managing configurations and data migration.

Chapter 7, *Solution Planning and Design*, helps you plan and execute functional design and technical design. It also contains tips and tricks with real-life examples of design patterns—both good and bad—to support best practices.

Chapter 8, *Integration Technologies, Planning, and Design*, covers integration planning and the integration tools and frameworks available in Finance and Operations, as well as best practices for integration design.

Chapter 9, *Customization and Extension*, helps you explore the things that you need to know before starting development, during development, and after development, such as the development environment, tools, technical concepts, build and versioning strategies, the development process, frameworks, best practices, and automated build and deployment processes.

Chapter 10, *Analytics, Business Intelligence, and Reporting*, covers the BI and reporting scenarios and tools. The chapter also covers how to use Azure Data Lake and Azure Synapse Analytics to define the analytics data strategy and integrations. It also explains the best practices in analytics, business intelligence, and reporting.

Chapter 11, *Testing and Training*, helps you understand the new features and techniques of testing. It also takes you through different testing scenarios and shows the readers some of the best practices in testing and training.

Chapter 12, *Managing Go-Live and Post Go-Live*, helps you to plan for a successful go-live and explains how you can support a production environment.

Chapter 13, *One Version Service Updates*, explores Finance and Operations One Version through topics such as update availability, update early adoption, service updates, quality update, and feature management.

To get the most out of this book

To get the most out of this book, you need to have a basic understanding of the ERP implementation process, IT project management, and software development life cycle. In addition, you should have access to the LCS portal and the development environment of Finance and Operations.

Readers who are part of ongoing implementation projects and have access to organization LCS projects and development or sandbox environments will get the most out of this book.

Readers who are not part of ongoing implementation projects can sign up for the Dynamics 365 Trial edition and deploy a demo development environment on the Azure portal via LCS. To try out the code discussed in the book, you must also have Visual Studio Professional or Enterprise license.

Software/Subscriptions required	URLs
Sign up to the Dynamics 365 Trial	`https://trials.dynamics.com`
Access to LCS	`https://lcs.dynamics.com/v2`
Azure portal subscription	`https://portal.azure.com/`

Visual Studio Professional or Enterprise Edition	https://visualstudio.microsoft.com/vs/
Office 365 trial	https://products.office.com/en-us/compare-all-microsoft-office-products?activetab=tab:primaryr2

If you are using the digital version of this book, we advise you to type the code yourself or access the code via the GitHub repository (the link is in the next section). Doing this will help you avoid any potential errors related to copy/pasting of code.

Disclaimer

All views, thoughts, and opinions expressed in this book belong solely to the author, and not necessarily to the author's employer, organization, committee, or other group or individual.

Download the color images

We also provide a PDF file that has color images of the screenshots/diagrams used in this book. You can download it here: https://static.packt-cdn.com/downloads/9781789950847_ColorImages.pdf.

Conventions used

There are a number of text conventions used throughout this book.

Bold: Indicates a new term, an important word, or words that you see onscreen. For example, words in menus or dialog boxes appear in the text like this. Here is an example: "**Feature testing,** also known as function testing, is the *standalone testing* of individual features performed by the QA resources or business analysts."

Warnings or important notes appear like this.

Tips and tricks appear like this.

Get in touch

Feedback from our readers is always welcome.

General feedback: If you have questions about any aspect of this book, mention the book title in the subject of your message and email us at customercare@packtpub.com.

Errata: Although we have taken every care to ensure the accuracy of our content, mistakes do happen. If you have found a mistake in this book, we would be grateful if you would report this to us. Please visit www.packtpub.com/support/errata, selecting your book, clicking on the Errata Submission Form link, and entering the details.

Piracy: If you come across any illegal copies of our works in any form on the Internet, we would be grateful if you would provide us with the location address or website name. Please contact us at copyright@packt.com with a link to the material.

If you are interested in becoming an author: If there is a topic that you have expertise in and you are interested in either writing or contributing to a book, please visit authors.packtpub.com.

Reviews

Please leave a review. Once you have read and used this book, why not leave a review on the site that you purchased it from? Potential readers can then see and use your unbiased opinion to make purchase decisions, we at Packt can understand what you think about our products, and our authors can see your feedback on their book. Thank you!

For more information about Packt, please visit packt.com.

Introduction to Dynamics 365 Finance and Operations

Every organization needs a system of records to manage data, control it, and use it for their growth. This often leads to embracing business applications for managing their resources well and to keep improving the business process. With cloud computing providing so many benefits, such as flexibility, efficiency, security, and more uptime, organizations are now looking to go for digital transformation to move from on-premises business applications to cloud-enabled business applications.

Dynamics 365 is a cloud service offering from Microsoft, combining several business needs into a single, scalable, and agile platform, allowing organizations to bring in this much-needed digital transformation.

This chapter will introduce you to Microsoft Dynamics 365 and share the details of various apps, solution elements, buying choices, and complementary tools. We hope you will get an insight into the various tools, offerings, and options provided by Microsoft in Dynamics 365. This may help you in your business transformation initiatives and solution and platform evaluation, spanning **customer relationship management (CRM)**, **enterprise resource planning (ERP)**, and **business intelligence (BI)**.

Let's explore the topics we are going to cover in this chapter:

- What is Microsoft Dynamics 365?
- Microsoft Dynamics 365 apps
- Exploring Power Platform
- Complementing/supporting tools with Microsoft Dynamics 365
- Dynamics 365 for Finance and Operations apps
- App source

Introducing Microsoft Dynamics 365

In the business application world, business leaders are always looking for a better business process automation to achieve digital transformation. The biggest challenge to achieve this is having various applications trying to work together to solve business process automation. Microsoft, for the past several years, has been focused on solving this problem by building intelligent applications infused with AI and analytics capabilities; these applications are built for a very specific purpose but, at the same time, can talk to each other and exchange data seamlessly.

Microsoft Dynamics 365 is the next generation of intelligent business applications in the cloud offered by Microsoft. It enables end-to-end business processes driven by unified navigation, has a core user experience in how these applications look and feel, and allows seamless integration with each other. Microsoft Dynamics 365 further extends Microsoft's commitment to being a cloud-committed company bringing in world-class business apps together in their overall cloud offering. These Dynamics 365 applications can be independently deployed. A customer can start with what they need, and as the business demands, they can adopt additional applications. Since its inception, Microsoft is making continuous efforts to make it better each day.

Microsoft Dynamics 365 has gained a lot of traction since its inception, and more and more companies are now adapting the applications from the Microsoft Dynamics 365 suite. Let's now explore the key deciding factors for adopting Microsoft Dynamics 365 in your organization's digital transformation journey, with the help of its usage benefits and salient features.

Microsoft Dynamics 365 salient features

What makes Microsoft Dynamics 365 stand apart from its competition and an enabler for organizations lies in its features, capabilities, and offerings.

Here's a quick glance at the salient features of Dynamics 365:

- A cloud-driven, browser-based application
- Seamlessly integrated with Office 365, all out of the box, to increase productivity and stand apart from others
- Built-in intelligence for predictive analysis and decision-making support
- Quick-to-adapt and easy-to-use business applications

- Releveled and revolutionized the traditional approach toward business solutions
- Easy to adopt new updates released by Dynamics 365 team

Dynamics 365 is the next generation of intelligent business applications in the cloud (public and private) as well as on-premises, expected to transform how businesses use technological solutions to achieve their goals.

Understanding Microsoft Dynamics 365 apps

The Microsoft Dynamics 365 approach to business applications unifies Microsoft's current CRM and ERP cloud solutions into one cloud service with new purpose-built business applications that work together seamlessly to help you to manage specific business functions.

Let's now get an insight at a high level into the various apps available in the Dynamics 365 family. Let's look at some of these apps, along with Dynamics 365 for Finance and Operations.

Dynamics 365 Customer Service

Dynamics 365 Customer Service is an omnichannel solution to unify the way customers and prospects experience your business. There are several dashboards in Dynamics 365 for customer service as well. The following screenshot depicts one of the dashboards:

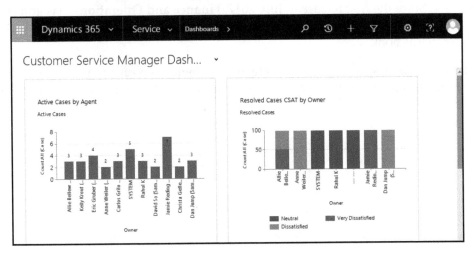

Users can create consistency and loyalty at all touchpoints across various experience channels such as self-service, peer-to-peer service, and assisted service. It also proactively addresses issues by detecting the customers' intent and social sentiment.

 Use the following link to learn more about Dynamics 365 Customer Service: `https://dynamics.microsoft.com/en-us/customer-service/overview/`.

Expect an increase in **CSAT** (short for **Customer Satisfaction**) and retention by providing personalized and consistent engagements and proactive addressing of service issues.

Dynamics 365 for Finance and Operations apps

Microsoft Dynamics 365 for Finance and Operations is now available as two separate products as Dynamics 365 Finance and Dynamics 365 **Supply Chain Management** (**SCM**) for licensing purposes. These two products are collectively called Dynamics 365 for Finance and Operations apps. If the customer buys licensing for both Finance and SCM, then they will get all of the features that were previously available in Dynamics 365 for Finance and Operations.

For the purposes of this book, we will call the product Microsoft Dynamics 365 for Finance and Operations.

Microsoft has done a complete re-architected Dynamics AX and introduced cloud-based Dynamics 365 for Finance and Operations to the world. Microsoft offers users an interface that is so natural to use that they just use it with an accelerated adoption, thereby raising productivity. Since the first release in July 2017, **Finance and Operations**, has gone through various updates, and introduced various new features and processes, which we will learn about later in this book.

The fact that it works seamlessly anywhere on any device and on any platform is among the key features that make Dynamics 365 for Finance and Operations very attractive to implement.

Dynamics 365 for Finance and Operations offers a wide variety of role-specific dashboards and workspaces to make work life easier for folks using it day in and day out. The following screenshot shows a dashboard that comprises several workspaces in Dynamics 365 for Finance and Operations:

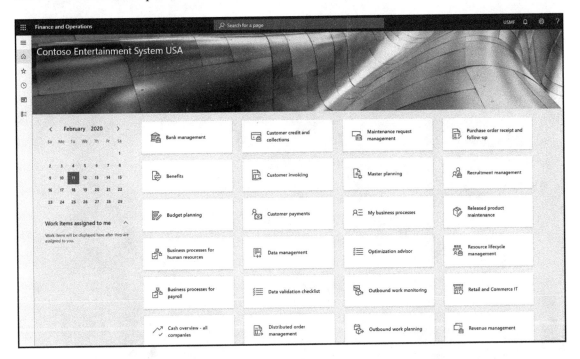

Dynamics 365 for Finance and Operations is a very flexible application, and it can be used for many scenarios as needed by any organization. Some examples are the following:

- **Enterprise**: An end-to-end solution that looks after the financials and core operations for a company
- **2-Tier Subsidiary**: Solution that handles the financials and operations for subsidiaries or business units and integrates with the headquarters ERP
- **Operational workloads**: Manages specific business functions/workloads of business and integrates with corporate systems

It would be very nice to get a glimpse of all workloads available in Dynamics 365 for Finance and Operations, suggesting their core functionality. The following diagram shows a full-suite visual for various workloads:

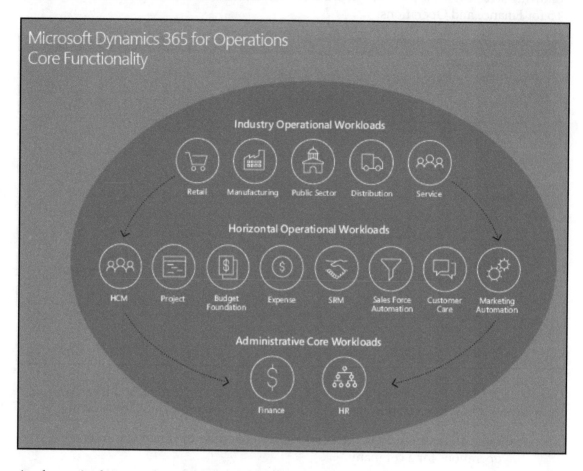

As shown in the preceding diagram, there are several modules/capability areas spanning different workloads, namely, vertical, horizontal/operational, and administrative.

We will be getting into the details of Dynamics 365 for Finance and Operations throughout this book; however, there are a few key features that are in line with other D365 business apps, as follows:

- Full-suite business management solution
- Multiple industry capabilities, namely, retail, distribution, manufacturing, public sector, and service industries; all built in a single solution
- Availability in 18 countries/markets with local compliance met and local language support
- Choice of deployment—in the cloud or on-premises
- Elevate business financial performance
- Run smarter with connected operations
- Automate and streamline supply chain process
- Innovate with a modern and adaptable platform
- Simplify configuration of your regulatory services

Several new navigation concepts are introduced in Dynamics 365 for Finance and Operations, and the following are the key ones:

- **Dashboard**: The dashboard is a new concept and is the first page that users see when they access the client. The dashboard contains tiles that show important details from the system.
- **Navigation pane**: The navigation pane provides access to workspaces, main menu elements, recently opened forms, and user-defined favorites.
- **Workspaces**: Workspaces are activity-oriented pages that are designed to increase a user's productivity by providing information that answers the targeted user's most pressing activity-related questions and allows the user to initiate their more frequent tasks.
- **Tiles**: A tile is a rectangular button that behaves like a menu item button. It is used to navigate to or open pages. In addition, tiles can display relevant data, such as counts or **Key Performance Indicators** (**KPIs**).

The following screenshot shows the navigation page:

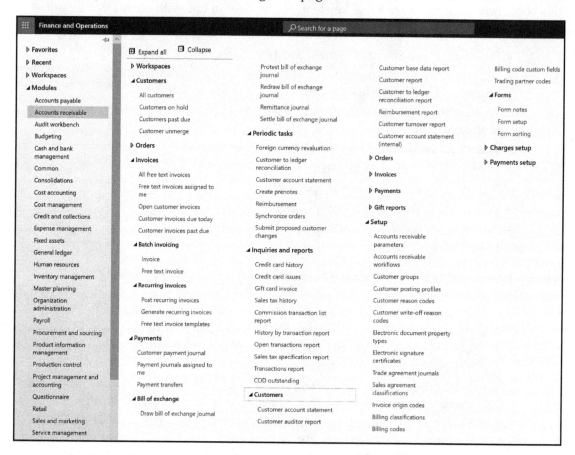

The following screenshot shows workspaces and various tiles used within workspaces in the Microsoft Dynamics 365 for Finance and Operations user interface:

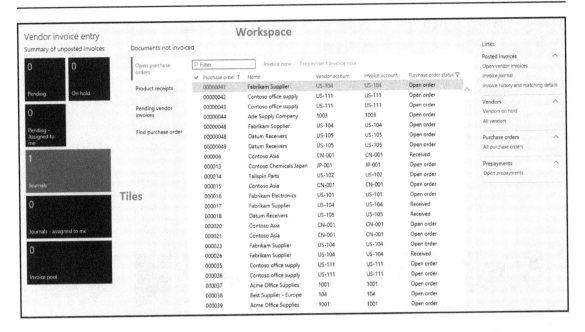

Use the following link to learn more about Dynamics 365 Finance:
`https://dynamics.microsoft.com/en-us/finance/overview/`.

Use the following link to learn more about Dynamics 365 Supply Chain
Management: `https://dynamics.microsoft.com/en-us/supply-chain-management/overview/`.

Let's move on to the next app that Dynamics 365 offers!

Dynamics 365 Business Central

Dynamics 365 Business Central is an accounting application offering from Microsoft, but it
is more than accounting software. It is a comprehensive business management solution for
small and midsized organizations that automates and streamlines business processes.

Microsoft Dynamics 365 Business Central also has dashboards similar to the role-driven dashboards in other Dynamics 365 apps:

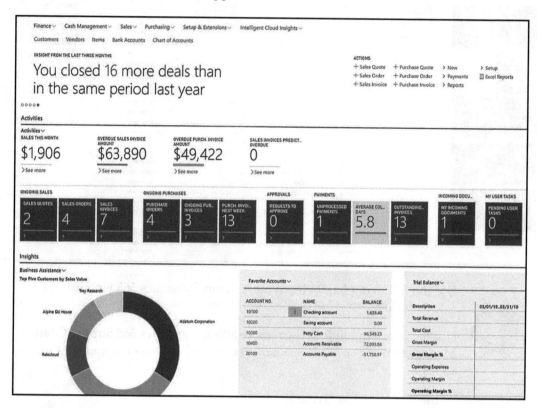

 Use the following link to learn more about Dynamics 365 Business Central: https://dynamics.microsoft.com/en-us/business-central/overview/.

Dynamics 365 Commerce

Earlier a part of Dynamics 365 for Finance and Operations, Microsoft Dynamics 365 for Commerce is now separated as its own application as part of the Dynamics 365 product portfolio. Microsoft Dynamics 365 for Commerce provides an intelligent platform to enable retailers to combine the best of digital and in-store to deliver personal, seamless, and differentiated customer experiences by empowering people and capturing insights to drive growth.

The following screenshot depicts a **Dynamics 365 Commerce** solution:

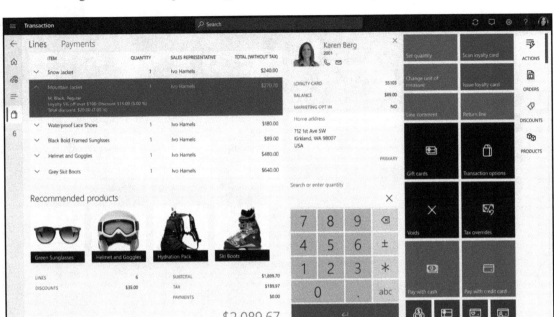

 Use the following link to learn more about Dynamics 365 Retail: `https://dynamics.microsoft.com/en-us/commerce/overview/`.

Dynamics 365 Human Resources

Microsoft Dynamics 365 Human Resources was an earlier part of the Finance and Operations and is now a separate SaaS-based independent offering out of Dynamics 365. Dynamics 365 Human Resources brings your human capital management to the cloud for a mobile, employee-focused, strategic HR approach that helps you to find and hire the right people, nurture success, and deliver high-impact, sustainable results.

The following is a talent solution dashboard showing various modules and capabilities:

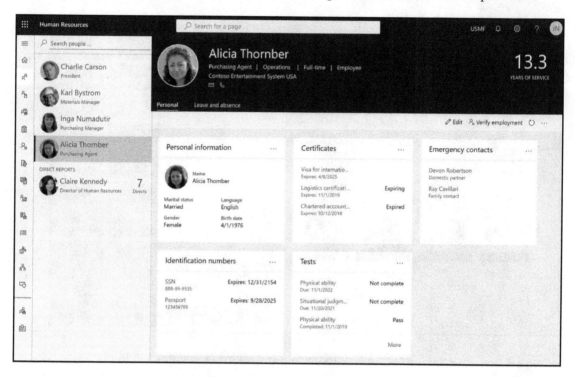

Use the following link to learn more about Dynamics 365 Human Resources: https://dynamics.microsoft.com/en-us/human-resources/overview/.

Microsoft is trying to make use of the Dynamics 365 suite easier by providing access to various tools that work very seamlessly with Microsoft Dynamics 365 business applications. These tools complement the Microsoft Dynamics 365 suite to make it more personalized and easy for information consumption and informed decision making. Let's have a look at these complementary tools in the following section.

Understanding Power Platform

Power BI, Power Apps, and Power Automate are all backed by the best-in-class cloud services for enterprise developers and IT professionals to quickly extend capabilities for Power users and scale to enterprise-wide manageability easily at any time.

Let's have a visual overview of additional apps/services/tools that could be utilized to measure information, act upon the task, and automate as much as possible. The following screenshot shows the Power BI, Power Apps, and Power Automate apps and how easy it is to build on top of it:

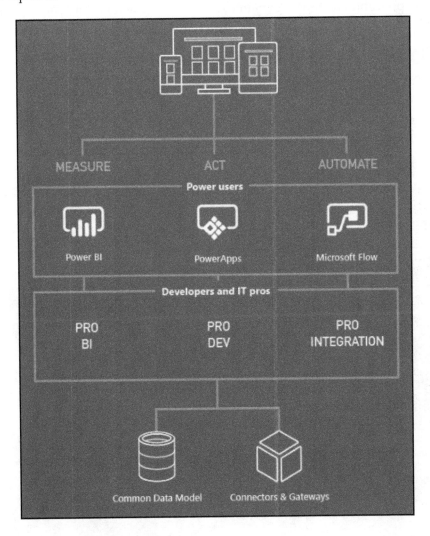

Let's now explore all of these tools one by one.

Power Apps

Microsoft has provided the Power Apps service, which can be used to build the new web/mobile apps that can connect to business data. It is the foundation to build any web/mobile application on top of Dynamics 365 solutions without writing any significant code.

Power Apps is a very strong tool that can be used in many ways; some are as follows:

- Building new apps
- Automate process
- Connecting data between various applications
- AI builder
- Creating new portals

Let's have a glimpse of a sample mobile app built in no time and ready for use by the business. The following screenshot shows an app built on top of Dynamics 365 for Finance and Operations and its data entities:

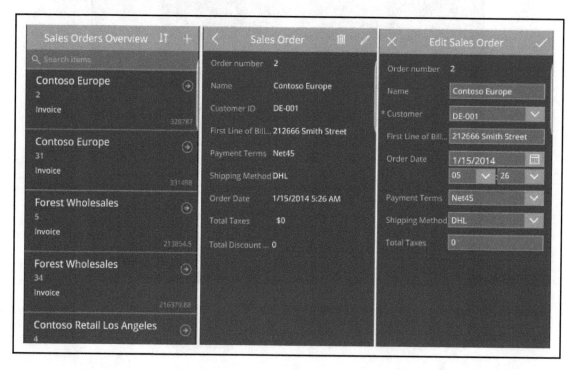

Use the following link to learn more about PowerApps: `https://powerapps.microsoft.com/en-us/`.

Power BI

Power BI is a powerful analytical visualization for Power users to quickly gain insights into information over the cloud or on their premises. It works with Microsoft Dynamics 365 to provide a self-service analytics solution. With Power BI built directly into Dynamics 365, you gain access to powerful business intelligence—real time on any device no matter where you are in the world—with rich visuals, charts, and graphics.

Power BI also has data warehouse capabilities including data preparation, data discovery, and interactive dashboards and can be embedded on most Azure Cloud platforms. Let's have a look at the following screenshot:

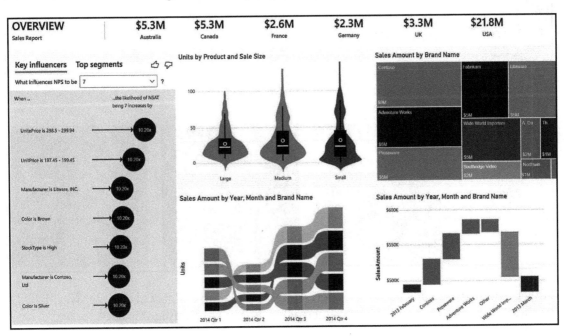

Here we see a sample dashboard from Power BI with several informational parts such as charts, trends, values, tables, and many more.

Use the following link to learn more about Power BI: `https://powerbi.microsoft.com/en-us/`.

Power Automate

Power Automate (previously known as Microsoft Flow) is the workflow engine of Microsoft Cloud, helping to quickly design any time-consuming task or process as either a complex multi-step process sequence or a simple one-step task. It is going to be seen more in areas of notifications, sync, and automating approvals. Let's have a look at the chain of events, which is very easy to establish in Power Automate, as follows:

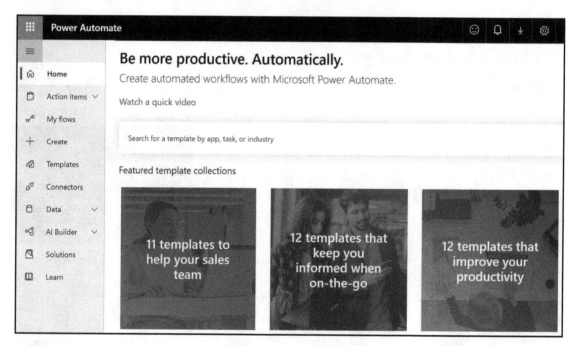

Power Automate supports a wide variety of data sources to connect to external world applications seamlessly and the list is increasing as you are reading this book.

 Use the following link to learn more about Power Automate (Flow): `https://flow.microsoft.com/`.

Common Data Service (CDS)

Common Data Service (CDS) is a shared database for storing business entities that connects to Dynamics 365, Flow, and PowerApps. It is the fabric behind Dynamics 365 and Office 365 to provide consistently structured entities across services spanning solutions within Dynamics 365 as well as external applications.

CDS gives a secure and encrypted business database, comprising well-formed standard business entities that can be deployed for use in your organization. It provides not only structured metadata, rich data types, auto numbering, lookups, and business data types such as address and currency, but also capabilities such as referential integrity through metadata configuration and cascade deletes, making a compelling functionality. CDS is licensed together with PowerApps as a stand-alone solution and is included in two different versions with Dynamics 365.

The following is a glimpse of managing entities within CDS with other tools such as connections, gateways, notifications, and others:

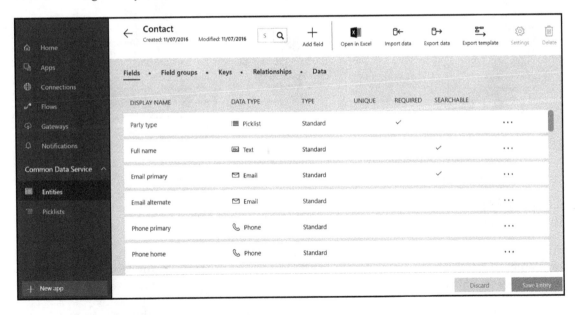

CDS makes it very smooth to communicate between different Dynamics 365 apps.

Microsoft AppSource

Think of an ecosystem in the cloud that can act as a single destination for business users to discover, try, and acquire line-of-business SaaS applications. That is what Microsoft AppSource is, and we see it as a great platform for partners having niche expertise in a specific subject to build, show, and sell their expertise and solution in the cloud.

Let's see how the AppSource landing screen looks. The following screenshot shows the AppSource search page along with solution offerings by partners related to one or many Dynamics 365 apps:

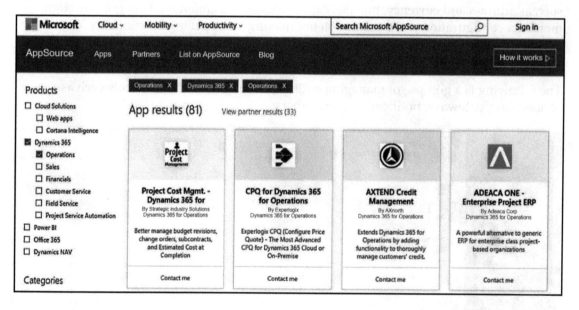

Consider AppSource an application store, where businesses will be able to find and try out line-of-business SaaS apps from Microsoft and its partners.

AppSource also provides a list of implementation partners who can assist customers in implementing these business apps. Currently, it hosts more than 80 apps for Dynamics 365 for Finance and Operations.

For customers, Microsoft AppSource is the place where you can find the apps from Microsoft and partners that drive your business. You can also request the trial through the implementation partner.

Microsoft AppSource is also a place for **ISVs** (short for **Independent Software Vendors**) to market your apps to business users. AppSource allows lead generation through using a proven system that Microsoft has built over several years. Use Azure's cloud services platform and tools to deliver differentiated apps to customers:

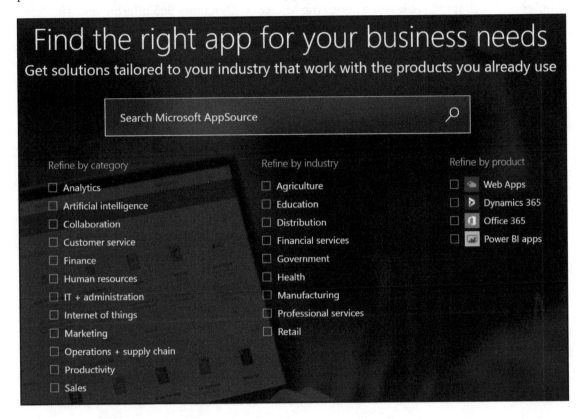

The preceding screenshot shows the AppSource landing page and solution across industry segments for ease in locating the perfect solution.

To learn more about it, you can visit https://appsource.microsoft.com.

Exploring Dynamics 365 for Finance and Operations

Earlier in this chapter, we learned about the Microsoft Dynamics 365 offering and all available different components and options. Our focus in this book is primarily on Dynamics 365 for Finance and Operations. Throughout this book, we will be focusing on Finance and Operations as a product and will go through different phases of the ERP implementation cycle in various chapters. We will discover specific tools and techniques applicable to implement it successfully in organizations. In this section, you will learn a little more about Finance and Operations and its history and highlights.

What is Dynamics 365 for Finance and Operations?

Microsoft Dynamics 365 for Finance and Operations is a modern ERP system built for cloud-first with two decades of proven business functionalities. Dynamics 365 for Finance and Operations may be a new name but it has been around for the last two decades. Finance and Operations, in the past, was known as Microsoft Dynamics AX and Axapta. Dynamics 365 for Finance and Operation is designed for midsized and large enterprise customers and is a multi-language, multi-currency enterprise resource planning solution. Finance and Operations is available in 138 countries and supports more than 40 languages and country-specific localization out of the box. On one side, the seamless integration of Microsoft Dynamics 365 for Finance and Operations with Office 365 takes productivity to a new level; on the other hand, out-of-the-box integration with Power BI, Cortana analytics, and machine learning takes the decision-making to another level.

Highlights of Dynamics 365 for Finance and Operations

The following topics describe the highlights of Dynamics 365 for Finance and Operations:

- **Modern**: Dynamics 365 for Finance and Operations is a modern, cloud-first, and mobile-first ERP solution. Microsoft has completely rewritten the technology platform and user interface from its previous version, Dynamics AX 2012. Just to name few advancements, the new version comes with cloud-first Azure deployment, modern HTML 5 client, mobile app, Power BI integration, and modern integration capabilities.

- **Work anywhere, anytime, and on any device**: The new user experience is optimized for multiple platforms and mobile apps. The clean, modern, and intuitive browser-based UI is a pleasure to use and easy to learn. All business logic is available any time, any place, on any device.

- **BI**: Dynamics 365 for Finance and Operations brings the power of the cloud to light up the state-of-the-art business intelligence options such as Power BI, Cognitive Services, and artificial intelligence. Dynamics 365 for Finance and Operations comes with a near-real-time operational data store called entity store for analytics and BI reporting. Entity store uses in-memory, **clustered columnstore index (CCI)** functionality that is built into Microsoft SQL Server to optimize reporting and queries. Dynamics 365 for Finance and Operations comes with many out-of-the-box Power BI content packs from Microsoft and provides the ability for partners and customers to author their own Power BI content pack and distribute it through the marketplace.

- **Productivity**: Microsoft Dynamics 365 for Finance and Operations keeps productivity as the core of its product and user interface design. Integration with productivity tools such as Office 365 has taken things to a new level, and the ability for business users to use their favorite apps such as Excel to export, edit, and publish data back to an application has never been so easy. The new concept of *workspaces* takes productivity to a new level by providing information around a process. All of the dependencies and answers to questions about a given process are available through a single page. Task guides make it easier to onboard new staff and train them on the process with step-by-step instructions while minimizing the learning curve.

- **Predictable and repeatable implementations**: Dynamics 365 for Finance and Operations brings **Lifecycle Services (LCS)** to the next level. With LCS, customers and implementation partners can manage their application lifecycle and move toward predictable, repeatable, and high-quality implementations. LCS is mandatory for any implementation project and allows customers and implementation partners to manage their implementation project from the project planning, deployment, and configuration, to monitoring and post-go-live support. LCS provides best practices and standards for implementation projects. With LCS, it has become very easy to manage and update Dynamics 365 for Finance and Operations.

- **Adaptable to any industry:** Dynamics 365 for Finance and Operations is a very flexible solution out of the box. Any industry can use Dynamics 365 for Finance and Operations due to its industry-standard features and flexibility to customize it to meet the needs of a particular industry. Microsoft is also learning from different industries and adding commonly used features to the standard product with each service update. Retail, manufacturing, distribution, public sector, finance, and IT are some of the industries where Dynamics 365 for Finance and Operations is used very frequently.

- **Feature management:** As part of a preview release, Microsoft releases some of the new features that are available only to targeted users. Features are added and updated in every release of Microsoft Dynamics 365 for Finance and Operations. The feature management experience provides a workspace where users can view a list of features that have been delivered in each release. By default, new features are turned off. Users can use the workspace to turn them on and view the documentation for them.

- **Service updates:** Microsoft has introduced the service update framework. With this framework, Microsoft has eliminated the tedious and painful task of upgrading the product every couple of years. Service updates enable customers to stay on top of newly coming updates to the product and adopt these updates easily through LCS. These service updates are continuous with new features and are released eight times per year. Customers may choose to get all eight of these service updates or just take the minimum required two service updates per year.

- **Automated testing:** Testing is a very big part of any product implementation. The same is true with Dynamics 365 for Finance and Operations; Microsoft has released the testing tool **RSAT** (short for **Regression Suite Automation Tool**), which can be used to automate the testing to reduce the cost for the UAT process. Users can create test cases and feed those test cases to RSAT to perform automated testing. By automating the testing process, customers can save a lot of time and effort that was previously taken in the past versions of the product.

Dynamics 365 for Finance and Operations deployment options

In today's modern world, everyone is focusing on cloud solutions where you don't have to worry about the infrastructure and other on-premises deployment issues like in the past. Microsoft is no different, and lately, a lot of focus has been on providing a better solution to the customer, which can be sustainable and scalable using cloud technology.

Previous versions of Dynamics 365 for Finance and Operations used to be just on-premises, but with the evolution of cloud technology, it is also available with cloud deployment. Let's have a look at the following table:

Capability	Cloud	On-premises
Infrastructure and data location	• Cloud service and data centers are fully managed by Microsoft	• Infrastructure is managed by partner or customer • Data resides locally • Disconnected data centers
Data trustee	• Microsoft	• Customer
Application lifecycle management (ALM)	• Microsoft managed • Customer and partner have access to ALM using Lifecycle Services (LCS)	• Customer or partner manages ALM using Lifecycle Services (LCS)
Cloud capabilities	• Microsoft backed data centers with high availability and disaster recovery system in place • Includes Sandbox environments	• LCS telemetry and automatic deployment
Intelligence and analytics	• Analytical workspace is ready to use • Option or pin the tiles and reports from PowerBI.Com • User can create and publish PowerBI reports	• User can create and publish PowerBI reports
Update and health monitoring	• Through LCS monitoring page	• Through LCS monitoring page
Licensing	• Subscription	• Subscription or through enhancement plan

Here, we see the comparison between cloud and on-premises deployment options for Dynamics 365 for Finance and Operations.

 Use the following link to learn more about deployment options for Dynamics 365 for Finance and Operations: `https://docs.microsoft.com/en-us/dynamics365/fin-ops-core/dev-itpro/deployment/choose-deployment-type?toc=/dynamics365/finance/toc.json`.

Dynamics 365 for Finance and Operations capabilities

Dynamics 365 for Finance and Operations has great capabilities that can be used to improve your business processes. Using the built-in features, you can see how the use of Dynamics 365 for Finance and Operations can make the user's life easier doing daily tasks. Dynamic 365 for Finance and Operations comes with many capabilities, and the following are some of the latest and greatest:

- Dynamics 365 Finance capabilities:
    - Use AI to drive important financial decisions.
    - Use powerful workspaces for faster decision-making.

- Use automation for your financial processes to reduce operational expenses.
- Use powerful localization to meet global financial complexity.
- Use Power BI for better reporting and analytics.
- Dynamics 365 Supply Chain Management capabilities:
  - Use powerful lean and intelligent manufacturing features to improve manufacturing operations.
  - Use IoT intelligence for production performance.
  - Use asset management to better maintain the assets.
  - Use advanced warehouse management with the latest improvements.
  - Use automation to streamline your supply chain.

 Use the following link to learn more about Dynamics 365 for Finance and Operations capabilities: https://dynamics.microsoft.com/en-us/finance-and-operations/capabilities/.

Trial of Microsoft Dynamics 365

New customers or consultants who want to get familiar with Dynamics 365 applications can leverage the trial provided by Microsoft to explore Dynamics 365. To start the free trial, simply follow the link https://trials.dynamics.com/, choose an app to explore, provide your work email address, and get started. The following screenshot shows the trial sign-up experience currently available:

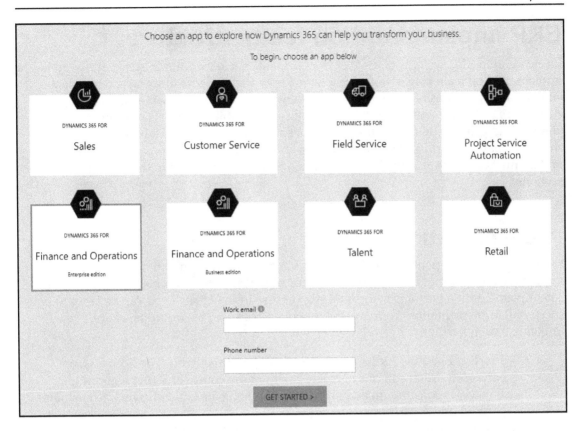

Depending on the application selected, you may have to provide additional details before the application can be provisioned for you. The trial application comes with guided experience and demo data to make it easy for new users to navigate, learn, and get familiar with the application.

Once you have seen the demo of the application and know that this will help to digitally transform your business, it is really important to build a team of smart people who will help you to make project implementation successful.

ERP implementation team structure

Implementing ERP systems takes a lot of effort, and it takes a team to successfully do it. The implementation team consists of people who know the business industry, are product experts, and have tons of experience implementing the product working along with the customer's own team. As a customer, it is your responsibility to select the right people, vendor, and product that fit your business need. In this section, we will talk about who should be part of your implementation team and how they can help you to succeed. Some of the important factors of the implementation team are discussed in the subsequent sections.

Implementation partner

When you are implementing any Dynamics 365 production, you will need an implementation partner to help you with your digital transformation journey. Dynamics 365 implementation partners bring a lot of expertise in the area so you can be assured of successful implementation. Here are the two main reasons you would need an implementation partner:

- **Product licenses**: As a customer, you cannot directly buy the licenses from Microsoft. Microsoft has partnered with many companies that work in the Dynamics 365 domain and sell the Dynamics 365 product licenses to customers through these partners.
- **Partner's expertise**: To become a partner with Microsoft, companies have to prove to Microsoft that they have the expertise to implement the Dynamics 365 products. Partners are the first layer of support to the customer. Microsoft relies on the partner's expertise to help customers with the implementation and support.

ISV solution

Dynamics 365 for Finance and Operations comes with great features to support many businesses from different industry areas. Most of the time, 80% of the business need can be fit with out-of-box features provided within Dynamics 365 for Finance and Operations, but there are those 20% of the requirements for which you might need to either change the business process or do some enhancement to meet that need.

When these business requirements become very common within an industry, sometimes ISVs develop the vertical solution that sits on top of standard Dynamics 365 for Finance and Operations. These ISV solutions are developed in such a way so it can be plug-and-play, which means as a customer/partner you wouldn't have to do much to implement these ISV solutions. Here are some examples of business areas that have ISV solutions:

- Sales tax
- EDI integration
- Multi-tier pricing

It is important to check for an ISV solution before you start on any big enhancement as there might already be a solution that may save you a lot of effort.

Solution advisors

Dynamics 365 for Finance and Operations implementation is a team effort. This team is made of the customer, the partner, Microsoft, and ISV solutions providers. The team needs to work like a well-oiled machine to achieve a successful implementation.

Sometimes customers hire an experienced independent solution advisor to work with the implementation team. Normally, a solution advisor has done many ERP implementations across various industries, which comes in very handy during the solution designs. The solution advisor's role is to keep customers and partners honest and keep them on their toes by checking each and every step of the project.

We cannot emphasize enough the importance of putting a good implementation team in place to make the implementation successful. Any decision taken during the implementation process can make a big difference, and a good implementation team can make sure you make good decisions.

Summary

In this very first chapter of this book, we started with learning about Microsoft Dynamics 365 and all of the different products that are part of it. We also briefly learned about all of the product offerings, different plans, buying, and trial options. Then, we shifted the focus to Dynamics 365 for Finance and Operations, which is the primary focus of this book, and we explored its history and key highlights.

In a nutshell, Dynamics 365 is a solution approach with a unified platform and data model. It's an end-to-end full -suite business application in the cloud. It's a win-win for customers, advisors, partners, and Microsoft, as they have enabled different channels of development, for example, drag-and-drop/wizard-like building capabilities for business users and analysts as well as pure development on Visual Studio, .NET, and BizTalk.

We look forward to Microsoft Dynamics 365 creating infinite possibilities and allowing organizations to leverage their finite resources and fixed timelines to be able to achieve more.

In the next chapter, we will start our journey of implementing Dynamics 365 for Finance and Operations and learn about the implementation methodology and tools.

Methodology and Initiation

2

In the first chapter, you learned about Microsoft Dynamics 365, its various apps/services/offerings, their capabilities, and the disruption in the way business apps are going to be leveraged. In this chapter, we will focus on implementation methodologies and best practices when initiating a project in Microsoft Dynamics 365 for Finance and Operations.

Once you have chosen to implement Microsoft Dynamics 365 for Finance and Operations in your organization and decided on the partner to assist you in this implementation journey, one major decision for the customer and the vendor is to decide on the implementation strategy. Let's now learn how to lay down the foundations for your project success. Whether it is an **ERP** (short for **enterprise resource planning**) implementation or any other major business transformation initiative, you must chalk out the path, rules, guidelines, processes, and milestones before embarking on your efforts. It is like the route of your journey, which is where a methodology comes into force. A methodology gives the much-needed direction and propelling force to drive your initiative.

Simply put, your project is your goal and the path to achieving it is enabled by the implementation methodology.

The following topics will be covered in this chapter:

- Importance of methodology
- Types of methodologies
- Project deliverables
- Initiation activities
- Team composition
- Ground rules
- Kickoff activities
- Best practices

Let's get into detail as to why a methodology is important and what all it does. This is important for all stakeholders who lay down the foundation of the project and set it on a course for success. So, this is a definite read for project managers, program managers, project owners, project advisors, and key team members.

Why select a methodology?

A methodology is a systematic theoretical analysis of methods applied to achieve one or many goals. This systematic study of methods with a clear process coupled with best practices ensures a higher success rate for goal attainment.

 A methodology as it is does not guarantee success and hence needs to be tailored and refined as per the enterprise needs to make it more suitable and adopted widely.

A methodology comprises various tools and techniques, such as phased workflows, individual process workflows, process procedures, templates, samples, aids, instructions, responsibility, accountability, authority, and risks and issues, all carried out in the interest of project's goal to deliver a product or service.

By managing programs undertaken in a repeatable manner, your team gains efficiency, works smarter, and can build an environment of continuous process improvement. In a nutshell, having a methodology provides enterprise initiatives with clear expectations and increases the probability and likelihood of its success.

Let's take a deep dive into the relevant methodologies for Microsoft Dynamics 365 for Finance and Operations in the next section.

Methodologies to choose from

The choice of methodology selection is limited but needs to be done carefully based on business goals and project/program goals. The primary methodologies we have seen being used in Microsoft Dynamics 365 for Finance and Operations are as follows:

- **Conference Room Pilot** (CRP): This methodology is a blend of agile and waterfall and can smartly use this to achieve goals of all sizes, big or small. This is widely used and accepted for various cloud-based initiatives.

- **Agile**: This methodology is good in select scenarios such as development, support, and enhancements. However, for a greenfield initiative of implementing Microsoft Dynamics 365 for Finance and Operations, this may not always be so useful. When the project duration is short and goals are clearly defined and non-changeable, this methodology will be found useful.
- **Waterfall**: This is a traditional methodology, which banks on clearly defined stages and deliverables, and is often used when the duration of the project is longer. This methodology carries some risk and in contrast to agile and CRP, the output is not seen early enough. Usually, big-bang project initiatives in implementing ERP are seen using this one. In the modern cloud world, getting early stakeholder buy-in is key to the high adoption of a new ERP and seeing the benefits of managing change within an organization.
- **Hybrid**: This is a mix-and-match kind of approach utilizing both agile and waterfall techniques. For different phases and different deliverables, sometimes agile could be used, while at other times waterfall could be used. Agile is closely related to the CRP methodology, however, it could be on a longer time horizon.

Let's learn about these methodologies in detail in the next subsection.

The Conference Room Pilot methodology

Prototyping models have long existed for testing and evaluation to see how the product performs before releasing. A **CRP** is very similar to a prototyping model. CRP is the ability to prototype out-of-the-box capabilities in a software product, including enhancements/customization, and it releases the solution/product to the end user in logically connected parts.

It also helps to break the bigger goal into smaller manageable goals and achieve them one by one over a period of time.

Following are salient features of a CRP methodology:

- The CRP methodology levers pilots, wherein each pilot is designed to target a specific stage, event, or business process of the enterprise during an implementation and should determine the success or failure.
- It's a recurring approach and is well utilized when a larger goal is divided into many manageable goals.
- It's a progressive approach that brings in smaller *time to value* in implementations and ensures early acceptance of a solution.

- It is very often said that *a picture is worth more than a 1000 words*; similarly, a CRP is an effective way to communicate the solution in a language that business **subject matter experts** (**SMEs**) can understand more effectively using visual aids and flows.

There are several benefits of using the CRP methodology in Microsoft Dynamics 365 for Finance and Operations implementations:

- Confirms and validates your understanding of business scenarios and requirements
- Less change management
- Higher adoption rate of incremental solutions
- Quicker go-lives
- A validated proposed solution with early feedback
- An iterative effort
- The opportunity for innovating, learning, and improving across delivery cycles
- The building of bigger solutions, bit by bit, in a highly efficient and successful manner

Let's now explore the various steps involved in using the CRP methodology.

Planning

This is the utmost important aspect of any methodology you would select. The planning process should address the core milestones in this approach, which spans scenarios, configured solutions with validation, and feedback, performed iteratively.

The following diagram shows the various steps and processes, with the flow of information involved in this approach:

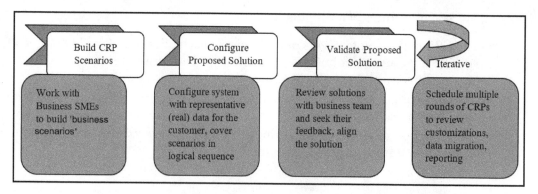

Considering that CRP's success lies in its pilots, the following factors should be leveraged in arriving at the number of pilots needed:

- Long-term as well as short-term goals of the initiative/program:
    - Use of top-down as well as bottom-up attainment of goals
    - Hierarchical map of goals, business processes, scenarios, and requirements
- Standard solution functionality fitment
- Customization/modifications needed
- Localization, country, or legal requirements
- Security and data privacy, or **Sarbanes-Oxley Act (SOX)**
- Connectivity (network latency) or performance
- Maintainability, deployment, or downtime for maintenance
- Licensing, support, and upgrade costs
- Shared services, intercompany transactions, and master data management
- Rollouts
- Enhancements

Execution

A good plan needs an equally good execution for goal achievement. As part of the execution, there are several iterative steps needed in CRP. Here are the steps we follow and that are recommended to execute in the CRP methodology:

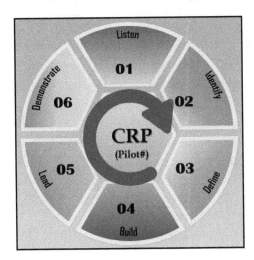

There are six steps and they are all iterative until you figure out the key steps making an impact and adding value to your implementation. The following is a brief guide to the CRP execution steps:

1. **Listen**: This involves giving an ear to all verbal and non-verbal business scenarios to cover in a CRP pilot.
2. **Identify**: This involves figuring out the core scenarios and preparing the solution options.
3. **Define**: This defines the scope for a pilot and gets it validated. This is crucial to the success of the CRP pilot. This must be done for both business scenarios and solution options.
4. **Build**: This step involves building prototypes, visuals, and a working solution once you have the stakeholders on-boarded with the scope and solution.
5. **Lead**: You must have a solution champion who leads the pilot from start to finish.
6. **Demonstrate**: This step demonstrates the solution to all of the stakeholders (business, solution, and IT) and seeks feedback for confirmation and optimization.

We would like to share select best practices in the CRP methodology to help you to manage and excel in your ERP journey.

Best practices in using CRP

Every methodology needs best practices as guiding stars in the implementation journey. Following are select best practices that we recommend:

- Always have a big picture agreed upon for the entire future-state solution.
- Use multiple CRPs for understanding and documenting business scenarios.
- Get early feedback on the business scenario understanding.
- Jointly work on the number of pilots needed.
- Build multiple solution options and validate them with stakeholders.
- Progressively add scenarios through a series of CRP workshops to gain the stakeholders' acceptance.
- Keep iterations short but still maintain the atomicity of each pilot.
- While feedback is important in CRP, it is a must to have agreed-upon change control and governance procedures.
- Maintain traceability of all artifacts.

One should add/modify the preceding recommendations based on unique business and project needs.

 There could be several CRPs based on the nature of the initiative and the goals to attain. It could be a pure business transformation or a functional, technical, or project-driven need, but you must tailor-fit the standards and processes accordingly.

In some scenarios, the agile methodology is also leveraged. Let's now take a deep dive into it.

The agile methodology

Agile is an iterative and collaborative process of applying processes and controls to achieve an objective. This methodology is highly popular in product development scenarios. Let's look at the following diagram for an end-to-end view of the agile methodology:

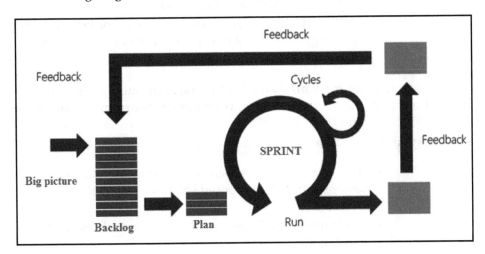

Let's look at all of the moving parts:

- While agile is focused on relatively quicker achievements than the other methodologies, the important aspect for its success is knowing the big picture well in advance.
- Using the big picture, a list of features/requirements/cases are elaborated and carved out into multiple plans.
- Each plan is then taken into execution, which is known as a sprint.

- A plan can have multiple sprints/sprint cycles.
- While executing sprints, feedback is taken and used in the backlog validation/updates.

Let's now learn salient activities in the agile methodology:

1. **Use case scenarios preparation**: This should be comprised of the solution core preparation, solution roll-out, support/sustenance, presales, and so on.
2. **Initial requirements analysis**: This is characterized by the following:

    - This is typically achieved initially in each sprint, led by an advisor/partner consultant, with sponsors, stakeholders, and key users.
    - A list of requirements and use cases needs to be prepared per sprint volume.
    - An ideal start would be to first prepare the requirements outline, covering everything at a high level.
    - In between sessions, you must document findings and solutions to make alignment upfront to ensure a smooth envisioning of the bigger solution.

3. **Solution-envisioning workshops**: This is one of the most critical phases where solution options using the **Strength, Weakness, Opportunities, and Threats (SWOT)** technique are discussed.
4. **Prototyping workshops**: This stage is characterized by the following:

    - These are workshop sessions with sponsors and users, demonstrating the proposed solution (fits, workarounds, and gaps).
    - This is used to validate the solution approach and its buy-in by stakeholders.
    - This phase is conducted in iterations/sprints so that the requirements and key decisions taken are well documented and are kept up to date with each prototype.

5. **Final system build**: This phase includes the following:

    - After ensuring sufficient confidence in the proposed solution, the final system can be taken for building.
    - This is iterative in nature and involves leveraging sprint cycles to deliver functionality incrementally.

- After this stage, the following are some key activities to be undertaken:

  - **System Integration Testing (SIT)**: Refer to Chapter 11, *Testing and Training*, for more details.
  - **The user acceptance testing (UAT)**: Refer to Chapter 11, *Testing and Training*, for more details.
  - **Training**: Refer to Chapter 11, *Testing and Training*, for more details.
  - **Cut over/transition**: Refer to Chapter 11, *Testing and Training*, for more details.
  - **Go-live**: Refer to Chapter 12, *Managing Go Live and Post Go Live*, for more details.
  - **Support**: Refer to Chapter 13, *One Version Service Updates*, for more details.

 Agile has some overlap with the CRP methodology, hence we are explaining it along with the overlapping components.

After understanding the CRP and agile methodologies, let's now learn about the traditional waterfall methodology.

The waterfall methodology

Waterfall is a classical sequential (non-iterative) approach, historically popular in large-scale packaged solution implementations globally. This has been used for initiatives/programs that are big, span multiple businesses, have a large number of requirements, involve complex single-site deployments, are developed by global/multi-site organizations, and so on.

Waterfall is simple to understand and has checkpoints/phases that must be completed before the next phase can start.

The following diagram shows the Microsoft Sure Step methodology with discrete phases and their deliverables to give an end-to-end glimpse of the waterfall methodology:

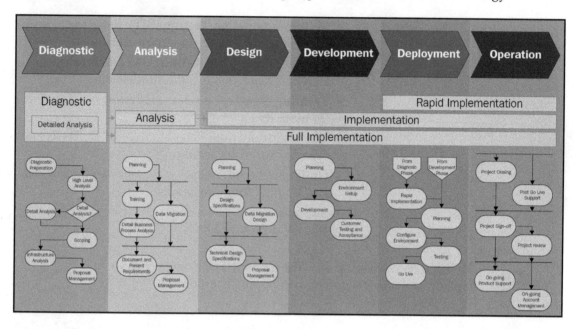

As shown in the preceding diagram, there are predefined stages and their associated deliverables. In a typical waterfall implementation, the following phases are expected:

- **Diagnostic**: This is primarily the presales phase or requirement-gathering phase.
- **Analysis**: This is the phase where an advisor/partner understands requirements and maps them with the solution. During this phase, the extent of solution fitment becomes known and the decisions to customize, buy, or build the solution verticals are made.
- **Design**: In this phase, a solution blueprint needs to be prepared, which in turn needs to be supported with other designs, such as functional, technical, data migration, and security. This is done for both fitment and solution gap areas.
- **Development**: In this phase, all gaps for which design documents are prepared in the earlier phase are undertaken for development and unit testing. Some implementations perform functional testing as part of this phase or in the subsequent phase.

- **Deployment**: This is the solution validation phase, where the solution is tested to fit the business requirements of the initiative. Preparation for go-live also happens in this phase and so do activities and deliverables related to data migration, security, training, and so on.
- **Operation**: This is the phase after go-live, often known as **support/sustenance**.

Let's now explore some key attributes of this methodology:

- This methodology is highly efficient when requirements are very clear, fixed, and well articulated.
- Requirements do not change much over a period of time.
- The scope for ambiguity must be minimum, as it would reduce the chances of success.
- Sometimes, implementations allow phases to run in parallel.
- There are some shortcomings of this methodology and they must be checked all of the time:
    - Ensure that the concept stage is finalized and signed off as, once the system goes into the testing phase, it is very difficult to go back and change anything.
    - The entire solution remains a black box and is seen only toward the later phase in the methodology life cycle.
- Reconsider your methodology when the requirements are to be elaborated out or when the program is an on going initiative:
    - There can be huge risks, assumptions, and uncertainties involved due to the inherent nature of the methodology.

Let's learn about common deliverables and phases across these methodologies in the following section and subsequent chapters.

Project deliverables

A project is successful when the expected outcome is achieved, which is measured by the deliverables. The knowledge of which deliverables are needed in which phase of the project is crucial.

Every phase must have a milestone before you hand it over to the next phase, and its achievement should be measured by the deliverables that resulted from the phase.

Hence, we are showing a diagram as well as calling out several key deliverables across phases in your Dynamics 365 implementation, as follows:

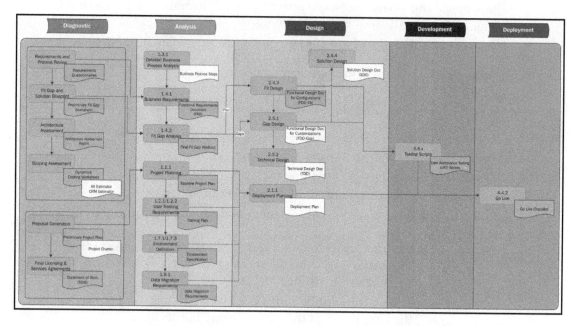

The preceding diagram is from Microsoft Sure Step online, depicting the phases and key milestones along with their deliverables. It documents in diagnostics the phase spans, project charter, project plan, **Statement Of Work (SOW)**, and so on.

Let's now learn about each deliverable in conjunction with its phase.

The planning phase

In the planning phase of the project, the implementation team should address the following milestones:

- Project charter: This is a formal document and the foundation on which the success of a project depends.
- SOW/contract: This contains a detailed scope covering all of the business processes as per the project goals and could be based on a scope document.

- Project plan: The project plan consists of the following planning components:
    - Communication plan: A plan of all the communication that needs to happen, when, and with whom
    - Test plan: A plan of the kinds of testing and the tools and techniques needed for it
    - Training plan: A plan to cover all aspects of training needs including delivery, content, location, and so on
    - Data migration plan: A plan that covers all aspects of managing the lifecycle of data from source to destination, including clean-up and conversions
    - Cutover plan: A plan for a pre-go-live checklist and data migration activities to bring needed last-minute data and transactions
    - Risk and issue matrix: A matrix to document, track, and plan for all risks and issues
    - Acceptance criteria: A list of all criteria by which to accept the system
- Ground rules: Ground rules are constraints and guidelines that are to be made by the project group and intended to help individual members.

Once the planning activities are completed, the scope of the project should be covered in the definition phase.

Requirements of the definition phase

In the definition phase of the project, the implementation team should address the following milestones:

- Business scenarios and processes: These are the list of processes defined in a hierarchical format.
- End-to-end process flows: These are all end-to-end information flow diagrams/visuals showing the start and end of a full cycle, for example, record to report, order to cash, and procure to pay.
- **Requirements Traceability Matrix (RTM)**: This is a matrix to maintain all requirements for tracking and closure purposes.
- As-is business flows: These are existing business flow visuals.
- To-be business flows: These are future state business flow visuals.
- Solution blueprint: This should represent the big picture of the solution meeting business needs.

After defining the scope, the implementation team should analyze each requirement in the analysis phase.

The analysis phase

In the analysis phase, the implementation team should address the following milestones:

- Fit gap analysis
- Workarounds and customization options
- Build versus buy evaluation
- SWOT analysis for workarounds and customizations/enhancements

Along with the analysis, the overall design of the solution needs to get started and continue in detail in the design phase.

The design phase

In the design phase of the project, the implementation team should address the following milestones:

- Out-of-the-box capabilities as fitment
- Functional and technical designs for any gaps in the present solution
- The best way of achieving business needs when it is not available out of the box in the solution
- Test scripts spanning:
  - End-to-end test scenarios for overall solution acceptance
  - End-to-end for a business process area
  - At least one test script per requirement
- Future-state solution blueprint
- Key decision matrix wherein every key decision is documented, explored options are mentioned, and the impact covered

After designing the solution, we should configure the representative capabilities in the configure phase.

The configure phase

In the configure phase, the implementation team should address the following milestones:

- A representative configuration of the business flow in Microsoft Dynamics 365 for Finance and Operations
- Sample data migration
- Demonstration scripts and videos
- High-level hands-on exercises

After acceptance of the prototype, any gaps, interfaces, or reports can be undertaken in the development phase.

The development phase

In the development phase, the implementation team should address the following development artifacts:

- **Entity-Relationship (ER)**
- Pseudo and actual code
- Technical designs
- Whiteboardings of data flow and code flow

There are some nuances in the development phase based on the methodology selected. For example, when using the waterfall methodology, the emphasis is on the overall design and then the actual development commences when the individual technical designs are ready. In the agile approach, the sprint determines the workload in development and the churn is expected to be done quicker.

After developing the solution, it is now ready for testing by the implementation team in the testing phase.

 Look for additional details of the required documents, artifacts, and code needs in subsequent chapters.

The testing and acceptance phase

In the testing phase, the implementation team should address the following:

- Test plan: This is a planning document that covers the details of what test scenarios are present, who will do test, and when the test is expected to be done.
- Test scenarios: These could be kept at end-end business processes, for example, record to report.
- Test cases: These are the breakdowns of test scenarios into their details to suggest what the test steps are, what inputs are to be used, and what the expected output should be.
- Issue logs: As part of the test result capturing, if a test fails, it should have a corresponding issue representing the details of failure for tracking purpose and closure.

After testing the solution, it is now ready for training the end users in the training phase.

In Chapter 11, *Testing and Training,* we will cover details of testing and various tooling available and the timing of the usage of such tools.

The training phase

In the training phase, the implementation team should address the following milestones:

- Training manuals: These are the user guides that are referred to when users start using the system. Be it testing, training, or go-live, training manuals are key in solution adoption and change management.
- User/task guides: These overlap with training manuals and mainly focus on solution steps and visuals.
- The actual training of super and end users: No training is complete without imparting hands-on training continuously to ensure project success.

You will learn more about the preceding in subsequent chapters.

After the training phase, the solution is now ready to go live.

The go-live phase

In the go-live phase, the implementation team should address the following milestones:

- Cutover checklist: This checklist covers everything from master data to opening balances and open transactions to be made available on day one of going live.
- Go-live readiness: This includes everything needed to prepare your organization for smooth transition to the new system:
  - Environment: This helps in knowing the whereabouts of the environment and its planning and distribution with needed stakeholders.
  - Access: Accurate access/security is key to ensure users can perform their work in the new ERP.
  - Communication mailers: This helps to keep everyone on the same page.

After a successful go-live, it is important to continue the journey and keep reaping benefits from the business platform while keeping it healthy.

The support phase

In the support phase, the implementation team should address the following milestones:

- Support/sustenance plan: This is an important aspect of keeping your solution healthy.
- Team spanning at varying levels to support needs: Maintaining a tiered support approach helps in timely and accurate issue resolution.
- Enhancement initiatives: Something is always chosen to be done later and having a product catalog for all changes/enhancements is key to ever-evolving your solution.
- Good-to-have business needs from RTM: After all must-have requirements are met, it is now time to cover good-to-have requirements.
- Issue portal: This is a single repository to manage issues and triaging and solutions and can be combined with knowledge management.
- Ongoing training, roll-out initiatives, and others: After the core solution is in place, it is now time to roll it out.

You will learn more about the preceding in subsequent chapters.

You should treat the aforementioned phases as a starting point, and we recommend that you leverage the CRP methodology concepts, PMI, and other useful resources to come up with your project-specific deliverables and milestones.

Now that you have gained information about all three methodologies, it is time to do a side-by-side comparison, which becomes your checklist for selection.

Comparative summary

Each methodology has both strengths and weaknesses, and no one size fits all in the ERP world. Hence, the project team should carefully evaluate the best-fitting methodology to achieve the business goal.

No one size will fit all situations; however, for easing your effort in choosing a methodology, we are sharing a comparative summary of the key attributes of the preceding methodologies:

Attribute/Scenario	CRP	Agile	Waterfall
End-to-end greenfield implementation of Microsoft Dynamics 365 for Finance and Operations	This is the latest and most widely used methodology in modern digital cloud initiatives. This blends the agile and waterfall approach to achieve the project goal.	Though this could be used, a lot of project management efforts will be needed, as it will not be able to handle all of the ambiguities that come with an ERP implementation. This is a good one to leverage with highly evolving solution needs.	The traditional approach, which is still OK to use, but the duration of the project is typically longer before you can start reaping benefits. Good for a known set of business needs and smaller time frame initiatives.
Enhancements and new feature implementations	This is very well suited to these initiatives.	Depending upon the delivery duration, clarity of requirements, and technical design, this methodology can be used.	Typically, this one is not used for a shorter duration due to the huge efforts involved.

Upgrades/migration	This is very well suited to these initiatives.	This methodology may be used in upgrades and has significant overlaps with the CRP methodology.	This methodology could be used; however, for faster ROI and buy-in from end users, either CRP or agile is preferred.
Support/maintenance	This is very well suited to these initiatives.	This methodology overlaps with the CRP methodology and is suited for support.	Typically, this one is not used for support.

What has worked for us is the CRP methodology, as modern ERP is no longer a traditional application, hence the traditional approach of waterfall is not the best fit. Agile is second in our list when the number of moving parts is high and when the project structure needs to be highly adaptable to changing business needs.

In the next section, we'll share the importance and best practices in project initiation.

Project initiation

A project is in place for something to be achieved, and any initiative in ERP adoption is considered a major undertaking. Hence, such initiatives should not be treated as mere IT programs but as organizational initiatives.

The definition of a strong start is important and may need to be personalized as per the size and complexity of the project. In essence, when project goals are committed from top to bottom and the vision is accepted by all of the stakeholders of the project, it is considered to be a strong start. Often, this is just like laying down the seeds of a plant and watering them with commitment. While detailed planning will happen shortly, emphasis needs to be given to pre-planning.

Business drivers and organizational goals often trigger the conceptualization of an initiative. Use these levers to pre-plan for the project and have a high level of execution throughout the process.

A strong project start is imperative in laying down the foundations for assured success. We can ensure a strong start by mixing in all of the key ingredients:

- Vision statement: This is super important and should be written in business language, in such a way that any person outside the project should also be able to read it and understand what the project aims to achieve. A project vision statement should always be tangible and achievable.
- Executive sponsorship: Securing involvement and push from top management is important.
- Benefits/value addition: Consider what benefits and value addition the project would help to accomplish.
- Timeline for going live and for realizing benefits: Setting realistic timelines is crucial to attaining them.
- Constraints and assumptions called out upfront and validated: These are important to be made known to everyone who could be impacted as it can alter the project's course if ignored.
- Identification of solution advisors and/or implementation partners: An important evaluation to ensure the right team mix, expertise, focus, and momentum is given to the project.
- Budgetary approvals: A must have before initiating a project as an ERP project needs that focus, being such a transformative initiative.
- SME: Identification of in-house **subject matter experts** (**SMEs**) and securing their time from regular work is key to project success.
- Change management: The ERP journey brings a lot of change and addressing change in a planned way helps smooth adoption.

Projects are accomplished by people and the right team composition is crucial. In the next section, we cover this in detail.

Project team composition

The formula for any project's success is to involve the right talent and have a strong team. A team working toward a common goal is a must and each member must be on board with project objectives.

Each team member must be trained in a matrix management style to get the best from them, as this form of organizational structure fosters collaboration unlike any other. Not just Dynamics 365, but any ERP project has so many moving parts that unless the team works in a united fashion, success can't be guaranteed.

Remember that no single cross-functional team is alike, as it is influenced by individual personalities, strengths, and weaknesses, coupled with the unique requirements of each initiative. This is what makes every Dynamics 365 implementation unique; hence, it is important for the project sponsor and the project manager to play the role of a binder to foster strong team dynamics.

A typical project team structure based on our experiences while implementing Dynamics 365 solutions and leveraging CRP methodology can be seen as follows:

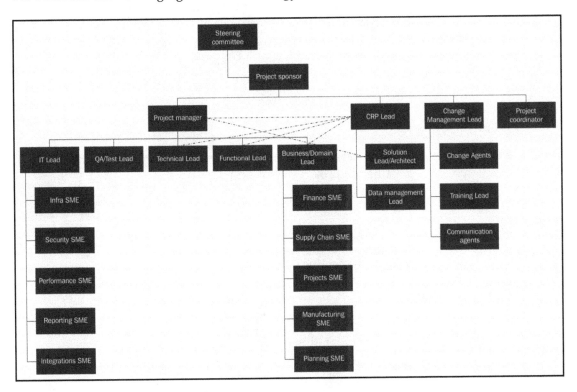

As shown in the preceding diagram, both sides of members need to function as one team, and hence, it typically becomes a matrix organization reporting with lots of dotted, as well as direct, reporting responsibility.

As ERP projects are usually large-scale initiatives, the support of external consulting partners and advisors is needed to form the right team for success. As described in the diagram, there are several full-time or part-time internal (client) roles as well as advisor/consulting partner roles highlighted.

We'll now share our knowledge on complete team composition, comprising groups and/or individuals, as follows:

- **Steering committee**:

    - These are the owners of providing resources, securing funding, and liaising with the executive management/board of the organization.
    - This role typically involves management representatives from the key departments of an organization.
    - This committee is expected to execute executive-level leadership, keeping the larger vision in perspective.
    - This committee needs to make policy decisions as necessary to ensure the success of the project.

- **Project sponsor**:

    - This role acts as a champion and gives a much-needed thrust to meeting the project's goals and objectives.
    - A project sponsor needs to be ahead of all of the project activities and is a single point of contact for all of the decisions needed for the project.
    - A project sponsor acts as a liaison to the steering committee and leads such meetings.

- **Project manager**:

    - The project manager is responsible for the overall management and implementation of the solution throughout its lifecycle.
    - The project manager leads the project planning activities and manages the execution of projects according to plan.
    - They manage relationships with stakeholders and keep them informed of the progress and issues.
    - They become the driving force for managing the expectations from all project deliverables.
    - The manager is the motivator of the team and enables and empowers the team members to deliver their best.
    - They create and maintain the project plan.
    - They manage and protect scope and creep.

- The project manager should always baseline the project plan in line with the objectives, changing conditions, and actuals.
- They manage the financial aspects of the project, ensuring accurate budgeting and estimates to the actual variance.
- They prepare the contingency plans, proactively work to identify triggering events for any issues/risk, and come up with an initial mitigation plan.
- They act as a single point of contact for sign-off-related activities.
- They are the knowledge champion of the project management methodology, standards, tools, processes, and procedures.

- **Business lead**:

  - This is an internal role and mostly comprises business experts, process owners, or SMEs.
  - Business leads are a central point of contact for a specific business process, and they need to carry end-to-end responsibility for the process.
  - They are responsible for translating the business needs into processes and requirement specifications.
  - They ensure that all of the current (*as-is*) and future (*to-be*) processes are incorporated in the solution scope.
  - A business lead is the owner of an end-to-end business process.

- **CRP lead**:

  - This is a cross-functional role involving knowledge of project management methodologies and the commitment to drive the project to success.
  - CRP leads are responsible for defining, planning, tracking, and managing every identified pilot.
  - They participate in the project planning activities and lead the execution of the pilot.
  - They manage relationships with project stakeholders, keeping them informed of the progress, issues, and deliverables in a pilot.
  - They are the owners of the business blueprint.

- **Advisor/partner/functional consultant/developer**:

  - These are external knowledge experts in the solution, whom we generally refer to as value experts.
  - They need to lead by example and carry multiple roles (namely architects, consultants, and so on).
  - They are the key link in enabling business transformation initiatives.
  - They are the owners of the solution blueprint.
  - They lead strategic discussions with stakeholders on matters of systems, business processes, and requirements.
  - They help to map business needs with solution features and where needed, fill in product gaps/whitespace with a custom solution.

- **Change management lead**:

  - Change management leads are the owners of all of the change management initiatives that spin off when implementing/adapting the Dynamics 365 solutions.
  - They chair the **Organizational Change Management (OCM)** discussion, and they provide advice for and direction in managing the changes arising from the project.
  - They assist the project manager and the CRP lead in identifying potential risks, and they create plans to mitigate the risks in plan execution.
  - They need to proactively identify new processes and changes to the existing business processes, and communicate these changes well through proper training.

- **IT lead**:

  - The IT lead is usually an information technology role, involving customer personnel.
  - The role supports all IT-related enablers in project execution.
  - They develop and review the technological scope.
  - They bring in technical direction and guidance.
  - They provide system and technical expertise to the project team.

Once you have a project team composed of the aforementioned roles, you have laid down a solid foundation for the success of your project. However, the preceding recommendations need to be mashed up as per the project's and organization's needs. We have seen exceptions to the preceding team structure and would like to call out the top two reasons for exceptions:

- Based on the project size, type, and complexity, a single person may perform more than one role. For larger initiatives, a dedicated **Project Management Office** (**PMO**) may also be formed, which enables the coordination of meetings, travel, activity collection, and project status distribution.
- Large enterprises also set up something called the service desk, which is typically an IT function that supports several IT operating processes, depending on the nature of the task. Also, if there are multiple initiatives, then each initiative can be treated as a project, which necessitates the dedicated role of a program manager.

ERP implementation is a long journey; you must implement measures to have continuity in all of the key resources, from beginning to end.

Project backbone

Every initiative needs to have a backbone structure that keeps things together. The project charter and project plan are among the top contributors to driving the project and keeping it together.

In this section, we will share insights into the project charter and project plan.

Project charter

The project charter is the foundation on which the success of a project depends. It must be complete and made as a formal document. All of the initial conceptual planning that triggers an initiative is expected to be taken as the key input.

Project initiation being the early stage, the project contributors/participants suggested in the earlier section must brainstorm, innovate, and commit in this formal document.

Following are the salient features of a project charter:

- It should clearly articulate and describe the project objectives in a **Specific**, **Measurable**, **Achievable**, **Repeatable**, and **Time-bound** (**SMART**) format.
- It should form a solid agreement between the sponsors and the project management team.
- This formal document should give the project manager the authority to manage the project.
- It should define the types of resources that will be needed across project activities.
- It should empower the OCM lead to drive the business process changes.
- This document should be able to give a top-level view of the initiative in focus and list all projects that are expected to be spun out of it.
- A project charter should define the high-level scope of the initiative.
- All critical success factors of accomplishing the goals must be called out, including the key milestones and target dates.
- This document is typically prepared by the project sponsors, along with the stakeholders involved in delivering the project.
- In a project charter, we must define a rough order-of-magnitude estimate for completing the project with some buffer as agreed with project stakeholders.
- It must mention the approved funding for the project and contingencies, if any.
- The selection of the project delivery process, that is, methodology, assumptions, constraints, known risks, and identified issues, along with the other key elements, must be suggested as guidelines of the project charter.

 A project charter should simply be seen as a map for everything that is expected to be achieved in the initiative and the direction for achieving this.

Often, a project initiation document is used along with a project charter to act as a level between the project charter and the project plan.

In larger initiatives, a project scope document is also prepared, which lays down the exact description of requirements and deliverables. This formal requirement document, scoped for an initiative along with the project charter, forms the basis for developing a project plan.

Project plan

A project plan is a road map document on how to achieve the objectives of the initiative as described in the project charter.

What needs to be accomplished should be in the project charter.
How the goals will be achieved should be in the project plan.

A project plan must facilitate concise and effective communication. This is important, as it ensures that all of the stakeholders are on the same page as to where their project stands at any point in time. A project plan is also a measurement to define outcomes, timelines, activities, resources, and commitments.

Any stakeholder at any point in time should be able to use the project plan and know what to expect by using the following fundamental questions:

- **Why**: The goals and reason for this initiative, typically coming from the project charter
- **How**: The list of all the activities needed to accomplish the project's goals
- **What**: The work expected to be performed in a specific activity
- **Who**: The person/team responsible for the individual work
- **When**: In a project timeline, when the work is expected to be completed
- **Which**: Which resources are needed

Let's take a look at some of the salient features of a project plan to implement Microsoft Dynamics 365 for Finance and Operations:

- Project implementation methodology must be selected, as recommended in the project charter.
- Must always have detailed scope, covering all of the business processes as per the project goals. This could be based on a scope document, also known as a **SOW** or contract, if prepared before the project plan.
- Must define the **Work Breakdown Structure** (**WBS**), which identifies all of the work that needs to be done to complete the project. Structuring the work into logical components and subcomponents is an important aspect of the WBS. The work definition should be at such a level of detail that it could be used to assign tasks to an individual.
- It must list the resources needed to contribute to the project. All internal and external resources must be maintained in the project plan.

- It should depict a schedule, laying down all of the scope items with their projected start and end dates, effort, and the duration needed. This is also where responsibilities are assigned. Always ensure and follow the **Responsible, Accountable, Consulted, Sign Off, Informed (RACSI)** matrix for responsibility assignment. A schedule is never complete until all of the resources necessary to complete the project have been committed or assigned.

- The project manager should always keep the critical path in check/updated in the project plan. A critical path is a set of activities in a path with the least slack and the longest duration. Activities that lie along the critical path cannot be delayed without delaying the finish time for the entire project. Hence, close monitoring and proactive measures are needed to ensure the timely attainment of project goals. You can use the critical path method to analyze the activities that have the least amount of scheduling flexibility.

- A project plan must be a living document and, hence, must be periodically updated with any changes in the due course of the project timeline.

- Each individual activity should also carry an estimate of the cost to complete the activity. This forms the basis of a project budget by summarizing the cost estimates for all of the activities in a project plan. Top-down budgeting involves allocating the overall cost estimates to individual work items to establish a cost baseline for measuring the project performance.

- A project plan should always be a perfect balance of the following various constraints in managing the scope:
  - Quality
  - Budget
  - Cost
  - Scope
  - Resources
  - Timeline

- A project plan must comprise the following sub-plans for effective management:
  - **Communication plan**: This is mostly a policy-driven approach for providing the project status information to the stakeholders. The plan should formally define who should be given what specific information and when the information should be delivered. We recommend that you also outline how such information should be disseminated and the form of communication matching the purpose: email, websites, printed reports, presentations, and so on.

- **Risk management plan**: Risks are impediments to project success. This plan is intended to cover all of the potential risks and issues, as well as suggest corrective options. Having a risk assessment matrix fosters the effectiveness of such a plan. Always maintain a log for **Risk, Assumption, Issue, and Dependency (RAID)**.
- **Quality and acceptance plan**: This plan enables securing the acceptance of the deliverables produced by the project from the required stakeholders (both internal and external). Identify the external dependencies, as these may directly or indirectly impact the project plan and hence may need to be kept in close check.
- **Change management plan**: A project plan must always incorporate all of the key decisions that could impact any activity. **Change Request (CR)** should also be captured in the due course of the project and be updated in the project plan after baselining it. Multiple levels of approval may not be a bad idea (for example, approvals for estimation, approvals for implementation, and so on). Often, the change itself may not be big, but its impact on the overall project may be huge. The impact on the testing and training aspects needs to be evaluated carefully in addition to the actual design and development. Understand the impact of timing of the change, as it is crucial; the later the change in the project lifecycle, the more costly and widespread impact it may have.

- Project plans must form the basis of all the project reporting requirements:
  - This includes a point-in-time position.
  - Dashboard reporting for project sponsors and the executive committee: This includes the following:
    - This should cover the overall progress in a percentage.
    - Phase-wise completion percentage.
  - Financials: This includes the following:
    - Project earned value
    - Current **Actual Cost (AC)**
    - Burn rate (the rate at which the project budget is being spent)
    - **Estimate to Complete (ETC)**: *ETC = Budget - Actual Cost*

- **Estimate at Completion** (**EAC**): The final forecasted value of the project when it is completed
- *EAC = actual costs (AC) + Estimate to Complete (ETC)*
- Budget
- Actuals (variance to budget)

- Detailed reporting for project stakeholders: This includes the following:
  - Activity-wise status for the phase in progress
  - The overall state of the project
  - Key risks and issues

Microsoft Project is a popular tool that can be used to prepare and maintain a project plan.

The following is a snippet of a project plan based on the CRP methodology, containing milestones, timelines, tasks, duration, a Gantt chart, and several other informative insights:

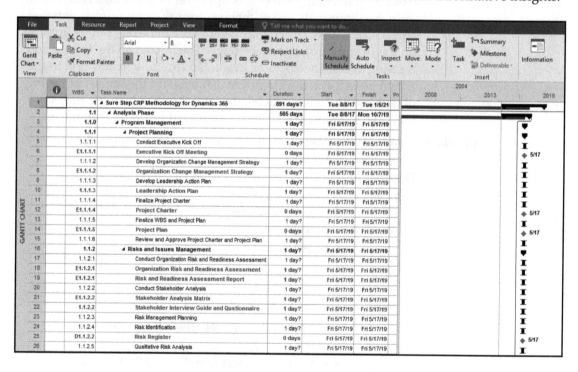

Even though the project manager has overall responsibility for developing and maintaining a project plan, a good plan cannot be prepared without the participation of the project team members.

A project plan must follow the established guidelines and standards and should always be baselined for all evaluation and reporting purposes.

Ground rules for a project team

Ground rules are constraints and guidelines that are to be made by the project group and intended to help individual members. They must be clear, consistent, agreed to, and followed by the team members. The purpose of ground rules is to adhere to the agreed style of working, which directly impacts the project's success.

We have seen that ground rules add value to the overall team communication, participation, cooperation, and support, as these are meant to address the behavioral aspects of project delivery.

The following are some of the top areas where ground rules are seen to be effective and, hence, should be created:

- Team meetings: For example, the ground rule for stand-up meetings could be just highlighting, in brief, the key accomplishments and challenges per track/lead.
- Communication: Verbal communications are a must and soft skills are important traits to have for the project team members. However, sharing relevant information with the impacted stakeholders in a formal mode is recommended as a ground rule.
- Team culture: We must ensure to factor in various cultural aspects while executing a project in the region intended and based on the various backgrounds of team members.
- Key decisions: A ground rule in communication could be to document all of the key decisions in a common repository, available to the concerned project stakeholders.
- Logistics: This includes ground rules for in-person workshops and virtual meetings.

- Terminologies and abbreviations: Team members must agree on any kind of abbreviations and terminologies and host the list in a team site accessible to all. This ensures less assumption in communication.
- Proactive management of risks and issues: Every team member must take up ownership of bringing up issues and risk proactively as well as potential ways of reducing/solving them. Risk and issues bring in a lot of unknowns. The lesser the unknowns in a project, the higher the chance of achieving timely success.
- Vacation and time off: A ground rule in project time off could be to seek leave approval from the project manager for any leaves of more than a week, and approval should be at least be two months in advance.
- Workload/priority conflicts: This is the single most important factor that could derail any project. Work prioritization ensures efficiency, stronger collaboration within and outside the team, and helps to bringing stakeholders together on the same page.

While several ground rules can be created, we recommend that you ensure agreement and commitment from the stakeholders before formalizing a rule.

These ground rules, the project charter, and the project plan are usually shared with the team in a kickoff meeting.

Kickoff meeting

Every project must have a kickoff meeting, which is about setting expectations, and clearly calling out and communicating goals. You must involve executives from all sides (partner and customer) in a kickoff meeting.

We would like to share our knowledge by outlining the key requirements for a successful kickoff meeting:

- Review the goals with the key stakeholders and ensure that you have the goals defined in the order of priority.
- Review the project goals and charter. Define and get a commitment on how success is going to be measured.
- Getting team commitment is key.
- Review the project plan in detail. Review the project milestones and deliverables, validate the team structure, roles, and responsibilities fitment with the resources, and emphasize the implementation methodology and the steps to success.

- Brainstorm and seek the team members' acceptance of ground rules. Communication and logistics are super important.
- Carry out the project communication plan and the risk management approach.
- Review the change control process.
- Ensure that all team members attend the kickoff meeting in person.
- For a geographically spread team, you may schedule a web conference or conduct another one for remote members.
- Optionally, tools that are going to be leveraged can also be included in the kickoff meeting.

Kickoff meetings should be simple and thorough and should enable team members to feel empowered, motivated, enthusiastic, energized, and focused. Kickoff meetings should be conducted at a common place for better alignment and commitment.

FastTrack

The FastTrack program is Microsoft's involvement after the licenses have been purchased to get you up and running fast on the cloud platform, which starts when the licenses have been purchased until the production system has been deployed.

In the FastTrack program, there is a role and responsibility that explains what is expected from the parties involved.

There are two programs for Microsoft Dynamics 365 Finance and Operations:

- Dynamics 365 FastTrack Business process applications: Gets a dedicated FastTrack solution architect
- FastTrack Essentials: Gets a shared FastTrack solution architect

FastTrack-recognized solution architects are an elite group of architects from our system integrator partners, who have consistently led successful implementations of complex scenarios.

For more information, refer to `http://fasttrack.microsoft.com/dynamics`.

Best practices in project initiation

Based on our practical experiences, the following are the recommended best practices that need to be evaluated for every project and its goals for effectiveness:

- Identification of the right stakeholders before project kickoff and keeping them up to date: You must have written and verbal commitments from all of the stakeholders toward meeting the objectives of the project and their contribution. You should also have a lot of team-building exercises throughout the duration of the project, as it facilitates the team members working more closely together.

- Ensure that your project charter has the following mentioned in detail:

  - The charter must be a formal document prepared from inputs from the key stakeholders. The project charter is not a legally binding document; hence, it is a great place for all stakeholders to openly contribute.

  - The objectives of the project must be explicitly mentioned in detail, in a clear and concise format. The goals should be quantifiable, realistic, time-bound, and should not contain any ambiguous elements. Using the SMART approach is very helpful to craft the project objectives.

  - The project charter must always be approved/signed off by the appropriate authority and should be easily accessible to all of the stakeholders in a collaborative workspace. The extent of details in a project charter to be shared with individuals may vary and should be factored in during sharing/access.

  - Get executive buy-in toward the business transformation initiative. Seek executive support in early communications in the project to create the much-needed excitement and commitment from all of the other stakeholders. Get the change management lead on board at the start of the project, as implementing Dynamics 365 impacts the existing business processes. To accelerate the implementation and ensure that the right approach and best practices are leveraged, make sure that an experienced, knowledgeable expert/advisor is on board.

  - For internal customer team members, always have a dedicated core team that would be working full time on the project. The core team should bring in the business process expertise from the customer side, and often, they are the SMEs as well. Getting part-time involvement is going to be a challenge going forward and slows down the whole initiative.

- For other internal team members (non-core team members), ensure that their work-life balance is planned in advance and expectations are set early. Some team members may see a spike in their average daily work, as they will now be doing more than one job. They would need to balance their existing daily job with implementation activities and any other additional role taken up in the project.

- Identifying a dedicated CRP/project leader is vital for a smooth journey. Strong communication, ability to handle ambiguity, commitment, passion, and so on, are some of the attributes that you should seek in your CRP leader.

- Avoid false starts. If any key information regarding the project is yet to be finalized, such as the project charter is not complete, the project goals are incomplete, the project manager is not identified, the CRP leader is not identified, the right stakeholders are not identified, or the funding not approved, then you should wait until all of these key attributes are clear to start the project.

- Prepare a resource-onboarding checklist, covering all of the information related to access, VPN, environments, SharePoint, distribution lists, and so on. Every resource should have its own dedicated account. There should never be a sharing of accounts/passwords, and no generic accounts, such as user1, user2, and so on, should be used.

- Have a published and centralized project calendar accessible to all of the stakeholders. Each stakeholder should keep the calendar up-to-date with their vacation plans, time offs, unavailability, and so on.

- Always have a key decision matrix/log throughout the project, as these decisions can alter the path and progress of the project. They also act as a knowledge repository. Leverage a user-friendly collaboration tool to maintain all of the project artifacts, deliverables, sign-offs, and so on.

Always remember that every project is unique; the objectives of each project vary and so do the challenges. Following the best practices would definitely benefit the project!

Summary

In this chapter, you learned about the importance of a methodology and the various choices of methodologies available. CRP is the clearly preferred and recommended option, while organizations can adapt to any other methodology depending on the organization's culture and project requirements.

It is important to keep your project plan up to date by keeping it in sync with the latest activities. You may use the baselining approach, which helps to predict the future set of activities and milestones.

Also, you learned about the need for a solid project start and how important it is to lay down the foundations for success early on. The key ingredients to be successful include forming the right team composition, laying down the ground rules (for behavioral aspects), and outlining the goals in the project charter.

After selecting the methodology and project initiation strategy, let's look at the toolsets available to help your project implementation. The next chapter provides an overview of **Lifecycle Services** (**LCS**) and all of the tools available and their use.

Lifecycle Services (LCS) and Tools

In the previous chapter, you learned about implementation methodologies, best practices in project initiation, and important project artifacts such as the project plan, project charter, team, and many others. However, this could soon become extremely challenging if they're managed by each customer and partner in their own way.

In this chapter, we'll share a list of tools and their importance and how they can help you in your journey with Microsoft **Dynamics 365 for Finance and Operations (D365FO)** One Version by looking at **Lifecycle Services (LCS)**, which are commonly used right from the start of going live to keep your solution healthy.

Some of the key topics that will be covered in this chapter are as follows:

- Introduction to LCS
- Tooling and libraries in LCS
- Project setup including onboarding and activities
- Ongoing use of D365FO system and LCS
- Monitoring and diagnostics
- Support system leveraging LCS

LCS

Microsoft Dynamics LCS provides a cloud-based collaborative workspace that customers and partners can use to manage implementations, upgrade, support, and many others by simplifying and standardizing the Microsoft D365FO implementations.

LCS helps in planning and executing Microsoft D365FO One Version projects in a repeatable and consistent way across implementations. It is an important tool, made as an Azure-hosted portal, and contains a set of services that allow us to perform various **Application Lifecycle Management** (**ALM**) activities easily. LCS acts as a common portal that provides shared resources for implementation partners and customers to collaborate together.

When a customer buys a subscription for Microsoft D365FO's One Version, what happens? What activities are supposed to be done, which resources can be leveraged, when would environments become available to them, how could the environments be managed, and would they get any tooling to support their implementation? There are going to be so many questions on how to keep the project on target and keep moving forward with the help of tools, which is where LCS plays a vital role.

LCS is one of our recommended tools for all Microsoft D365FO implementations and it helps in improving the predictability and quality of implementations, thereby enabling business value faster. The goal of Microsoft is to bring in LCS is to deliver the right information at the right time and to the right people. This helps in ensuring repeatable and predictable success with each rollout of an implementation, update, or upgrade.

LCS is available to customers, partners, as well as prospects. While customers and partners get access to learning, implementation, and other purposes, prospects can get access for trial purposes. The following table suggests various ways of getting LCS access:

For an existing customer of the older version of Dynamics AX	For partners of Microsoft D365FO	For customers of Microsoft D365FO
Sign in to LCS using the CustomerSource credentials	Sign in to LCS using PartnerSource credentials	Sign in to LCS using Microsoft **Azure Active Directory** (**Azure AD**) credentials

Now, let's have a look at various common tooling options that are available in LCS that are project-specific.

LCS tools

We would like to highlight some of the frequently used common tools in LCS that can be used across multiple projects:

- Manage methodologies
- Organization users
- Globalization portal
- Translation service

- Preview feature management
- Manage incidents
- Shared asset library
- Solution management

These common tools are available to all LCS projects, while project-specific tools need to be set up per project, as mentioned in the next section.

Project-specific tools

We would like to highlight some of the frequently used project-specific tools from LCS:

- Project settings
- Project users
- Cloud-hosted environments
- **Business Process Modeler (BPM)**
- Alert service
- Translation service
- Configuration and data manager
- Support
- Asset library
- Upgrade analysis
- Environment monitoring
- System diagnostics, and many others

With so many tools available, it may easily become confusing if you don't know when and where to use them. We intend to cover this aspect with the help of the following table, which highlights various tools along with their classification and details:

Segmentation	Tools	Details of the tooling
Foundation	Methodologies	Methodologies provide a tool that you can use to ensure a more repeatable and predictable implementation of projects.
Foundation	Projects	Projects are the key organizers for your experience in LCS. Projects let you invite your partners to collaborate with you, and they also let you track their progress.

Foundation	Upgrade analysis	Upgrade analysis helps you plan your upgrade to the latest version of Microsoft D365FO by analyzing the code artifacts from Microsoft Dynamics AX 4.0, Dynamics AX 2009, or Dynamics AX 2012.
Ongoing	BPM	BPM lets you create, view, and modify standard process flows.
Ongoing	Cloud-hosted environments	A cloud-hosted environment is a tool that you can use to deploy and manage Microsoft Dynamics environments on Microsoft Azure.
Ongoing	Configuration and data manager	The configuration and data manager lets you copy a configuration from one instance to another.
Ongoing	Alert service	This service enables ISV/partners to alert Microsoft of upcoming new legislations.
Support	Issue search	Issue search helps you find the existing solutions and workarounds for known issues in Microsoft Dynamics products.
Support	Cloud-powered support	Cloud-powered support helps you manage support incidents.
Support	System diagnostics	System diagnostics helps administrators monitor Microsoft Dynamics environments.

When to use which tool is an important decision. We would recommend having a good read of the subsequent sections, where we share our knowledge of important tools and concepts.

Now that you've learned about the various common and project-specific tools from LCS that can be leveraged, the next step would be to apply/use them when setting up a project.

Setting up a project in LCS

All projects must go through a series of steps, guidelines, and tools from Microsoft that leverage LCS. These projects span the following use case areas:

- **Prospective presales**
- **Migrate, create solutions, and learn**
- **Implementation** (only available when a subscription is bought for live implementation)

There are some resources and tools that are needed at the beginning of the project and some that are needed as part of an ongoing basis. Now, let's explain the process in sequence, right from an invitation from Microsoft to setting up your D365FO project in LCS and onward.

In LCS, you start by setting up a new project yourself via an invitation from Microsoft, or you can create one for your organization. The ability to create an implementation project in LCS is provided by Microsoft only. However, a project can be set up by yourself or your partner/advisor for learning, testing, demonstration, and so on.

Please refer to the following screenshot, which shows various options in LCS project creation:

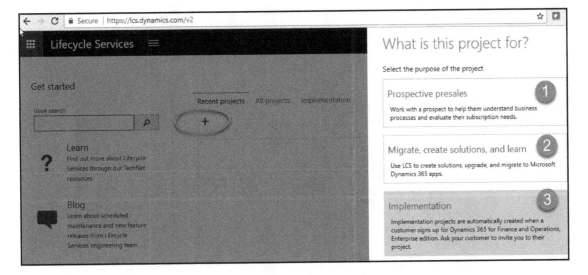

In LCS, projects are the key organizers and lay down the foundation for your goals. It is here that the methodology connection happens, and the rest of the execution follows this methodology using phases and tasks such as your project phases, activities, and milestones.

The following screenshot shows a form where you have to select from various options to set up a project in LCS:

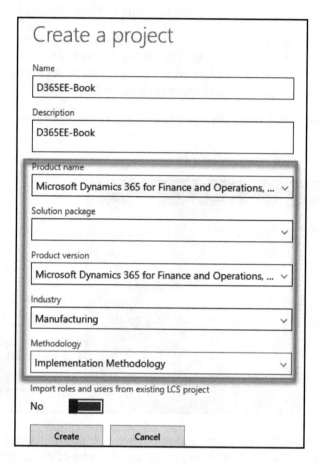

Note that you can create your own methodology for a non-implementation project. For an implementation project, you can only make limited changes to the existing phases and tasks provided by Microsoft; however, you can add as many phases and tasks as you'd like within them.

The following screenshot shows how to share a sample visual for a project and its implementation methodology in LCS:

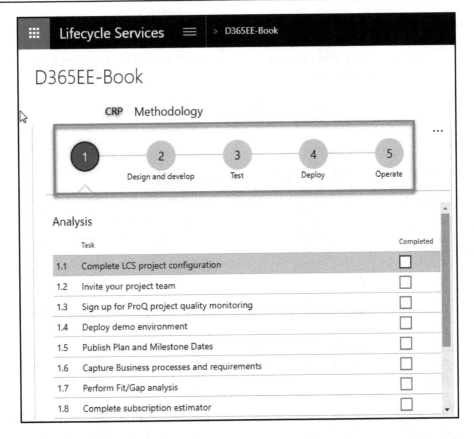

Before a phase can be marked as complete, you must complete the specified mandatory tasks and their dependent tasks.

 For more details on LCS and setting up a project, please visit `https://docs.microsoft.com/en-us/dynamics365/unified-operations/dev-itpro/lifecycle-services/lcs-works-lcs`.

Once the required project requisites have been defined in the LCS methodology, it is going to be helpful for team members to understand expected deliverables at various stages. Typically, deliverables are common in some types of implementation methodology being followed, and we'll share these deliverables and best practices while keeping the CRP methodology in focus.

A project contributor (be it from the customer's side or the partner's side) must complete the mandatory steps outlined in the implementation methodology and follow a go-live readiness checklist to gain access to the production environment on the cloud.

Now, let's learn about the various tools and capabilities in LCS that can be used to lay down a strong foundation for project success.

Tools for a solid project foundation

Now, we are going to cover the key foundation-related tools for your project's implementation. These are typically one-time setup tools and the structure remains the same throughout the life cycle of the project, though the data within them can be updated/changed.

The select tools are as follows:

- **(Project) methodologies**: Pre-assigned from Microsoft for implementation projects. This is similar to your project plan containing a list of phases, activities, milestones, dates, and many others. You can add additional phases and activities/steps to an implementation project but cannot modify existing ones from Microsoft. For other project types, customers or partners can set up their methodology to drive their project to success.
- **Project**: Pre-created from Microsoft for implementation projects; for other project types, customers and partners can create their own and give them a name. Microsoft has provided an onboarding tool that helps customers and partners in a guided way to set up everything related to the foundation of your implementation project in LCS.
- **Project users**: To give access to users to work on an LCS project, they need to be set up as users in LCS and given appropriate access. The project owner is typically your Office 365 admin who was invited to set up D365FO service, while for other project types, it is the user who creates the project. You can add or change users using the project users tool.
- **Project setting**: This is one place where settings related to the project are defined. These are comprised of customer's Azure subscriptions, DevOps settings, SharePoint settings, and continuous update settings.

Some of the other tools include the following:

- Preview feature
- Shared asset library
- Subscription estimator
- Asset library

Now, let's look at some select tools and their methodology.

Methodologies

Methodologies provide you with a tool that you can use to ensure more repeatable and predictable implementation projects.

The following are the salient features of a methodology in LCS:

- You can use one of our methodologies or create your own.
- By using a (project) methodology and various LCS tools, you can easily track and report on your progress.
- Always keep the objective of using best practices to simplify and standardize the implementation process in the adoption of your solution.
- Methodologies can be edited or appended.
- You should not change the methodology for implementation projects as there could be severe consequences of changing the methodology mid-flight, and this may require a lot of effort to get it back on track.
- Methodology is super important when the customer is ready for production deployment. We need to identify the gold build. It is mandatory for an organization's user to sign off and complete the provisioning checklist to do so. The user will also be added as the admin user in Microsoft D365FO as an *admin*.

The following is a sample visual of what a methodology looks like in LCS for an implementation project:

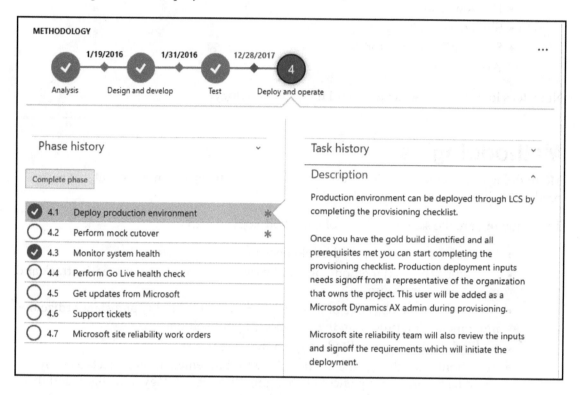

In a methodology, you can define a number of phases, phase-specific activities, descriptions, add references, add attachments, and so on.

LCS projects

Projects are the key organizers of your experience in LCS. Projects let you invite your partners to collaborate with you, and they also let you track the project's progress.

The following are the salient characteristics of a project in LCS:

- Each customer who purchases Microsoft D365FO will receive one LCS implementation project. Customers can then add their partner/CSP/VAR as a user to those LCS projects.
- Based on the offer selected by the customer, the features in this project's workspace will be enabled.
- Environments included in the offer will be deployed and managed by Microsoft.
- The **Action** center will guide you through the required actions that must be completed, including upcoming updates.
- A new methodology experience includes locked tasks as you progress through the implementation.
- A more complete audit trail specifying who completed each methodology phase and what tasks.
- Milestones can be used to track critical project dates.
- The organization that owns a project must maintain a valid service plan to keep the project active and is responsible for all the charges related to the project.
- Partner users can see the implementation project for each customer using their credentials.
- Before kicking off, you should complete the required configuration for LCS for SharePoint and Azure DevOps/Visual Studio Team Services.

Now, let's have a look at the new onboarding experience, which helps in ensuring the accuracy and the coverage of settings that's needed for your project.

Project onboarding

There is a new, simple, and structured onboarding method you can use for your project for Microsoft D365FO One Version on LCS.

Follow these steps to learn how to configure your project once you embark on your journey of D365FO:

1. Sign in to LCS using the account that is notified that your implementation project is ready to be configured.
2. Open the **Project onboarding** tool.
3. Follow the wizard/guide to configure your project by providing the necessary details.

4. The following screen is the first screen you'll see, and shows a welcome message. On the right of every screen, there is a details pane that provides more information, useful tips, and a URL:

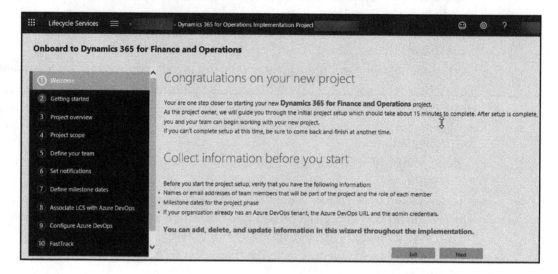

5. Select your deployment type and users by type (**Operations users**, **Team members**, **Activity users**, and so on):

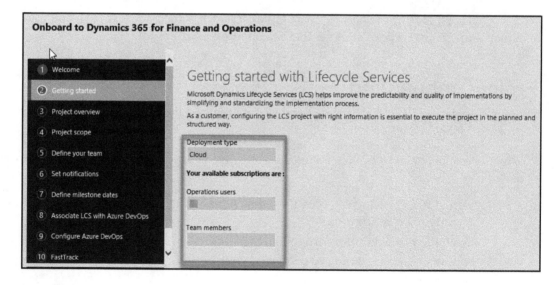

6. Give your project a name and provide partner details:

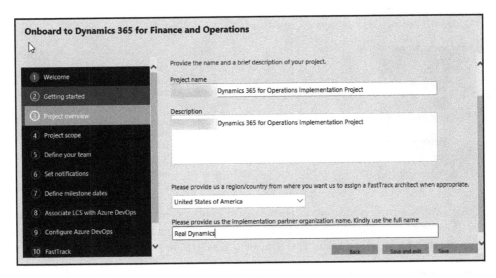

7. Select the industry and implementation type (new implementation, upgrade from a prior version, and many others)
8. Also, provide information about whether it would be using a **warehouse management system** (**WMS**) and/or retail and/or interfaces, and many others:

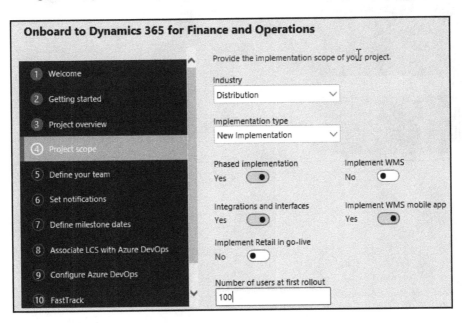

9. Create and grant access to team members for useful operations on LCS:

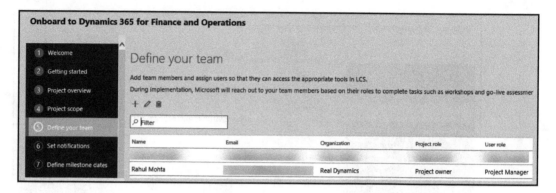

10. Provide milestone dates. These can be viewed on the main project screen and are super important for several reasons including capturing the start and completion dates for requirements and analysis, design, development, UAT, and go-live:

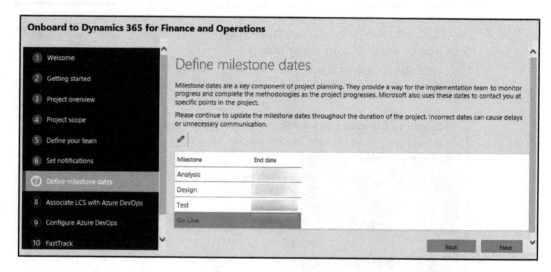

11. Next, link your LCS project with your DevOps (earlier known as VSTS) project:

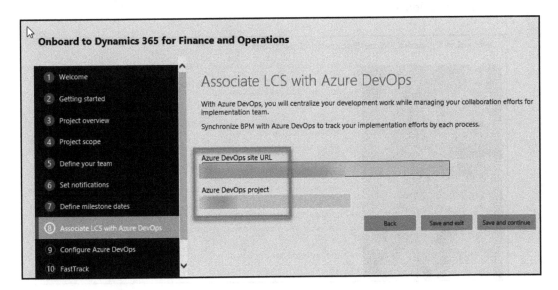

12. Review the FastTrack program and also what to expect based on your user count:

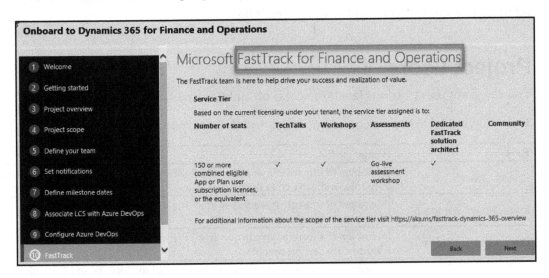

13. Lastly, review all the important links and resources that can help smoothen your D365FO journey:

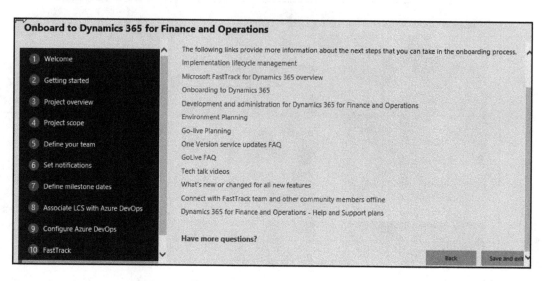

Now that your project has been onboarded, let's learn about the different users that can be set up to work in LCS throughout the project's life.

Project users

You can grant users various levels of access on an LCS project.

The following table lists various access roles and their purpose:

Role	Usage
Project owner	Members of this role have access to all the tools in LCS, can add other users in any role, and can delete the project.
Environment manager	Members of this role have access to all the tools in LCS and can manage cloud-hosted environments.
Project team member	Members of this role have access to all the tools in LCS but can't manage cloud-hosted environments.
Project team member (prospect)	Members of this role have limited access to all the tools in an LCS project: • Prospects are users who have been added to a project, but who don't have an account in VOICE or an Azure AD account. • You can identify that a user is a prospect because a prospect is listed as his or her organization.

Apart from users needing access to a project, you can also create additional types of users (organization users), as explained in the next section.

Organization users and roles

By default, membership in an LCS organization is controlled by organization membership in CustomerSource or PartnerSource. All users that are members of the CustomerSource or PartnerSource organization are added to LCS. You can also create organization users that are not affiliated with CustomerSource or PartnerSource. Some of the key factors to be considered in user creation are as follows:

- Users can access organization-specific information, such as business process libraries and methodologies
- Organization users do not have access to specific projects until they have been invited to join them

Along with the LCS project role, you can also classify the user among one of the following user roles:

- Project manager
- Functional consultant
- Technical consultant
- Architect
- Business user

Now, let's go through the options of enabling unreleased features available for just preview.

Preview feature management

Preview feature management is also known as beta feature management and has the following salient characteristics:

- If you've been invited to try an LCS preview, you can enter a code or enable the preview here.
- Public previews are available for any LCS user.

- Private previews are only available to users and organizations that have been invited to participate.
- To get involved in LCS previews, you need to sign up for the Microsoft D365FO feedback programs.

Now, let's look at the usage profile/subscription estimator, which is important for sizing your environment.

Usage profile/subscription estimator

This is a sizing tool that uses a usage profiler, which is a data-gathering tool that helps you describe your projected or current usage of a Microsoft D365FO implementation.

The usage profile that is generated can be used for various purposes, such as hardware sizing for a production environment by Microsoft and support.

This tool seeks information in the following three sections:

- Deployment details
- Instance characteristics
- Retail and commerce

The Microsoft Dynamics Lifecycle Services subscription estimator provides an automated estimate of the subscription that's needed for your Microsoft D365FO instance. It does the following:

- It uses the user license details and the transaction count to infer the subscription's needs.
- There can be multiple versions of estimates and one of them can be marked as *active*, which in turn is used by Microsoft for production sizing purpose support.

Now, let's go through an important tool that we can use to pull resources to your LCS project.

Shared asset library

You can maintain a lot of assets in a common organizational library for the purpose of reusability and productivity.

The following are the shared asset types:

- Configuration
- Deployment
- Model store
- Model database
- Business database
- Localized financial report

While the preceding are shared and available across LCS projects, each project builds its own artifacts over a period of time, all of which are maintained in the asset library.

Asset library

The asset library is a single repository that maintains all the artifacts related to your implementation of Microsoft D365FO and the project in LCS.

There are several asset types that can be used to store, use, reuse, and deploy the following artifacts:

- **Cortana intelligence application**: These are Microsoft-provided machine learning and recommendations-related components that are installed in your environment via the LCS asset library repository, which brings insights derived from the Cortana intelligence suite components using machine learning right within Dynamics 365.
- **Data package**: Data packages are used for loading data using the LCS asset library repository in your Dynamics 365 environment.
- **Microsoft D365FO database backup**: This procedure can only be used in non-production environments. In this tool, a Microsoft D365FO database backup is uploaded as a file in the LCS asset library repository and then reimported in the same or another instance in order to quickly use the system.
- **GER configuration**: This involves uploading and leveraging the **Electronic Reporting (ER)** configuration in an asset library repository in Microsoft LCS and subsequently using it in your Dynamics 365 environment.
- **Localized financial report**: Any country/region-specific localized solutions that have been prepared by developers and ISVs can be created as a solution and added in the LCS repository, which could subsequently be used in other implementations by the partner/advisor who owns it.

- **Marketing asset**: Here, organizations can upload their logo of different sizes in the LCS asset library repository for subsequent use in other environments.
- **Model**: This is a code repository and consists of a group of elements that typically constitute a distributable software solution. Model is a design-time concept; for example, a warehouse management model.
- **Power BI report model**: This is explained in detail in `Chapter 10`, *Analytics, Business Intelligence, and Reporting*.
- **Software deployable package**: This is explained in detail in `Chapter 6`, *Configuration and Data Management*.
- **BPM artifact**: Use this repository within the LCS asset library to manage and reuse your business process libraries.
- **Process data package**: This is explained in detail in `Chapter 6`, *Configuration and Data Management*.
- **Solution package**: Here, you can obtain solution packages published from Microsoft and use them during your environment spin-up time.
- **NuGet package**: Here, you can obtain NuGet packages published in the shared asset library or import new ones so that you can use them in your D365FO environment. Microsoft D365FO Visual Studio projects allow X++ code to interact seamlessly with code written in other .NET languages.

You can make a copy of an asset directly from the asset library. Also, you can ship a new version of any file in the asset library and provide release notes when you publish an asset. This is useful when you have assets that have been published by your organization's users.

Organization users can now get additional versions of the same file and check what has changed with each version from the release notes before they download a specific version.

SharePoint online

Managing documents in a SharePoint library is very convenient, and leveraging the same with your implementation methodology in LCS is a great combination. LCS provides you with the ability to perform SharePoint online integration with an LCS project. Let's look at how to do this:

1. To set up a SharePoint online site in an LCS project, go to the **Project settings** tile.
2. On the **Project settings** page, click the **SharePoint Online library** tab.
3. Enter the SharePoint Online site URL belonging to your Office 365 tenant and then click **Next**.
   Clicking **Next** will open the following screen, which shows the URL of your SharePoint online site:

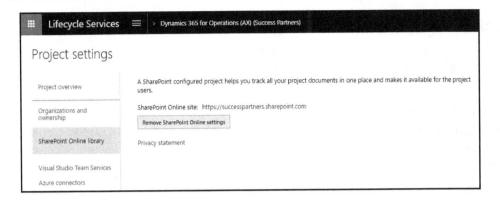

The preceding screenshot shows the LCS project settings screen's **SharePoint Online library** tab. Here, you need to assign your SharePoint online site in order to integrate with LCS so as to keep your LCS documents in sync with it. Once the SharePoint online site URL has been accepted by LCS, you are ready to upload documents to any step in the LCS methodology.

The integration between LCS cloud services and SharePoint uses OAuth user authentication.

So far, we've covered setting up your project with all the necessary bells and whistles so that you can use it effectively on a day-to-day basis.

Now, let's go through the tools and options that are helpful for day-to-day activities using LCS.

Ongoing day-to-day activities

The following are the key tools in LCS for ongoing usage in your initiative. These tools are expected to be used frequently and, hence, the information within keeps evolving:

- BPM
- Cloud-hosted environment
- Code upgrade
- Configuration and data manager
- Localization and translation and the alert service

We'll look at these in detail in the subsequent sections.

Business process modeler

BPM lets you create, view, and modify standard process flows inside Microsoft D365FO. One of the top goals for BPM is to standardize the process flows, their documentation, and their usage throughout the initiative.

BPM helps in aligning your Microsoft D365FO One Version processes with industry-standard processes, as described by the **American Productivity and Quality Center (APQC)**, and can also perform fit-gap analysis between the business needs and the default processes in Microsoft D365FO One Version.

By linking BPM with DevOps, you can generate a consolidated list of gaps and import them manually into DevOps as work items that include a reference to the process flow.

BPM also leverages Microsoft Word and Microsoft Visio to generate documentation for business processes and export business process maps to Visio files, respectively.

The following are the key usages and benefits of using BPM:

- Align Microsoft D365FO processes with industry-standard processes, as described by the APQC.
- Identify the fit and gaps between user requirements and the default functionality that Microsoft D365FO provides.
- Use the synchronize option in the BPM library hierarchy with your VSTS project.
- At the time of writing, this is a one-way sync from LCS to VSTS, which will keep your VSTS work items (epics, features, and so on) updated with any changes that are made in the LCS BPM library.
- There are three kinds of libraries where BPM can be maintained:
  - **Global library**: Available to all LCS users
  - **Corporate library**: Available to all organization users
  - **Project library**: Available to users within the LCS project with appropriate access

The following screenshot shows a global library from Microsoft:

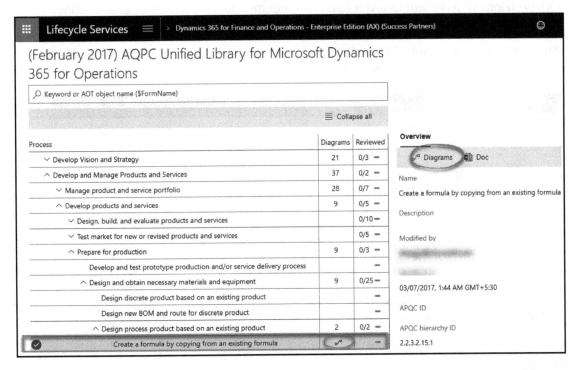

As shown in the preceding screenshot, you can create and maintain the hierarchical flow of business processes and requirements by leveraging branching and segmenting.

Please refer to `Chapter 5`, *Requirements and Process Analysis*, and `Chapter 6`, *Configuration and Data Management*, for more details on LCS BPM.

 LCS BPM can be synchronized with VSTS, where more detailed information, processing, and various workflows can be implemented.

Now, let's learn how to manage cloud-hosted environments using LCS.

Cloud-hosted environments

Cloud-hosted environments can be used to deploy and maintain Microsoft D365FO environments on Microsoft Azure.

When you use cloud-hosted environments, you must select the type of Microsoft D365FO One Version environment in order to deploy a demo, developer/test, or production environment.

The following screenshot of an LCS cloud-hosted environment depicts the environments and their types in an implementation project:

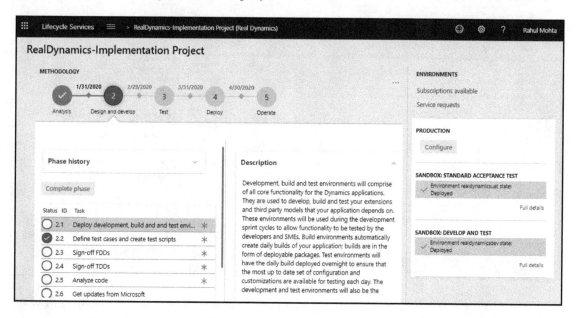

The following are the types of cloud-hosted environment that you can choose from:

- A customer-own Azure subscription.
- A two-sandbox environment that's provided as part of a subscription needs to be configured in a self-service way.
- The production environment, as part of the subscription, will be deployed by MS toward the very end upon completing the go-live assessment checklist, which is typically shared by the FastTrack team.

Based on your selection, the cloud-hosted environments tool provisions the appropriate number of **Virtual Machines** (**VMs**) in Azure through LCS. These VMs have the components (and all their prerequisites) of Microsoft D365FO already installed on them.

You can get details of your deployment status, the URL for Microsoft D365FO, the URL for retail Cloud POS, and local VM credentials, along with domain accounts and system diagnostic information from the LCS environment monitoring page.

 Other than the production environment, customers that are interested in resizing their VM once it has been deployed from the LCS can only do so from the Azure Portal.

Code upgrade

The code upgrade tool helps you plan your upgrade to the latest version of Microsoft D365FO One Version by analyzing code artifacts from the prior versions of Microsoft D365FO (for example, 8.x or 7.x) or Dynamics AX 2012.

It can also be just run for estimations so that you can receive analysis reports. When only the estimation is used, the exported and upgraded models will not be checked in to Azure DevOps/Visual Studio Team Services and will not be available for download.

These are the brief steps that must be followed when upgrading from Dynamics AX 2012:

1. Create an upgrade analysis job (the task you are performing now).
2. Export your AX 2012 model store.
3. Zip (compress) the model store file.
4. Upload your compressed model store.
5. After the job has completed, download the metadata file, `UpgradedMetadata.zip`, or connect to the Azure DevOps/Visual Studio Team Services project containing the upgraded code. We expect Microsoft to release a data upgrade service as well for the previous versions.

Configuration and data manager

The configuration and data manager lets you copy a configuration from one instance of Microsoft D365FO to another.

You can copy from and to Microsoft D365FO environments that meet the following criteria:

- They are managed as part of an LCS project.
- They run on the data management framework in Microsoft D365FO and can leverage data packages (containing entities).

- You can also create groups of data packages called **Process Data Packages** (PDP) and use them for all kinds of deployments to any environment in the LCS project being worked on. Please refer to `Chapter 6`, *Configuration and Data Management,* for more details.

Translation service

Microsoft Dynamics 365 Translation Service (DTS) is hosted in LCS to enhance the experience for partners and **independent software vendors** (ISVs) when they translate their solutions or add a new language.

The following screenshot shows the service in action. It shows the translation service request ID in a chronological way. The user can click on the ID to get more details:

Users need to upload a file in **Localization Interchange File Format** (XLIFF), which goes through Microsoft's machine translation service and provides output in a file.

Alert service

The Dynamics ERP regulatory alert submission service is designed to support the localization community in reporting changes in a country/region legislation, which impacts the Microsoft-supported localized country/region solution.

If there is an upcoming regulatory change in your Microsoft-supported country/region that you are aware of, you can now flag it to Microsoft by submitting a regulatory alert. The following screenshot shows a list of alert submission samples from `https://docs.microsoft.com/en-us/dynamics365/fin-ops-core/fin-ops/index`:

Dynamics Regulatory Alert Submission

+

🔍 India ✕

ID	Title	Country/region	Law enforced date	Date submitted
0000020285	IN-Business process for GST refund	India	2016-09-30	2015-10-19
0000020284	IN-Business Process for GST Payment	India	2016-09-30	2015-10-19
0000020283	IN-GST Registration	India	2016-09-30	2015-10-19
0000020282	Adoption of IND-AS	India	2016-03-31	2015-10-19
0000020273	IN-FVU (file validation utility tool) version 4.8 for e-TDS/TCS return	India	2015-09-28	2015-10-14
0000020196	Test - Tax format report change for India	India	2015-12-31	2015-08-12
0000010136	Central Excise and Service Tax - Digital Signature and e-records	India	2015-07-15	2015-07-13
0000010118	IN_New FVU tool version 4.7 for TDS/TCS return	India	2015-06-20	2015-06-30

The solution to this is based on a simple four-step wizard that will take you through the regulatory alert submission:

1. Searching for the alert or associated feature
2. Associating business processes with the regulatory change
3. Alert details
4. Submission confirmation

The Microsoft Dynamics 365 translation service is designed to improve the experience of the partners and customers when translating the Microsoft Dynamics product UI into existing and additional languages.

The following are some additional capabilities of the localization and translation services in LCS:

- The solution can also be used to translate custom features that have been developed by partners.
- The solution is based on the Microsoft Translator Hub and the Multilingual App Toolkit.

- It provides customized machine translation as the starting point of the translation process, reducing the effort of post-editing and review.
- A major benefit of the solution is that Microsoft Linguistic Assets are made available through the Microsoft Translator Hub.

Now, let's go through support-related activities involving key support tools that can be used to keep your project healthy.

Ongoing support

The following are the key tools in LCS for ongoing support. These tools are expected to be used frequently right after going live, while some can also be used for ongoing activities:

- Issue search
- Support
- Work items
- System diagnostics
- Updates

Let's look at each of these tools in detail, starting with Issue search.

Issue search

Issue search helps you find existing solutions and workarounds for known issues in Microsoft D365FO.

You can see which issues have been fixed, which issues remain open, and which issues have been resolved as unable to be fixed.

Now, let's go through all the options of raising and managing support in your day-to-day project activities.

LCS support options

LCS has several options that can help you manage various support incidents.

The support options are as follows:

- **Manage incidents**: This is a single window that you can use to view all the support incidents that have been raised with Microsoft from your organization across projects. These incidents are classified as premier and non-premier and are based on your support agreement with Microsoft.
- **Open work items**: This provides a list of the currently open work items.
- **Support issues**: The project team or business users can submit an issue from within the Microsoft D365FO client or manually create an issue in the LCS. Issues can be investigated by a customer or partner team and can also be raised to Microsoft.
- **Service request**: All service requests are raised with the **Dynamics Service Engineer (DSE)** for any matter related to the production environment.
- **Hotfix request**: When business users encounter an issue while using the Microsoft D365FO client, they can search to find out whether Microsoft has published any hotfixes regarding the issue. If so, the business user can submit a request for a hotfix, which will be available under this section. The system administrator can assign the request to the IT team for further evaluation.
- **Self-service tools**:
    - **Deploy sandbox**: Deploy your cloud VM as part of the subscription for Tier-2
    - **Code deployment**: Deploy code packages
- **Move database**
- **Restart services**

It is recommended that you rightly classify the severity of the issue when submitting to Microsoft as they will ensure that you are on top of the issue and that you know the background of it well so that you can get the support team on the same page, hence providing a better chance for an accurate and early resolution.

You will find out more about using LCS to monitor performance, SQL monitoring, and other self-service tools in `Chapter 12`, *Managing Go-Live and Post Go-Live*.

Work items

This is another view that shows all the open work items. These work items are available on Visual Studio online services, which have to be configured for the LCS project.

The following are the two modes of work items usage in LCS:

- When you choose the storage location of LCS, then you can create new work items in LCS, but then, there is no VSTS integration.
- When you configure the VSTS integration in your LCS project, then you need to link it to a specific VSTS project. When you create work items in the linked VSTS project, then the work items will be seen in your LCS project/work items. You can open the work items from LCS by clicking on the ID link.

In various types of work items, certain types of bugs or tasks that have been created within VSTS are visible in LCS.

Environment monitoring

Environment monitoring is used to monitor, diagnose, and analyze the health of the Microsoft D365FO environments.

Microsoft uses telemetry data to show monitoring and diagnostics information on LCS. This data is used in three scenarios:

- **Monitoring**: Helpful in finding out whether your environment is up and running (availability) and its health.
- **Diagnostics**: Helpful in troubleshooting user issues and getting insights into production SQL usage and some SQL troubleshooting tools.
- **Analytics**: This is currently only available to Microsoft. It is used to perform analytics to gauge and understand feature usage and performance using Microsoft Power BI.

The following screenshot shows environment monitoring in LCS:

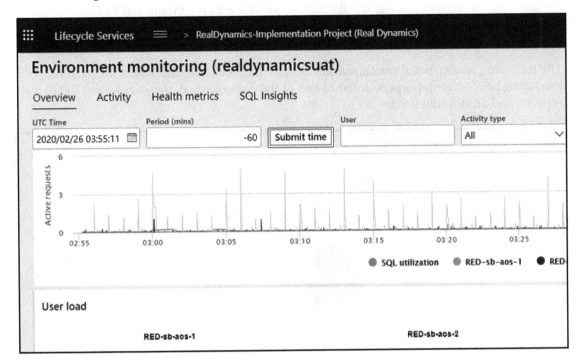

For a subscription-based production environment, Microsoft is responsible for actively monitoring the health of the production environments at all times.

For all the other environments that are hosted by customers/partners, they need to actively monitor the health.

After monitoring, another important tool to leverage at select intervals of project duration is system diagnostics.

System diagnostics

System diagnostics helps administrators monitor Microsoft D365FO environments:

- The dashboard provides a visual indication of the number of hosts in the selected environment that encountered errors when running rules and also displays the last five messages.
- It also indicates whether any collector jobs have encountered errors while running.

Only production environments that have been deployed through LCS in a Microsoft Managed Subscription will be actively monitored by the Microsoft Service Engineering team. All other environments, such as Sandbox environments, do not have the monitoring features turned on.

The following screenshot shows a sample system diagnostics dashboard with sections providing brief information about the health of the environment, messages, jobs, detailed reports, and admin functions:

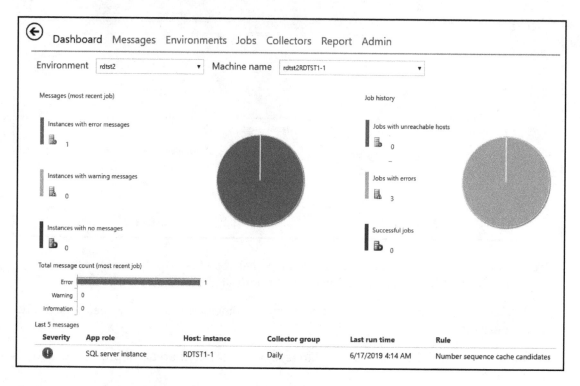

As we can see, the system diagnostics dashboard gives administrators quick insights into the health of the environment in an easy, visual, and actionable way.

Updates

Updates are provided in the action center on LCS's project main page. The default settings that can be applied to a multi-tier sandbox and production environment for Microsoft D365FO environment is provided in the **Project settings**, as shown in the following screenshot:

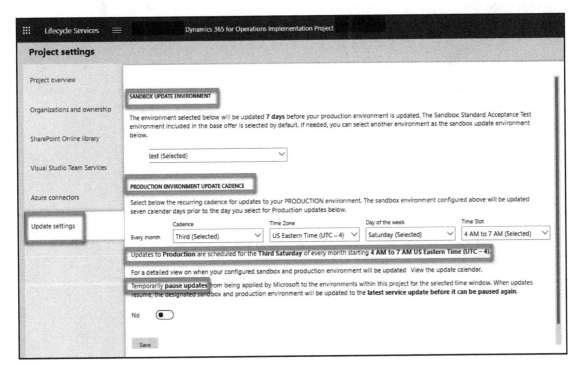

Here, you can suggest the preferred update cadence for the production environment and, if needed, can pause the updates.

Please refer to Chapter 13, *One Version Service Updates*, for more details on managing continuous updates coming from Microsoft.

Summary

In this chapter, you learned about various tools that you can use to embrace Microsoft D365FO. It is extremely important to know about all the tools and options you can use to effectively manage and drive the project to success, and LCS has a plethora of tools that you can benefit from and that derive value from your implementation. We expect and continuously see Microsoft enhancing these tools' existing capabilities for every customer and partner. We also expect new functionality additions that will benefit customers and partners worldwide and that lay a strong foundation of successful adoption of Microsoft D365FO.

Understanding the architecture of a system is critical if we want to know how it works. In the next chapter, you will learn about the architecture and the various components of Microsoft D365FO. You will also learn about deployment.

Architecture, Deployment, and Environments

4

Enterprise resource planning (**ERP**) software such as Dynamics 365 for Finance and Operations is a massive software application that supports global enterprises in providing information across all the functional units of a business entity. Understanding architecture is critical in order to know how the system works. Software architecture is fundamental to answering the following questions:

- How does a software application work?
- What different components are part of the software, and how do they interact?
- Can software grow as a business grows?
- What infrastructure do we need to deploy the software?
- How can a software application be deployed and managed?

When you are planning to implement Dynamics 365 for Finance and Operations in your organization, it is imperative to understand the architecture of the product and how it can fit within your organization. To get the answers to the preceding questions in relation to Microsoft Dynamics 365 for Finance and Operations, this chapter covers the following topics in detail:

- Understanding architecture
- Understanding application components and architecture
- Understanding deployment options
- Understanding cloud deployment and environment planning

Understanding architecture

The Dynamics 365 for Finance and Operations architecture is built for the cloud, to embrace the investment and innovation happening in the Microsoft Azure cloud. The architecture uses modern user interface, integration, and web technologies. Dynamics 365 for Finance and Operations can be deployed on cloud or on-premises. Cloud deployments use Microsoft Azure, and the production environment is fully managed by Microsoft, while on-premises deployments are deployed locally on the customer's own data center. To understand the overall architecture of the Finance and Operations product, let's start with understanding the conceptual architecture of the product.

Conceptual architecture

From the conceptual architecture perspective, both cloud and on-premises deployment options use the same application stack, clients, development environment, and **Application Lifecycle Management** (**ALM**). The difference is primarily in the infrastructure, database, and identity provider used. The following diagram represents a high-level conceptual architecture of Dynamics 365 for Finance and Operations:

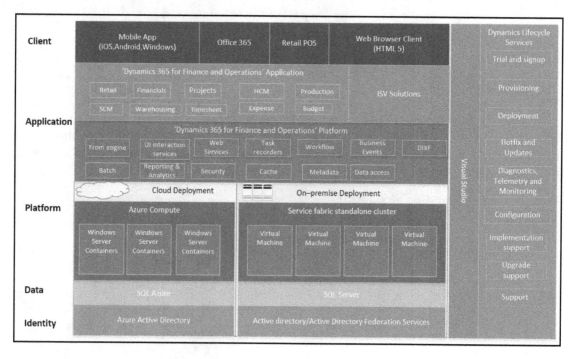

Let's try to understand different components of the preceding architecture diagram, starting from the bottom stack:

- **Identity**: At the very bottom of the architecture is the identity layer. This component represents the identity and authentication management of Dynamics 365 for Finance and Operations. In cloud deployment, **Azure Active Directory** (**Azure AD**) is used for authentication, while on-premises deployment relies on on-premises **Active Directory Federation Services** (**AD FS**) for authentication.

- **Data/storage**: The next layer after the identity layer is the data or storage layer, which represents the database used to store the core business configuration and transaction data. In cloud deployment, Azure SQL is used as the database. On-premises deployment uses Microsoft SQL Server 2016 Standard edition or Enterprise edition.

- **Platform**: On top of the data layer is a platform layer that represents the Azure compute infrastructure, operating system, and applications to host the various components of Dynamics 365 for Finance and Operations. Cloud deployment uses Azure compute through Windows Server containers. On-premises deployment uses on-premises infrastructure and **virtual machines** (**VMs**) to deploy the various components through the Service Fabric standalone cluster.

Starting from October 2019, Microsoft is migrating cloud deployment compute from virtual machines to Hyper-V containers. This feature is also known as migration to self-service deployment.

- **Application**: This layer in the architecture diagram represents the Dynamics 365 for Finance and Operations application components, metadata, and code. The core application components of Finance and Operations are the same, irrespective of the deployment choices.

- **Client**: The client layer is the topmost layer in the architecture diagram. This represents the various client components to access Dynamics 365 for Finance and Operations, such as the browser client, mobile app, and Office 365.

- **Development tools**: In the preceding architecture diagram, Visual Studio is shown as a vertical layer to the overall architecture diagram. Visual Studio is the exclusive development environment for a developer to extend the existing application logic or build new features.

- **Lifecycle Services**: Finally, the **Lifecycle Services** (**LCS**), which are used to manage the application's life cycle, including deployment, monitoring, and support for the cloud, as well as on-premises deployments.

To understand the architecture better, we need to go deeper into each of the preceding layers and try to understand different application components and their architecture. But before that, let's first understand how the conceptual architecture diagram shown previously maps to the physical environment deployed for Dynamics 365 for Finance and Operations.

Deployment architecture

The deployment architecture depicts the mapping of a conceptual architecture to a physical environment. The physical environment includes the computing nodes and services, and how they connect with each other to make the final environment. In this section, let's explore the deployment architecture of Dynamics 365 for Finance and Operations.

The cloud deployment architecture

The Dynamics 365 for Finance and Operations architecture is built for the cloud, which is the recommended and preferred option of deployment. Cloud deployment uses Microsoft Azure, managed by Microsoft, as the cloud platform. The following diagram shows an example of the production environment deployment architecture:

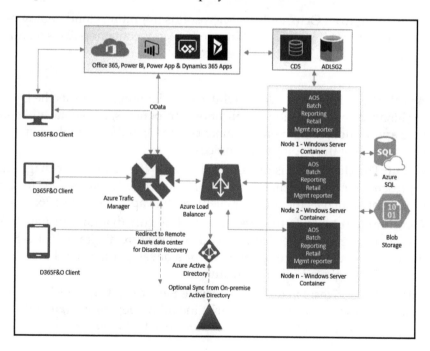

To understand the diagram, let's walk through the image from left to right, and explore the various components and their roles, as follows:

- **Client devices**: Client devices such as workstation computers, tablets, and mobile devices connect Finance and Operations through the web browser or mobile apps. Other applications, such as Office 365, Power Apps, Power BI, and Dynamics 365 applications, can connect Finance and Operations data using **Open Data Protocol (OData)** or via **Common Data Service (CDS)** and Azure Data Lake Storage Gen2.
- **Azure Traffic Manager**: Azure Traffic Manager is used for **Domain Name System (DNS)** resolution and Azure region identification. It also redirects to remote Azure data centers in disaster recovery scenarios.
- **Azure Load Balancer**: An Azure load balancer provides a higher level of availability by spreading incoming requests across multiple nodes.
- **Azure AD**: Azure AD provides identity management and authentication for Finance and Operations. Optionally, you can use Azure sync to sync identities from your on-premises AD.
- **Windows server container nodes**: All core application components, such as **Application Object Server (AOS)**, batch server, retail server, reporting services, management reporter, and many others, are deployed as Windows Server container nodes. Container nodes are deployed in **high availability (HA)** mode (at least two in the availability set), and can be scaled out based on demand.
- **Data layer**: Finance and Operations uses Azure SQL Database for transaction workload and Azure Blob Storage to store files. Optionally, master and transaction data can be synced to the customer's own CDS and Azure Data Lake Storage Gen2 environments.

 This architecture diagram is just an example to help you understand the architecture; your actual deployment design will vary according to your resources and requirements.

On-premises deployment architecture

The on-premises deployment option uses Finance and Operations components running on the premises, leveraging Service Fabric standalone clusters. The following diagram shows an example of the on-premises deployment architecture with the minimum recommended nodes for Dynamics 365 for Finance and Operations:

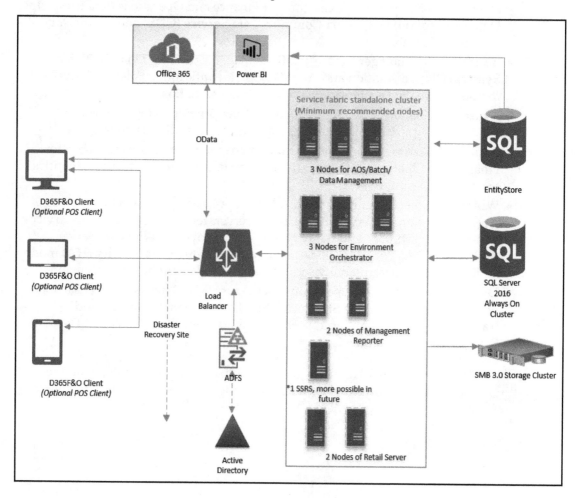

Let's again walk through the preceding image from left to right, and explore the various components, as follows:

- **Client devices**: Similar to the cloud environment, various devices use a web browser or mobile application to access Dynamics 365 for Finance and Operations. Office 365 uses OData for communication.
- **Load balancer**: The network load balancer is used for balancing the load between application nodes and redirecting the disaster recovery scenario.
- **Active Directory Federation Services** (**AD FS**) **and AD**: AD FS is used along with the on-premises AD for authentication.
- **Application VMs**: In on-premises deployment, all the core components of Finance and Operations are deployed using the Service Fabric standalone cluster. In addition to the regular application VMs, another set of VMs is needed for on-premises environment management from LCS.
- **Database layer**: All databases are created on Microsoft SQL Server 2016 Standard edition or Enterprise edition. The **Server Message Block** (**SMB**) 3.0 storage cluster stores unstructured data on the **Application Object Servers** (**AOS**). An optional dedicated data store for reporting and analytics (**EntityStore**) is available to all customers on version 10.0 and later.

> This architecture diagram is just an example to understand the architecture; your actual deployment design will vary according to your resources and requirements.

> Microsoft Dynamics 365 for Finance and Operations is built for the cloud first. Therefore, many features are not implemented or need to be configured differently to the on-premises deployments. For the latest details on the on-premises deployment option, refer to `https://docs.` `microsoft.com/en-us/dynamics365/unified-operations/dev-itpro/` `deployment/on-premises-deployment-landing-page`.

Understanding application components and architecture

In the previous section, we explored the conceptual and deployment architecture of Dynamics 365 for Finance and Operations. Now, it's time to go deep into each layer of the conceptual architecture and understand the various components involved, their role, and how they interact with each other. Let's start with the bottom-most layer of the conceptual architecture diagram: the identity layer.

Working with identity management

Dynamics 365 for Finance and Operations cloud deployment uses Azure AD for identity management and authentication. Microsoft Azure AD is a modern, cloud-based service that provides identity management and access control capabilities for your cloud applications. You can use **Azure AD Connect** to integrate and synchronize with an on-premises Windows AD and provide the **Single Sign-On** (**SSO**) functionality to the user and devices. The following diagram shows the high-level capabilities of Azure AD:

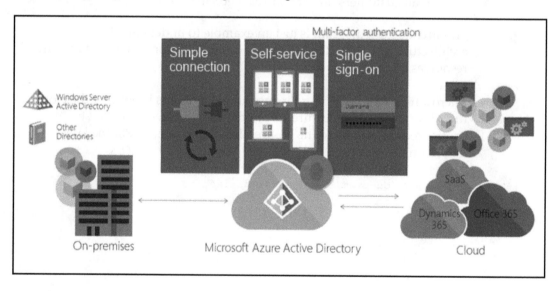

Cloud deployment of Dynamics 365 for Finance and Operations uses Azure AD and the **SAML** 2.0 (short for **Security Assertion Markup Language**) protocol for the authentication and authorization process. The following diagram depicts in five simple steps how this happens:

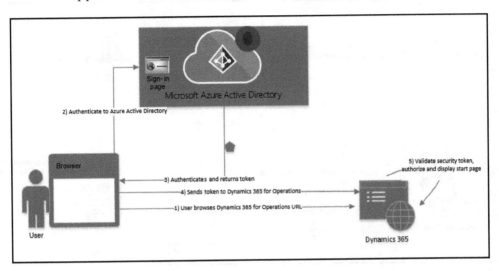

As shown in the preceding diagram, the authentication process happens in the following sequence:

1. The **User** logs on to Dynamics 365 for Finance and Operations using a browser.
2. The user session gets redirected to the Azure AD login page for authentication. The user logs in to Azure AD using the user ID and password.
3. Azure AD authenticates the user and generates the SAML 2.0 token.
4. The user session gets redirected to Dynamics 365 for Finance and Operations with security tokens.
5. In the end, Dynamics 365 for Finance and Operations validates the security token, authorizes the user (if the user is registered as a valid user in the application), and displays the start page.

The on-premises deployment option uses AD FS for authentication and AD for identity management. The following diagram shows the authentication flow in on-premises deployment:

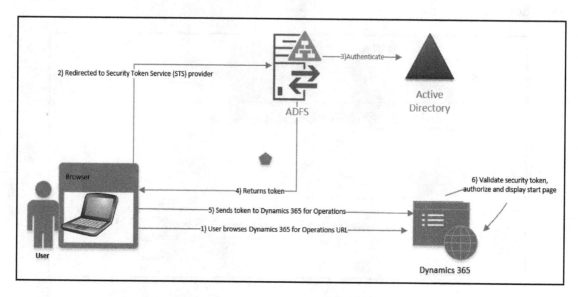

As shown in the preceding diagram, the authentication flow for on-premises deployment is similar to cloud deployment. The only difference is that for the cloud, Azure AD is used as an **STS** (short for **Security Token Service)** and identity provider, whereas for on-premises deployment, AD FS is used as the STS provider and AD as the identity provider.

 An STS is a software-based identity provider that issues security tokens in a claims-based identity system.

Understanding the data layer components

The cloud deployment option of Dynamics 365 for Finance and Operations uses the Azure SQL Database for primary read and write workload, and Azure Blob Storage to store files. Cloud deployment utilizes Azure SQL's **ReadOnly Secondary** feature to offload read-only workload. Azure SQL geo-replication is used for disaster recovery scenarios.

The following diagram shows the various data layer components used in Dynamics 365 for Finance and Operations and their purposes:

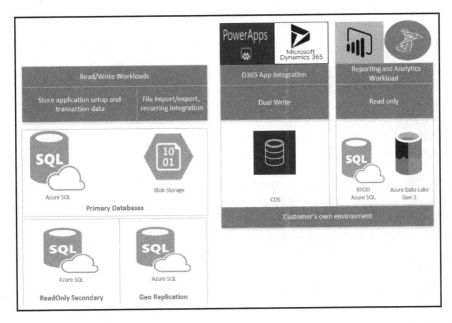

In the cloud deployment, application and transaction data can be synchronized to the customer's own CDS, **BYOD** (short for **bring your own database**) Azure SQL Database, and Azure Data Lake Storage Gen2 for integration, reporting, and analytical workload.

The following diagram shows the data layer in an on-premises deployment option. It uses SQL Server as a primary database and the SMB 3.0 storage cluster for unstructured data such as files:

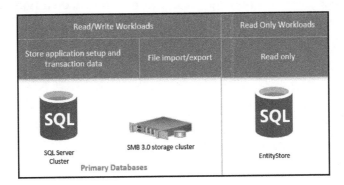

Optionally, customers can configure **EntityStore** as a dedicated database for the analytical and reporting workload.

Understanding the platform-layer components

The Microsoft Dynamics 365 for Finance and Operations platform layer represents the compute, operating system, and applications to host the various components of Dynamics 365 for Finance and Operations. Finance and Operations comprises multiple applications, such as AOS, Batch Service, Data Import/Export Service, Retail Server, Management Reporter, and SQL Server Reporting Services. The following is a list of the various application components and their corresponding usage:

- **AOS**: AOS is a core component deployed as web app on **Internet Information Server** (**IIS**) to enable the Finance and Operations application functionality to be run in the client.
- **Batch Service**: Batch Service is deployed as a Windows service to provide background batch scheduling capability to the Finance and Operations application.
- **Data Import/Export Service**: The Data Import/Export Service is deployed as a Windows service to provide data import/export capability to the application.
- **Retail Server**: This provides stateless services and business logic for Retail **Modern Point of Sale** (**MPOS**) and e-commerce clients.
- **Management Reporter** (**MR**): MR is deployed as a web app on IIS to provide financial reporting functionality in the application.
- **SQL Server Reporting Services** (**SSRS**): This is deployed as WebApp on the IIS and provides document reporting functionality.

In cloud deployment, these components are deployed and run on a Windows Server container. The following diagram shows a logical view of the containers deployed in the cloud deployment model:

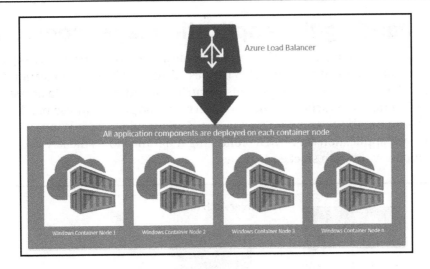

In the local business data or on-premises deployment, all the application components are deployed using Microsoft Azure Service Fabric standalone clusters on the customer data center.

 Service Fabric is a next-generation Microsoft middleware platform for building and managing enterprise-class, high-scale applications. Service Fabric standalone clusters can be deployed on any computer that runs on Windows Server.

On-premises deployment needs an additional component called an **environment orchestrator** to enable the on-premises environment management from LCS. The following diagram shows the logical architecture of on-premises deployment:

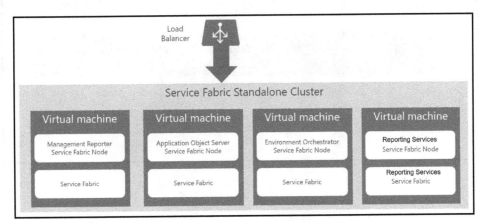

Understanding the application layer components

The Dynamics 365 for Finance and Operations application layer is primarily represented by application runtime, known as **AOS**. AOS runs as an ASP.NET web application hosted on IIS. AOS has all the core kernel components (security, metadata, and data access), forms engine, user interface interaction service, web services endpoints, and so on. Asynchronous batch processing capability and data management are provided by a Windows service running on each application server. The following diagram shows the key components of the server and how they are stacked together:

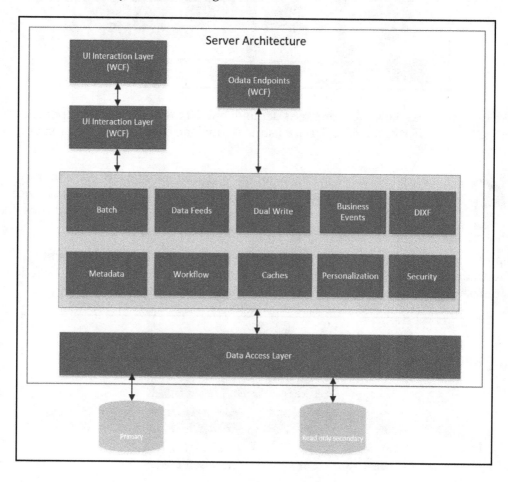

The Dynamics 365 for Finance and Operations application stack is divided into multiple packages and models. Splitting the application code stack into multiple packages provides many benefits, such as modular code, and better servicing models, as shown in the following diagram:

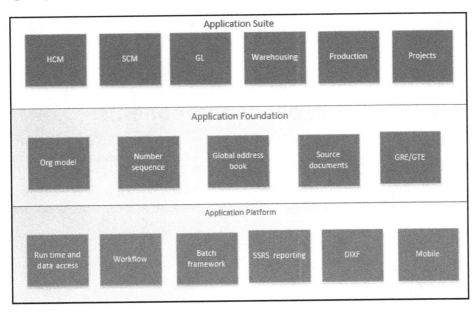

As shown in the preceding diagram, the following are three key packages representing the application stack:

- **Application Platform**: This is the lowest-level package and contains application code, handling the core application functionalities, such as runtime and data access, workflow, batch framework, SSRS reporting, **Data Import/Export Framework (DIXF)**, business events, data feeds, task recorder, and mobile framework.
- **Application Foundation**: This contains a shared application code used by the different modules in the application, such as number sequence, global address book, source document format, **generic report engine (GRE)**, and **generic tax engine (GTE)**.

- **Application Suite**: This is the top-level package containing the code of the basic application functionality for each module. Customers, partners, and **independent software vendors** (**ISVs**) can extend the application suite to add additional functionality, to fulfill their unique business requirements. The Application Suite started as a monolithic big package containing the entire application area; however, over time, this got divided into multiple packages to modularize code and create independent applications out of Dynamics 365 for Finance and Operations.

Understanding the client components

The user experience is fundamental to the success and adoption of ERP systems. If an ERP application is not easy and pleasant to use, the end user starts showing resistance to using the ERP system and starts using legacy tools and processes. An intuitive and enjoyable user experience naturally increases productivity. Dynamics 365 for Finance and Operations comes with a browser-based HTML 5 client and purpose-built mobile apps for iOS and Android devices. The browser client integrates with Office 365 to increase productivity and usability for the end users.

Browser client

The primary client for Dynamics 365 is the web browser. The Dynamics 365 for Finance and Operations client supports many browsers, such as Internet Explorer, Microsoft Edge, Google Chrome, and Safari.

The following are the key highlights of the browser client:

- Use of pure web technologies: HTML 5, CSS, and JavaScript.
- All communication is via HTTPS, using the RESTful protocol in the JSON data format.
- All code runs on the server within the context of the ASP.NET web app.

From an architecture point of view, the following diagram shows how the browser and the application server interact when the user interacts with Dynamics 365 for Finance and Operations in a browser:

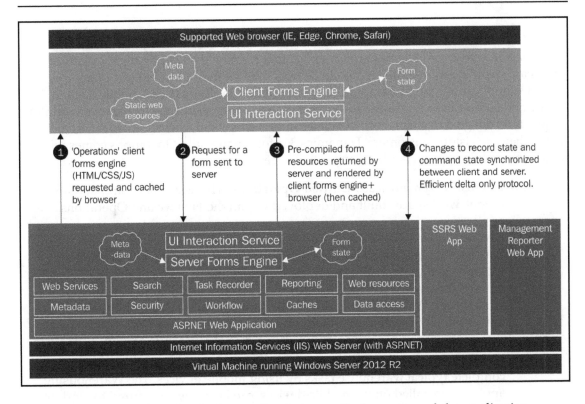

The following steps describe the interaction between the browser and the application server, as shown in the preceding diagram:

1. As the very first step, when the user browses the application page, the user gets authenticated and redirected to the home page of Dynamics 365 for Finance and Operations. If the user is using Dynamics 365 for Finance and Operations for the first time, then the **application form engine** is requested and cached by the browser.

2. When the user navigates to a form within Dynamics 365 for Finance and Operations, the browser sends the **form request** to the server.

3. In response to the form request, the server returns **precompiled form resources**. Form resources are rendered by the browser and client form engine and then cached locally by the browser.

4. Now, the changes made by the user on the form—such as changing the data, and clicking a button—are **synchronized** between the client and the server, using delta changes.

Mobile app

In the last few years, mobile has grown so fast that it's now the leading digital platform. Users are spending more time on mobile devices than on their personal computers. Business applications are also impacted by this trend. Employees need mobile apps to create and submit their timesheet and expenses; managers need apps to approve workflow requests on the go; sales reps need customer information, and can create orders on the go when they are visiting customers. Dynamics 365 for Finance and Operations comes with the following mobile apps on Android and iOS devices:

- **Microsoft Dynamics 365 Unified Operations**: This is a generic app that hosts mobile workspaces built and deployed within the Finance and Operations application.
  Several mobile workspaces are available out of the box, such as Invoice approval, Expense management, and Purchase approval. In addition, Finance and Operations mobile workspace frameworks enable developers and IT administrators to customize the existing workspace and build new mobile workspaces. We will be covering the architecture and key capability of this app in the following section of this chapter.

- **Microsoft Dynamics 365 for Finance and Operations – Warehousing**: The Warehousing app is a purpose-built application for warehouse workers to complete typical warehouse tasks by using mobile devices. The Warehousing app, once installed on the mobile devices, can be easily configured to work with your Dynamics 365 for Finance and Operations instance, and supports features such as Material handling, Receiving, Picking, Putting, Cycle counting, and Production processes.

- **Microsoft Dynamics 365 Project Timesheet**: The Microsoft Dynamics 365 Project Timesheet mobile app is a purpose-built app to submit and approve timesheets for projects. This mobile app surfaces the timesheet functionality that resides in the Project management and Accounting area of Dynamics 365 for Finance and Operations, improving user productivity and efficiency as well as enabling timely entry and approval of project timesheets.

Microsoft Dynamics 365 Unified Operations – mobile app

As described earlier, this app is a generic app that automatically pulls mobile workspaces deployed in the customer's environment. The following are key highlights of this mobile app:

- **Offline capability**: You can view, edit, and operate the mobile app when your device is connected to the network and while your mobile phone is completely offline. If a user creates or updates data while their device isn't connected to the Finance and Operations server, temporary records are created in the local cache. When your device re-establishes a network connection, your offline data operations are automatically synchronized.

- **Build and deploy**: IT admins can build and publish mobile workspaces as per the organization's requirements. The app leverages your existing code, business logic, and security configuration. IT admins can easily design mobile workspaces using the point-and-click workspace designer that comes built in with the Dynamics 365 for Finance and Operations web client.

- **Business logic extensibility**: IT admins can optimize the offline capabilities of workspaces by utilizing the business logic extensibility framework. Using this, you can provide additional business logic and render support by adding a JavaScript file with the application workspace metadata.

The following screenshot provides an overview of the Dynamics 365 for Finance and Operations mobile application user interface:

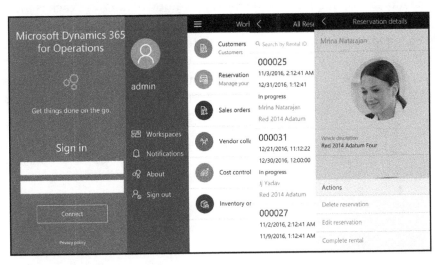

The following diagram shows the various user and system interactions within the mobile application framework:

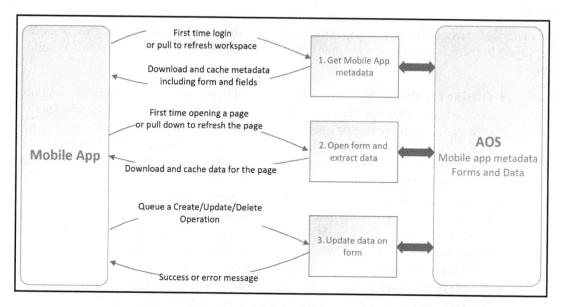

As shown in the preceding diagram, user and system interaction can be explained as follows:

1. Mobile app metadata, forms, and data are all stored on the application object server. When the user logs in for the first time or pulls to refresh the dashboard, the mobile app requests the metadata, and downloads and caches the workspaces and pages.

2. When the user opens the page or pulls to refresh the data on the page, the mobile app opens the form, downloads the data for the page, and caches it.

3. Any operation—such as editing the data or taking an action that results in a create, update, or delete operation—goes into the queue and is subsequently executed on the AOS, with the result synchronized.

Office 365

The Office integration capabilities of Microsoft Dynamics 365 for Finance and Operations enables end users to interact with the Finance and Operations data in their favorite Office application, such as Excel and Microsoft Word. In Excel, the Microsoft Dynamics Office add-in allows users to export, edit, and publish data back to the Finance and Operations application. In Word, the add-in allows users to build templates and upload those templates to the Finance and Operations application. A user can then trigger document generation to populate Dynamics 365 data to Word, which can be used for light reporting.

The Microsoft Dynamics Office add-in is a lightweight Office web add-on available for free in the Office store. The Office add-on is built using the Office web JavaScript API and HTML and uses OData to interact with the data entities of Dynamics 365 for Finance and Operations.

The following diagram shows the architecture of the Dynamics 365 for Finance and Operations integration with Office 365:

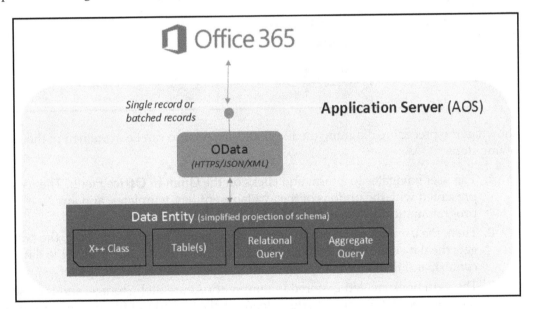

The following screenshot represents the interaction between Dynamics 365 for Finance and Operations and the Office add-in when open in Excel:

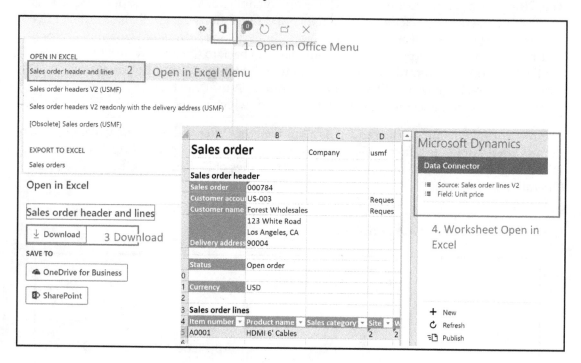

As shown in the preceding diagram, the Excel add-in scenario can be explained in the following steps:

1. The user navigates to a form and clicks on the **Open in Office** menu. The user is presented with the options of the available entities, templates, and any programmatically added integrations.
2. Then, the user selects the entity and clicks **Open in Excel**; in this step, the system gets the data entity and the field context, creates a workbook, inserts the data context, and then inserts the connector manifest and the server URL.
3. The workbook created is stored in temporary Azure Blob Storage, and the user is presented with the option to download the file to the local filesystem or save to the cloud, such as OneDrive for Business or SharePoint Online.
4. When the user downloads the file and opens the Excel workbook, Excel runs the data connector app, makes a connection to the server URL, reads the table binding, calls the OData service to retrieve the data, and—finally—fills the table binding with data.

All interactions with the Excel add-in scenario use the current user login and, hence, the security context. Users can only read or update data to which they have access.

After understanding the various components of the core application, let's delve into learning how LCS are used with Finance and Operations.

Using LCS

LCS are one of the most important components of the Dynamics 365 for Finance and Operations architecture. LCS are a Microsoft Azure-based collaboration portal that provides a unifying, collaborative environment, along with a set of regularly updated services that help you manage the application life cycle of your Microsoft Dynamics 365 for Finance and Operations implementations.

The following diagram shows the various services supported by LCS during the implementation, update, and support phases of Dynamics 365 for Finance and Operations:

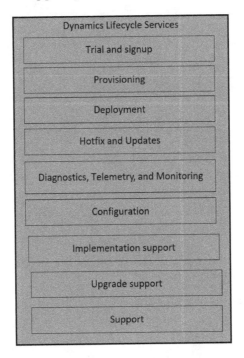

As is clearly evident, LCS are used throughout the life cycle of the project. You will learn about the different tools available in detail throughout this book.

The ALM for on-premises deployments is also orchestrated through LCS. Customers can use LCS to help manage their on-premises deployments. The following diagram shows the on-premises ALM process through LCS:

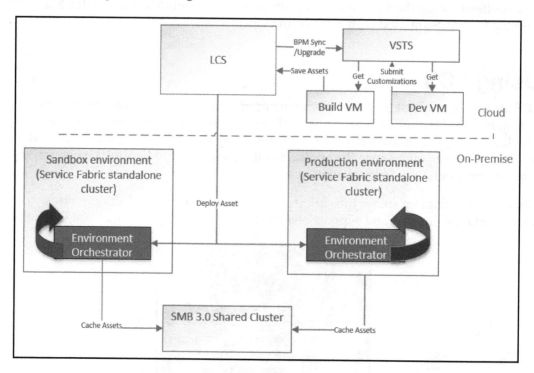

As shown in the diagram, similar to cloud deployment, LCS can be used to synchronize the LCS project artifacts to **Visual Studio Team Services** (**VSTS**). The developer can use the one-box cloud machine or already downloaded machines to get the latest code in their development environment. Once done, the code is checked in the VSTS. The cloud build environment can pull the latest code and generate the deployable artifacts that can be uploaded to the LCS asset library. The on-premises, production, or sandbox environment can be serviced directly through LCS with the help of the environment orchestrator within the Service Fabric standalone cluster node.

As mentioned earlier, LCS is one of the most important components of the overall Dynamics 365 for Finance and Operations architecture as it is used throughout the life cycle of the implementation project and beyond. We have dedicated Chapter 3, *Lifecycle Services (LCS) and Tools*, to covering various other features of LCS.

Understanding development architecture

ERP applications are built for generic industry requirements, and most of the customers implementing an ERP system need some level of customization application to satisfy their unique business requirements. The Microsoft Dynamics 365 for Finance and Operation development environment uses Visual Studio as the only **integrated development environment** (**IDE**) for development. The Finance and Operations Visual Studio extension provides a full set of development capabilities within the Visual Studio Code editor.

The following diagram shows the development environment architecture:

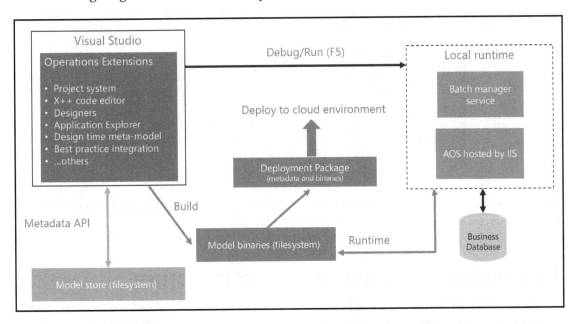

The following are key highlights of the Finance and Operations development architecture:

1. **Operations Extensions** provides the developer, application explorer, X++ code editor, project system, user interface designer, debugger, and other tools to extend the existing functionalities and add new ones.
2. The source code is stored in the development environment filesystem as XML files (**Model store**) and used by the **Metadata API** of the Visual Studio extension for the editing and design experience.
3. The build process compiles application source code to .NET CIL/DLL files (**Model binaries**).

4. In Dynamics 365 for Finance and Operations, X++ is a 100% managed language running in the .NET **Common Language Runtime** (**CLR**).
5. Local runtime is deployed on the development machine to provide a debugging experience.
6. Visual Studio can also be used to create a deployable package to promote the application code to the test and production environments.
7. Visual Studio can be configured with Azure DevOps for source control, and then Azure DevOps build and release pipelines can be used for automated build and automated deployment to the test and production environments.
8. There are distinct source code, design time, and runtime concepts in Dynamics 365 for Finance and Operations, as shown in the following screenshot:

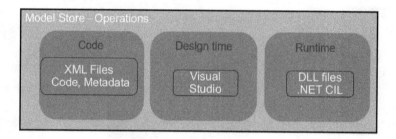

We will discuss the development environment, development concepts, and practices in more detail in Chapter 9, *Customization and Extensions*.

Understanding integration architecture

Dynamics 365 for Finance and Operations supports numerous integration models to help integrate with third-party applications, as well as built-in native integration with Office 365, Power Platform, and Dynamics 365 applications. The following diagram shows the integration architecture concepts in Dynamics 365 for Finance and Operations:

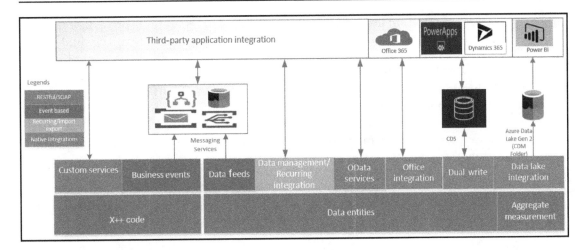

As shown in the preceding diagram, there are various integration options and concepts available in Finance and Operations. These integration concepts can be better explained with the following categories:

1. **HTTP bases RESTful:** Dynamics 365 for Finance and Operations provides an OData REST endpoint for all the data entities that are marked as public. It supports complete **CRUD** (short for **create, retrieve, update, and delete**) functionality that can be used to integrate with any third-party applications. Along with OData, custom X++ business logic can be exposed as a RESTful or **Simple Object Access Protocol** (**SOAP**)-based service.

2. **Event-based**: The business events and data feeds feature can send near real-time event notification and data changes to generic consumers, such as Azure messaging services. External business applications and systems can subscribe to specific business events or data feeds using Azure messaging services and receive close to real-time events and data update from Finance and Operations.

3. **Recurring import/export**: Dynamics 365 for Finance and Operations provides APIs for recurring data integration for bulk import/export integration scenarios. Recurring data integration patterns are based on the data management platform also used for application life cycles, such as configuration management and data migration.

4. **Native integration:** Dynamics 365 for Finance and Operations provides built-in integration with Office 365 applications such as Excel and Word. The dual-write feature enables customers to integrate Finance and Operations data into their own CDS. This enables direct integration with Power Apps, and Dynamics 365 applications such as Sales, Services, and Talent. The **Data Lake integration** feature enables incremental export of Finance and Operations master and transaction data into the customer's own Azure Data Lake Storage Gen2 environments in **Common Data Model** (**CDM**) folder format, which can be further used by Power BI dataflows to built rich analytical reports.

Integration for business applications is a big topic and cannot be covered in a couple of paragraphs. We have a dedicated chapter, `Chapter 8`, *Integration Technologies, Planning, and Design*, to learn more about integration architecture, concepts, and best practices.

Understanding security architecture

An ERP system provides unified business functions to organizations by integrating data and processes from different departments, such as human resources, accounts receivable, accounts payable, inventory management, and general ledger. Since the ERP system stores all the company data, ERP security is extremely important. Dynamics 365 for Finance and Operations provides a comprehensive security model to secure application access and defines the security policy for business users using security roles and data security policies.

The following diagram provides a high-level view of the security architecture used in Dynamics 365 for Finance and Operations:

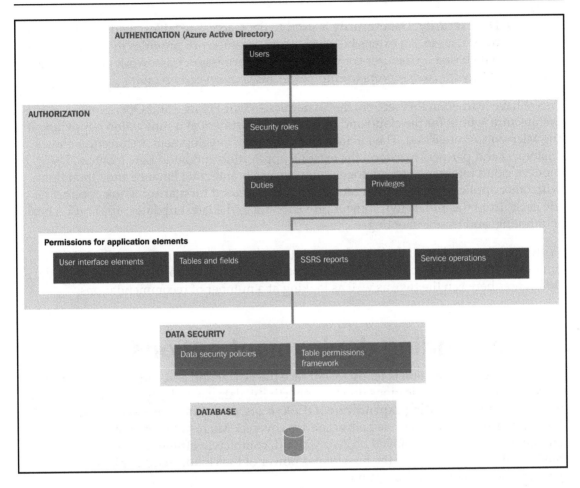

As shown in the preceding diagram, there are three components of security architecture:

- **Authentication**: As discussed earlier in this chapter, Azure AD is used for the authentication process in Dynamics 365 for Finance and Operations. If the user is not authenticated, the connection to the application will be closed.
- **Authorization**: Authorization is the control of the application access. Once the user is authenticated, the Finance and Operations application determines what the user can see based on the security role they are assigned. Security roles comprise duties and privileges that are designed to secure individual user interface elements, tables and fields, reports, and service operations. The privileges defined in the application also define the access levels, such as delete, read, and write. Based on the access level, the application element access is controlled for the user at runtime.

- **Data security**: Data security is used to deny access to tables, fields, and rows in the database. An extensible data security framework provides the ability to filter data based on the user context. The table permission framework provides the ability for AOS servers to enforce permissions on certain tables.

As we have learned in this section, the Dynamics 365 for Finance and Operations architecture is built for the cloud and utilizes the investment and innovation happening in the Microsoft Azure cloud. The Finance and Operation development architecture allows customers and partners to extend the existing application and build new features. Using modern cloud integration technologies, you can easily integrate Finance and Operations with other applications in your organization. LCS are used for managing the application life cycle, from the initial environment provisioning to the latest updates, application health monitoring, and troubleshooting.

With an understanding of the complete architecture, let's now learn Dynamics 365 for Finance and Operations cloud and on-premises deployment options and understand the differences between the two, as well as looking at a number of recommendations.

Understanding deployment options

Whether your organization is ready to embrace the power and ease of the cloud or still prefers on-premises applications due to connectivity, data sovereignty, **capital expenditure** (**CAPEX**) versus **operating expenditure** (**OPEX**) costs, or any other reason, Dynamics 365 for Finance and Operations has both scenarios covered. Microsoft Dynamics 365 for Finance and Operations can be deployed on Azure cloud, completely offline, and on-premises (local business data). To maximize the benefit and power of the cloud, cloud deployment is the preferred and recommended option.

Cloud

The cloud deployment option enables the deployment of Dynamics 365 for Finance and Operations on the Microsoft Azure cloud platform. There has been an unprecedented adoption of cloud ERP systems by mid-sized and large organizations. Cloud deployment is the preferred and recommended option, as Microsoft is committed to its cloud first approach in business applications, and continues to invest more in cloud services.

The following are the key highlights of cloud deployment:

- Fully managed by Microsoft's cloud service
- Subscription pricing—pay per user per month
- System of intelligence
- Scale-out as needed with the help of Microsoft's support team
- ExpressRoute as an add-on

ExpressRoute lets customers connect their on-premises infrastructure to Azure data centers using a dedicated, private connection that's highly available, highly reliable, has low latency, and is supported with a published 99.95% financially backed **service-level agreement** (SLA).

The following diagram depicts the idea of a cloud deployment model, where the application—as well as the configuration and customization, telemetry, and diagnostics, and business data—are all in the cloud. Microsoft is a data trustee and manages the environments. The customer and partner do not have direct access to the production infrastructure but can access ALM, telemetry, and diagnostics data through LCS. The customer and partner have full access to the development, build, and sandbox environment, and can log in to the environment using a remote desktop:

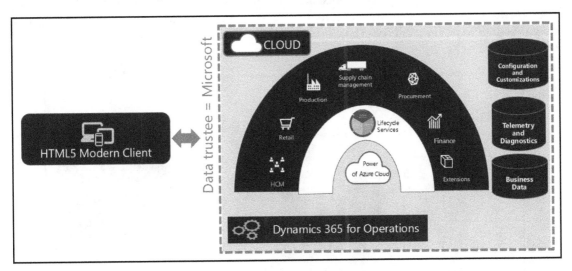

Specific scenarios where cloud deployments are desirable include the following:

- An organization desires to move their operations to the cloud completely to save on-premises infrastructure cost and maintenance.

- An organization has already been using Office 365 or Dynamics 365 products, such as customer engagement, and wants an integrated view.
- You'd like to innovate faster and utilize the power of the cloud with Microsoft cloud services, such as Power BI, machine learning, and the **internet of things (IoT)**.

Local business data or on-premises

Some organizations do not want to store their data on infrastructure they don't fully control. Local business data deployment is a choice for them. Local business data deployment is a deployment model whereby the key components of Dynamics 365 for Finance and Operations are deployed on the customer's local data center. This model is suitable for customers who are not ready for the cloud journey due to regulatory reasons or their existing data center investments.

As explained earlier in this chapter, local business data deployment still uses LCS for deployment and management of Dynamics 365 for Finance and Operations. However, there is no business data processing outside the customer's or their partner's data center. In this model, the customer/partner is responsible for managing the infrastructure and disaster recovery. Power BI or cloud intelligence is optional for local business data, as these options need business data in the cloud. Customers will have an option to enable it by allowing the business data to be replicated in the cloud. The following diagram represents a local business data deployment model:

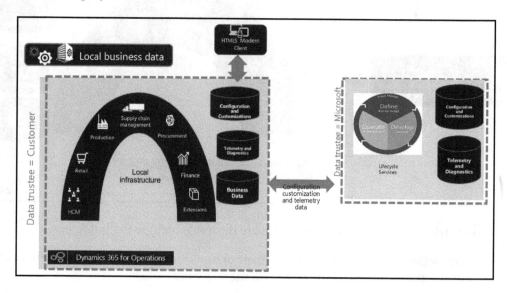

As shown in the preceding diagram, local business data means that the finance and operations application deployment is limited to the customer data center. LCS in the cloud are still used for deployment and management, where the configuration, customization, and telemetry data is synchronized to the cloud to enable management and diagnostics.

The following are the key highlights of local business data deployment:

- Disconnected data centers
- Local data residency
- Capitalize hardware investments

> Many Finance and Operations features are built for the cloud-only version and are not supported—or need to be configured differently—in the on-premises version. To see feature comparison between the on-premises and cloud version, follow this link: `https://docs.microsoft.com/en-us/dynamics365/unified-operations/fin-and-ops/get-started/cloud-prem-comparison`.

> We recommend you always get the latest information from these links:
>
> - `https://docs.microsoft.com/en-us/dynamics365/unified-operations/dev-itpro/deployment/setup-deploy-on-premises-environments`
> - `https://docs.microsoft.com/en-us/dynamics365/unified-operations/dev-itpro/deployment/on-premises-deployment-landing-page`

Comparing cloud and on-premises deployments

Earlier in this section, we have discussed the cloud and on-premises deployment models. The following table highlights and compares the key differences between these two deployment models:

Capabilities	Cloud	On-Premises
Infrastructure	Full Microsoft-managed cloud service	Customer/partner managed Not supported on any public cloud infrastructure, including Azure
Data residency	Microsoft-managed data centers	Local data residency

Application Lifecycle Management (ALM)	Managed by Microsoft Customer/partner have access to telemetry and ALM data through LCS	Managed by customer/partner using LCS
Licensing	Subscription: Per month per user cost	License with software assurance/business-ready enhancement plan or subscription
User count	Minimum 20 users	No minimum user requirement (minimum hardware is scoped based on 250 users)
Intelligence and analytics	Author and publish Power BI reports Ready-made analytical reports Pinning tile and reports from PowerBI.com (`https://powerbi.microsoft.com/en-us/`)	Author and publish Power BI reports
High availability (HA) and Disaster Recovery (DR)	Included in enterprise offer and managed by Microsoft	Customer-managed
Internet connectivity	Must	Periodic connectivity for deployments and servicing

While it helps customers to have on-premises deployment as an option, the cloud deployment is, however, the preferred and recommended option.

Let's learn the environment-planning aspect of cloud deployment projects in the next section of this chapter.

Understanding cloud deployment and environment planning

In a typical implementation project, you need to separate environments to develop customization, configuration and test the solution before you can deploy the final solution in the production environment. For successful ERP implementation of Microsoft Dynamics 365 for Finance and Operations, it's important that you plan your environment early in the project.

Environment planning for on-premises implementation projects is a big subject, as it is not only planning different environments during the implementation but also includes planning for sizing and procurement aspects of each environment.

Environment planning for a cloud deployment option gets a little easier, as Microsoft takes care of the production environment configuration and sizing based on customer's transaction and user load needs. Cloud deployment also has a pre-defined environment typologies and sizing for non-production scenarios. In this section, we will cover the environment planning aspect of a cloud implementation project.

Type of environment

With cloud implementation of Dynamics 365 for Finance and Operations, there are a few different topological and sizing configurations available for non-production scenarios. Let's briefly touch base on the different types of environment configurations and their use cases.

Tier-1 - Development or Build

A Tier-1 environment is a single-box environment and is typically used as a development and build environment. The architecture of the Tier-1 environment is different from a production environment. In this environment, the SQL Server database is used, and all components such as AOS, batch, database, management reporter, and many others are installed on the same server.

The Business Application October 2019 release plan includes features to enhance the development tooling to enable development using local computers, instead of a pre-configured Tier -1 environment. It is also planned to replace the build process as a standard Microsoft DevOps process. These features, when available, will eliminate the need for the Tier-1 environment for development and build purposes.

Tier-2 - Standard Acceptance

The Tier-2 environment is a multi-box instance that customers can use for **user acceptance testing (UAT)**, integration testing, and training purposes. The architecture of this environment is the same as the production environment, with smaller capacity and sizing. Similar to the production environment, the Tier-2 environment uses Azure SQL Database. However, this environment is not configured for disaster recovery.

Tier-3, Tier-4, and Tier-5 environments

Tier-3 or higher environments are similar to the Tier-2 environment, with higher capacity and sizing. A Tier-3 or higher environment is suitable for performance testing and data migration testing scenarios.

Production

The production environment is provisioned before the project go-live activities start. The production multi-box instance includes disaster recovery and high availability.

Project type and environments

Now that we know different environment type classifications, let's look at how many environments you need for your project.

The following screenshot shows a sample template that highlights different environments and sizing tiers you may need, depending on the project's complexity:

Environment purpose	Simple projects	Medium projects	Complex project	Environment tier
Development	X	X	X	1
Build	X	X	X	1
Test	X	X	X	2
Golden config		X	X	2
Pre-production data migration		X	X	2
Performance testing			X	4 or higher
UAT			X	2 or 3
Training			X	2
Production	X	X	X	Based on sizing

As shown in the preceding screenshot, the number of environments you need and sizing requirements typically depend on the complexity of the project. In a simple project, you can reuse one environment for multiple purposes. For example, the test environment can be used for pre-production data migration, UAT, and training purposes during the different phases of the project. However, for a complex project, you should plan a separate environment for their purpose.

Now, let's learn in the next section about the environments that are provided by Microsoft when you buy a Finance and Operations license.

Finance and Operations standard cloud offer

Each Dynamics 365 for Finance and Operations standard cloud offer includes three environments:

- **Tier-1 environment: Develop and test**—One develop/test instance is provided for the duration of the subscription. This instance is a non-production, single-box instance that the customer can use as an automated build environment, or to customize Finance and Operations and do unit testing for the changes. Additional develop/test instances can be purchased separately as an optional add-on.

- **Tier-2 environment: Standard Acceptance Testing**—One Standard Acceptance Testing instance is provided for the duration of the subscription. This instance is a non-production multi-box instance that customers can use for UAT, integration testing, and training. Additional sandbox/staging instances can be purchased separately as an optional add-on.

- **Production environment**: One production instance is provided per tenant. The production multi-box instance includes disaster recovery and high availability. It will be provisioned when the implementation approaches the Operate phase, once the required activities in the Microsoft Dynamics LCS methodology and a successful go-live assessment are completed.

In summary, for cloud deployment options, the following table illustrates different environment tiers, and their typical use, deployment, and cost structure:

Tier	Topology	Used for	Deployment	Cost
Tier-1	One-box environment	Development, Build, or Test	Customer or partner or Microsoft subscription	One Build, one Dev environment in MS subscription. Can buy an additional subscription or deploy as many as you need in your own Azure subscription.
Tier-2	Multi-box	Test, Golden configuration, UAT	Microsoft subscription	One comes with a license in Microsoft subscription and you can buy additional if you need it.
Tier-3 – Tier-5	Multi-box	UAT, Performance testing	Microsoft subscription	Additional cost.
Production	Production	Production	Microsoft subscription	Comes with license.

In summary, Microsoft provides one development, one build, one Tier-2 environment, and a production environment that might be good enough for simple projects. For a medium or a complex project, you will need to purchase additional add-on environments. Microsoft is working on features to minimize the need and cost of additional add-on development and build environments. For more details, follow this link: `https://docs.microsoft.com/en-us/dynamics365-release-plan/2019wave2/dynamics365-finance-operations/developer-tools-as-installable-components`.

Summary

In this chapter, we started with understanding the architecture of Dynamics 365 for Finance and Operations. We covered the conceptual architecture, various components, their roles, and how they function. Dynamics 365 for Finance and Operations embraces modern architecture built for cloud deployment. The new architecture, when deployed in the cloud, uses Azure AD for the identity model and Azure SQL as the database, and the application components get deployed using Windows Server containers. On-premises deployment uses AD FS for authentication, SQL Server 2016 for database, and a Service Fabric standalone cluster to deploy application components. In the new architecture, the AOS is hosted on IIS, and batch operations run as a Windows service. Application logic is now modular and separated into an application platform, application foundation, and application suite.

Dynamics 365 for Finance and Operations clients now comprises the modern HTML 5-based web client and mobile app and have seamless integration with Office 365. They use an exclusive development platform on Visual Studio. LCS are used to manage the cloud as well as the on-premises deployment application life cycle—from project inception to upgrade.

You also learned about the deployment choices available: cloud and local business data. The cloud deployment option is the preferred and recommended option, while the local business data option can be useful for an organization having reservations about moving to the cloud due to regulatory or other challenges.

The next chapter is about building the foundation of your implementation project by collecting requirements, and conducting fit-gap analysis of the solution requirement.

Requirements and Process Analysis

5

In the previous chapter, you learned about the building blocks of a project by defining a project charter and a project plan. The next step is to build the foundation of your implementation project by collecting any requirements, their analysis, and their fit-gap. The following are the key objectives of the requirement-gathering or analysis phase of the project:

- Understanding the customer business process and goals
- Defining the project scope
- Identifying the fit and gaps
- Developing a solution blueprint

In this chapter, we will explore requirements, processes, and solution blueprints while emphasizing their need, as well as various other moving parts for managing the scope of your project.

The following topics are covered in this chapter:

- Requirements scoping
- The hierarchy of business processes and subprocesses
- LCS BPM and Azure DevOps/VSTS
- Requirement-gathering techniques
- **Requirement Traceability Matrix (RTM)**
- Requirements segmentation and ownership
- Analysis of requirements
- Solution blueprint
- Key decision logs
- Best practices in managing requirements

Requirements scoping

Where can we start to collect and document requirements? What kind of requirements need to be collected? How do we ensure that all the requirements are collected?

You might be wondering about the previous questions, which are common for all ERP implementations. For a successful project, laying down a strong foundation right from the start is needed and collecting accurate and documented requirements is one such activity.

Even before engaging a solutions partner/advisor, a lot of organizations internally come up with a requirements list for their business transformation. The size of the organization, the businesses involved in the transformation, and the future state goals all play a significant role in driving requirements, and it is a project in itself. In any implementation methodology, exhaustive requirement collection and analysis is a must to be successful.

 Often, organizations engage external firms and advisors to support them in the requirements gathering, as this is like defining the goal of your journey.

The focus of requirements collections should cover all the aspects of the existing business processes, as well as the future state of business processes. The requirement-gathering and understanding process is a highly scientific approach that needs niche expertise and the ability to pay attention to important details.

Hierarchy of business processes and subprocesses

There must always be an explicit link between business processes and requirements.

It should start at a high level for the coverage perspective, but the requirements must be collected in detail. Asking the five *Ws* is always a good idea to ensure that enough details are collected.

 The six *Ws* are *Why*, *What*, *Where*, *Who*, and *When*, as well as *Which*. When solution envisioning is performed, another crucial question, *How*, is answered.

All the business processes that will be part of the initiative and each of their subprocesses must be considered in order to prepare the requirements list. There should never be a requirement without it being linked to one or many processes; alternatively, there should not be any process/subprocess that does not have any requirements. Any such situation wherein a requirement does not belong to any business process should be validated with the out-of-scope criterion and addressed by the change control board.

We recommend that you follow a hierarchical approach while gathering and documenting requirements. The following diagram represents one such approach and depicts the goal leading to the business process, which, in turn, leads to a subprocess and, ultimately, the requirement:

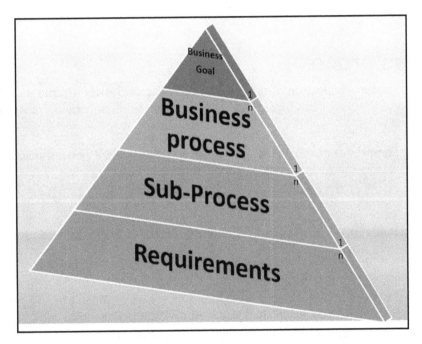

The hierarchical way of recording requirements is a proven approach to orienting and structuring the requirement-gathering process and ensuring that each requirement has downstream usage. Systematic success warrants the manageability of the project scope and, hence, a hierarchy. The project benefits when the stakeholders can clearly understand the big picture as well as the activity-level details. Empowering team members with scope clarity is a solid foundation for collaboration and achieving goals.

Now that we've laid the foundation using a hierarchical approach, we'll explain the elements that are involved in achieving it.

Business goals

This is the highest-level view of the project. This is the big picture for anyone within or outside the project so that they know what the project is going to achieve at a high level. As we explained in the previous chapter, project goals are defined in the project charter and the approach to achieving these goals is defined using the project plan.

A quick mathematical expression for viewing a project from top to bottom is as follows:

- *1* goal: *n* business processes
- *1* business process: *n* subprocesses
- *1* subprocess: *n* requirements

Business process

A business process is a collection of related, structural activities/requirements that are interconnected and that can be represented in a flowchart comprising of decision points and dependencies.

To find out more about business processes and ERP, do a quick Google search – there is plenty of information out there!

Many organizations follow the industry-specific nomenclature of business processes:

- **Record to report**: This domain describes the process of managing financial and ledger information for any organization.
- **Order to cash**: This domain describes the process of receiving and processing customer sales and its entire lifecycle until their payment.
- **Procure to pay**: This domain describes the process of ordering and processing vendor invoices and its entire lifecycle until payment settlement.
- **Plan to produce**: This domain describes the process of creating and building products/services and its entire chain from demand to supply.

Business processes are best described using flows and visuals and have several uses, such as training, testing, solution acceptance, and so on. Each business process comprises one or many subprocesses in the functional domain.

The following visual suggests the set of business processes that need to be followed, as per a generic industry nomenclature:

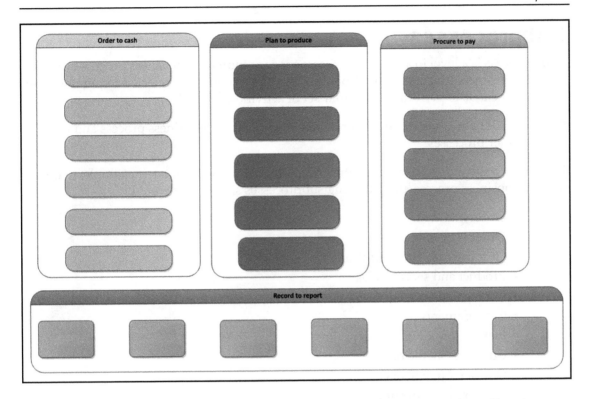

 Always leverage industry-specific business processes to gain uniformity and consistency.

As an example, order-to-cash processes may cover lead generation, prospect identification, opportunity creation and management, order management, order fulfillment, order returns, and so on.

 Refer to the following links for more details about the generic end-to-end business processes that occur in various domains regarding to order to cash and procure to pay:

- https://en.wikipedia.org/wiki/Order_to_cash
- https://en.wikipedia.org/wiki/Procure-to-pay

Once you have identified and documented all the business processes of the project visually, the next step is to define their subprocesses.

Subprocesses

A **subprocess** is a level in a business process for each individual business process function. Detailing business functions starts from this level. One or many connected requirements are needed to be able to perform a particular set of activities.

Subprocesses help in visualizing inter dependencies within a business process and have links to other processes.

Each subprocess must constitute all the grouped functions within it. For example, in order to cash a business process, the following subprocesses should be covered:

- Order intake
- Order processing
- Order release and credit checks
- Product and service sales
- Pricing and term agreements
- Consignments
- Picking, packing, and shipping
- Customer invoicing
- Customer payments
- Intercompany documents
- Returns

 Selecting grouped results/subprocesses varies per customer and should always be tailor-made to fit their business model.

Subprocesses are well documented in visual tools such as Microsoft Visio.

The following diagram depicts a sample subprocess with swim lanes showing the involved departments/roles and their inter dependencies:

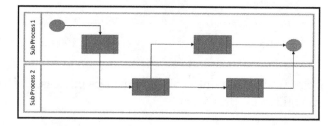

Make sure that you have the happy path of an end-to-end business scenario for every initiative. This will allow everyone to connect the dots to the big picture of the project, and this happy path process will be utilized at various milestones, for example, testing, training, and so on.

A subprocess could be dedicated to a single functional area or it could be a cross-functional area as well. Some may go a level deeper than the requirements to the activity level, the decision for which depends on the type, complexity, and nature of the initiative. Essentially, in process-flow documentation, there should be a clear definition and depiction of information flow with inputs, outputs, decision points, and roles involved.

Now, let's deep dive into the requirements.

The requirements of the business process

A requirement is a series of activities/steps within a subprocess. Often, organizations may leverage use case scenarios to explain the requirements clearly. Typically, a use case is a pattern of behavior and a sequence of related activities. Every organization must have the goal of collecting the requirements in the most structured way possible as this smooths out the rest of the project activities, thereby securing success.

Our recommendations for requirement-gathering for a Microsoft D365FO implementation are as follows:

- Requirements should be defined as **Specific, Measurable, Achievable, Realistic, and Time-bound (SMART)**.
- Business processes and requirements should contain detailed information about business needs.
- Each requirement is typically expected to be executed by one person.
- Requirements can be shared and reused in multiple subprocesses.
- In the CRP methodology, it's beneficial to have the business blueprint, business processes, and subprocesses all prepared before the start of the initiative.
- All the requirements can be collected at the start, or they can be collected as per the CRP pilot.
- The documentation of the requirements is a must, and various techniques can be leveraged for this.

- Typically, an RTM should be leveraged, which hosts the laundry list of requirements and is used for tracking, linking to activities, and deliverables in a project.
- Ensure that each requirement can be tested and a positive test can be performed on it.

There are several factors to consider while preparing process flows. Based on our experience, we recommend the following factors to leverage while preparing them:

- **Related**: Document all the related flows that directly or indirectly impact the business process at hand.
- **Well-structured**: Always bring in a systematic approach of documentation and start with the various inputs and triggers for process flow.
- **Uniform**: Ensure consistency and uniformity across the flows.
- **Consistent**: There may be several team members who may be documenting such process flows and details, and it helps to prepare a guideline and an outline for the entire project to follow.
- **Clear and unambiguous**: Business understanding may be completed right away in one session and so must the process flow documentation. Consider preparing the base flow of the process first, ensuring absolute clarity and no ambiguity or assumptions.

There are a lot of tools available for managing business processes and requirements; for example, BPM, DevOps, SharePoint, Excel, and so on. However, we recommend that you leverage LCS BPM along with Azure DevOps to manage these more effectively in the context of Microsoft D365FO.

Now, let's learn how LCS BPM can be leveraged to manage your entire set of processes and requirements.

LCS BPM and Azure DevOps

You may be wondering where and which tool to use to capture detailed information about business processes and requirements. While traditionally Excel, SharePoint, DevOps, and various other tools were being leveraged, there came a need to have a tool that would facilitate this information quickly and with high productivity. The place for such a tool has been filled with BPM in LCS.

It's easy to manage your business process, subprocess, and requirements in LCS BPM and use them throughout the implementation and after implementation. Based on our experience, the following are the top-level steps involved in utilizing LCS BPM in your implementation:

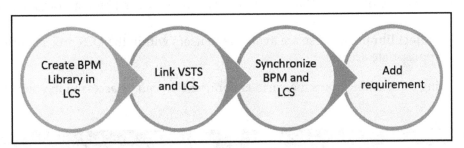

As shown in the preceding diagram, using LCS, you can create business processes that are specific to your implementation project. The next step is to set up the Azure DevOps/VSTS project and link it with Azure DevOps/VSTS. You can further synchronize BPM with LCS and then add the requirements. Synchronization with Azure DevOps/VSTS provides a collaborative environment for further planning and tracking work throughout the lifecycle of the project. In the following subsections, we'll take a deeper look into the BPM library and the Azure DevOps/VSTS integration and synchronization features in LCS.

Business process modeler

The BPM tool comes with a set of public libraries that allow you to leverage them as a reference. Alternatively, you can create a new one from scratch. Often, advisors/partners come up with their existing business process libraries as a starting point and modify them according to your industry and organization's needs.

By using the BPM, you can achieve the following goals:

- Standardize the process flows and business requirements so that they're maintained as a library.
- Align the Microsoft D365FO, Enterprise Edition processes with industry-standard processes, as described by the **American Productivity and Quality Center (APQC)**.
- Prepare a hierarchy of business processes and their associated requirements, all under one repository.

There are three types of libraries in BPM, as follows:

- **Global libraries**: These are available from Microsoft, and can be used as a starting point so that you can build your own.
- **Corporate libraries**: These are libraries that are owned by your organization for any organization user to leverage.
- **Project libraries**: These are available to users within the LCS project with appropriate access.

The following screenshot shows the various libraries that can be accessed in your LCS project:

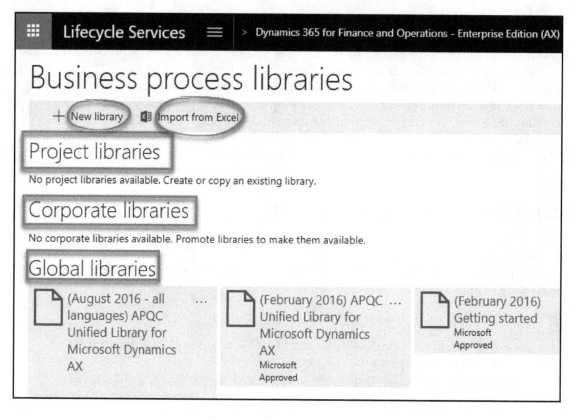

 Microsoft regularly updates LCS and, at the time of writing this book, has recently released a new interface for BPM. This new interface will be used throughout this book.

The following screenshot shows a global library from Microsoft leveraging an APQC cross-industry business model:

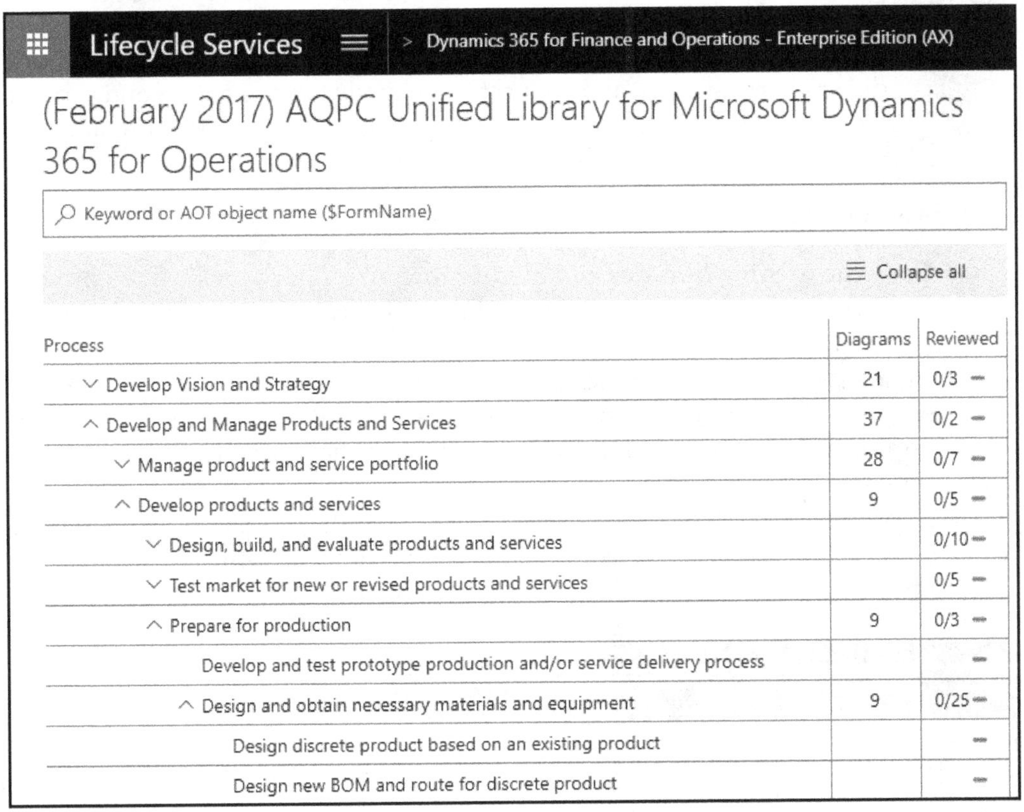

The preceding library is divided into three sections, as follows:

- **Core view**: Here you can edit, review, and combine your hierarchy with the configuration and data manager tool.
- **Process hierarchy**: Here, you can view/build your business process and requirements hierarchy.
- **Process details**: Here, you can maintain more information for a specific reference/line in the hierarchy and include details such as a process applicable to a list of countries where the customer has a business presence as well as a list of industry verticals, and so on. You can also identify the fit and gaps between user requirements and the default functionality that Microsoft D365FO, Enterprise Edition provides.

APQC stands for **American Productivity and Quality Center**, a recognized non-profit organization working in benchmarking, best practices, process and performance improvement, and knowledge management. APQC functions with its member organizations to identify best practices, discover effective methods of improvement, broadly disseminate findings, and connect individuals to one another and provide the knowledge, training, and tools they need to succeed. Refer to `https://www.apqc.org/about` to find out more.

You can create a new BPM library in the following ways:

- **Copy the existing libraries and modify them**: You can copy libraries provided by Microsoft or your organization and modify them to suit your project-specific processes.
- **Create a new library from scratch**: You can create a new library from scratch by either adding steps one by one or importing them as an Excel file. You can also import and add steps from the existing libraries that are accessible in your LCS project.
- **Import from Excel**: Use the **Import from Excel** button, which opens a dialog, as shown in the following screenshot. Click on **Download template**, prepare your library in Excel, and then import it back to create your BPM library:

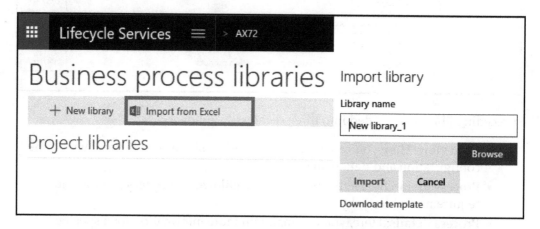

Now, let's create a new library from scratch and learn about the steps that are involved. Click on the **Create library** button. A new dialog box will open, where you can enter your library name and click **OK** to create the library. Once the library has been created, you can open the library. A new library will always have two default processes. You can rename those processes and then add additional processes as children or siblings, as shown in the following screenshot:

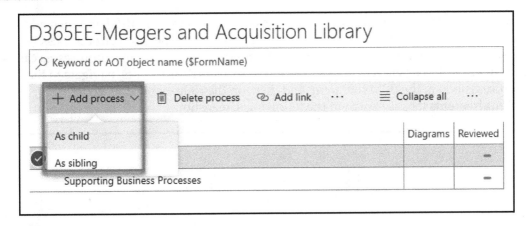

There is also the option to import from other available BPM libraries, which can be the fastest way to build your library.

The following screenshot shows an example of importing the **Deliver products and services** process and its subprocess from the APQC library:

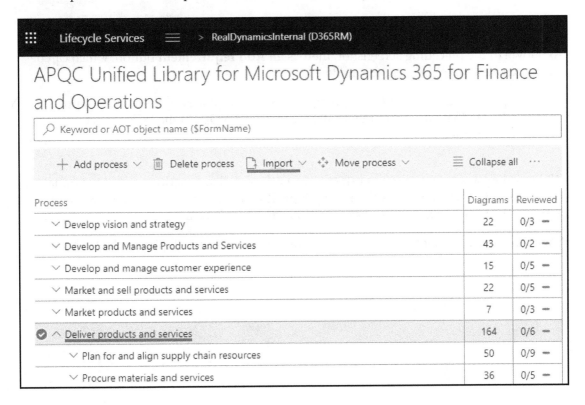

We recommend that you build your processes and subprocesses in BPM and then add requirements within that structure. This ensures the completeness of your business processes, as per the project's objectives. Adding requirements within subprocesses can be done either in BPM or via Azure DevOps/VSTS. To add requirements, navigate to the subprocess node in the BPM hierarchy and then, on the right-hand side, go to the **Requirements** tab, as shown in the following screenshot:

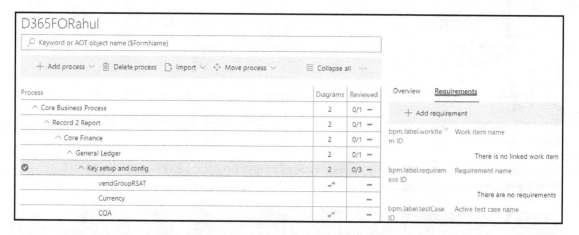

As shown in the preceding screenshot, there is an **Add requirement** button, which can be used to create requirements at this node.

 Remember that the requirement level in BPM is supposed to be mapped to the requirement work item in Azure DevOps in the LCS project settings.

While adding a requirement, you can specify a title, detailed description, and the initial assessment, and whether it is a fit or a gap type. If you're unsure of whether it's a fit or a gap type, just leave it as **Not assessed**, which is the default value.

The following screenshot shows the requirement pop-up screen depicting the fields:

If requirements are not maintained using LCS BPM in a hierarchical format, then it will be tough to manage them as a flat list, thereby adding cost and tenure to the overall project, along with a lot of risks.

In addition to creating and importing a process, you can delete a process, create linked processes, rearrange them by moving them up or down, and make them a sibling or child.

You can also add additional information to the process node, as follows:

Properties	Description
Description	Add a detailed description of the process.
Keywords	Add keywords that can be used for an easier search.
Links	Link external links; you can use a link to provide external documentation for related processes.
Industries	You can select one or more applicable industries where a particular business process is applicable.

Countries	If you are working with a multi-country implementation, it is not uncommon to have country-specific business processes. You can select one or more countries where the business process is applicable.
Activity diagram	You can associate an activity diagram with a business process. Activity diagrams are used to describe how a business process or task is completed in a proposed software solution. There are three types of activity diagrams: • **Task recordings**: You can upload the business processes task recording to automatically generate activity diagrams and process steps. Refer to the link for more details on task recorder, at https://docs.microsoft.com/en-us/dynamics365/fin-ops-core/dev-itpro/user-interface/task-recorder. • **Microsoft Visio**: You can associate a business process with a Visio diagram by manually uploading a Visio file. • **User-defined**: You can manually create flowcharts as a BPM activity diagram.

The following screenshot is an activity diagram for a business process. It can be edited and updated with elements from the left, as well as saved and published:

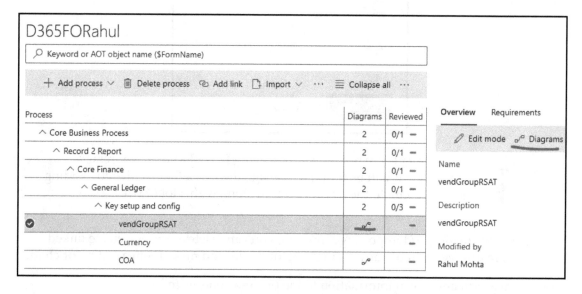

You can create process-specific flowcharts or import a Visio diagram after clicking on the **Diagrams** button, as highlighted in the preceding screenshot.

To see the action pane in the diagram, you need to right-click on the canvas to see the toolbar at the bottom with the options for **Edit**, **Save**, **Export**, and **Gap list**, as shown here:

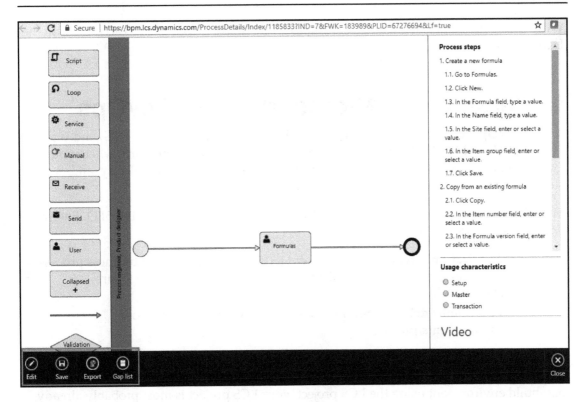

Once your business processes are complete, you can export a business process node as a Microsoft Word document and use it as a training manual in the later phases of the project.

Clearly, the BPM tool helps you easily define and manage your business processes and requirements during the analysis phase of the project. Integration with Azure DevOps/VSTS and in-product help takes this to the next level since you can utilize these business processes in the later phases of the project.

 With LCS being a cloud service, Microsoft releases new features and enhancements on a monthly basis. To find out about the latest features and capabilities, follow the *What's new* documentation of LCS on the Microsoft official documentation site at `https://docs.microsoft.com/en-us/dynamics365/unified-operations/dev-itpro/lifecycle-services/whats-new-lcs`.

Managing the business hierarchy in LCS has one more advantage: it has out-of-the-box synchronization with Azure DevOps/VSTS. Here, you can synchronize the LCS BPM library hierarchy with your Azure DevOps/VSTS project as a one-time push, and from there on, maintain all project delivery-related information in Azure DevOps/VSTS.

With your BPM library defined, let's configure your Azure DevOps/VSTS account with the LCS project.

Understanding Microsoft Azure DevOps

Azure DevOps was formerly known as **Visual Studio Team Services** (**VSTS**) and is also known as **Visual Studio Online** (**VSO**). It's a single collaboration platform where you can manage all the aspects of your project, including planning, execution/delivery, and support.

The top two benefits of leveraging Azure DevOps/VSTS with Microsoft D365FO, Enterprise Edition and LCS are as follows:

- **Application Lifecycle Management** (**ALM**): Management of business processes and requirements in LCS while using the same for delivery in Azure DevOps/VSTS
- **Continuous delivery**: Seamless code and data movement across environments/projects

To connect and manage your BPM library artifacts in Azure DevOps/VSTS, the LCS project must be linked to Azure DevOps/VSTS. If your project team has already deployed a dev/build environment using the LCS project, your LCS project is most probably already linked to Azure DevOps/VSTS. You can utilize Azure DevOps/VSTS capabilities to manage all configurations, data, business, integrations, reporting, or any other requirements in your Dynamics 365 implementation.

Now, let's look at the steps that are involved in setting up your LCS project and Azure DevOps/VSTS:

1. Log in to `https://www.visualstudio.com/` and create a new Azure DevOps/VSTS account.

2. Create a new Azure DevOps/VSTS project to be hosted in your account and select the tenant to host your project at `https://visualstudio.microsoft.com/`. Also, select how to manage your code (Git or TFS), as shown in the following screenshot:

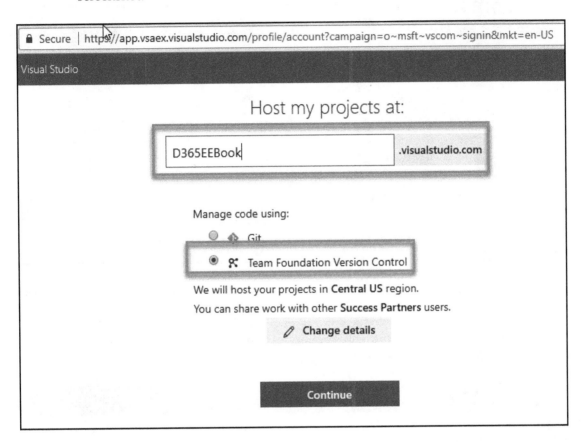

3. Selecting the right code repository is important. Here, we're using **Team Foundation Version Control**.

4. If your project needs Git, that is supported as well.

5. Verify whether the new project has been created in Azure DevOps/VSTS by verifying the URL of the project. This typically ends with your project name, as highlighted in the following screenshot:

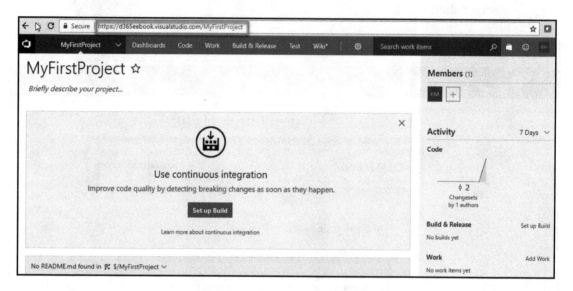

4. Now, we need to link the LCS project with Azure DevOps/VSTS. The LCS project needs to be connected to the Azure DevOps/VSTS account and project from the **Project settings**. Go to the section for Azure DevOps/VSTS and click on the **Setup Visual Studio Team Services** button to set up the LCS and Azure DevOps/VSTS project link:

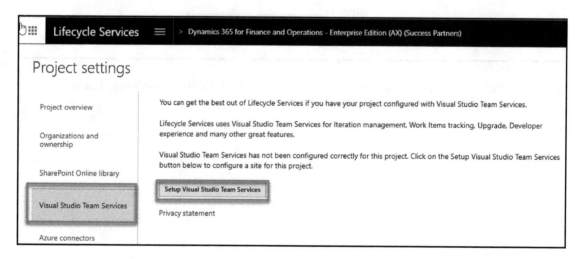

Ensure the URL is in the legacy VSTS format; for example,
`https://<<Your organization>>.visualstudio.com`.

5. For the LCS to access the Azure DevOps/VSTS account, it needs to be provided
   with a personal access token, which can be accessed from the Azure
   DevOps/VSTS **Security** settings:

6. You can create a token valid for a set duration in Azure DevOps. To do so, go to
   your DevOps security settings, and then to **Personal access tokens** to get one.
   This can be seen in the following screenshot:

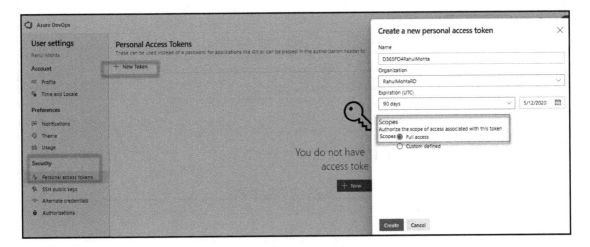

7. This token should be copied and pasted in the LCS BPM – Azure DevOps screen, along with your Azure DevOps account URL:

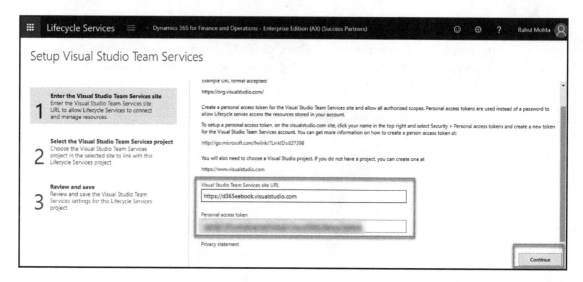

8. Once you click on **Continue**, the LCS will be allowed to access the projects in this account. Here, you need to select one of the projects from Azure DevOps/VSTS:

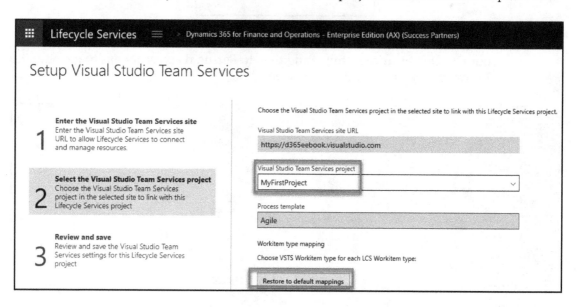

9. After selecting a project, the work items mapping can be selected by clicking on **Restore to default mappings**, as highlighted in the preceding screenshot. These work items can be changed between BPM and LCS.

10. Associate Azure DevOps/VSTS work item types with LCS items based on the process template being used in the Azure DevOps/VSTS project:

- For the **Capability Maturity Model Integration (CMMI)** process template, the following is a mapping of work items:

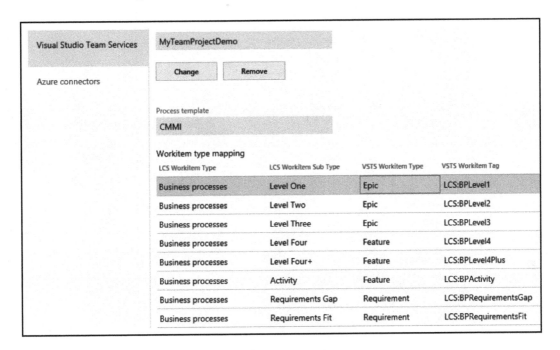

Visual Studio Team Services	MyTeamProjectDemo			
Azure connectors	Change Remove			

Process template
CMMI

Workitem type mapping

LCS Workitem Type	LCS Workitem Sub Type	VSTS Workitem Type	VSTS Workitem Tag
Business processes	Level One	Epic	LCS:BPLevel1
Business processes	Level Two	Epic	LCS:BPLevel2
Business processes	Level Three	Epic	LCS:BPLevel3
Business processes	Level Four	Feature	LCS:BPLevel4
Business processes	Level Four+	Feature	LCS:BPLevel4Plus
Business processes	Activity	Feature	LCS:BPActivity
Business processes	Requirements Gap	Requirement	LCS:BPRequirementsGap
Business processes	Requirements Fit	Requirement	LCS:BPRequirementsFit

- For the **Agile** process template, the following is a mapping of work items:

LCS Workitem Type	LCS Workitem Sub Type	VSTS Workitem Type
Process template		
Agile		
Workitem type mapping		
Business processes	Level One	Epic
Business processes	Level Two	Epic
Business processes	Level Three	Epic
Business processes	Level Four	Epic
Business processes	Level Four+	Epic
Business processes	Activity	Feature
Business processes	Requirements	User Story
Risks		Issue
Issues		Issue
Change Requests		Issue
Functional Design Docu...		Task
Technical Design Docum...		Task
Development Deliverable		User Story
Development Tasks		Task
Development Tasks	Upgrade Tasks	Task
Test Cases		Test Case
Test Tasks		Task
Bugs		Bug
Operate Issues	Monitoring alerts	Task
Operate Issues	Support Issues	Task

11. Once the Azure DevOps/VSTS project process template has been selected and the work item has been mapped, you can turn on synchronization from LCS BPM to the Azure DevOps/VSTS project backlog.

12. Use the backlog capability to keep items in the correct order and connected to the right things, as well as to keep items in your backlog linked to epics or scenarios you're using to drive your business.

 As per the mapping that we've done in the LCS project settings, the levels of BPM are reflected as features and stories in Azure DevOps/VSTS. For any other project template, although it would be mapped or asked to manually to map, and it may not allow to fully use the downstream features, such as the **Regression Suite Automated Test (RSAT)**.

Here are some acronyms that are used in Azure DevOps/VSTS:

- **Epic**: This is a virtual package that can span across releases and allows you to group features.
- **Feature**: This is a simple explanation of business needs.
- **Stories**: This explains features in more detail, based on several constraints and conditions.

Now, let's learn how to synchronize BPM with Azure DevOps/VSTS and see what it looks like on both sides.

BPM and Azure DevOps sync

You can synchronize the BPM library hierarchy into your Azure DevOps/VSTS project as a hierarchy of work items (epics, features, and so on) by clicking on the **VSTS sync** option:

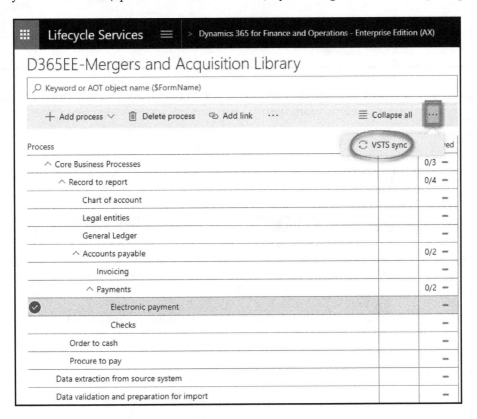

This is a limited two-way sync from LCS to Azure DevOps/VSTS that will keep your Azure DevOps/VSTS work items updated with any changes that are made to the LCS BPM library. Only when the requirements have been added to the right level can Azure DevOps/VSTS be synchronized with BPM.

Once the work items have been synchronized, you will notice a new requirement tab that's visible to your work item in BPM, showing the Azure DevOps/VSTS requirements ID:

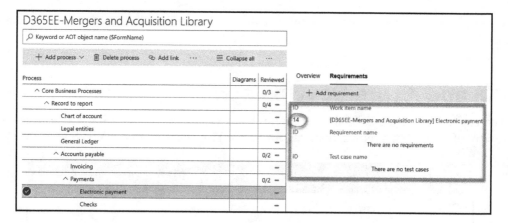

 The hyperlink is shown in blue in the highlighted text, which on clicking takes to DevOps work item.

Inside Azure DevOps/VSTS, the sync work items can easily be seen under the work section of the project and under the **Backlog** features:

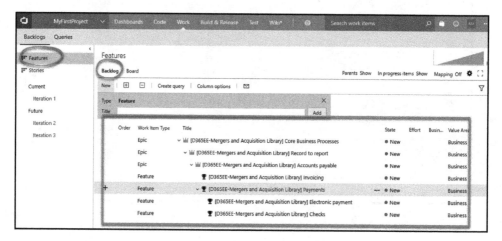

Once the work item is available in Azure DevOps/VSTS, as shown in the preceding screenshot, you can perform all the necessary steps and actions to update it with additional information, links, documents, and so on and use them for various purposes throughout the project (such as reporting, tracking, status, planning, and so on). The following screenshot shows a sample BPM library work item being edited in Azure DevOps/VSTS and an example of a work item type called feature:

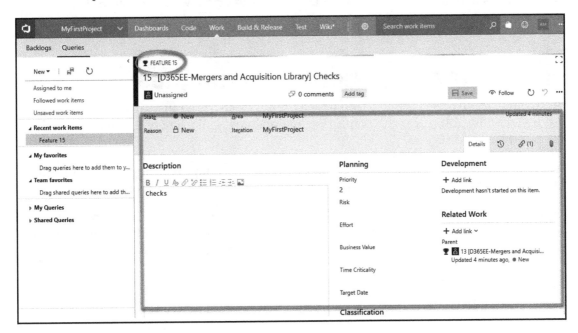

Note the acronyms and their relationship between Azure DevOps/VSTS and BPM:

- *1* (LCS) project: *n* (Azure DevOps/VSTS) epics
- *1* (Azure DevOps/VSTS) epic: *n* (Azure DevOps/VSTS) features
- *1* (Azure DevOps/VSTS) feature: *n* (Azure DevOps/VSTS) stories
- *1* (Azure DevOps/VSTS) story: *1* LCS BPM (requirement)

Continuous reporting and Azure DevOps/VSTS

Are you wondering how you can get the right insights with so much information involved? We recommend that you leverage the Azure DevOps/VSTS content pack for Power BI to gain insights into your team projects with automatically built dashboards and reports that are available quickly.

For more details, refer to `https://powerbi.microsoft.com/en-us/documentation/powerbi-content-pack-visual-studio`.

Now that you've understood the background details of creating business processes and requirements in BPM, let's learn about the various techniques we can use to collect and analyze them.

Requirement-gathering techniques

Achieving requirements is the reason why a project exists. You must always ensure you have a lot of due diligence when capturing, maintaining, and using requirements to drive the project toward success.

In the CRP methodology, you must conduct several workshops focusing on requirements collection, understanding validation, and having a solution to the approach.

How good the requirements are depends on how they were collected; the purpose and technique of gathering requirements is a significant contributor. Based on our experiences, we recommend that you leverage a technique that uses the following three verbs:

- Listen
- Lead
- Negotiate

You can use any technique that facilitates information collection and understanding the process based on industry- and customer-specific situations; however, the verbs listen, lead, and negotiate, are expected to be leveraged one way or the other.

Listen

As the first step in the requirement-gathering phase, you must listen to the customer regarding what they need/want to accomplish.

If you are a customer, you must ensure you convey all the business requirements to your Dynamics 365 solution advisor/partner/consultant. The business process owners are among the best to communicate requirements.

Some clients may seek external professional help from companies that specialize in **Business Process Reengineering (BPR)** or the likes of the *Big 5* consulting firms.

For any Dynamics 365 implementation, we recommend the following tools to make listening smoother:

- A questionnaire
- *As-is* business processes
- Calculations and examples
- Existing templates and formats
- A walkthrough of the existing system

Prepare questionnaires to collect information and have the business SMEs fill it out. At this stage, you are giving them the opportunity to provide you with details of what the business needs and their view of the requirements it needs to meet.

The questionnaire should be tailored for the client by the domain, functional area, and role. If you are an implementation partner/advisor, you should use industry templates, the business process libraries in LCS, and any other tool that provides a good starting point for questionnaires.

You will have to tailor them while considering the client's business, scope, and requirements based on the proposal and the client's organization structure. Always make a note of your understanding.

The quality of your questions makes a difference in requirements understanding and collection. Ask the process owners/SMEs to explain the entire process, and after it's over, ask open-ended questions – for example, what would you like to have in the new system?

A thorough understanding of your business process is important for your advisor/partner. We recommended that they are prepared well in advance. Doing detailed homework will help leverage their knowledge about the topic and also in gaining the customer's confidence. It also reduces the chances of missing any areas during discovery and the time the customer has to spend explaining the process to you.

The following are our expectations from a solution advisor and implementation partner/consultant, as part of this process:

- Seek/get examples of complex calculations (for example, revenue deferrals, royalties, commission, and pricing calculations).
- Seek all the possible scenarios and the factors that influence the outcomes.

- Understand the current business process flows (*as-is* processes) thoroughly.
- Ask for any work instructions or operations manuals to document their current process, to help in understanding the current business process.
- Ensure that all present and expected interfaces are well documented with clear handover criteria, as well as clear success and exceptions factors. Integrations are important in a modern hybrid environment, wherein business applications must always exchange information with other best-of-breed systems to ensure they meet the expected goals of an organization.
- Get samples of the reports, especially external-facing documents (invoices). Sometimes, customer invoices can become a project by themselves (checks, customer statements, packing slips, shipping labels, and so on, as applicable).
- Schedule an existing system walkthrough, especially for areas that are unique for the customer's business.
- Take screenshots and document the *as-is* as well as the *to-be* processes.
- Clarify whether any changes have been made to the existing processes and provide recommendations regarding changes to be made in the processes.
- When working on global projects, ensure that the SMEs from different locales come up with unified processes and share their requirements, which may be unique.

With the listening process complete, it's time for the solution owners to move on to the requirement-gathering phase.

Lead

Upon collecting information from the customer in detail, it's time to analyze and come up with your understanding of what they need. Document all the open questions you want to discuss further to get ready to lead the discussion about requirements. It's a must to understand the requirements in depth, and this can be easily achieved by engaging the customer and asking the right questions.

 We recommend that you seek future state (*to-be*) business processes and subprocesses in flow charts, as well as detailed requirements from the client in order to get started with existing (*as-is*) business processes.

In the leading process, we expect the solution advisor and implementation partner/consultant to be on top of the following activities:

- Seeking the business process flow in detail and asking for a walkthrough.
- Getting the business rules defined at various decision points in the flow chart.
- Validating the completeness of requirements coverage, dependencies, and business rules.
- Understanding and documenting the pain areas and asking questions to clarify if you have any doubts.
- Never assume a requirement; always get it validated.
- Avoiding discussions about solutions in the requirements meetings; this will dilute the purpose of the requirements workshop.
- Avoiding spending time discussing the out-of-scope areas until the client has approved the change order.
- Project derailment happens when scope creeps are allowed.
- It is in the interest of the customer and external stakeholders of the project to keep the requirements/scope in check.
- Capturing the details of reporting, security, integration, and data migration, along with the other requirements discussions.
- Non-functional requirements play a key role in shaping project success.
- Avoid using Dynamics terminologies or acronyms (for example, posting profile, value models, and so on during CRP discussions).
- Using short forms early in the discussion activity should be avoided, as these may prolong or confuse the stakeholders' understanding; they may be unaware of such terminologies or acronyms.
- Once the requirements have been heard and you have led the discussion, it's time to strike a balance between business and project goals and constraints.

Upon listening to and leading the business conversations, it is time to get back to the drawing board to work out all the solution capabilities that are available as per the project's scope and then initiate the next activity of negotiating.

Negotiate

This technique, in requirements workshops, is also known as solution brainstorming in CRP methodology. You may use knowledge of industry best practices to push back on requirements that do not add value to the business.

As part of this negotiation, you need to provide insights into why a specific feature is not needed anymore and what the replacement is as part of the new process. Also, always seek and negotiate the necessity and impact of requirements. Knowing this allows the project delivery team to prioritize the activities.

Often, requirements come from *how it works* in the current system (this does not always mean how it should work). Even worse is the fact that challenges/bugs in the current system become requirements for implementation in Dynamics 365. Consultants accept these as requirements and provide custom solutions. Understand what problem you are trying to solve and get to the bottom of the issue and then brainstorm the solution using the artifacts and information that's been collected.

 Finding the bottom of the issue is also known as **Root Cause Analysis (RCA)**.

Use the power of *why. Why do you do this as part of your process?* Often, when you get to the *why*, it is due to the current limitation and it can expose a requirement that is not adding value. In most cases, customization is a convenient way of providing solutions as an analyst – you are just taking the solution from the existing system and pushing your work to the developers in terms of customization.

Let's go over an example of a requirement that you should push back. We had a customer requirement to post an out-of-balance general journal entry. D365FO, Enterprise Edition doesn't support it. The reason users were asking for this to be a requirement was because the previous system had a bug that would post an out-of-balance entry in certain scenarios and then accountants had to use this *feature* to correct it.

Requirements are always needed and they keep coming back; hence, you should document them in your RTM and **Business Requirements Document (BRD)**. As the list of requirements in a typical Dynamics 365 implementation is long, we recommend that you segment them rightly and have a clearly defined owner.

Requirements Traceability Matrix (RTM)

In Microsoft D365FO implementations, there are many business processes involved that contain several scenarios and potentially many requirements per scenario. Also, a relationship/connection exists among them. To closely manage these many-to-many requirement relationships, formulating a comprehensive network of requirements for a process is a must for a project's success.

One easy way of remembering this could be by using the following definition: The RTM is a single repository/document that collects all the requirements, their relationship with other requirements, and their role in business processes – all pertinent information related to the solution, its development, and go-live.

The RTM is one live matrix that should be kept up to date throughout the lifecycle of the project and is often used by the project manager to re-baseline the project plan as needed.

The following is suggested as an end-to-end goal for requirements collection, analysis, and closure:

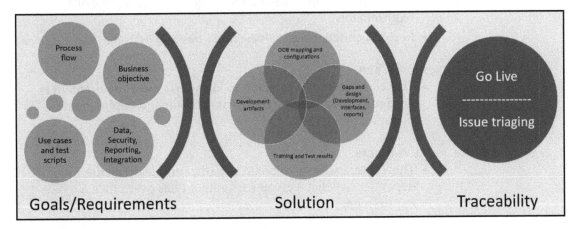

The preceding diagram shows the goals described as requirements belonging to a process/subprocess and how they influence the solution's analysis.

Solution acceptance becomes easier when an RTM is used. Also, stakeholders can validate and confirm whether each identified requirement meets the solution being delivered by leveraging the RTM and solution artifacts.

Now, let's learn how to collect, define, and scope the requirements.

Requirement segmentation and ownership

During requirement-gathering, an important aspect is to rightly classify them. Classification plays a vital role in the lifecycle of a requirement and how it's addressed downstream. Accurately classifying requirements helps project stakeholders use them adeptly and see them from various sides.

We recommend that you use the following techniques for classifying requirements and tailor-fit them based on the size, complexity, and business situation of your Dynamics 365 project:

- Ask the question **What**:
    - What kind of requirement is this? For example, functional process-oriented, non-functional security, decision making, and so on.
    - Impact on the business (must-have or good to have).
- Ask the question **Why**:
    - This classification is oriented to weigh the importance of a requirement.
    - Recommended usage values: must-have, good to have.

- Ask the question **When**:
    - This classification is oriented to know when the requirement is needed so that it can be taken for solution and deployment planning in the CRP.

- Ask the question **Where**:
    - This classification is oriented to gather and learn all the dependencies that a given requirement has over other requirements.

- Ask the question **Who**:
    - This classification is oriented to always ensure that there is an owner of the requirement.
    - Usually, ownership is made by subprocesses, and all the requirements within the process should inherit from them.
    - There should be at least four owner types for every requirement, as follows:
        - Business owner/SME
        - Project core team owner from customer
        - Project core team owner from advisor/partner
        - Technical owner

- Ask the question **Which**:
    - This classification is oriented to gather all the resources that are needed for a requirement.
- Ask the question **How**:
    - This classification is solution-oriented, and if a solution that was already committed or agreed upon is available, then it should be captured as well.

 There are a number of details that go into a requirement, so analysis is an important activity that may overlap or happen right after requirement collection.

When collecting details and classifying, watch out for loops and ensure that ambiguity, if any, is validated with the right owner. Also, ensure that all potential scenarios/outcomes of the requirement are collected, along with the exceptions.

Segmentation of requirements with the definition of an owner is important if you want to assist in analyzing the requirements effectively.

Now, let's explore the typical areas of collecting requirements while implementing Microsoft D365FO and their representative sections, as follows:

Type	Subtype	Requirement area
Generic/foundation	Generic/foundation	This includes collecting requirements about the companies involved, business verticals/industries involved, countries, sites, locations, solution instances, and so on.
Functional	Finance and accounting	This includes collecting requirements about general ledgers with a chart of accounts, financial reports, financial dimensions, posting rules, currencies, country-specific taxation and compliance, financial periods, month-end, fiscal close, accounts payable, accounts receivable, invoicing and payments, fixed assets, bank, cash flow, electronic payments, budgeting, allocation, provisions, and so on.

Functional	Supply chain and distribution	This includes collecting requirements about products and their lifecycles, engineering change management, bill of material or formula management, stock-keeping units, sales order processing, purchase order processing, warehousing and transportation, returns, inventory management, inventory costing, customer service, **Maintenance, Repair, and Operations** (MRO), and so on.
Functional	Manufacturing and planning	This includes collecting requirements about production processing and control, scheduling, resources management, quality control and assurance, demand planning, forecasting, and so on.
Functional	Projects	This includes collecting requirements about contract management, professional services, project management, project types and their accounting, project budget, grants, and so on.
Functional	Human resources	This includes collecting requirements about talent/workforce management, leave management, skill management and training, payroll, and so on.
Functional	Mobile workforce	This includes collecting requirements about timesheet management, expense management, self-servicing, and so on.
Non-functional	Security	This includes collecting requirements about the business function and security roles, user interface-based security, data-dependent security, policy-based security, read-only versus transactional security, and so on.
Non-functional	Data migration	This includes collecting requirements about configurations, master data, data volume, data validations, migration from other systems, open transactions, historical and closed transactions, and so on.

Non-functional	Data warehousing and reporting	This includes collecting requirements about single source of truth reporting across systems, day-to-day reporting, analytical reporting, dashboard, interactive information exploration, and so on.
Non-functional	Integration	Middleware and integration, **Electronic Data Interchange** (**EDI**), workflow, and so on.
Industry-specific business needs	Specifics	Industry-specific requirements.

The preceding table is just a representative sample of what to expect when requirement-gathering. The scale, depth, and coverage vary from customer to customer and industry to industry, so you must ensure that all the requirements related to the contract/scope are well captured and classified.

After collecting and segmenting the requirements across various areas, we need to analyze these requirements and capture the entire process in RTM so that it can be used throughout the initiative.

Analysis of requirements

Requirement analysis is supposed to be done by experts of the Dynamics 365 solution. This expert could be an external advisor/partner or an internal team member and should bring in their much-needed experience alongside solution guidance options.

Customers must push their advisors/partners/consultants to seek solution options, both in the form of workarounds and in the form of customizations or extensions when a requirement can't be met with out of the box capabilities. Even when requirements are envisioned to be met out of the box, their mapping must be documented and should be validated during the learning/prototyping phase in the CRP approach.

When a requirement can't be achieved with out-of-the-box capabilities in a Dynamics 365 solution, then the solution analysis stage starts. Poor analysis will add more time, effort, and cost to the project. Every time you get a requirement that needs customization, try to think about how the other Dynamics 365 customers are using it. Ask why Microsoft (the principal) did not build the feature, and you will find pointers to push back.

When a requirement is a must-have and is legitimate enough to break a process, then the customization route should be taken. Care must be taken not to customize the Dynamics 365 solution beyond 50% of the core functionality as it would be similar to the situation of a magician who has several balls to juggle at the same time. You should certainly try to avoid such a conundrum.

We recommend that you do the following when analyzing the requirements as well as gaps from solution fitment:

- Classify the gap and its impact:
    - Here, the extent of the gap from a customization perspective should be captured.
    - Some usage examples include simple, medium, and complex.
    - The impact of a gap is essentially two-fold: an impact on other business processes and requirements and an impact on the overall solution. Both impacts should be well thought of and documented for the solution planning phase.
    - Ensure that you capture both the extent and impact as they are like two sides of the same coin. Both are needed to evaluate the solution options, feasibility, acceptance criteria, and other highly influential elements of a project's success.
- Perform a workaround analysis:
    - Before any customization is brainstormed, ensure that the solution owner has exhausted all possible workarounds to solve the gap.
    - When possible, look for multiple workarounds, come up with a SWOT analysis, and jointly discuss in a project.
    - When an approach is seen as a major decision, it is recommended that you use a key decision log, along with making updates to the requirement.
    - After careful evaluation of all workarounds, when no alternative exists, then solution brainstorming in order to customize the solution should be done.
    - Often, when thinking of solutions, there are situations when the solution may not be comprehensive enough.
    - You should capture all risks, issues, and potential side effects, along with the customization approach.
    - It is recommended that you always get the right stakeholder buy-in for all the major gaps with their solution propositions.

- Make ballpark estimates for customization:
    - Preparing estimates for customization could be done at the time of customization envisioning or, subsequently, upon finalizing the customization approach.
    - Estimation techniques are out of the scope of this book; however, you should always explore the best-recommended estimate techniques that are applicable to your project.
    - Look at the available partner solution assessment for gaps by checking Microsoft AppSource. There, you can search for all solution providers and their capabilities. For more details, please refer to `https://appsource.microsoft.com`.
    - When customization is the last resort, look for the estimates, extent, and impact of the gap to ascertain if it makes sense to get a ready-made solution that addresses all or most of the gaps.
- Build or buy a decision for gaps:
    - Based on the estimate, complexity, and comfort level of the partner solution versus the in-house capabilities of customizing the solution, you should be able to make the decision of make or buy.
    - Similar situations may still have a varied effect on decision-making, so it is advised that you always evaluate every project that's undertaken in the Dynamics 365 world.

Having analyzed the gap and with the solution options discovered, it's time to build the entire solution proposal from the bottom up.

Solution blueprint

A solution blueprint is the ultimate visual in a project. It's a midway checkpoint, and its acceptance means that the project now changes from the assessment phase to the building phase. A solution blueprint is always best when represented in an end-to-end flow diagram that shows all the solution elements that have been envisioned and agreed to be leveraged from here on out.

A typical business blueprint must cover everything that the business is going to leverage in their future state operations. The solution blueprint is now the central and most important element when making any key decision and adjusting the scope, and going forward, it will be leveraged in almost all the deliverables in the project.

All project stakeholders should have access to it, must have a voice to suggest optimizations, and must be involved in accepting the solution blueprint.

A much more detailed document called the **Solution Design Document** (SDD) is also recommended for in-depth documentation of the solution details, and the solution blueprint should be used as its foundation.

The following diagram is a sample solution blueprint that spans all the business processes, tools, legacy applications, and top subprocesses:

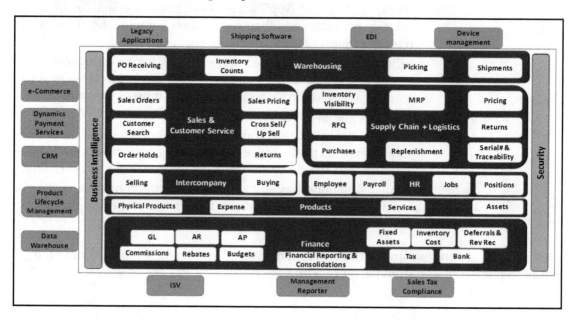

We, as solution advisors, often take the preceding solution blueprint one step forward and align the Dynamics 365 terminology in order to leverage the fit-gap analysis of requirements.

We recommend the following checklist for a typical solution blueprint:

- Are all the business processes and subprocesses covered?
- Are all the requirements (functional and non-functional) addressed?
- Has any other solution in the solution matrix been depicted and documented?
- Are all the interfaces specified?
- Are all the solution elements or apps specified?
- Are all the pilots or phases in a CRP covered?
- Has a supporting SDD been prepared?

Arriving at the solution blueprint is a long process, and during this journey, several decisions need to be made in the project, which leads to our next topic of maintaining a key decision log.

While preparing the solution blueprint and during the requirements analysis, decisions need to be made. We recommend leveraging a key decision log to register them.

Key decision log

Based on our experience, one of the top issues in project delivery is the availability and usage of a key decision log. This is a binding matrix that can streamline communications and expectations and bring in a lot of delivery efficiency.

Once the solution blueprint and the solution design document have been prepared, people seldom go back to the original requirement, that is, the **Business Requirement Document (BRD)**, the situation, use cases, and exceptions to understand, or people seldom recall what happened previously to trigger a particular approach. Hence, it is crucial to always maintain a key decision log that can be accessed by all the relevant project stakeholders.

Any decision that could alter the course of the project and impact its objectives must be documented. Also, the circumstances of making the decision should be noted as this will complete the entire story of the decision. A decision may impact one or more requirements, so all the impacted processes must be mentioned in the key decision as well. This will allow the various owners of the project to participate in the impact analysis and, hence, the decision-making process.

Best practices in managing requirements

Based on our experiences, when managing requirements, you should always keep the following best practices in mind:

- A business transformation initiative is not a destination; rather, it is a journey that must constantly evolve. Hence, you must always keep the requirements up to date. This includes key decisions that are made in a process/requirement. They should be easily available in the RTM.
- Always capture the requirements in a SMART format. They should not have abstract details.

- Never assume any requirement; always get it validated. Validation is the best when it's documented and signed off.
- Requirements change over time and how you handle such changes decides the fate of the project. Scope management and change requests should be the key levers for a project manager/CRP lead.
- Requirement collection and documentation is a zero-sum game; both parties (on the business and solution sides) should participate well and the RTM should be a living document that is easily accessible, simple to understand, and can be leveraged throughout the lifespan of the project.

 If you can tell and trace the life of a requirement, then it is a strong foundation for success. Subsequently, this traceability can be referenced in all business documents. It empowers the change management initiative and, ultimately, project success.

Summary

In this chapter, we explored scoping, defining requirements, and the RTM, along with their connection to business processes and subprocesses. While some implementations may consider a requirement document a good enough artifact to be able to continue with the project, we have seen that with a structured approach to documenting requirements, maintaining their traceability ensures that the entire project team has bonded with the goals they need to reach, which means there is a greater chance of achieving success.

While sharing insights of various requirement-gathering techniques, we highlighted the need to listen well, lead the discussion, and negotiate the must-have requirements. The answers to the fundamental business questions (*why, what, when, where, who,* and *how*) and requirement ownership ensures that a proper analysis is performed. This leads to selecting the right solution mapping, approaches, **Independent Software Vendor** (**ISV**) solutions, enhancements, and so on, thereby leading to the preparation of the solution blueprint, which is the backbone of the project.

The key deliverables from this chapter that we expect you to address are RTMs (comprising business processes and requirements), solution blueprints, and key decisions that are captured in a log.

In the next chapter, we will cover addressing configurations and data management by defining strategies and planning for them. You will also learn about golden configuration, various data management techniques, data cleansing, and quality validation recommendations. We will cover these topics from a solution perspective regarding data entities and data packages, the LCS configuration and data manager, **Process Data Packages** (**PDP**), and Azure DevOps/VSTS.

6
Configuration and Data Management

In the previous chapter, you learned about the importance of requirements gathering, business processes, solution blueprints, and requirement traceability.

In every implementation project, there are two primary data management activities that a project team needs to deal with, as follows:

- **Configuration data**: Configuration means setting up the base data and parameters to enable your functionalities, such as financial, supply chain, taxation, and project management.
- **Data migration**: Data migration means migrating data from the existing legacy system to a new ERP system. Typically, it includes master data such as customers, vendors, and products, and open transactions such as opening balances, open receivable, open payable, open orders, and on-hand inventory.

Effective management of data can be achieved with the help of the right scoping, tool selection, techniques for migration, validation, and well-defined acceptance criteria. Configuration and data management is often the most complex and underestimated area in ERP implementations. This chapter is about the tools, techniques, and best practices you should use when doing configuration and data management for Finance and Operations projects.

We will be covering the following topics in this chapter:

- Explaining configuration management
- Managing data migration
- Introducing data management tools
- The data management framework
- Data management scenarios
- Best practices in managing configurations and data migration

Explaining configuration management

Configuration management is an ongoing process of identifying and managing changes to system configuration during the lifecycle of the project.

The following are the key activities that are performed during the configuration management process:

- **Planning**: This step involves planning the scope, identifying the configuration, and the resources, tools, and techniques to set up, test, and manage the configuration data.
- **Setup and testing**: This phase usually starts early in the requirement gathering phase and continues until user acceptance testing. In the beginning, a functional consultant in the project usually studies the customer's legacy system and gathers key information such as legal entities, chart of accounts, financial dimension, number sequences, and master and reference data and configures the CRP environment. As the CRP phase continues, the key decision that's made during these phases inspires new and updated configuration. Most of the configuration is finalized once the functional and design documents have been completed; however, configuration updates continue during the development and testing phase of the project to reflect new custom configurations and address quality issues.
- **Tracking and controlling change**: One of the important aspects of configuration management is to ensure that changes to the configuration are tracked and controlled. Tracking and controlling the configuration data ensures that the system is tested with the same configuration in the different environment during various phases of the implementation project. As an example, configuration usually starts with the CRP environment and then moves to system testing, **user acceptance testing (UAT)**, and finally the production environment.

In summary, configuration management revolves around identifying and setting up the right configuration and tracking and managing the changes throughout the project. One of the proven techniques you can use to track and control the configuration data is using a golden configuration environment. A golden configuration environment is an environment where are all key system configuration is set up and maintained. All the other environments, such as system testing and the UAT environment, are seeded from the golden configuration environment periodically to ensure that the configurations are tested before they move to production. In the following subsections, we will learn about more key aspects of configuration planning and the golden configuration environment.

Planning configuration management

Planning is key for configuration management. This revolves around identifying the scope of the configuration, such as a list of modules, parameters, references, and master data. Implementation teams typically build a repository of all the configurations in Excel files, which are then imported to the relevant environments. We recommend that you leverage the following key considerations in your configuration planning:

- Create a list of configurations that are needed for the project and identify and assign the resources responsible for configuration. As a part of this list, identify the cross-functional module configuration and add the secondary responsible resources.
- Build a list of environment-specific configurations. Some of the configurations, such as links between applications talking to each other, need to have different values in different environments. For example, you need to ensure that the test instance of Dynamics 365 for Finance and Operations is pointing to the test instance of the shipping solutions and that the payment gateways have been configured in the test mode.
- Try to automate the changes to configurations and their movement across environments to avoid the risk of human errors.
- Maintain a list of company-specific configurations. When you are planning global rollouts, define a global template and maintain a list of configurations that need to be revisited for every company.
- Create a configuration template to collect data for the setup of each module, and describe the purpose of configuration and its usage for tracking purposes.

Now, let's look at the various environments that are used in configuration management, especially the golden configuration environment.

The golden configuration environment

Let's learn about the environmental factors in configuration planning since several environments are usually involved. One of the biggest challenges that an implementation team faces is moving the configuration from one environment to another. If configurations keep changing in every environment, it becomes more difficult to manage them. Similar to code promotion and release management across environments, configuration changes need to be tracked through a change control process across environments to ensure that you are testing with a consistent set of configurations.

The objective is to keep track of all the configuration changes and make sure that they make it to the final cut in the production environment. While all environments are important and have a purpose, the golden environment is a special one and should always be pristine (without any transactions). As part of the configuration management process, once configurations have been accepted/tested/approved in the test environment, they should be moved to a golden environment. This golden environment can also be turned into a production environment, or the data can be copied over to the production environment. The golden environment is usually the starting point for various environments, for example, UAT, training, and pre-production.

The advantages of a golden environment are as follows:

- A single environment for controlling all configuration-related information.
- Base environment to set up other tools for initial solution validation.
- Template environment to span other environments, thereby reducing chances of any configuration changes or data corruption, which could directly impact testing or any other related activity.

The one factor that you should remember is to keep the code base of the golden configuration alongside the latest approved code base for production so as to keep this environment in sync with the latest updates.

Let's summarize all the activities involved in configuration planning:

- It should leverage industry best practices that are relevant to the customer organization for configuring your Finance and Operations solution.
- It should define and document everything that constitutes configuration.
- You should identify the environments that manage the configuration and data.
- In the project plan, you should define the acceptance criteria for the golden configuration and ensure they are user-accepted, tested, and ready to move to production.
- For repeatable and assured success, keep the project goals in context and use them as references.
- Configurations evolve over time; hence, proper versioning should be maintained:
    - Based on the business objectives, define a baseline for initial configuration.
    - All intermediate versions should be well thought of, and key decisions should be captured and tested before marking them ready for production use.
- Identify and leverage the tools provided with Dynamics 365 for Finance and Operations for data management.

- The data exchange with Microsoft Dynamics 365 for Finance and Operations happens via data entities and it is important to map them with the business needs and migration requirements:
  - This will help us find out whether all the entities are available out of the box or whether some need to be built.
  - Also, by knowing these entities, you can start planning your sequence of loading and leverage the same during the actual migration.
- It is often difficult to perfect the configuration, data dependencies, and their sequencing in any implementation. Hence, you should build and leverage a reusable library of configuration and data templates. Reusability brings in predictability and accuracy, and you don't need to start from scratch all the time; rather, you could just use a template and build the delta (data) on top of it.
- Also, a strategy for the building blocks of configuration is needed. This helps in manageability and the controlled movement of configurations.

 Configurations are the base elements that help tailor solutions so that they suit the business/project needs. Some configurations are non-reversible; hence, utmost care must be taken when arriving at such decisions. Experts in the solution can help you accurately plan for the right configuration without much rework.

A lot of advisors and partners are creating their own industry-specific configuration templates and offerings for Microsoft Dynamics 365 solutions, which should be explored by customers and other partners in their implementation to maximize their returns on investment, so that they are benefitted.

Now, let's learn about planning related to data migration.

Managing data migration

Similar to configuration management, data migration is an important activity in any project. By data migration, we mean the data that you need to migrate from the legacy system, such as master data and opening balances. Data is needed for any kind of task and has multiple attributes. Hence, to ensure that it is managed and utilized well, we need to employ a systematic approach.

In the context of implementing a Dynamics 365 solution, we are focusing on overall data management and would like to share a graphic for an end-to-end understanding of all the activities involved in planning for data:

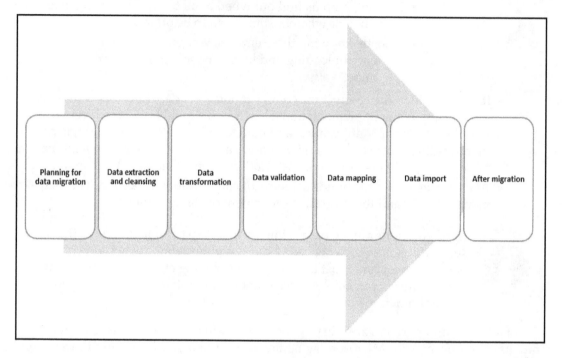

The full suite of activities involved in data migration are as follows:

- **Planning for data migration**: This involves planning the scope, tools, techniques, volume, and environment.
- **Data extraction and cleansing**: A data extraction script should be created to extract the required data in the appropriate format. Often, the quality of the data in the legacy system is not very good, so attention should be given to cleanse the extracted data.
- **Data transformation**: Applying appropriate transformation logic to prepare the data for its final import into Dynamics 365 for Finance and Operations.
- **Data validation**: Maintain a checklist of validation criteria for the business for extracted data.

- **Data mapping**: This mapping is per entity level; for example, the customer entity can span account-related information, contacts, and addresses. You must ensure that you have found a home for entity information so that it can be exchanged at the field level, including any transformation needs on the data.
- **Data import**: Maintain a log of what data and which records have been extracted, cleaned, validated, and migrated.
- **After migration**: Always confirm with the business about data accuracy and completeness.

Data migration may just seem like a one-time activity of moving data from the source to the Dynamics 365 Finance and Operations, but it goes through the same lifecycle as that of any other requirements in a project. Planning for data migration is a must in order for us to be able to systematically identify and execute a number of activities spread over time with multiple stakeholders. It also eases out potential unknowns and makes it easier to know what to expect next.

We recommend that you start negotiations from point zero so as to condense huge data migration needs to a minimum of only what is a must. For example, when discussing customer transactions, start the discussion to bring only open records for active customers and not all the historical transactions.

To be successful, involve business users and data experts right from the start of the project. Based on the size, complexity, and nature of the customer business, you may also need to include a data governance strategy in data migration planning.

Scoping the data migration

Rightsizing the scope is among the first steps toward a successful initiative. The scope must be well-documented and agreed upon by all the relevant stakeholders to ensure smooth and accurate data migration.

Often, implementation teams either do not consider data migration at all or have unreasonable expectations regarding the data migration requirements.

Even if the original sales proposal has explicit data migration requirements that have been identified, many of the project team members and stakeholders may not be aware of what was specified or may not agree with the scope.

We recommend that you always have a dedicated data scoping activity planned, which should give both sides the opportunity to be on the same page and leave very little room for any assumptions. This scoping activity can be achieved by answering the following set of questions:

- **What is needed to keep the business running efficiently?**

  Define the business goals with this question in mind, and then approach the issue of what information needs to be migrated to meet these goals or what solutions can be provided to meet the goals without migrating the data. For example, a customer may say that they need to be able to collect their receivables and run aging for customers. This is the business goal. This means that you only need to migrate Open AR for the customers, along with the due date.

- **Is there an alternative to bringing the existing data over?**

  Reporting out-of-legacy systems or data warehouses and defining a manual process, if it is going to be used only for inquiries over a short period of time, are some potential alternatives.

- **How much of the data present in the legacy systems is up to date, validated, and good for future use?**

  Do you want the new system to have the same issues that you are trying to solve in the current system?

- **How many records are involved or what volume of data migration is needed to accurately pinpoint the tool and technique for loading?**

  Ensure that the ballpark numbers of record counts are defined for each area during scoping (for example, 4 million products, 200,000 customers, and 2,000 open orders). This will help you select the right tools.

- **How often will you be asked to retrieve this data?**

  Usually, the activity of configuration and data migration is an iterative exercise, so the need to leverage/build reusable capabilities to address this iterative nature is required.

Identify and document the business needs clearly and accurately, with examples where possible. You can avoid the cascading effect and carve out the critical pieces of data that you need frequently in order to limit the scope. For example, just migrating the open balance of each customer invoice rather than trying to bring the complete line item detail requires less effort. If a customer service needs the invoice line detail to research a customer issue that happens once a month on average, this detail would generally not be worth the effort of trying to migrate it.

Part of the data migration planning process involves educating business stakeholders about the cost of migration and focusing on migrating information that would enable better business decisions, better servicing of customers, and information insight. In principle, you should avoid migrating historical transactions, such as posted sales invoices, posted purchase orders, individual general ledger transactions, and inventory transaction history.

It is important to facilitate a scoping exercise with the project team and remember that every record that needs to be migrated comes at a cost; the question is not whether it can be done, but should rather be whether is it worth it.

The effort to clean and transform data is a humongous task and an expensive proposition. Certainly, historical transactions are needed for various purposes, such as compliance, regulatory requirements, business analysis, and customer support. However, there are other solutions available as alternatives for migrating all the legacy data. These solutions/tools can be selected based on the size of the dataset, transformation requirements, and storage and access needs. Here are some common tools that we have used for our customers for historical transaction insights:

- Extract and store the historical information from the legacy system for reporting purposes. Leverage an existing or new data warehouse to meet the reporting/analysis requirements. Use tools such as Power BI for historical analytical reporting.
- Storing data on the cloud, such as Azure SQL, and then show it in reports (SSRS).
- A shared folder or a SharePoint site to store the extracted files from the source system in various formats, such as Excel, CSV, and PDF.

- Set the security of the legacy system to read-only and do historical lookups there. Make sure that support contracts and an exit strategy are part of any discussion regarding this option so that the customer is not paying for multiple systems indefinitely. This is a good option for a stable legacy system where support is still available (without paying a hefty annual support price) and also helps ease the transaction for the legacy system support vendor.

- Consider extracting and storing legacy data in the Data Lake or relational database without having to do a mapping or cleansing process. As part of business intelligence and analytics planning, you should factor combining the Dynamics 365 for Finance and Operations data with historical data to combine and deliver reports involving historical transactions.

Common data migration areas

In any implementation, there are quite a number of common business areas that need to be migrated. Let's explore some of these business areas, along with our recommendation for how they should be scoped.

The following table is an example that you can use as a starting point to help validate the decisions to be agreed upon in a data migration requirements session:

Functional area	Guidance for scoping
General ledger history	• **Prior years' history**: Periodic balances for 2 years • Current year until a set date, periodic balances
Customers	• All the active customers (and addresses) • Has performed a transaction in the last 18 months, has an open balance, or has open sales orders
Vendors	• All the active vendors (and addresses) • Has performed a transaction in the last 18 months, has an open balance, or has open purchase orders
Products and prices	• All the active products and prices • Products have been created in the last 6 months, there is stock in hand, the product has open purchase, sales, or production orders, or the product was sold in the last 12 months • **Prices**: All the active and future prices for customers and vendors • Trade agreements and sales/purchase agreements in Dynamics 365 for Finance and Operations terminology
Open AP	• Migrate all the open documents: Invoices, payments, and debit notes • **Key fields**: Vendor ID, open amount, description, due date, invoice number, document number, document date (original invoice date), method of payment, PO/reference, or any other information that you need in order to pay the vendor • You should be able to run vendor aging and pay the vendors (1099 reporting considerations)

Open Accounts Receivable (AR)	• **Migrate all open documents**: Invoices, payments, and credit notes • **Key fields**: Customer ID, open amount, description, invoice number, original date, due date, method of payment, customer PO number, and reference to sales order number • You should be able to run customer/AR aging and collect payments from the customers
Inventory (on hand)	• Migrate in-hand inventory for each product by dimensions • Are your product's numbers changing (this would mean changing labels in the warehouse)? • Cost for each lot and dates for batch numbers • Review the impact on inventory costing
Open orders	• Open sales orders and open purchase orders – orders that haven't been delivered yet • Discuss the returns (you may need to refer to the old system for a short period of time) • Orders that are delivered but yet not invoiced
Bank balances	• The last-reconciled balance • Unreconciled transactions
Fixed assets	• **The active assets**: Assets that are in the possession and in the books • **Key values**: Fixed asset number, acquisition price, accumulated depreciation till date, remaining periods, acquisition date/put-in-service date, date depreciation last run, serial number, assigned to, dimensions, and so on

Planning data migration

Data is both qualitative and quantitative in nature; hence, your data migration strategy should include a concrete and measurable success definition to determine when data migration can be considered complete. Now that you have a solid plan for configuration and data management, you should now explore all the available techniques that will assist you in accomplishing the plan.

The following is a suggested list of key activities you should factor into your data migration plan/strategy:

- Collect the requirements for data migration with measurable factors
- Identify all the data elements/entities and their sources
- Understand and keep the target solution/system schema in perspective
- Develop a governance strategy for leadership and direction
- Define data quality and integrity parameters
- Identify all the data validations and rules
- Identify and assign an owner for every type of data
- Define data conversion needs (if any)
- Agree on a data cleansing approach

- Collect data volumes per entity
- Identify when full data loads are needed and when the incremental approach needs to be taken
- Identify all the post data migration checkpoints
- Identify and leverage the tools provided by Microsoft/principal

Now, let's consider a list of items to factor in for your data migration plan:

- **Environment**: You need to plan for an environment to run the data migrations iteratively. You don't want the test environment to be messed with every week while the data migration team is still trying to stabilize the data migration processes.
- **Cycles**: You need a plan for multiple cycles of data migration that are a few weeks apart. This gives us time to validate the data, fix issues, and improve the performance of the migration processes.
- **Resources**: Business resources will be required to help extract and validate the data for each cycle. They may be needed to help cleanse the data if you run into issues with the legacy data. IT resources will be required to extract, import, and validate the data.
- **Training**: It is a good idea to train and utilize dedicated resources in the data conversion process as this is an iterative process. It also gives you experienced resources focusing on improving the process based on the feedback received from data validation.
- **Verification**: Data quality in the source system has a huge impact on the number of data migration iterations that you have to perform during tests.
- **Testing**: Complete a full data migration prior to starting system integration testing, UAT, and training. These migrations should be performed by following the data migration process documentation, and the time for each step needs to be recorded. As a part of this process, have the migrated data validated by the business prior to starting the tests in these environments.
- **Automation**: Come up with iterative/automated processes, including data extraction from legacy systems. This makes the cycle time for data migration shorter, improves its quality, and provides consistent results. For some extractions, you could use reports from the legacy system that the business uses. For example, if a business uses a detailed **Accounts Receivable (AR)** aging report, you can use that report as an input for migration rather than building a separate job for data extraction.

- **Teamwork**: The team should record the timing for each process and arrange dependencies and processes that can be run in parallel.
- **Communication**: Document the migration process end to end – from data extraction and intermediate validation to migration (the development team that writes the code should not be the one executing it). With a documented process, you can get more team members to execute the repetitive data migration processes.

The next step after planning is ensuring that you have a smooth and spot-on execution.

Executing the data migration

There is no single technique in managing data that can be leveraged all the time in a typical Dynamics 365 implementation. Discipline, ownership, and a process for master data governance are critical success factors for the sustainability of a system. Data management is not a one-time affair, so it should always be closely monitored, optimized, and executed as per your plan. **Extract, Transform, and Load** (ETL) is one of the most common approaches in data migration planning, and you will be using it in one way or the other, no matter which solution/application is in focus.

The following steps are involved in ETL:

1. Identify all the source systems, as per the data migration requirements.
2. Build data templates to extract information from the source system:
    - When volumes are high, you can leverage a SQL database as a common repository to extract the information.
    - For smaller data and configurations, you can directly leverage Excel as the mechanism.
3. Prepare for data export from the source system into the staging places.
4. Perform data cleansing and validation activities:
    - System validations and automation should be leveraged wherever you can generalize a rule for validation and cleansing. You should use it to put the staging data in a format that can be imported into the target system.
    - When human decisions are involved, then introduce manual checkpoints for data validations in the staging system, for example, mandatory data, data types, and data length.
    - Leverage the tools that are available in the Dynamics 365 solution to import data.

Now, let's learn about data mapping and transformation considerations:

- **Cleanest data**: If the data is stored in multiple places in a legacy system, you should pick the cleanest one to extract a copy from. Consider the update timings in the source and add dependencies in the go-live plan to get the source data updated, prior to starting the extraction.
- **Business rules in transformation**: Define and validate the field mapping between the legacy systems and Dynamics 365 for Finance and Operations, along with any transformations that need to happen between the extraction and the import process. Define rules in the target system or in the source systems (for example, bad addresses and phone numbers) to enable automation and transformation as much as possible.

 Identify the areas that need data cleansing earlier in the planning stage so that these cleansing efforts can start early and the datasets can be made ready well ahead of time.

Leveraging the aforementioned techniques, let's evaluate the various tools and see how we can benefit from them.

Introducing data management tools

Dynamics 365 for Finance and Operations provides comprehensive functionality within the application and LCS to manage the configuration and data migration process. The best practices, from a systems' perspective, are already baked into them, so using these tools should be included in planning.

In Dynamics 365 for Finance and Operations, the implementation team can use various tools and frameworks for data management. The following image shows the different tools and frameworks available for data management:

Data Entity and Packages Framework	Database Operations	Cross Company Data Sharing
• Initial data configuration • Copy data across environment • Data migration	• Backup/Restore/Refresh/Point In Time Restore	• Sharing parameter and reference data

The data entity and packages framework is the primary and most useful tool for handling various data management scenarios. This tool helps the implementation team perform the initial data configuration, manage configuration data within the environment, copy the configuration across environments, and migrate the data from legacy systems.

Database operations, such as backup, restore, and point-in-time restore, are another set of tools that can be used to quickly set up a new environment and to even move your final golden configuration environment to production for the first time.

The cross-company data sharing tool can be used in an implementation scenario where multiple legal entities are involved in sharing common parameters and reference data, for easier and effective data management.

Now that we have introduced the various toolsets, let's explore these toolsets in detail.

The data management framework

The data management framework in Dynamics 365 for Finance and Operations is based on **Data Import/Export Framework (DIXF)**. This tool, along with the other tools in LCS, helps the customers and partners quickly set up their initial environment from blank data, manage the configuration data throughout the lifecycle of the project, plan and execute data migration, and move the data from one environment to another.

There are several tools and concepts that constitute the overall data management platform in Dynamics 365 for Finance and Operations. Some of these tools are within the Finance and Operations application, while the others are available in LCS. Let's learn about these tools and concepts and how they can be used for various data management scenarios.

Data management concepts

First, let's understand the various concepts that are used within the data management framework, since it forms the core element that is used in any data-related activity.

The data management workspace

The data management workspace in Finance and Operations provides a single entry point for the data administrator to configure, plan, export, import, and monitor data projects. The data management workspace is available in the Finance and Operations, system administration area, or from the dashboard.

The following screenshot shows the data management workspace in Dynamics 365 for Finance and Operations:

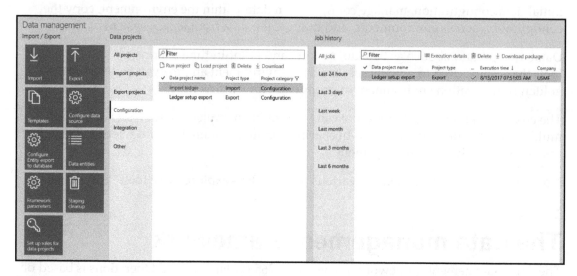

The data management workspace has several functions that can be be used to import data, export data, and facilitate other useful capabilities and views so that you can quickly manage your data flow.

Data entities

Data entities are the foundation bricks of a data management platform and serve many other purposes, such as integration, analytics, and office integration. Data entities provide a conceptual abstraction and encapsulation of the underlying table schema that represents the data concepts and functionalities.

For more details on data entities, please refer to Chapter 8, *Integration Technologies, Planning, and Design*. You can also refer to the Microsoft documentation at https://docs.microsoft.com/en-us/dynamics365/unified-operations/dev-itpro/data-entities/data-entities.

From a data management perspective, data entities enable scenarios for configuration data provisioning and data migration, as shown in the following image:

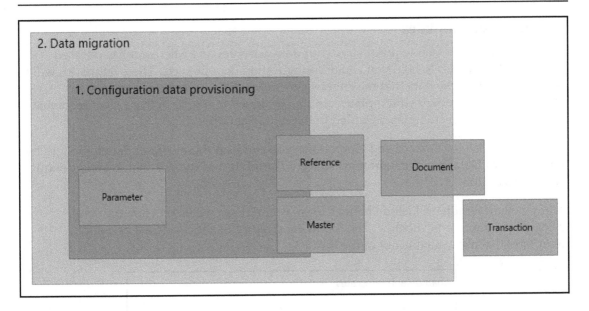

As shown in the preceding image, activities related to setting up a company, its parameters, and selecting reference and master data are within the boundary of the configuration data provisioning, where a number of tools are available.

The migration of open documents, master data, and supporting data could also be done using tools in LCS or using data management within Dynamics 365 for Finance and Operations.

Configuration data templates

Configuration data templates are predefined lists of entities for each module area that can be used in a data project. You can create, view, and modify these templates by using the template page in the data management workspace. The **Template** page in the data management workspace provides tools that let you create a template of entities. Similar to exporting data projects, you can create data templates by adding one entity at a time or adding multiple entities. You can also use the **Open in Excel** button to open the contents of the grid in a Microsoft Excel workbook. Modify the entities as you require and then click **Publish** to upload the changes back into Dynamics 365 for Finance and Operations. You can also use any existing data projects to create a template.

Default data templates

Templates make it easier to jump-start your data activities and Microsoft has released predefined templates to help you create configuration data projects. These templates will be sequenced so that the data that the entities generate will be processed in the correct sequence. These predefined templates are also designed to maintain the correct sequence when more than one template is added to the same data project.

In Dynamics 365 for Finance and Operations, you can load these default data templates by navigating to **Data management workspace** | **Template** and then using the **Load default templates** button.

Many default templates include entities for master data as well as customers, vendors, released products, and suchlike. The following screenshot shows the list of default templates that are available out of the box:

Load default templates

✓	Template ID ↑	Description
	010 - System Setup	System setup
	020 - GL Shared	General ledger shared
	022 - Workflow	Workflow
	025 - General ledger	General ledger
	100 - Bank	Bank
	120 - Accounts payable	Accounts payable
	130 - Tax	Tax
	140 - Accounts receivable	Accounts receivable
	150 - Fixed assets	Fixed assets
	160 - Budgeting	Budgeting
	300 - Inventory	Inventory
	310 - Product information ma...	Product information manage...
	320 - Procurement and sourci...	Procurement and sourcing
	330 - Sales and marketing	Sales and marketing
	395 - Quality management	Quality management
	400 - Warehouse management	Warehouse management
	405 - Transportation manage...	Transportation management
	410 - Production control	Production control
	412 - Process manufacturing	Process manufacturing
	418 - Product configuration ...	Product configuration models
	420 - Costing	Costing

[Load selected] [Load all] [Cancel]

For more details on data templates and their sequencing, please refer
to `https://docs.microsoft.com/en-us/dynamics365/unified-`
`operations/dev-itpro/data-entities/configuration-data-templates`.

Data templates are reusable artifacts and are used to create data projects quickly, as
explained in the next subsection.

Configuration data project

A data project or configuration data project contains configured data entities, their source
data format (Excel, CSV, and XML), mapping, and default processing options (execution
sequence or dependency). Configuration data packages are created by using the data
import and export projects in the data management workspace. Data projects support the
following scenarios:

- **Export of configurations**: Create configurations of entities and use the data
  management framework to export them into a package.
- **Import of configurations**: Upload a configuration package and use the data
  management framework to import the package.

To export data packages, you simply click on the **Export** tile in the data management
workspace, which opens the configuration data project page, as shown in the following
screenshot. You can name the project and add entities to create the data project:

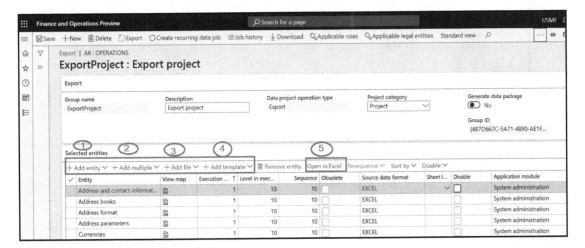

As highlighted and numbered in the preceding screenshot, there are a number of ways you can add data entities to your export data project:

1. **Add one entity**: Enter the first part of the name of the entity until it appears in the lookup.
2. **Add multiple entities**: Enter any part of the entity name, use the lookup for the module, enter any part of the tag name, or use the lookup for the entity category to show a list of entities. Press *Tab* to move the focus away from the lookup field and activate the filter. In the grid, select the entities to add.
3. **Add a file:** Browse to a file that contains a name that matches the name of an entity and a file name extension that matches the file name extension that is in your data sources.
4. **Add a template:** Select from a list of templates that you've loaded in your instance.
5. **Open in Excel:** Another option is **Open in Excel**, which you can use to edit and publish it back.

After you have added the list of entities in your configuration and sequenced them, you can click on the **Export** button to export the data project and create a data package. During the export, you can view the execution history of the data project, as follows:

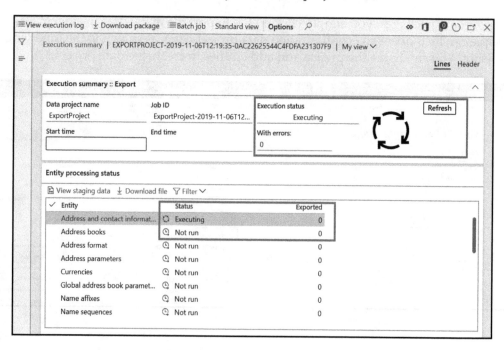

After the export has completed, you can download the packages locally by clicking the **Download package** button.

Once the configurations have been exported in a data package, they can be imported into another company or environment. The following screenshot shows the setup of such an import project:

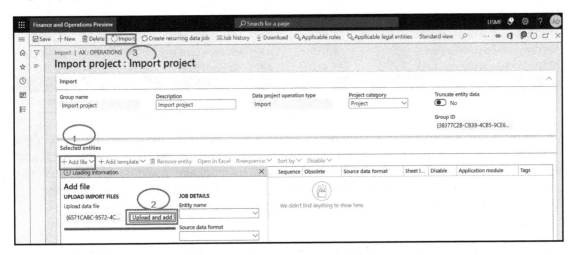

As highlighted in the preceding screenshot, to import a data package, you need to simply create the import project and click on the **Add file** button, then click **Upload and add** and locate the package file, and finally click the **Import** button. The import process will begin asynchronously and you can monitor the execution progress on the summary page.

As you've learned, exporting a data project generates the output as a data package that can be imported back into another environment. Details around the data packages concept are explained in the next section.

Data packages

A data package typically consists of one-to-many data entities. A typical data package consists of a group of entities for a particular task, process, or function. For example, the data entities that are required for general ledger setup may be part of one data package. The format of a data package is a compressed file that contains a package manifest, a package header, and any additional files for the included data entities.

The following screenshot shows the content of a sample data package, which contains sample configuration data for the data validation checklist process:

Name	Size	Packed	Type	Modified	CRC32
..			Local Disk		
Data validation checklist.xlsx	8,589	6,237	Microsoft Excel Wo...	5/24/2019 8:54...	826F8319
Data validation project task.xlsx	9,689	7,347	Microsoft Excel Wo...	5/24/2019 8:54...	132F2A67
Data validation task area.xlsx	8,637	6,291	Microsoft Excel Wo...	5/24/2019 8:54...	60CDD2EC
Data validation task status.xlsx	9,473	7,128	Microsoft Excel Wo...	5/24/2019 8:54...	9522FD04
Manifest.xml	19,748	1,134	XML File	5/24/2019 8:54...	6BB5A700
PackageHeader.xml	854	306	XML File	5/24/2019 8:54...	0B46C668

Data Validation Checklist.zip - ZIP archive, unpacked size 56,990 bytes

In a typical implementation scenario, when you start to set up the initial configuration data, you create data packages with entities containing standard business data, sample data, and entities without any data. You can then decompress the package, use data spreadsheets to collect the business data, and compress them to create the final data package. You can import this data package into your environment to complete the initial set of configurations.

Data packages can be directly imported using the data management workspace or uploaded to the LCS asset library and applied to the same or another environment through the data configuration manager. These concepts will be covered in the next subsection.

LCS Project | Asset library | Data packages

Once the data packages have been downloaded from your initial configuration environment and the data has been finalized, you can upload these data packages to your LCS project library. As shown in the following screenshot, the LCS asset library can be used as a repository for the data packages:

Asset library

Select asset type		Data package files							
BPM artifact (10)		+ ✎ 🗑 IMPORT 📋 Copy SAVE TO MY LIBRARY VERSIONS							
Cortana intelligence application (0)		✓ Name	Valid	Version	Scope	Status	Release candidate	Modified date	Size
Data package (17)		140 - AR_1	✓	1	Project	Draft		8/14/2019	386 KB
Database backup (0)		120 - AP_1	✓	1	Project	Draft		8/14/2019	386 KB
Dynamics 365 for Retail SDK (0)		020 - GL shared_1	✓	1	Project	Draft		8/14/2019	5 MB
GER Configuration (1)		100 - Bank_1	✓	1	Project	Draft		8/14/2019	161 KB
Localized financial report (0)		130 - Tax_1	✓	1	Project	Draft		8/14/2019	198 KB
Marketing asset (0)		025 - GL_1	✓	1	Project	Draft		8/14/2019	275 KB
Model (0)		Financial data sharing templates	✓	1	Project	Published		8/14/2019	4 KB
Power BI report model (3)		100 - Bank	✓	1	Project	Draft		8/14/2019	161 KB
Process data package (7)		120 - AP	✓	1	Project	Draft		8/14/2019	386 KB
Software deployable package (6)		130 - Tax	✓	1	Project	Draft		8/14/2019	198 KB
Solution package (0)									

The following are the key features of data packages in the LCS asset library:

- **Upload new data packages**: You can use the + button to create new data packages and upload the data package file.
- **Save it in your shared asset library**: Similar to the other asset types in LCS, you can save the data package as a shared asset. A shared asset can be imported into other projects within your organization.
- **Import**: Using the **IMPORT** option in the **Asset library** project, you can import the assets shared with you. While importing the assets, you can see all the data project assets that have been shared within your organization or shared by Microsoft.
- **Maintain version**: You can use the LCS asset library to manage the different versions of the asset file. You can also view the previous versions and pick a previous version to import it back if needed.

Configuration data packages

To reduce the implementation time, Microsoft releases multiple base data packages that you can use as a starting seed for your implementation projects. These packages contain the elements that are required in each module/area in order to meet the minimum requirements. For advanced business processes, you may have to add more entities to the list of packages.

The configuration data packages are available in LCS in **Asset library | Data packages** and can be imported into your implementation project data package asset. These data packages contain configuration entity spreadsheets based on the best practices data from Microsoft, which can be used to create an initial golden environment.

The entity spreadsheets include three types of data:

- **Business data**: The spreadsheet contains standard business data for a sample mid-sized company, combining the best practices and business standards to be used as a starting point for your initial configuration.
- **Sample data**: The spreadsheet contains data that can be used as an example for business-specific data. This data can be imported and used as an example, but it is expected to be changed in the spreadsheets itself, before loading it.
- **No data**: This spreadsheet doesn't contain any data. Several areas of the product are unique to each business and its business practices; hence, these spreadsheets must be reviewed and updated as per the organization's needs.

Data entities in configuration data packages are sequenced appropriately to guarantee a successful single-click import of the data, thereby ensuring data dependencies. These configuration data packages are great starting points to accelerate the configuration of your solution on Microsoft Dynamics 365 for Finance and Operations.

 Please refer to the following link for detailed information on configuration data packages and listing packages with their entities and content in the spreadsheets: https://docs.microsoft.com/en-us/dynamics365/ unified-operations/dev-itpro/data-entities/configuration-data- packages?toc=dynamics365/unified-operations/fin-and-ops/toc. json#data-packages-system.

LCS – configuration and data manager

Configuration and data manager is a tool in LCS that helps you apply data packages to your Dynamics 365 for Finance and Operation environment.

The following screenshot shows the configuration and data manager tool in LCS:

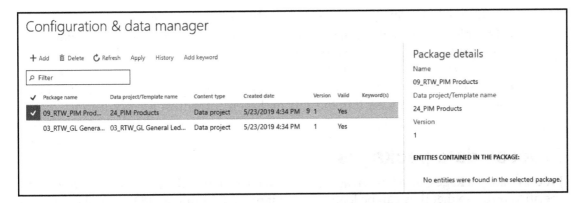

The configuration and data manager tool shows all the validated data packages that are available in the project asset library. Using **Configuration & data manager**, you can select one or more data projects and click **Apply**. This opens up a dialog where you can select the environment and a legal entity, and then click **OK**. This will apply the selected data packages to your environment.

When applying multiple data packages, you can choose to apply concurrently or sequentially, based on the dependencies, as shown in the following screenshot:

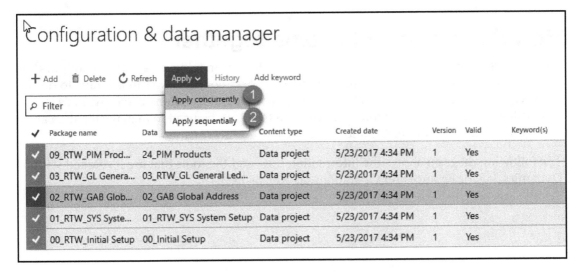

Once the data package has been consumed, you can view its status in one of three ways:

- In LCS, select a data package and click **History** to review its status.
- The information that's shown as part of the status includes target environment, company, package name, start and end times, status by data entity, and the overall status of the data package.
- To see the details of any errors that occurred, you need to sign in to the target environment and view it in the data management workspace job history.

Process data packages

Process data packages, also known as **PDPs**, are a collection of data packages arranged in a specified order so that they can be loaded into a target environment. PDP consolidates data packages into a unified bundle. The PDP is then used to configure a business process or a group of business processes in one business process library.

From our personal experience in implementation projects, the data management framework within Finance and Operations is mostly used to seed environments. PDP can be helpful in provisioning environments data for demo purposes. To find out more about PDP, go to `https://docs.microsoft.com/en-us/dynamics365/unified-operations/dev-itpro/lcs-solutions/process-data-packages-lcs-solutions#consume-a-pdp`.

How these concepts come together

As you learned in the preceding sections and chapters, managing data and its configuration is highly important and Microsoft has provided a lot of tools that we can leverage to do so. However, selecting the right tools for the right purpose must be done carefully. Let's look at an end-to-end visual of all the tools and elements that can be used to manage the data and configuration in your implementation and beyond.

The following diagram shows the information flow and the tools that are leveraged within Dynamics 365 for Finance and Operations, as well as LCS:

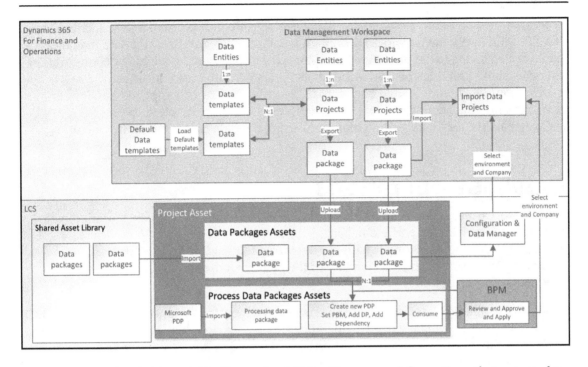

The sequence of activities within Dynamics 365 for Finance and Operations that are used to manage the data and its configuration starts with the identification and creation of data entities. Once the data entity and related entities have been identified, they can be grouped together in a data package, where the dependencies can also be assigned. These data packages are built using a data project.

For an implementation initiative, when you need to start from ground zero, the identification of these entities could be time-consuming. This activity can be avoided using the default data templates provided by Microsoft or by creating your own data templates. These templates are meant to be reused to create data projects, whether you need to load the information in the same environment or another environment.

While the full suite of data and configuration activities can be done entirely in Dynamics 365 for Finance and Operations, Microsoft has provided more tools in LCS. These tools in LCS primarily start with data packages. These are the same data packages that are created in Dynamics 365 for Finance and Operations that could be added to the LCS asset library and used to import the data and configuration in an environment.

You can directly execute these data packages in LCS or combine them and sequence them in a PDP and apply them to an environment using the configuration and data manager. You can also leverage the predefined templates from Microsoft, available as configuration data packages, which can be downloaded and updated with customer-specific information/data and uploaded back into LCS so that they can be applied to an environment. These configuration data templates can also be directly processed in Dynamics 365 for Finance and Operations using the data management framework.

Database operations

There are occasions when, instead of working on a particular data or configuration, you may need to work on the entire database. Such scenarios could come up while creating a new environment and seeding it with the data from the golden environment, or while requesting Microsoft to use the database of the golden environment and populate production for the first time.

In any cloud sandbox environment (Tier-2 and above), customers and partners can use LCS self-service tools to initiate database operations. Database operations are available on the LCS environment detail page, under **Maintain** | **Move database**, as shown in the following screenshot:

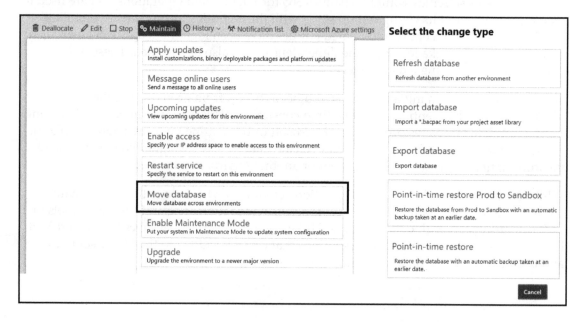

Let's briefly look at the various database operations options:

- **Refresh database**: You can use this option to refresh the data of the current environment data from another sandbox or production environment in the same implementation project. During the implementation project, this option can be used to quickly spin up a new environment for training or UAT from by refreshing the data from the golden configuration environment or existing test environment. After going live, this option can be used to refresh production data in the test environment to troubleshoot any ongoing production issue or to keep your test environment data in sync with production.

- **Import database**: This option lets you import a `.bacpac` file from your LCS asset library. This option is useful in scenarios where your golden configuration environment is maintained as a Tier-1 environment. In such cases, you can export the Tier-1 environment database as a `.bacpac` file and upload that in the LCS project asset library under a database backup. After that, you can use the import database option from the Tier-2 environment to restore the database from the backup.

- **Export database**: This is simply the reverse of the import database option. This option lets you export your current Tier-2 database in your project asset library. You can download the `.bacpac` file and import it into a Tier-1 environment.

- **Point in time restore prod to sandbox**: As its name suggests, using this option, you can refresh your sandbox environment from a production backup that was taken on an earlier date. This option can be extremely helpful in a scenario where you are trying to reproduce a production issue that happened on an earlier date.

- **Point in time restore**: This option lets you restore the current database with a backup taken at an earlier date. These options can be useful if you wish to reproduce the issue that happened at an earlier date in the same environment.

In summary, using these self-service data movement operations, you can simplify and speed up configuration and data movement across the environments.

Cloud sandbox environments and tiers are described in Chapter 4, *Architecture, Deployment, and Environments*, in the *Cloud deployment – environment planning* section.

To see the latest information about database operations and tutorials on how to use them, go to `https://docs.microsoft.com/en-us/dynamics365/unified-operations/dev-itpro/database/dbmovement-operations`.

Cross-company data sharing

Cross-company data sharing is a mechanism that's used for sharing reference and group data among companies in finance and operations deployment. This feature simplifies the master data management for customers with multiple legal entities. For example, if your implementation project is dealing with multiple legal entities but some setup and parameter data is common across the legal entities, you can use this feature to share the data. When a particular table is added to a master data sharing policy and the applicable legal entities have been mapped, the data in the underlying tables is synchronized over to the other legal entities seamlessly.

The business user does not have to worry about maintaining this setup data in multiple legal entities. You can simply create, update, or delete these records in one company, and the system will instantly synchronize the changes to all the other applicable legal entities. This feature supports configuration (such as parameter tables) and group tables (methods of payment, payment terms, customer groups, and so on).

 Detailed documentation on cross-company data sharing is available on Microsoft's official documentation site: `https://docs.microsoft.com/en-us/dynamics365/operations/dev-itpro/sysadmin/cross-company-data-sharing`.

Data management scenarios

These are some typical data management scenarios a project goes through. Let's explore the tools and processes to use in each scenario.

Initial configuration in a blank environment

Your implementation project has just started and you have created your first environment. To set up the initial configuration, we recommend that you leverage the data management framework within Microsoft Dynamics 365 for Finance and Operations and start with the base data packages that have been released by Microsoft. We can download the base data packages from LCS, extract the data files, fit them to the customer's business needs, and then load them in the initial environment.

Many partners and ISVs are investing in creating industry-specific data packages that they intend to use over and over again in various implementation scenarios. These data packages can also be used to seed the initial configuration environment.

Once you have applied the base data packages, you can save them as data templates. You can also load the default template provided by Microsoft. You can add and remove entities, according to your requirements, and maintain the data template in order to create future data projects.

Data migration from legacy systems

After your initial Dynamics 365 for Finance and Operations environment has been configured, it is time to perform data migration from the legacy system. Once again, data management is the right tool to use if you wish to load legacy system data in Finance and Operations. However, data migration from legacy systems can be complex, depending on the legacy architecture and its age. The following diagram depicts the data migration process that can be used in your implementation project:

As shown in the preceding diagram, data migration activities start from identifying data entities in Dynamics 365 for Finance and Operations and the corresponding data in your legacy system. Once the data elements have been identified, you need to work on mapping these data elements. Data templates in Finance and Operations can be used to define the mapping rules and default values. Often, the data in a legacy system is not in a very clean state and you do not want to bring unnecessary data to your new system. If possible, clean or filter such data in the legacy system.

For large data migration scenarios, you may need custom or ETL tools for data extraction and data cleansing. You can use these tools to create data files and data packages as needed for Dynamics 365 for Finance and Operations. Once the data packages have been prepared, you can validate and load the data into Dynamics 365 for Finance and Operations.

Data migration is usually not a one-time process; it needs to be repeated multiple times to get to a clean state. Repeat this process multiple times in the development environment and every other environment, such as training, testing, and UAT, to catch any errors.

 If you are migrating to Finance and Operations from a previous version of Dynamics AX, such as AX 2009, **Data migration tool** (**DMT**) can be leveraged to plan and execute data migration.

Remember that for production to going live, data migration activities usually need to be performed during system downtime. Apart from a successful run, another aspect that you may have to manage is the total time to run the data migration activities. This time must be measured and optimized to fit your overall downtime window.

Copying the company configuration within an existing environment

If your implementation project involves multiple legal entities, you can configure one base company and then use the data management **COPY INTO LEGAL ENTITY** feature to copy configuration data to other legal entities in the same instance.

Also, for the customer who is going live with multiple legal entities in different phases, you can create and maintain a template company and use it periodically to set up new legal entities quickly.

The following screenshot shows the **COPY INTO LEGAL ENTITY** data project operation type:

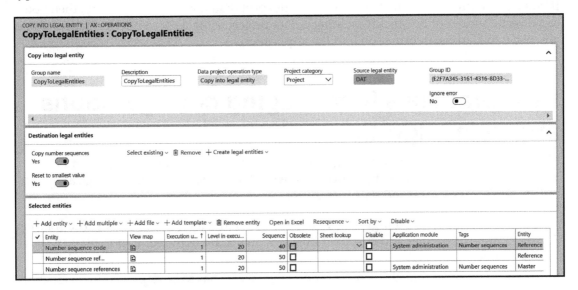

As you can see, using this feature, you can define a source legal entity and multiple destination legal entities. You can also copy the number sequence code to destination legal entities.

For more information on configuration copying across companies, please refer to `https://docs.microsoft.com/en-us/dynamics365/unified-operations/dev-itpro/data-entities/copy-configuration`.

Copying data between environments

If your golden environment is already ready, and the data and import processes have been validated, then we recommend that you use the database copy functionality to seed any other environment, including production.

For any incremental data load, you may directly utilize data management tools such as data entities or data packages within Microsoft Dynamics 365 for Finance and Operations.

Ad hoc data loading

If you have to process any new load or import/export data for a new data entity, then you can directly process it by quickly creating a data project using a data entity or data package and use it to load the information into the application.

Best practices in managing configurations and data migration

Managing configuration and data migration is a complex task and must implement learning from the past and best practices. We would like to share our knowledge and best practices of configuration and data migration:

- Always have a configuration management and data migration plan. The solution advisor/partner and customer business owner are both required to play an active role.
- Always baseline the configuration whenever it has to be deployed in production. Be it a full configuration set or delta, it must be tested with all the potential use cases, and the test result should be baselined.
- Collaboration tools should be leveraged as a repository with track changes enabled for traceability.
- There is a lot of decision-making that happens in configurations and data migration, and it should always be updated in the key decision matrix.
- Align your configuration and data migration plans with the implementation methodology.
- Ensure sign-offs on business requirements toward data migration.
- Always ensure that you have a golden environment in your plan and use it to seed the other environments.
- Keep multiple data migration strategies for the following:
  - Initial system load
  - Key configuration masters
  - Business-specific master data
  - Open transactions
  - Regular and cut-over time
- The migrated data must always be verified, tested, and accepted as part of system acceptance.

- Ensure that the mapping and transformation logic is tested for sample data before running it full-fledged for all the data. Always try and keep the transformation as simple as possible with very few conversions.
- The data to be imported should always be reviewed, validated, and cleansed by the business before being imported.
- Do not forget the sequencing of data load; this is one activity that can bring in a lot of rework if it's not managed carefully.
- When making key decisions on configurations and data migration, ensure that they are taken up in the **Change Control Board** (**CCB**) for their validation/approval.
- Never run short of documentation and tracking, as these activities evolve with time.
- Always ensure that naming conventions have been defined for the configuration and data migration elements and that they are used consistently throughout the project.
- Conduct human and system data integrity checks post data migration.

 Configuration and data migration are like icebergs in an implementation initiative. They may look simple at first glance, but they deserve a lot more attention.

Summary

In this chapter, you learned how to manage configuration and data. The strategies that were suggested for managing configuration and data are based on our experience, and they lay a strong foundation for configuration and planning, including migration. It is super important to have the right data management strategy as it has a direct impact on everyone who's going to use the system, on decision making, on driving daily operations, and on achieving the project objectives. As there are a number of data management techniques and tools, it is highly important to select the right one to effectively manage your configuration and data in Microsoft Dynamics 365 for Finance and Operations. Understanding the solution capabilities of data entities and their usage in the solution directly, as well as through LCS using data packages and PDP, are must-haves in your configuration and data planning.

With the growth of LCS, it has become imperative to leverage capabilities such as data packages and self-service data movement tools to ensure faster and on-time delivery of your project.

From the next chapter onward, we will explore how to best address the various design patterns, key deliverables, and development approaches. We will start with the key design documents, that is, the functional design document, the solution design document (which is also known as the big picture), and the technical design document, based on the latest architecture stack of Dynamics 365 for Finance and Operations. We will also cover resources such as AppSource for your ISV solutions evaluation and selection. We will discuss the recommended features in Dynamics 365 for Finance and Operations to be leveraged, so as to avoid customization.

Solution Planning and Design

7

The solution design process begins once the analysis phase has been completed. By now, the project plan is ready, the requirements document has been signed off, the **Conference Room Pilot** (**CRP**) has been completed, and the fit-gap exercise has been completed and documented as part of the analysis phase. In the fit-gap activity, if the team has decided on using some **Independent Software Vendor** (**ISV**) solution to fill the gaps, then you may need to evaluate the best ISV solution. For any other gaps, the implementation team needs to document the overall solution and produce functional and technical design documents to address the gaps through customization and extension. However, before starting on writing design documents, a functional and technical consultant also needs to know the standard features that can be used to fill the gaps or complement the solution design they are proposing.

Solution planning and design of your custom feature are very critical for the success of the ERP implementation project. Design documents produced in this phase help to define the baseline for the custom solution and provide clarity to the developer on what to build. Design documents also help to better estimate the cost, timeline, and resources required for the project.

In this chapter, we will cover the following topics:

- Finding the right app for your business needs
- Understanding common product features
- The functional design document
- The solution design document
- The TDD

Finding the right app for your business needs

After the business requirements are identified and the fit-gap analysis is done, one crucial decision the project team has to make is whether to build the required customizations or buy an existing solution to bridge the solution gap. During the fit-gap analysis, you can use the LCS **Business Process Modeler** (**BPM**) libraries and add the requirements associated with the business process. You can specify whether the element is a fit or gap, and you can determine a high-level estimation. You can then use the LCS BPM library to view all of the processes and gaps to identify the areas that require ISV solutions.

There are a great many ISV solutions available in the Dynamics 365 ecosystem that can help you to bridge the gap between the standard product and the required industry-specific functionality. Usually, if someone already has a solution that has been used by multiple customers, it will be less risky than developing your solution—you don't want to reinvent the wheel.

Solution architects and the technical and functional teams need to act like the customer's advocate in choosing ISV solutions. Getting the right ISV solution is essential for your success.

Microsoft AppSource has made it super easy to find the right ISV solution. As shown in the following screenshot, visit `https://appsource.microsoft.com`, refine your search by category, industry, and product, and you'll get a list of ISV solutions available as per your criteria:

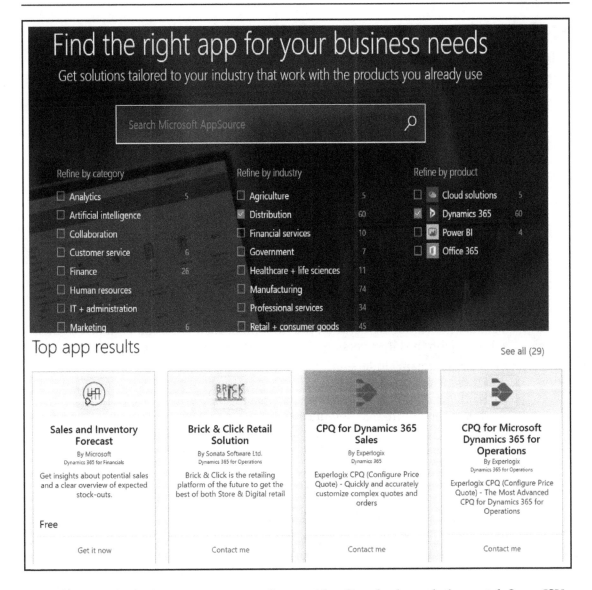

Find the right app for your business needs

Get solutions tailored to your industry that work with the products you already use

Search Microsoft AppSource

Refine by category

☐ Analytics	5
☐ Artificial intelligence	
☐ Collaboration	
☐ Customer service	6
☐ Finance	26
☐ Human resources	
☐ IT + administration	
☐ Marketing	6

Refine by industry

☐ Agriculture	5
☑ Distribution	60
☐ Financial services	10
☐ Government	7
☐ Healthcare + life sciences	11
☐ Manufacturing	74
☐ Professional services	34
☐ Retail + consumer goods	45

Refine by product

☐	Cloud solutions	5
☑	Dynamics 365	60
☐	Power BI	4
☐	Office 365	

Top app results

See all (29)

Sales and Inventory Forecast	Brick & Click Retail Solution	CPQ for Dynamics 365 Sales	CPQ for Microsoft Dynamics 365 for Operations
By Microsoft	By Sonata Software Ltd.	By Experlogix	By Experlogix
Dynamics 365 for Financials	Dynamics 365 for Operations	Dynamics 365	Dynamics 365 for Operations
Get insights about potential sales and a clear overview of expected stock-outs.	Brick & Click is the retailing platform of the future to get the best of both Store & Digital retail	Experlogix CPQ (Configure Price Quote) - Quickly and accurately customize complex quotes and orders	Experlogix CPQ (Configure Price Quote) - The Most Advanced CPQ for Dynamics 365 for Operations
Free			
Get it now	Contact me	Contact me	Contact me

Using the search result, you can contact the provider directly through the portal. Some ISV providers allow you to sign up for the trial version of their solution right from the portal. AppSource indeed makes it easy to search the ISV solutions; however, it is not that easy to decide on one. Let's dig further to understand essential considerations before choosing an ISV solution.

Before choosing ISV solutions

It is indeed easy to find all of the ISV solutions available as per your requirements. However, before selecting an ISV solution, consider the following points:

- **Build versus buy analysis**: Sometimes, going with an ISV solution may look like a quick win. However, it comes with a cost. When evaluating the cost of the ISV solution, you must consider the total cost of ownership and not just the cost of licensing. Others may include code integration, support, training, and so on. High-level estimation on the original requirements and gaps can help you to evaluate the cost of building these customizations yourself and compare that with the cost of an ISV solution in the long run.

- **Benefits and percentage of fit**: Understand all of the benefits that the ISV product has to offer and identify the rate of fit that you have with the requirements. If you still have to customize for more than 20-30 percent of the scenarios, you may be better off building the whole solution by yourself.

- **The readiness of the One Version model**: The ISV product must follow the Microsoft One Version model and continuously update the story. With the One Version model, the ISV solution provider must ensure the compatibility of their solution with the latest version of the Finance and Operations release.

- **Product roadmap**: Understand the product roadmap and features. Make sure that these deadlines are mentioned as part of the contract. For example, ISV currently provides tax calculations only for the US. However, Canada is on the roadmap. Make sure that you understand the deadlines for Canada and have those documented as part of the contract to ensure that your project doesn't suffer due to delays from ISV. Also, review the roadmap for the upcoming cumulative updates.

- **D365FO release plan**: Be aware of any new functionality that Microsoft is working on for new releases. You can find the features that Microsoft is already working on in the Dynamics release plan documentation (`https://docs.microsoft.com/en-us/dynamics365/release-plans/`). Will these features replace the ISV solution? How easy would it be to upgrade your solution and take advantage of the new features? Would it be more cost-effective? How will it affect the business if you wait for the new features versus if you do temporary customization or implement the ISV solution?

- **Architectural review**: Have detailed architectural reviews done by the technical architect on the team as part of the evaluation to ensure that there are no architectural gaps and that the solution is scalable.

- **References**: If you don't have an existing relationship with the ISV, ask for customer references, and discuss the recommendations before making a decision.

- **Company size and support**: Evaluate the ISV solution provider's size, financial strength, and any risk associated with the long-term support of the product.
- You don't want to involve too many ISV solutions as part of the overall solution. It will increase the dependencies for upgrades and take away time from your core implementation team in managing conflicts and testing.

If there are a lot more features included in the ISV solution than the customer may ever need, it may not be the best fit.

After evaluating the ISV solution, let's assume you have decided to pick the ISV solutions that are best suited to address all of the solution gaps. Let's now discuss what you should do after selecting the ISV partner.

After selecting the ISV partner

Consider the following after partner selection:

- If possible, try to reduce dependency as much as possible. Have a single partner/advisor who manages ISV and the development partners.
- Get the budget approved and have all of the invoices billed through the partner. This way, the customer doesn't have to deal with multiple parties.
- Share your project plan with the ISV partner and align their delivery dates according to your schedule. Update your project plan to include the key ISV deliverables.
- Have them attend weekly meetings for status updates (if they are working in parallel on building the solution).
- Plan the code and configuration changes from ISV that must be incorporated into your development and other environments.

Many organizations have unique business requirements, which are not easily fit to the core product or ISV solution and need to be addressed with extension by the customer or implementation partner. In some cases, the customer may want to go for building the solution themselves instead of going with the ISV solution. While developing new features, it is vital to understand and have knowledge of standard features in Finance and Operations. You can use these features as possible workarounds to avoid customization or use them as part of your custom solution to provide a consistent user experience. In the next topic, let's discuss using standard features in Finance and Operations.

Understanding common product features

During the fit-gap analysis sessions, the consultant and product experts should try to find workarounds for every possible gap. Utilize the LCS BPM library to identify the standard business processes and best practices. There are many common features in Finance and Operations, applicable across the system. These features, if carefully examined, can address several gaps or helpful to be considered in your custom solution. In this section, we will briefly cover some of these standard features.

Personalization

Customization is often requested by business users to simply add, hide, move, or rename fields displayed on the forms. To handle such requirements, Microsoft D365FO comes with a powerful personalization feature.

With personalization, a user can change how certain UI elements are displayed in their version of Finance and Operations to best serve their needs. The following are key highlights of the personalization feature:

- Users can add, hide, move, or rename fields on the form.
- It is possible to personalize a page and share it with other users by directly exporting the personalized page and asking the other users to navigate to the customized page and import the personalization file that you've created.
- If a user has admin privileges, they can also manage personalization for other users.
- While the user can make the screens morph the way it suits them to help their productivity, these personalization changes do not impact other users or the underlying code base.
- The following screenshot shows how users can manage personalization in D365FO:

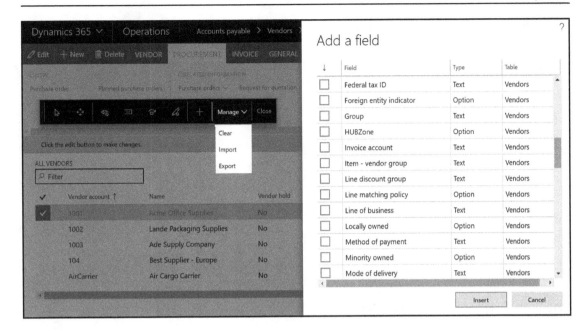

> To learn in detail about the personalization feature, visit the URL at `https://docs.microsoft.com/en-us/dynamics365/operations/get-started/personalize-user-experience`.

Integrating with Office

Office integration is another excellent feature in D365FO that can cut down many customization requests related to user productivity. The Excel Data Connector add-in makes Excel a seamless part of the user experience within the user interface. The application uses data entities and OData services to interact with Office add-ins and to provide the ability to export static data available on the page and perform template-based export. Moreover, you can modify the data in Excel and push it back.

The following screenshot shows various Excel integration options in Finance and Operations:

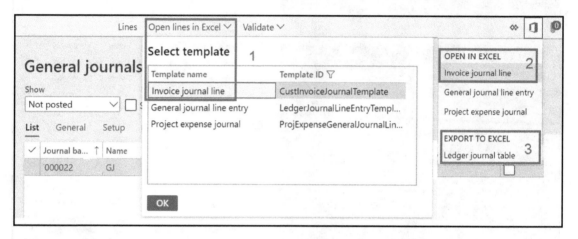

The preceding screenshot shows three options to export or edit data in Excel:

1. **Open lines in Excel**: These are the options that are added by code using the export API. These options can be custom-generated exports or custom template exports.
2. **OPEN IN EXCEL**: These options are automatically added to the data entities and entity-based templates that share the same root data source as the current page. These options make it easier to read data in Excel and publish the data changes back to the Finance and Operations application using OData services.
3. **EXPORT TO EXCEL**: These options are automatically added to all of the visible grids on the page. These options are static exports of data from a grid.

Excel integration can be used as an option to fill the gaps related to data import/export and ad hoc reporting done by business users. You can also use these features by building data entities for the custom features in you build as part of your solution. The documentation provides in-depth coverage of the concept, features, and how you can extend the solution to add open lines in Excel, at `https://docs.microsoft.com/en-us/dynamics365/operations/dev-itpro/office-integration/office-integration`.

Document handling

The **document management feature** (also known as **document handling**) enables users to attach documents to a particular transaction or a master data record in D365FO. It can be used to attach supporting documents, such as an invoice copy received from a vendor, purchase order quotes, and contracts. Different document types can be created and configured to be used across solution areas. Normally, separate document types are created for use by departments, as you can limit who can see the notes by the document type. You can save the notes and print them on output documents, such as purchase orders, packing slips, and invoices. The files that are attached can be viewed using the **Attachment** option on the Finance and Operations screen.

For sophisticated needs, for example, if you are using **Optical Character Recognition** (**OCR**) to capture the vendor invoices, a side-by-side attachment viewer is available on exception-handling forms, pending invoices, and journal inquiries. The following screenshot shows the side-by-side document view of vendor invoices:

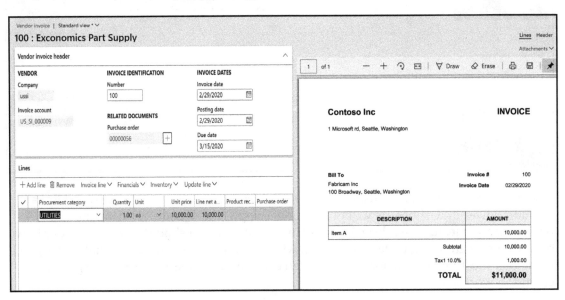

You can utilize these document management capabilities in your custom solution easily to deliver a consistent user experience and increase productivity.

Using workspaces

Workspaces are activity-oriented pages that are designed to increase the user's productivity. A workspace provides information that answers most of the targeted user's activity-related questions and allows the user to initiate more frequent tasks. As shown in the following screenshot, a workspace usually contains tiles (displaying counters or KPIs to answer a set of questions), a collection of relevant lists, and action buttons (to initiate activities), graphs, charts, or Power BI dashboards, and a set of links to pages that are important but not frequently used for this activity:

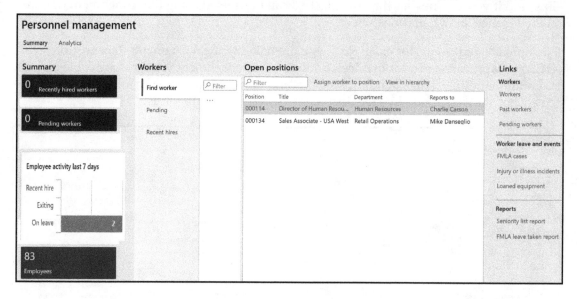

The best part is that you can create a new workspace; add counters, list pages, and links; and add Power BI dashboards without writing a single line of code, all using the personalization feature. While creating custom solutions, you should always consider how business users are going to use the system, what common questions they usually have, and what their most frequent actions are. You can combine all of these into a single page by creating a workspace.

Electronic Reporting

Electronic Reporting (**ER**) is a feature that you can use to configure the formats for electronic documents in accordance with the legal requirements of various countries/regions. ER simplifies the creation, maintenance, and upgrade of electronic document formats by enabling business users to create these reports through configuration. Because you configure formats, not code, the processes of creating and adjusting formats for electronic documents are faster and easier.

The ER engine has the following capabilities:

- It represents a single standard tool for electronic reporting in different domains and replaces more than 20 various engines that do some type of electronic reporting for Microsoft D365FO.
- It makes a report's format insulated from the current D365FO implementation.
- It supports the creation of a custom format that is based on an original format. It includes capabilities for automatically upgrading the customized format when changes to the original format occur because localization/customization requirements are introduced.
- It becomes the primary standard tool to support the localization requirements in electronic reporting, both for Microsoft and Microsoft partners.
- It supports the ability to distribute formats to partners and customers through Microsoft Dynamics **Lifecycle Services** (**LCS**).

Many requirements that need customization through code, for example, payment file to bank and remittance report, can now be delivered through configuration using the ER model. Electronic reporting can support a range of functions in D365FO, including the following:

- Financial auditing
- Tax reporting
- Electronic invoicing
- Payment formats

The best part is that, in most cases, you do not have to create these formats from scratch; Microsoft has already delivered the base version of an electronic report format and will continuously provide updates through LCS. The partners or customers can utilize the base model and create their own version, as per their requirements.

For more details, read more about electronic reporting at `https://docs.microsoft.com/en-us/dynamics365/operations/dev-itpro/analytics/general-electronic-reporting`.

Tax engine

Similar to electronic reporting, Microsoft has introduced a **Global Tax Engine** (**GTE**) to set up and calculate taxes from a code-based approach to configuration.

Currently, the GTE functionality is only available for India but may be available for other countries in the future.

The GTE is highly configurable and lets business users, functional consultants, and power users configure tax rules that determine tax applicability, tax calculation, posting, and settlement, based on the legal and business requirements. The GTE covers the following functional scopes:

Functional area	Scope
Tax administration	• Tax registration • Tax authority • Tax-related information on master data • Tax invoice and voucher numbering
Tax applicability	• The application scope of a tax • Applying taxes on transactions
Tax calculation	• Determination of tax basis and tax rate • Calculation and distribution of tax amount
Tax accounting	• Accounting treatment of the calculation and distributed tax amounts
Tax documentation	• Tax invoice
Tax settlement	• Output tax and input tax assessment • Tax adjustment • Tax payment, carry forward, and refund
Tax return	• Tax inquiries • Tax report • Filing and e-filing

Just like electronic reporting, the GTE feature can be leveraged to implement tax-related requirements through configuration.

Configurable business documents

One of the top customization requests on almost every implementation project by customers is to modify the Finance and Operations printable business documents such as purchase order confirmations, sales order packing slips, sales invoices, and many others. With the October 2019 release, the **Configurable business document** feature makes it possible for super users to customize the business document by using Microsoft Office-based templates.

The following screenshot shows the **Business document management** workspace in Finance and Operations, where you can find all available business document configuration:

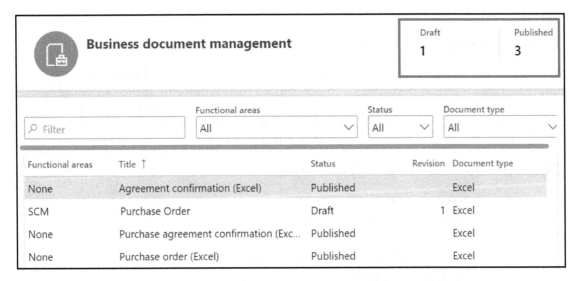

The configurable business documents feature is built on top of the **ER** framework and provides out-of-the-box templates for several reports across the module. To learn about these out-of-the-box document templates and how to customize them further, check the page at `https://docs.microsoft.com/en-us/dynamics365/unified-operations/dev-itpro/analytics/er-business-document-management`.

Batch framework

The batch framework provides an asynchronous, server-based batch processing environment that can process tasks across multiple instances of the **Application Object Server** (**AOS**). Any transaction that needs to be executed asynchronously can run using the batch framework.

Performance scaling of volume-intensive operations or actions to be performed periodically are the typical uses of batch jobs, for example, invoicing shipped orders every 15 minutes, daily export of positive pay files, and inventory recalculation or close process.

In batch jobs, tasks are created to perform the necessary actions, and these tasks can be multithreaded to utilize the available resources fully. You can also create dependencies between batch tasks, for example, when you want products to be imported before importing the product pricing information. To achieve this, you can set up a product pricing import task to run only when the product import job is completed successfully. Other usages of batch jobs include workflow execution, recurring data export/import, scheduling reports execution, and so on.

Workflows

Workflows are the mechanisms by which business rules and approval processes are implemented in the solution. You can direct certain transactions for approvals using workflows. Some examples of documents for which built-in workflows can be set up are AP invoice journals, purchase requisitions, expense reports, budget planning processes, general journals, customer payments, and free text invoices.

The usage of workflows includes the following:

- Assigning a transaction for review
- Assigning a transaction for approval
- Automation of a business step
- Conditional decisions on business data, which the next steps are dependent upon
- Multiple levels of approvals
- Approval type selection, such as based on role, based on position, and managerial hierarchy
- Workflows can be delegated and/or escalated after a specific time frame

Always keep the workflow implementation as simple as possible. Many organizations move from paper or manual approval processes into systematic workflows and come up with complex rules. It becomes difficult to build and maintain such workflows as organizational changes occur and, eventually, these workflows are abandoned.

Database logging

The database log is a feature that helps in auditing. It keeps track of the changes made by users. You can enable *tracking* of specific actions, such as insert, delete, and update. For updates, you can turn on the monitoring for specific fields. It keeps track of who created or modified the record and when. In the case of updates, you can see the previous value and the new value.

This is typically used in areas where audit tracking is required, such as customer credit limit updates, vendor bank account updates, and many others. Standard reports are available for reviewing any changes made.

The database logging feature is powerful and valuable from a business perspective but can be expensive with regard to overall system performance when enabled for transactional tables. It is recommended to use the database logging feature only for master and reference data tables.

The Finance and Operations mobile application

D365FO come with a generic mobile application that can be utilized for requirements where you need to serve a mobile workforce. The Finance and Operations mobile app can work even in offline mode and automatically synchronize when connected to the internet. The best part is that, as an IT admin, you can build and publish mobile workspaces as per the organization's needs. The app leverages your existing code, business logic, and security configuration. You can easily design mobile workspaces using the point-and-click workspace designer that comes built in with the web client of D365FO. You can further optimize the offline capabilities of workspaces by utilizing the extensibility framework for business logic. Using this, you can provide additional business logic and rendering support by adding a JavaScript file with the application workspace metadata.

Microsoft has already shipped and is continuously shipping several common-use, out-of-the-box mobile workspaces; however, you can further extend or create new mobile workspaces as per your specific requirements.

Common Data Services, Power Automate, and Power Apps

Common Data Services (CDS), Power Automate, and Power Apps are another set of solutions that can play a significant role in your custom solution design. As you may already know, CDS is the Microsoft Azure-based business application platform that enables you to build and extend applications with your business data efficiently. Using Power Automate connectors, you can bring data from multiple data sources, including Finance and Operations and other applications from the Dynamics 365 family. On top of this data, you can build modern low-code apps using Power App or the CDS SDK.

In an implementation project, you can explore whether requirements could be best suited to be a Power App using the CDS platform. Typically, the applications that you build using CDS and Power App are last-mile applications that are not fundamental parts of the ERP system but are either managed in spreadsheets or different third-party systems. Using CDS and Power Apps, you can build these applications very quickly and integrate them easily with Finance and Operations. You can also embed the Power Apps applications within the Dynamics 365 application as personalization, which provides the ability to access PowerApps within the Finance and Operations user interface.

The following are some scenarios we think will be best suited to be developed using the CDS platform to cover last-mile situations and to integrate business processes:

- An independent solution with a low dependency: For example, this could be a service desk app that can be used by employees to request products or services, and once it is approved by managers, it can be used to go and create purchase orders in the application.
- A solution that requires data from multiple sources: For example, this could be an app for salespeople who go out to the field to manage collections. They need to pull data about the customer from Finance and Operations, sales, and social media to understand the full picture of the customer before the meeting.
- A sophisticated solution that utilizes the power of Azure Cloud infrastructures, such as Azure Machine Learning and Azure IoT, along with data from D365FO: For example, this could be a plant management system for the manufacturing industry that collects IoT data related to machines used at the production site. The app can provide sophisticated functionalities that are specifically associated with the plant management system; however, it can also pull operations data, such as machine details, purchase orders, and supplier and warranty details.

Now, building customization in the Power Platform has become much easier, with the introduction of the dual-write feature, which automatically synchronizes data between Finance and Operations and CDS. Dual-write brings out-of-the-box scenario-based integration between Finance and Operations and other Dynamics 365 products such as Dynamics 365 for Sales and Customer Service. You can also use dual-write to synchronize your custom data entities to CDS to build the external application.

With this understanding of standard features in Finance and Operations, now let's delve into the best practice of writing design documents in Finance and Operations projects, starting with the solution design document.

The solution design document

A **Solution Design Document** (**SDD**) includes information about the elements of the overall solution, including D365FO standard features (fits), gaps, and integrations. It is essential to get the entire solution depicted in a pictorial representation. The BPM in LCS is an excellent tool with which to put together the SDD.

Overview and objectives

An SDD is primarily referred to by the core team members of the implementation team. The following are the critical objectives of solution design documentation:

- The details of the business flow in the future solution, based on Microsoft D365FO
- Solution validation
- A single point of reference for future value additions, issues, and troubleshooting
- Documenting at the high level
- Business and solution flow diagrams

Guidelines for the SDD

Solution design is a solution binder that brings together all of the aspects of the solution. The following are suggested coverage areas that a solution design should comprises:

- There should be an end-to-end pictorial flow of the entire business process by function, for example, one end-to-end flow diagram for the supply chain, one end-to-end flow diagram for financials, and likewise for the other business functions.
- The end-to-end flow must have starting/entry points, ending/closure points, and handover to other process diagrams.
- All of the decision points that can bring in additional business scenarios should be included.
- There should be steps that are manual or automated.
- The roles expected to perform the function in Microsoft Dynamics in a swim lane view should be present.
- Fundamental security and integration solution components should be included.
- All of the artifacts and configurations that will be needed to deploy the solution in production should be included.
- The critical takeaway from the SDD is that the core implementation team (especially customer members) is on board with the overall solution flow and design.
- The SDD must be able to convey the entire set of business processes in the scope of the project. These may include, but are not limited to, the following:
    - Record to report
    - Order to cash
    - Procure to pay
    - Plan to inventory
    - Others

Also, it must contain the core processes that enable the previously mentioned processes, as follows:

- Legal entities
- Number sequences
- Languages
- Users
- Countries involved
- Systems involved

The SDD is a highly important artifact in implementing Dynamics 365; it is your single point of reference to know anything about the solution. In simple words, an SDD connects all of the dots together.

In a medium and complex project, along with the overall solution design document, you would need a detailed functional and technical document to outline how a customized feature is supposed to work. In the next sections, let's understand the critical aspects of writing functional and TDDs.

The functional design document

In the previous section, you learned how to provide solutions for the identified feature gaps by using ISV solutions or utilizing some of the standard features and tools available. The next step is to start the design process for the requirement gaps that still do not have a home in the overall solution. The **Functional Design Document** (**FDD**) describes the features of the desired customizations. The document can include things such as flowcharts, screenshots, and wireframes. At a minimum, an FDD will contain an organized list of requirements that can be used for development, testing, and customer sign-off.

Before going further with the details of why functional design is essential, what it should cover, and best practices, let's first learn about the process of the fit-gap review session, which is critical before moving forward with writing an FDD.

The fit-gap review session

The fit-gap document is the primary input document to write the FDD. It is imperative to review the fit-gap document in detail before starting with the FDD. The following are a few pointers to take note of when conducting a successful fit-gap review session:

- The fit-gap review session should involve the functional and technical solution architects, project managers, and customer **Subject Matter Experts** (**SMEs**).
- It is important to remember that this is a fit-gap session, so the fit should also be analyzed. Any degree of customization identified in the fit should be recorded.
- Often, you may find gaps listed that aren't really gaps, as the solution can handle the requirement. The review session should discuss each requirement in detail and consider all possible alternate solutions.

- All gaps should be recorded and assigned a unique number. The Microsoft LCS business modeler tool enables you to document your business processes and record gaps.

- Take a detailed look at how the gaps are going to be addressed. Outline the testing/review process for customizations/extensions and how the testing will be administered.

- By focusing on these topics, you will soon learn where the team stands with regard to the appropriate documentation and its approach to the customization process.

Now, in the next heading, let's gets back to the FDD. Why is it necessary, and what purpose does it serve?

Why write an FDD?

Functional design documents help developers, testers, and customers to understand the customizations in detail. The following are key benefits of FDDs:

- FDDs help the development team to understand the feature and provide a clear scope and definition of what to develop. Function design documents streamline the development process. The development team working on the feature has a clear understanding and answers to all their functionality-related questions to start development. Since this document is approved by the customer, the developers only develop customizations/extensions that are authorized.

- FDDs help the testing team to understand the feature under development and to develop a test plan around it.

- FDDs provide the customer with a clear vision and definition of the feature being developed. Also, it helps the entire project team to visualize and see the solution long before it is built.

- FDDs provide the baseline of the training documentation for the application support team and business users.

Now let's understand important pointers for a project manager in the design phase of the implementation project.

Project management aspects of design

The following are a few pointers for project managers to consider during the design phase of the project:

- The fit-gap analysis, requirements analysis, and the project plan need to be signed off to start the functional design phase. You can break them up into areas and start sooner if you have specific areas signed off.
- Make the team put together the overall functional architecture and the flow across applications, and review with the respective stakeholders.
- Start with the functional design for areas on which the rest of the solution has a dependency. For example, customer and product masters are essential for the downstream supply chain, invoicing processes, and others.
- Dedicate resources for large, complex functional areas early on. Also, make sure to have dedicated time from business users.
- Based on the fit-gap analysis, the implementation team, along with solution advisors, should prepare a plan of approach to address the critical gaps.
- Divide responsibilities by area and try to have smaller FDDs created for each area. This will help to manage them better.
- While the FDD work is in progress, assign the development and QA teams for each functional area. Engage them in reviewing the functional design, and support the respective business analysts early on.
- You need to plan for multiple iterations and reviews. Functional designs are very crucial. Upfront reviews can save a lot of development hours and rework while also increasing the overall quality of the deliverables.
- Identify all of the cross-functional requirements; the solution architect should lead them to suitable designs.

Cross-functional reviews are critical in larger projects. Have recurrent meetings every week or twice a week (as needed) to review the functional designs with all of the functional team members together. Prioritize the reviews for foundation items, such as customer-master and product-master changes, which will impact other functional areas.

Cross-functional reviews will help to improve the solutions (the rest of the team may have inputs on doing the same thing in a better way or with less customization). Also, more importantly, you will be forcing the team to review each other's designs by pulling them together into a room.

Engage business SMEs early on for reviews (set up a design walkthrough, provide deadlines for getting feedback, and seek a sign-off for each of the functional designs).

Depending on the complexity, involve SMEs external to the project for an independent review and recommendations. For example, when you start auditing the financial results of the company, your accounting practices will automatically improve as people know that they are going to be audited.

Next, let's explore important considerations while writing the FDD.

Things to know before writing an FDD

FDDs speak the application language and terminology, so business analysts writing FDDs must understand the D365FO application and functionality. A lack of product knowledge and understanding can keep the document at a high level, pushing the design aspects to the developers, which deviates from the purpose of the document.

Always ensure that all of the key decisions made during the design time are recorded in the key decision log and signed off by the project team. Recommended areas where key decisions are mostly taken are as follows:

- Financials
- Inventory costing
- Adjustments
- Integrations
- Reporting

Also, all assumptions should be documented and validated with the concerned stakeholders to ensure a solution built to purpose.

Microsoft Dynamics Sure Step provides good templates to write FDDs. Create your own version with the sections relevant to your project and have the team follow the template.

Always have one or many requirements in the **Requirements Traceability Matrix (RTM)** corresponding to the FDD. A RTM is a foundational element in ERP implementations, as it ensures consistent delivery against contract and business requirements.

Another important aspect to consider before starting to write the functional design document is to know the feasibility of the solution. With the release of D365FO version 8.0 (April 2018), customizations are possible through extensions only. The extension is a development model where the developer can utilize events and hooks within the application code to include additional functionalities without impacting the Microsoft code. What this means from a solution design perspective is that, unlike earlier versions, there will be a scenario when a requirement cannot be customized.

To make sure that your custom solution is feasible, consider the following points:

- There could be a customization requirement that it may not be possible to develop through extensions.
- If there are no options available in the product to extend the requested functionality, find a workaround or take Microsoft feedback. Ultimately, if it's not feasible, say no to the customer.
- If you think your requirement is common, suggest it to Microsoft using the idea portal; it might become a part of the core product in future releases.
- Also, check the Microsoft roadmap for upcoming features and to see if those can fill the gap.

 Extension capabilities in D365FO are being improved with every release. Follow Microsoft's official documentation page to know more about extensibility, at `https://docs.microsoft.com/en-us/dynamics365/unified-operations/dev-itpro/extensibility/extensibility-home-page`.

Finally, let's discuss some common dos and don'ts you should consider during the design phase.

Dos and don'ts

The following are some dos and don'ts while writing FDDs:

- Do not repurpose the unfit features to avoid customization. You will end up causing unforeseen issues down the road or blocking any future use of the functionality related to the feature.
- Do keep the architecture simple and easy to follow. The more complexity you add to the solution, the more difficult it will be to implement and support.
- Do try to reduce the duplication of data in multiple places; avoid unnecessary/complex integrations.
- Do design the solutions around standard functionality, without touching the core system. For example, if the customer wants to automate the creation of allocation journals based on the allocation rules defined in the general ledger module, as a functional consultant, I will design a separate customization that will extend the functionality of the core Finance and Operations allocation process rather than changing standard forms and features.

After the functional design document is completed and signed off, the development team needs to start writing a TDD. Let's learn about the TDD in the next topic.

The technical design document

A **Technical Design Document** (**TDD**) includes information about the programmatic approach of how a particular requirement will be implemented.

TDDs are prepared primarily by the technical solution architect or technical lead for the final development. They are also used by the testing team to write detailed test cases. The following are the key objectives of technical design documentation:

- The details of feature architecture and design goals
- Solution and data validation
- Documentation of the code (high-level)
- Process and data flow diagrams

Guidelines for the TDD

Technical design is about planning the solution and putting together a skeleton of the technical solution. Putting together good design documentation will help you to avoid development rework and improve the quality of code by allowing you to think through several facets of the solution before you start coding. TDD speaks the language of applications and, often, the code and technology, to achieve the solution. It is incumbent on the solution architect and technical leads writing the TDD to have expert knowledge about the system, design patterns, limitations, and the recommended customization approach.

Consider the following guidelines when writing TDDs:

- Follow the Microsoft roadmap as to where the overall solution is headed—what new features are on the roadmap and what features will be deprecated in the future.
- Utilize the innovation happening in the cloud. There are many Azure cloud solution platforms such as the Power Platform, Logic App, Azure Data Factory, machine learning, and many others that can be utilized with Finance and Operations to solve complex problems.
- Utilize the standard solution frameworks as much as possible and extend if required.

- Be cognizant of the cloud-first solution approach; consider the edge and on-premises scenarios in your custom solution.
- Consider recommendations and best practices when designing a solution.
- The technical design typically starts after the sign-off of the functional design. It can also start early for a functional area where the requirements are clear.
- Engage the technical lead early on during functional designing to understand the functional requirements and flow.
- Plan brainstorming sessions among the team to discuss different solution ideas.
- Plan separate technical specs for integrations and data migration.
- Plan communications within the team to handle cross-functional designs.

Things to consider while writing TDDs

A TDD not only helps the developer to develop the solution but is also a key document for the quality team to validate the final solution. The TDD must cover various aspects of software development, such as the following:

- **Brainstorming**: There are multiple ways to solve a problem—discussions and brainstorming led to the identification of the best possible one.
- **Process flow**: Depict the overall process flow for the functional area so that it is clear to the developer what the final outcome is and how to reach it.
- **UI and usability**: Keep in mind the users and processes that will be using the new forms. Is it the workers on the floor or a person in the accounting department? Is it a repetitive function, such as shipping sales orders or invoicing POs, or is it a batch process, such as invoicing sales orders? Use familiar UI patterns, considering the users of the functionality.
- **Scalability of the solution**: Think about how the solution can be scalable, that is, more controlled by parameters and data instead of code. Having it controlled by parameters will help you in global environments. For example, you can turn off the functionality for companies that don't want to use it. Also, should you have an issue in production with a recently released functionality, you can have the option of turning it off by using parameters.
- **Apply generic design patterns**: Utilize solution ideas and frameworks offered within the product. The goal is not to rewrite the product; you are just extending its capability for business use. Follow the design patterns of the standard pages for custom pages.

- **Performance**: Identify the volume of transactions in the current production and the anticipated growth in the next few years. The solution should consider the performance requirement early on. Design a prototype and generate sample data to test the performance.
- **Exception handling**: Identify exceptional scenarios and document them. Build enough controls to avoid mistakes by users (you don't want to leave flaws that would let users hurt themselves). On the other hand, you don't want to spend too much time on building an extremely idiot-proof system.
- **Security**: Consider the security aspects as part of the technical design.

In the end, the TDD must be reviewed with solution architect and functional leads to ensure that any errors, misunderstandings, or ambiguities are detected and corrected.

Summary

In this chapter, we reviewed the design aspect of an implementation project. After the requirements have been collected, the document is signed off, and the fit-gap process is completed, the consultant starts the design documentation process. We started this chapter with the topic of finding the right app for your business needs and discussed the evaluation, selection criteria, and engagement of ISVs solutions on the project. Many common features can fill the gaps further or complement your custom solution design; we went through them briefly to understand how you can use them in your solution design. We learned to plan and execute the design documents effectively and about common mistakes and how to avoid them along with the best practices to be followed for design patterns considering multi-company, support, and upgrade aspects.

In the next chapter, we will learn all about integration technologies for planning and design in D365FO. We will explore Finance and Operations integration topics such as basic concepts, integration architecture, integration tools, planning, design, development, and best practices.

8
Integration Technologies, Planning, and Design

To get the most benefit out of an ERP system, it needs to be integrated with other enterprise systems in the organization. Integration with other systems enables accuracy and timely updates when it comes to business data, which is very important for business success and growth. The differences between the architecture and age of integrated systems often make integration difficult and challenging. It is vital to ensure that the technical analysts and developers in your project are familiar with integration technologies in Dynamics 365 Finance and Operations, so that they can develop the best integration solution possible for any given integration needs.

This chapter is about understanding the integration architecture and the concepts and technologies available in Dynamics 365 for Finance and Operations.

The following topics will be covered in this chapter:

- Basic web integration concepts
- Learning about the integration architecture
- Integration concepts in Finance and Operations
- Integration scenarios and planning
- Integration design and development
- Best practices and recommendations

Basic web integration concepts

To understand the integration concepts in Dynamics 365 for Finance and Operations, it is important to know about the basic web integration concepts. In this section, we will learn about basic web concepts such as RESTful APIs, SOAP, OData, JSON, OAuth, and the event-driven architecture pattern.

RESTful APIs

REpresentational State Transfer (**REST**) is an architecture style that relies on six guiding constraints: stateless, client-server, cacheable, layered system, code on demand (optional), and uniform interface. Web service APIs that adhere to the REST architecture are called RESTful APIs.

Many modern internet applications, such as Microsoft Azure, Twitter, LinkedIn, Google, PayPal, and Amazon, use the RESTful architecture style in their APIs, which allows easy integration over the HTTP communication protocol. The primary reason RESTful APIs are useful in cloud and web applications is that the calls are stateless. This means each request or interaction is independent. Nothing has to be saved that has to be remembered by the next request, and any request can be directed to any instance of a component.

A RESTful API explicitly takes advantage of HTTP methodologies. They use GET to retrieve a resource, PUT to update a resource, POST to create that resource, and DELETE to remove it. A resource can be an object, file, or a table row in a database. HTTP-based RESTful APIs are defined by the following key aspects:

- **Base URL:** Such as http://YourWebApplicationAPIURL/
- **Media type:** Such as application/JSON and application/XML
- **Standard HTTP methods:** Such as GET, PUT, POST, and DELETE

SOAP APIs

The **Simple Object Access Protocol** (**SOAP**) is a specification for exchanging structured information for web service implementation. SOAP uses XML as a message format and relies on application layer protocols, such as HTTP, TCP, and SMTP, for message transmission and negotiation. SOAP defines a message format based on the envelope, header, and body. All request and response messages must be serialized in this message format.

The following diagram shows the structure of a SOAP message:

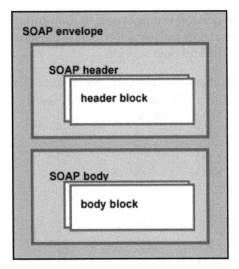

A SOAP message always starts with an envelope that contains the mandatory SOAP header block and SOAP body block. The SOAP header contains the application-related information, such as message ID and soap action. The SOAP body block contains the actual message intended for the recipient.

SOAP versus REST

There is always a discussion among integration experts with regards to which one is better: SOAP or REST. How do they compare? The following list highlights some of the comparisons between SOAP and REST:

- SOAP is a protocol, while REST is an architectural style.
- SOAP defines standards to be strictly followed, while REST doesn't define too many standards.
- SOAP requires more bandwidth and resources than REST.
- SOAP defines its own security; RESTful web services inherit security measures from the underlying transport layer.
- SOAP permits the XML data format only; REST permits different data formats, such as plain text, HTML, XML, and JSON.

In summary, REST is lighter and simpler for integration, especially with cloud web applications.

JSON message format

JavaScript Object Notation (JSON) is a lightweight data-interchange format. JSON is self-describing and easy for humans to read and write. It is the most commonly used data format on the web and for RESTful web services.

The following is a simple example of the JSON format describing customer group data containing two customer groups with customer group IDs of 10 and 20, with the additional Description and PaymentTermId fields:

```
{
  "CustomerGroupId":"10",
  "Description":"Wholesales customers",
  "PaymentTermId":"Net30"
},
{
  "CustomerGroupId":"20",
  "Description":"Retail customers",
  "PaymentTermId":"Receipt"
}
```

Another little complex example of the JSON data format describing personal details is shown here. The following example represents personal details, including address, phone number, and children and spouse details:

```
{
  "firstName": "John",
  "lastName": "Smith",
  "isAlive": true,
  "age": 25,
  "address": {
    "streetAddress": "21 2nd Street",
    "city": "New York",
    "state": "NY",
    "postalCode": "10021-3100"
  },
  "phoneNumbers": [
    {
      "type": "home",
      "number": "212 555-1234"
    },
    {
      "type": "office",
      "number": "646 555-4567"
    },
    {
      "type": "mobile",
```

```
        "number": "123 456-7890"
      }
  ],
  "children": [],
  "spouse": null
}
```

As we mentioned earlier, this is easily readable by humans, and at the same time, lighter and easy to parse by a computer program. These characteristics make JSON the preferred data type for web and cloud applications.

OData protocol

OData stands for **Open Data Protocol**, which is an open protocol that enables the creation of REST-based data services, which allow resources to be published and edited by web clients using simple HTTP messages. The OData protocol was initially developed by Microsoft in 2007 and is now a standardized protocol of the OASIS OData technical committee.

OData provides the following benefits:

- It lets developers interact with data using RESTful web services
- It provides a simple and uniform way to share data in a discoverable fashion
- It enables broad integration across products
- It enables integration using the HTTP protocol stack

For more information on OData, please refer to the following web links:

Topic	Link
OData standards	http://www.odata.org/documentation/
OData introduction	https://msdn.microsoft.com/en-us/library/dd541188.aspx
OData by example	http://www.odata.org/odata-services/

OAuth authentication model

OAuth is a modern authentication standard used by many popular web applications such as Facebook, Twitter, LinkedIn, and Google. OAuth is an open standard for token-based authorization and authentication on the internet. It provides client applications with secure, delegated access to server resources on behalf of a resource owner. It specifies a process for resource owners to authorize third-party access to their server resources without sharing their credentials. OAuth was first released and used by Twitter in 2007, and the latest version of OAuth is OAuth 2.0.

The following diagram shows how authentication works with OAuth 2.0:

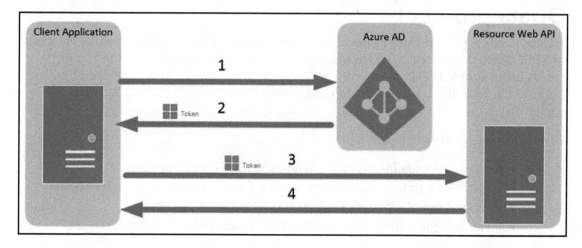

As we can see, the OAuth authentication flow starts with the **Client Application** requesting a token from the identity provider, such as **Azure AD**. The identity provider authenticates the client application and returns the token to the calling application. The **Client Application** then presents the access token web application. The web application validates the token and returns the request.

Event-driven architecture

The **event-driven architecture** (**EDA**) is a software architecture pattern that promotes the production, detection, consumption of, and reaction to events. An event can be defined as **a significant change in state**, for example, when a sales order status changes from *open* to *shipped*. The system architecture may treat this state change as an event whose occurrence can be made known to other applications within the architecture.

An event-driven architecture consists of event producers that generate a stream of events and event consumers that listen for the events:

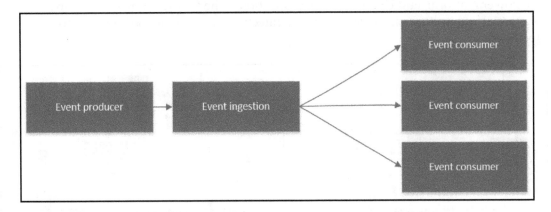

The event-driven architecture pattern has the following benefits:

- Events are produced in near real-time so that consumers can respond to events as soon as they occur.
- Event producers and consumers are decoupled.
- There's no point-to point-integration. It's easy to add new consumers to the system.
- Highly scalable and distributed.

Now that we have covered the necessary integration concepts, let's delve into learning about the integration architecture of Finance and Operations.

Learning about the integration architecture

As enterprises move toward using more and more specialized applications, rather than having an ERP do everything for them, you need a robust framework and strategy to manage integrations within the ERP system. Dynamics 365 for Finance and Operations provides robust frameworks and functionalities that can be integrated with third-party applications using modern techniques.

Dynamics 365 for Finance and Operations supports numerous integration models to help us integrate with third-party applications, as well as built-in native integration with Office 365, Power Platform, and Dynamics 365 applications. The following diagram shows the conceptual architecture of the integration architecture in Dynamics 365 for Finance and Operations:

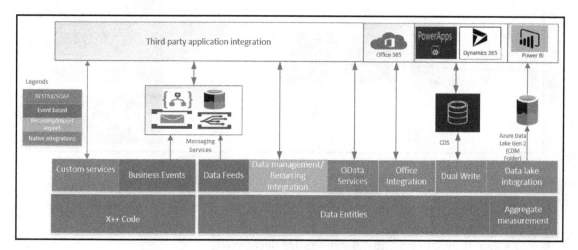

As shown in the preceding diagram, the following are the key categories for the integration options in Finance and Operations:

1. **HTTP-based RESTful/SOAP**: Dynamics 365 for Finance and Operations provide OData REST endpoints with complete **create, retrieve, update, and delete (CRUD)** functionality that can be used to integrate with any third-party applications. Along with OData, custom X++ business logic can be exposed as a RESTful or SOAP-based service.

2. **Event-based**: Business events and data feeds can send near real-time event notifications and data changes to generic consumers, such as Azure messaging services. External business applications and systems can subscribe to specific business events or data feeds using Azure messaging services to receive close to real-time events and data updates from Finance and Operations.

3. **Recurring import/export**: Dynamics 365 for Finance and Operations provides an API for recurring data integration for bulk import/export integration scenarios. The recurring data integration pattern is based on the data management platform that's also used for application life cycles such as configuration management and data migration.

4. **Native integration**: Dynamics 365 for Finance and Operations provides built-in integration with Office 365 programs such as Excel and Word. The dual write feature allows customers to integrate Finance and Operations data into their own **Common Data Services** (**CDS**). This enables direct integration with Power App and Dynamics 365 applications such as Sales, Services, and Talent. The Data Lake integration feature provides incremental exports for Finance and Operations master and transaction data into customer's own Azure Data Lake Storage Gen2 environment in **Common Data Model** (**CDM**) folder format, which can be further used by Power BI Dataflows to build rich analytical reports.

As shown in the preceding diagram, data entities are the key components of integration frameworks in Dynamics 365 for Finance and Operations, and serve multiple integration patterns through data management platforms and OData endpoints. Features such as Office integration, data feeds, and dual writes also use data entities. In addition to data entities, **X++ business logic** can be used to create custom services with the SOAP and JSON endpoints, as well as business events for event-driven integration models.

There are various ways we can integrate a third-party application with Finance and Operations. To understand these options better, let's take a deep dive.

Integration concepts in Finance and Operations

In the preceding section, we understood the basic integration concepts used in modern cloud- and web-based applications. Finance and Operations uses these concepts as part of the core integration architecture. On a high level, there are several key integration components, such as data entities, OData services, custom services, recurring integrations, business events, data feeds, dual write, and Data Lake integration. In this section, we will explore these components, concepts, and terminologies in detail, and we will also explore how to use these technologies while building integration solutions in our implementation projects.

Data entities

Data entities are the most important concept for integration in Dynamics 365 for Finance and Operations. In Dynamics 365 for Finance and Operations, data entities are first-class citizens, and they enable data management, data migration, OData integration, Office integration, and Power BI integration.

What is a data entity?

A **data entity** is an abstraction over underlying tables and a simplified projection of the schema that is more conceptual in nature than the physical tables underneath. All business logic resides in the entity or in the underlying tables. Entities can expose both relational as well as aggregate data.

To summarize this, data entities provide conceptual abstraction and encapsulation (denormalized view) of the underlying table schema to represent key data concepts and functionalities.

The following diagram shows the current normalized model for customer data in Dynamics 365 for Finance and Operations and the corresponding denormalized customer entity:

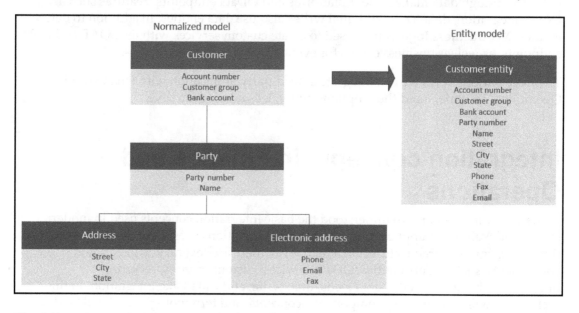

The following are the key highlights regarding data entities in Dynamics 365 for Finance and Operations:

- First-class citizens and defined as metadata objects.
- In the database layer, data entities are represented as updatable views.
- Serves multiple purposes, such as OData services, recurring integrations, Office integration, and data management.

OData services

In Dynamics 365 for Finance and Operations, OData services are used for integration. The OData REST endpoint exposes all the data entities that are marked as public. The **IsPublic** design-level property is all that it needs to determine whether the data entity needs to be exposed as the OData endpoint.

The following screenshot shows `CustCustomerEntity` in Visual Studio, with the **IsPublic** property set to **Yes** to expose the entity as the OData endpoint:

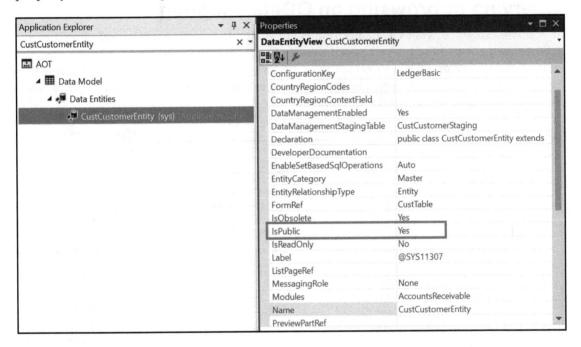

Dynamics 365 for Finance and Operations ships more than two thousand data entities out of the box, which includes more than 1,500 public data entities.

> The list of data entities is growing with every major release of Dynamics 365 for Finance and Operations to cover missing areas and new functionalities and integration points.

In addition to the out of the box data entities, customers and partners can easily extend the existing data entities or create new data entities, as per their data management and integration requirements.

An entity marked with the **IsPublic** property set to **Yes** is automatically available as an OData endpoint and can be consumed for various tools and purposes, such as third-party client applications for integration, Microsoft Office for data export/import, or any other client applications that can consume OData feeds.

In the next few sections, we'll explore how to query, browse, and consume OData services for Dynamics 365 for Finance and Operations.

Querying or browsing an OData endpoint

If you want to know what OData endpoints are available in your Finance and Operations environment, or want to query a specific entity to get the data, you can simply browse using a web browser. OData provides a simple query format that we can use to browse the resources using a web browser. The following table describes a few basic query formats for accessing OData resources and entity data:

URL	Description
`[Your Organization Root URL]/data/`	Get a list of data entities
`[Your Organization Root URL]/data/Customers`	Get a list of all the customers
`[Your Organization Root URL]/data/Customers?$top=3`	Get a list of the first three customer records
`[Your Organization Root URL]/data/Customers?$select=FirstName,LastName`	Get a list of all the customers, but show only the first name and last name properties
`[Your Organization Root URL]/data/Customers?$format=json`	Get a list of all the customers in JSON format that can be used to interact with JavaScript clients

The OData protocol supports many advanced filtering and querying options on entities, such as `$filter`, `$count`, `$orderby`, `$skip`, `$top`, `$expand`, and `$select`. Many built-in operators are available to `$filter` data, such as equals, not equals, greater than or equal to, less than, less than or equal to, and, or, not, addition, subtraction, multiplication, and division.

For more details about the filter and query syntax and its capabilities, go to `http://docs.oasis-open.org/odata/odata/v4.0/errata02/os/complete/part2-url-conventions/odata-v4.0-errata02-os-part2-url-conventions-complete.html#_Toc406398092`.

Consuming OData services

It's good that you can browse the OData services using a browser and evaluate the response; however, real-life integration is always system to system, running in the background. Let's try to understand how these real-life integrations can be built using Dynamics 365 for Finance and Operations' OData services.

OData services can be consumed by the client application in two ways:

- Using the pure HTTP communication model, where you build URLs, build request messages, parse and handle responses, and do error handling. Doing all this from scratch can be complicated and unnecessary.
- Using the already available libraries. There are various libraries and tools available to encapsulate OData HTTP communication in different programming languages.

The following table features many such OData libraries for various development platforms, such as .NET, Java, and JavaScript:

Library	Platform	Description
OData client for .NET	.NET	LINQ-enabled client API for issuing OData queries and consuming OData JSON payloads.
`Simple.OData.Client`	.NET	A multiplatform OData client library supporting .NET 4.x, Windows Store, Windows Phone 8, Silverlight 5, iOS, and Android.
SDL OData frameworks	Java	Open source Scala/Java-based SDL OData framework that aligns with the v4 specifications.
Apache Olingo	Java	Apache Olingo is a Java library that implements the OData.
ODataJS beta	JavaScript	The Apache Olingo **OData Client for JavaScript** (**ODataJS**) is a library written in JavaScript that enables browser-based frontend applications to easily use the OData protocol for communication with application servers.

The OData official website page (`http://www.odata.org/libraries/`) features many more libraries, including documentation and download links.

Now, let's explore how we can use the OData client to get the .NET library to build a client application using the C# programming language and consume Finance and Operations OData services. The following diagram describes the high-level steps that a developer needs to follow to consume OData service endpoints:

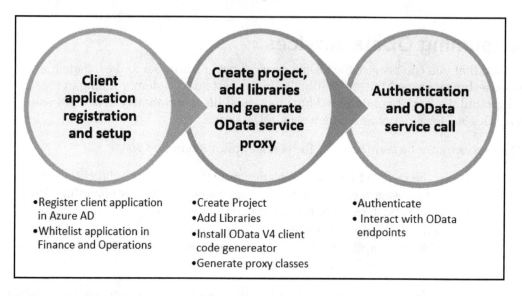

As we can see, consuming OData endpoints is done in three stages. Let's explore these in more detail.

Client application registration and setup

To consume Dynamics 365 for Finance and Operations' OData services, the client application needs to know the following:

- **OData service endpoint URI:** Your Dynamics 365 for Finance and Operations base URL; for example, if your environment is XYZIncDEV, your base URL will be `https://XYZIncDEV.cloudax.dynamics.com`.
- **Authentication details:** Your Azure AD organization tenant ID, such as `XYZInc.com`, and credentials for the connection.

OData services in Dynamics 365 for Finance and Operations use the OAuth 2.0 authentication model, as described earlier in this chapter. The client application can either use a valid Finance and Operations user ID and password or use the service-to-service authentication model. In cloud deployment, the service-to-service authentication model is the recommended option as you do not have to store the real username and password in the client application. Let's take a look at how to do this:

1. To use service-to-service authentication, a client application must be registered under your organization Azure active directory and given the appropriate permissions. The following link describes the steps for registering an application in the Azure portal: `https://docs.microsoft.com/en-us/azure/active-directory/develop/quickstart-register-app`.

2. Next, you need to add Dynamics ERP API permissions to the new application and create a client secret. Note down the application ID and secret value, which will need to be configured in your client application for authentication.

3. Then, whitelist the application ID in Finance and Operations and map it to a valid application user for authorization. The following screenshot shows a visual of the mapping application ID with a Finance and Operations user:

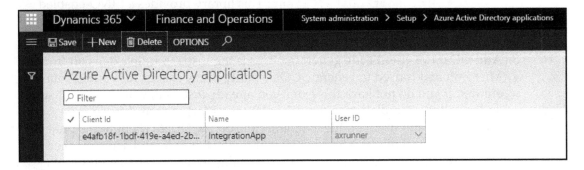

Setup is available under **System administration | Setup | Azure Active Directory applications**.

Creating a project, adding libraries, and generating an OData service proxy

Once you are done with the application registration process and have collected all the necessary details, you are ready to create your client application. In this example, we will create a console C# application so that we can interact with Dynamics 365 for Finance and Operations OData services. The following steps describe how to create the client application:

1. **Create the C# console application**: To start, use Visual Studio to create a C# console project.

2. **Add reference libraries**: To authenticate and consume Finance and Operations OData services, you need at least the following two library packages. You can use the NuGet package manager in Visual Studio to install these libraries in your project and add references:

   - `Microsoft.IdentityModel.Clients.ActiveDirectory`: This package contains the binaries of the **Active Directory Authentication Library** (**ADAL**). ADAL provides a .NET standard class library with easy to use authentication functionality for your .NET client.
   - `Microsoft.OData.Client`: This library provides a LINQ-enabled client API for issuing OData queries and consuming OData JSON payloads.

3. **Add OData v4 client code generator**: This is the Visual Studio extension from Microsoft and is used to generate OData entity proxy classes for your OData entities. If you do not have this extension already installed, you can download and install this template from the Visual Studio Marketplace. After you've downloaded and installed the tool, you can add the OData client to the project. This will create a file with an extension of `tt` (text template). Then, you need to update the `MetadataDocumentUri` string value in the `tt` file to your OData metadata endpoint. The following diagram illustrates the steps that you need to take to add the OData Client's `tt` file and update `MetadataDocumentURI` in Visual Studio:

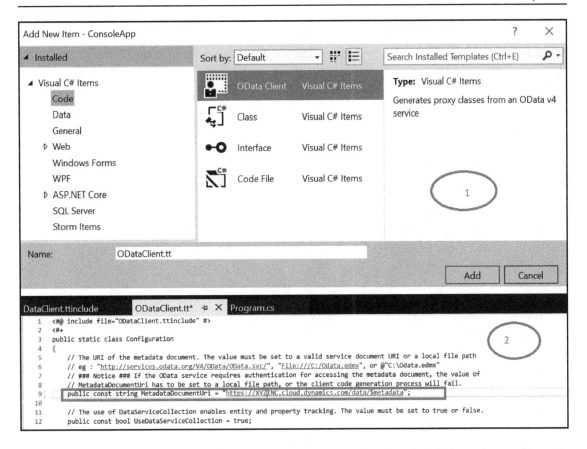

Once the metadata endpoint URL has been updated, right-click on the `tt` file and choose to **Run custom tool**. This will read the metadata and build proxy classes for all the OData services. This step generates a library that contains all your OData services and their operations with names such as `<YourProjectNameSpace>.Microsoft.Dynamics.DataEntities`.

Authentication and OData service call

Once the required packages have been added to your project and the entity proxy has been generated, the next step is to implement the code to authenticate and consume OData entities. An OData Service call will need an authorization token passed as a header on the service request. You can implement this as follows:

1. Using the ADAL library, retrieve the authentication token from the Azure Active directory.
2. Using generated proxy classes, you can instantiate the data entity objects, set properties, and call methods to interact with the OData endpoint.

The Dynamics 365 for Finance and Operations product team has developed sophisticated examples of consuming OData services in C#, which are available on GitHub. The sample code can be downloaded from `https://github.com/Microsoft/Dynamics-AX-Integration`.

 To learn more about Azure Active Directory authentication using the ADAL library, take a look at the Microsoft documentation site: `https://docs.microsoft.com/en-us/azure/active-directory/develop/active-directory-authentication-libraries`.

In this section, we learned how to consume Finance and Operation OData services in the C# programming language. Similarly, you can use OData libraries and Azure active directory authentication libraries in various other development platforms, such as Java, JavaScript, Node.js, PHP, curl, and many others to consume Finance and Operations OData services.

Now, let's explore another popular programming model in Finance and Operations called custom services.

Custom services

Custom services are programming models through which a developer can convert the X++ business logic into a service. Using this model, any existing X++ code can be exposed as a custom service simply by adding an attribute to it. There are standard attributes that can be set on the data contract class and methods to automatically serialize and deserialize data that is sent and received.

In Dynamics 365 for Finance and Operations, the custom service programming model supports SOAP and JSON endpoints. Custom services are always deployed on two endpoints; the following table shows the endpoint URIs:

Type	Endpoint URI
SOAP endpoint	`https://<host_uri>/soap/Services/<service_group_name>`
JSON endpoint	`https://<host_uri>/api/Services/<service_group_name>/<service_group_service_name>/<operation_name>`

Most of the custom services that are available out of the box in Dynamics 365 for Finance and Operations are system services that are utilized for internal application processes or integration with various components, such as DIXF, retail, and warehouse web application. There are various functional services available, for example, `FormLetter` services and `financialDimensions` services, which can be used for third-party integration scenarios.

The following bullet points summarize the custom services programming concepts in the Dynamics 365 for Finance and Operations application:

- Custom services are based on the data contract defined by developers and the service contract can be controlled.
- The existing business logic can be utilized and exposed as a service.
- Custom services are good for simple requirements, which are not otherwise easy to achieve using data entities.
- Custom services are best suited for an action to be triggered by third-party applications, such as PO receiving/posting and packing slips.

Business events

Business events introduce an event-driven integration model in Dynamics 365 for Finance and Operations. Business events occur when a business process is executed in the application. Some example business events could be a sales order being shipped or a purchase order being confirmed.

The following diagram illustrates how business events work in Dynamics 365 for Finance and Operations:

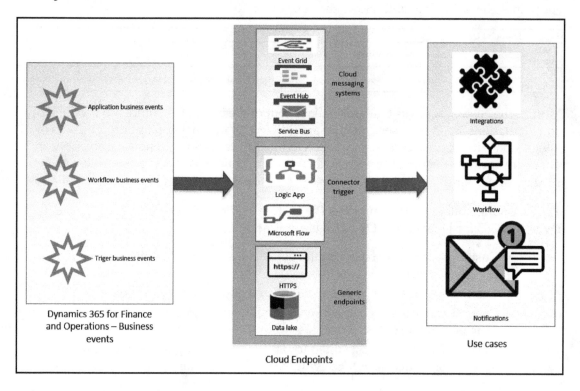

In Finance and Operations, business events are implemented in some business processes out of the box. These business events can be typically classified as application business events and workflow business events. The alert feature, which is typically used by users to notify others of data changes in the application, can also be configured for business events. The administrator can configure these in order to send business events to Azure messaging services such as Azure Event Grid, Event Hub, and Azure Service Bus. External business processes or applications can subscribe to those events and act on such events for various use cases such as integration, workflow, or notification.

Business events are also available as triggers in Finance and Operation connectors with the name *When business events occur*. This trigger can be used in Power Automate or Logic Apps to subscribe to any of the business events that are available in the target instance of Microsoft Dynamics 365 for Finance and Operations.

Now, let's explore the key concepts related to business events in Dynamics 365 for Finance and Operations.

Business events catalog

The business events catalog lists the business events that are available in your Finance and Operations application. The business events catalog can be accessed from **System administration | Set up | Business events**.

The following screenshot shows the user interface of the business events catalog in Dynamics 365 for Finance and Operations:

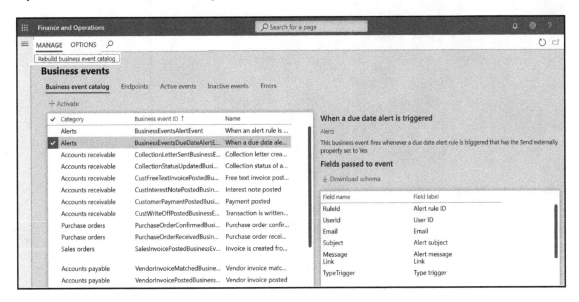

The business events list is built during the code deployment process of the Finance and Operation environment. However, if an explicit update of the catalog is required, this can be done using the **MANAGE | Rebuild business events catalog** option.

Each business event that's available in the catalog contains a category, business event ID, and description. It also contains the payload that will be generated when business events occur. You can also download the payload schema in JSON format.

In summary, the business events catalog helps identify the business events that are required for implementation purposes. It also helps identify the schema for each business event.

Business events endpoints

Endpoints basically define the destination where business events are sent. Before you can activate and use business events, you must configure an endpoint. The following screenshot shows how to create an endpoint:

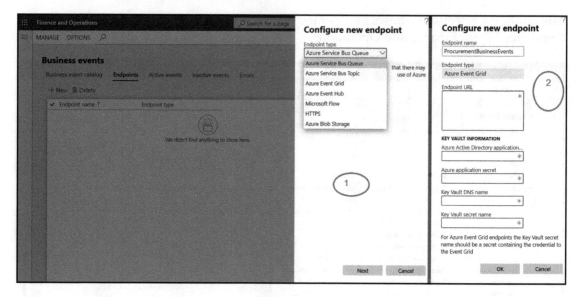

The following types of endpoints are currently available out of the box:

- Azure Service Bus Queue
- Azure Service Bus Topic
- Azure Event Grid
- Azure Event Hub
- HTTPS
- Microsoft Flow (Power Automate)
- Azure Blob Storage

To configure an endpoint in Finance and Operations, follow these steps:

1. Create Azure-based endpoint destinations such as Azure Event Grid or Azure Service Bus in your Azure subscription.
2. Set up the Azure Key Vault to provide the secret to the Azure messaging resource.

3. Store the Azure messaging service connection string value as a Key Vault Secret value.

4. Set up **Azure Active Directory** (**Azure AD**) and get the application ID and application secret.

5. Add the Azure AD application to the Key Vault Access policies with access to Secret Management.

6. Configure an endpoint in Dynamics 365 for Finance and Operation by providing an Azure AD application key, Application secret, Key vault DNS name, Key vault secret name, and additional destination details if needed.

The purpose of using an Azure key vault is to securely store the sensitive connection strings of the Azure messaging resource. Finance and Operations connects to the Azure Key Vault using the key vault's information to retrieve the connection string. It then uses its connection string and other parameters to create a connection with the messaging resources to deliver the payload.

Business events processing

Business events in the business events catalog aren't active by default. Business events can be activated from the Business events catalog form, by selecting the **Activate** button and providing legal entity and endpoint details. If you leave the **Legal entity** field blank, the selected business events will be activated in *all* legal entities.

When business processes such as purchase confirmation run and the corresponding business event, that is, `PurchaseOrderConfirmedBusinessEvent` is active, a business events payload is generated as part of the transaction and stored in the business events queue.

Delivery of the business event payload to the endpoint is done in an asynchronous manner. Dedicated threads are allocated to process business events by the system, which ensures faster processing of business events. In case of failure of delivery (such as if the messaging service is down), business events are available in the failed queue and can be processed manually.

Available business events and extensibility

In Finance and Operations, business events are implemented in some business processes out of the box. These business events include some common business processes in different modules of the application. Generic workflow business events are generated at various points when processing a Finance and Operations workflow. Power Automate or Logic Apps can be used with workflow business events to build rich notification and approval scenarios. Similar to the workflow business events, alert business events can also be used cross-module with enhanced notification and system integration scenarios.

At the time of writing this book, the business events framework was a new feature. Take a look at the business event home page to get a list of available business events and new capabilities: https://docs.microsoft.com/en-us/dynamics365/unified-operations/dev-itpro/business-events/home-page.

The programming model of the business event framework is quite easy and extensible and can be used by the customer and partner developer to create any new business events or even extend payload information of out of the box business events.

As a developer, you can also extend endpoint types and add your own endpoint if needed. For more information on developing new business events, take a look at the Microsoft documentation page: https://docs.microsoft.com/en-us/dynamics365/unified-operations/dev-itpro/business-events/business-events-dev-doc.

Benefits and use cases

The business events feature is based on the event-driven architecture pattern and has the following benefits:

- Business events are produced in near real time, which means they enable faster notifications and integration scenarios.
- Consumers of business events are decoupled from Finance and Operations.
- No point-to point-integrations. It's easy to add new consumers to the system.
- Highly scalable and distributed.

At a high level, business events are most suitable for business events notifications, third-party integration, and automating business processes through the workflow. The Microsoft product team is doing a tremendous job in documenting various potential use cases for business events in detail. Go to https://docs.microsoft.com/en-us/dynamics365/unified-operations/dev-itpro/business-events/potential-use-cases to get the latest information on this.

Data feeds

Data feeds enable near real-time incremental exports of Dynamics 365 for Finance and Operations data to Azure Data Lake. Data feeds follow a similar architecture model to business events, except here, the data feed is tied to data change **create, update, and delete (CUD)** events on tables rather than business processes.

The following diagram shows the conceptual architecture model of data feeds:

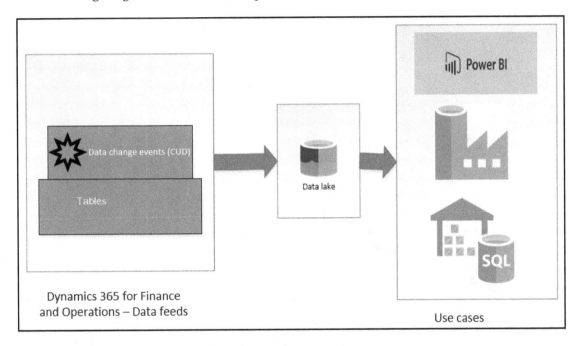

As shown in the preceding diagram, data feeds track insert, update, and delete events at the table level and send data changes to Azure Data Lake. Finance and Operations data that's ingested in the Azure Data Lake follows **Common Data Model** (**CDM**) format, which can be further consumed by Azure data services such as Azure Data Factory, Azure Synapse Analytics, and Power BI for reporting and analytics purposes.

The following screenshot shows the user interface in Finance and Operations to Configure data feeds to Data Lake:

Configure data feeds to Data lake (preview)

Choose Tables   Choose using Entities   Active   Deactivated

+ Add Tables

✓	Table display name	System name	↑ License code	Table group	Status
	Accountants	Accountant_BR	General ledger	Main	Initializing
	Accountant location relati...	AccountantLogisticsLocation_BR	Trade	Main	
	Accountant location roles	AccountantLogisticsLocationRole_BR	Trade	Main	
	Accounting distributions	AccountingDistribution	General ledger	Transaction	
	Accounting distribution t...	AccountingDistributionTemplate	General ledger	Group	
	Accounting distribution t...	AccountingDistributionTemplateDetail	General ledger	Worksheet	
	Accounting event	AccountingEvent	General ledger	Transaction	
	Cost center type	ACOCostCenterAttributeValue_BR	General ledger	Miscellaneous	
	Journal names	ACOJournalName_BR	Not specified	Group	
	Journals	ACOJournalTable_BR	Not specified	WorksheetHeader	
	Journal lines	ACOJournalTransOverHead_BR	Not specified	WorksheetLine	
	Cost absorption paramet...	ACOParameters_BR	Not specified	Parameter	
	Production - costing	ACOProdCostTable_BR	Not specified	TransactionHeader	
	Absorbed costs	ACOProdOverHeadCostTrans_BR	Not specified	TransactionLine	
	ActualWorkItemEntry	ActualWorkItemEntry	Not specified	Miscellaneous	
	BLWI country/region	AddressCountryRegionBLWI	Trade	Main	

The form lists all the tables in the system that are available for the data feeds. Before you can configure any tables for the data feeds, you have to bring your own Azure Data Lake, store the Azure Data Lake connection string in an Azure Key vault secret, and setup **Data connections**, on a Data feeds parameters form as shown in the following screenshot:

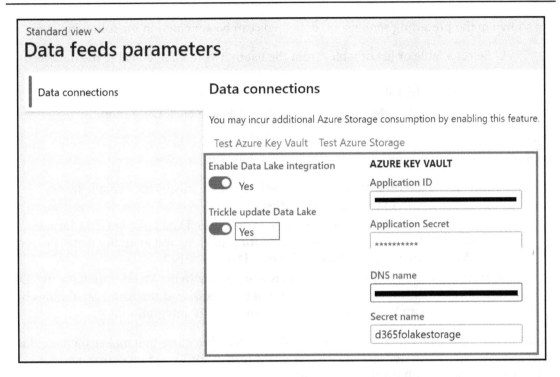

Once the data connection has been setup, you can configure the tables for the data feeds service. The following mock-up screenshot shows the user interface and the steps you need to follow to configure the data feeds:

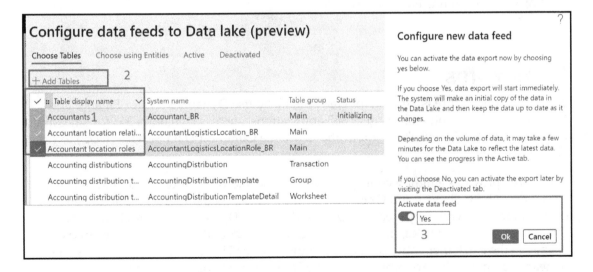

As shown in the preceding screenshot, data feeds can be activated in the following steps:

1. Select a table or list of tables from the list that you wish to enable the data feeds for.
2. Click the **Add Tables** button.
3. Select **Activate data feed** radio button to **Yes** and click **Ok** button.

Similar to the business events feature, data feeds is based on the event-driven architecture pattern and has all the event-driven architecture's benefits, as follows:

- Data feeds are produced in near real-time, which means they enable faster notifications and integration scenarios.
- Incremental data is delivered directly to an Azure Data Lake in CDM format, which enables automatic consumption for reporting and analytics using Power BI, Azure Synapse Analytics, and Azure Data Factory.
- Having Finance and Operations incremental data in an Azure Data Lake in CDM format not only enables powerful out of the box BI and reporting capabilities but also enables a plethora of scenarios for third-party integration.

In summary, data feeds are based on an event-driven architecture that makes incremental data available in the Azure Data Lake in the CDM format for BI and reporting, and for effective integration with third-party systems.

 At the time of writing this book, the data feed feature was not generally available. The information listed here may change or work differently when this book is released.

Dual-writes

The dual-write feature is exciting for customers who use Dynamics 365 for Finance and Operations and also other Dynamics 365 applications, such as Dynamics 365 for Sales and Dynamics 365 for Talent. These applications use the **Common Data Service** (**CDS**) to store and secure data.

Dual-write provides a tightly coupled near real-time and bidirectional integration between Dynamics 365 for Finance and Operations and the common data service. Once an entity is enabled for dual-write, any create, update or deletes in Dynamics 365 for Finance and Operations results in writes, in near real time, to the CDS and vice versa. For example, a change in the Customer entity data in Dynamics 365 for Finance and Operations is reflected in near real time in the Account entity in the Dynamics 365 for Sales, and vice versa.

Dual-write not only provides direct in-built integration between Dynamics 365 for Finance and Operations and other Dynamics 365 systems but also allows us to add new entities or customize the mapping of existing entities, as per our business requirements.

Even when you are not using Dynamics 365 for Sales or other Dynamics applications, you can still synchronize Finance and Operations data into CDS instance and use Power App on top of CDS to build custom business applications.

The following diagram shows the conceptual architecture of the dual-write feature:

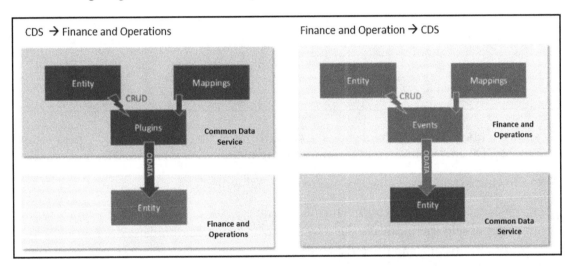

As shown in the preceding diagram, the dual-write feature tracks data change events at the data entity level using native features such as plugins in CDS and data events in Finance and Operations. As the changes happen in the application, dual-write applies data mapping and writes the data back to other applications using the OData protocol. In scenarios where one environment is down for maintenance and other activities are available, we can pause it and replay the integration when the environment is available again.

The dual-write administration experience is embedded into Dynamics 365 for Finance and Operations and available under the data management workspace, as shown in the following screenshot:

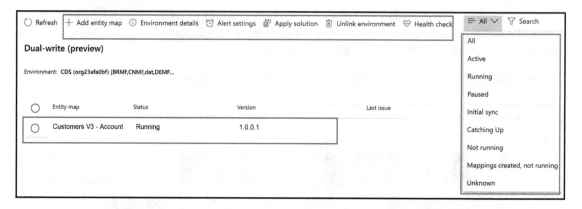

As shown in the preceding screenshot, the administrator can use Finance and Operations to link to the CDS environment, add an entity, set up mapping, and monitor integration.

The following list highlights the key features of dual-write:

- Near-real time and bidirectional integration
- A simple and intuitive user interface to enable and administer dual-write
- Support for standard and custom entities (map)
- Ability to customize entity (map) and field mappings
- Ability to filter and do basic transformations
- Consolidated view to review entity (map) activities and errors

Microsoft is also working on making setting up dual-write an out of the box experience through LCS. This will allow CDS environment provisioning and linking as part of the Finance and Operation environment creation experience.

> The dual-write feature is an evolution of the Data Integrator platform (`https://docs.microsoft.com/en-us/power-platform/admin/data-integrator`), which was used to integrate Dynamics 365 applications with Finance and Operations.
>
> At the time of writing this book, the dual-write feature is not generally available. The feature's details and their capabilities may change in the final version.

Data management and the batch data API

In ERP systems, it is a very common and important integration practice to handle high-volume integration in asynchronous patterns. Dynamics 365 for Finance and Operations allows us to configure how we export or import data in files using a recurring schedule. This integration pattern is based on data entities, the data management platform, and RESTful batch data APIs.

The following diagram shows the batch data API conceptual architecture in Dynamics 365 for Finance and Operations:

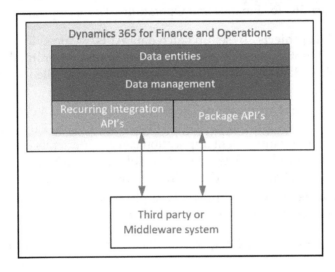

As we can see, there are two sets of APIs at the top: data entities and data management.

The following table summarizes the key differences between both APIs so that you can decide on which one works best in your integration scenarios:

Key point	Recurring integration API	Data package API
Scheduling	Scheduling in Finance and Operations	Scheduling outside Finance and Operations
Format	Files and data packages	Only data packages
Transformation	XSLT support in Finance and Operations	Transformations outside of Finance and Operations
Supported protocols	SOAP and REST	REST
Availability	Cloud only	Cloud and on-premise

The following diagram describes the process of setting up and consuming the recurring integration using RESTful services:

As highlighted in the preceding diagram, the next heading describes how to set up batch data API in Dynamics 365 for Finance and Operations. These steps are as follows:

1. **Create data projects**: To set up batch data APIs, we need to set up data projects. This step involves creating the data project for export or import and then adding the required data entities with the appropriate source file format and defining the mapping.

2. **Set up the client application**: The next step is to set up a client application. Both recurring integration and package APIs use the OAuth 2.0 authentication model. Before the integrating client application can consume this endpoint, a client application must be registered in Microsoft Azure AD, granted permission, and whitelisted in Dynamics 365 for Finance and Operations.

3. **Call the APIs**: Now, the third-party application or middleware system can use the RESTful APIs to send and receive messages.

The following table describes the integration APIs that are available for recurring integration:

Type	API name	Description
Import	Enqueue	Submit the files for import
Import	Status	Get the status of import operations
Export	Dequeue	Get the file's content for export activities
Export	Ack	Acknowledge the dequeue operation

The following table describes the list of APIs that are available when using package APIs:

Type	API name	Description
Import	GetAzureWriteUrl	Used to get a writable blob URL.
	ImportFromPackage	Initiates an import from the data package that is uploaded to the blob storage.
	GetImportStagingErrorFileUrl	Gets the URL of the error file containing the input records that failed at the source and sends them to the staging step for a single entity.
	GenerateImportTargetErrorKeysFile	Generates an error file containing the keys of the import records that failed at the staging step to the target step for a single entity.
	GetImportTargetErrorKeysFileUrl	Gets the URL of the error file that contains the keys of the import records that failed at the staging-to-target step of the import for a single entity.

Export	ExportToPackage	Exports a data package.
	GetExportedPackageUrl	Gets the URL of the data package that was exported by a call to ExportToPackage.
Status check	GetExecutionSummaryStatus	Used to check the status of a data project execution job for both export and import APIs.

The Microsoft product team has made a console application that showcases the data import and data export methods that are available on GitHub. For more information, go to `https://github.com/Microsoft/Dynamics-AX-Integration/tree/master/FileBasedIntegrationSamples/ConsoleAppSamples`.

Azure Data Lake Storage Gen2 integration

Azure Data Lake Storage Gen2 (**ADLSG2**) is a set of capabilities dedicated to big data analytics, built on Azure Blob Storage. Using Azure Data Lake integration in Finance and Operations, customers can configure and export master and transnational incremental data to their own Data Lake in the CDM folder format. Once data has been staged in the Azure Data Lake in CDM format, you can use the Power BI dataflow feature to build interactive Power BI reports.

The following screenshot shows the user interface that's used to configure Azure Data Lake integration in Finance and Operations:

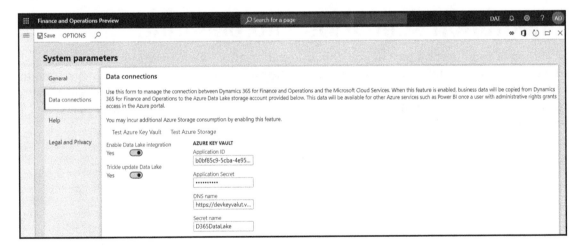

To configure Finance and Operations integration to the Data Lake, the following steps must be performed:

1. Create a new Azure Data Lake Storage Gen2 account or use an existing one. Get the storage account connection string.
2. Create a secret in the Azure Key Vault and store the storage account's connection string.
3. Create an Azure AD Application and generate an application secret.
4. Using the Azure Key Vault access policy, grant access to the Azure AD application to manage the Azure Key Vault secret.
5. Enable Data Lake integration and configure the Data Lake's details in the **Data connection** tab under **System Administrator | Setup | System parameters** in Finance and Operations.
6. Select and enable aggregate measurement for an automatic refresh in Finance and Operations under **System administration | Setup | Entity store.**

Azure Data Lake integration is a big topic for analytics and Power BI integration with Dynamics 365 for Finance and Operations. We will cover Azure Data Lake Gen 2 integration in more detail in the Chapter 10, *Analytics, Business Intelligence, and Reporting.*

Integration scenarios and planning

Planning is an important part of any data integration effort. Data integration planning requires identifying integration scenarios and the high-level requirements of integration. In this section, we'll cover common integration scenarios, common questions to be asked for gathering integration requirements, and selecting the right integration strategy based on your requirements.

Integration scenarios

Every project is different, and integration requirements will vary, depending on the scope and needs of a project. However, there are some common areas where most businesses have processes that require integration. The following table shows the common integration points and possible scenarios:

Integrations	Possible scenarios
Customers	Customers need to be maintained in the CRM system, which needs to be synced with the ERP system.
Sales orders	Integrating web orders with the ERP system, which includes delivery notification, invoicing, and payments or with customer systems directly (for example, EDI integration).
Product and inventory (on hand)	Receiving product data from a PLM system. Sending the product-and-inventory-on-hand data to external systems or customers, for example, e-commerce, Amazon, Marketplace, and so on.
Price list	Sending a product price list to external systems or customers, for example, e-commerce, marketplace, and so on.
Sales tax	Sales tax integration with sales tax solutions (to calculate the sales tax based on the product, customer, ship to, price, and other relevant parameters).
Purchase orders	Purchase order, including ASN and AP invoice, integration with the vendor systems.
Employee and positions	Receiving employee and reporting relationship information from the HR system or sending employee information to the payroll or expense systems.
Chart of accounts and financial dimensions	Sending the chart of account and financial dimension data to other internal systems, such as the payroll system, expense system, and others.
Exchange rates	Downloading daily exchange rates from exchange rate providers, such as OANDA.
Payment integration with banks	Sending AP payments such as check, ACH, and wire to the banking systems or automating bank reconciliations.
GL integration	Importing GL journal entries that occur outside of the Finance and Operations system, such as expense, payroll, loan accounting systems, or other divisions using a different accounting system (acquisitions).

In the next section, we'll look at the common integration requirements you should collect during the analysis phase.

Integration requirements

In a typical integration scenario, the implementation team works with the business users, internal IT, and in some cases, representatives of the applications that have been identified for integration to determine the requirements in detail. The following questions must be answered and documented so that you have a successful integration solution. Often, the answers to these questions are not clear-cut and will require modeling the different scenarios to develop the best solution. That being said, starting this process early on in the project is the key. Let's take a look at some of these questions:

Questions	Example values	Effects on design
What type of data needs to be integrated?	Sales orders, purchase orders, and so on.	This will help you determine whether you can use any existing data entities or need to create a new one.
What kind of integration type will the other applications support?	XML, web services, and flat file.	This will help you determine the technology to be used.
What is the availability of the systems that are being integrated? What are the requirements of real-time data exchanges?	Asynchronous or synchronous.	This will help you determine the integration technology and configuration requirements.
Is the integration based on the pull model or the push model?	Pull, push, or event-driven.	This will help you determine the technology and configuration of the exchange event.
What is the volume of transactions?	Number of transactions (daily, weekly, monthly, or yearly).	This will help you determine the scale of integration, suitable integration technology, and deployment options.
What will be the frequency of data exchange?	Timing per second, minute, and hour.	This information helps you determine how to configure the integration solution.
What business rules are associated with the data?	The sequence of events and exception handling.	This will help you determine the customization required for the document exchange.

Does the data need to be transformed? Will the transformations be performed before data is sent or when data is received?	The extent of transformation – field-level mapping, value mapping, and flat file to XML or vice versa.	This will help you determine which integration configuration and transformations need to be used.
Is the external system an in-house system or an external trading partner?	Security and encryption requirements.	This will help you determine how the users and security need to be configured.

Making a decision regarding what synchronous or asynchronous integration pattern to use is key. Now, let's take a look at the pros and cons of each.

Synchronous or asynchronous?

One of the key decisions to be made is whether integration should be real-time (synchronous) or asynchronous. The following table analyzes both messaging approaches and describes the scenarios when one should be selected over the other:

Type	Pros	Cons	Good for	Examples
Synchronous	Fail-safe communication. Error/exception handling.	Tight coupling between systems. Blocks sender until the receiver is finished. Network dependency; calling system must be available.	Transaction processing across multiple systems.	Mobile app/handheld for PO receiving, SO picking, inventory on-hand, and so on.
Asynchronous	Decoupled systems. Does not block sender. The integrating system doesn't need to be available. Messages can be queued.	Reliability. Error/exception handling.	Publish and subscribe. Request reply. Conversation.	General ledger, sales order, purchase orders, and master data integrations.

In general, asynchronous messaging architectures are preferred and recommended for enterprise integration as it allows for a loosely coupled solution. The asynchronous integration pattern overcomes the limitations of remote communication, such as network latency and the unreliability of the connected systems. The issues of reliability and exception handling in asynchronous messaging can be overcome by utilizing acknowledgments, status checks, and logging features.

Integration strategy

Previously, we learned about the various integration concepts and technologies that are available in Dynamics 365 for Finance and Operations. In this section, we'll highlight the available integration technologies, integration solutions, and best practices for Finance and Operations.

The following table lists the available integration technologies, integration types, integration patterns, and what type of integrations these technologies are best suited for:

Integration technology	Integration type	Integration pattern	Best suited for
OData	Inbound/Outbound	Synchronous	Low to medium volume, a real-time, system to system integration
Custom services	Inbound/Outbound	Synchronous	Low to medium volume, a real-time, system to system integration
Batch data API	Inbound/Outbound	Asynchronous	High volume asynchronous import/export
Business events	Outbound	Asynchronous	High volume status event notification, workflows, and outbound integrations
Dual-writes	Inbound/Outbound	Asynchronous	Integration with Dynamics 365 Apps
Data feeds	Outbound	Asynchronous	High volume data integration for data analytics and integrations
Data lake integration	Outbound	Asynchronous	High volume data integration for Analytics

Now that we've learned about the various integration strategies that are available within Finance and Operations, let's explore the middleware applications we can use to complete the end-to-end integration solution.

Integration middleware/messaging services

Using RESTful APIs and the OData service, any third-party application can directly integrate with Finance and Operations. However, when using asynchronous integration patterns or the event-driven architecture, you must use messaging services or middleware as an integration broker to integrate with Finance and Operations.

In the previous, section, we learned that many Azure messaging services are supported out of the box when using business events and data feeds. There are several other middleware integration tools that can be used to integrate Dynamics 365 for Finance and Operations with third-party applications. This section will briefly talk about these technologies and middleware systems.

Logic Apps

Logic Apps is a cloud-based **Integration Platform as a Service (IPaaS)** that can simplify and implement scalable integrations solution in the cloud, on-premises, or both. Logic Apps provide a visual designer that can model and automate your process as a series of steps known as a workflow. The Logic Apps comes with hundreds of connectors across the cloud and on-premises to quickly integrate across services and protocols.

For advanced integration scenarios, Logic Apps come with Enterprise Integration Pack connectors. This allows you to easily include validation, transformation, and message exchange through industry-standard protocols, including AS2, X12, and EDIFACT. You can also secure messages with both encryption and digital signatures.

Using an on-premises data gateway with Logic Apps, you can connect to your on-premise resources, including SQL Server, BizTalk server, filesystems, DB2, Oracle database SAP application server, SAP message server, and many more.

Logic Apps has a built-in connector for Dynamics 365 for Finance and Operations, along with triggers and actions, both of which can be used in a variety of integration scenarios.

To find out more about the Logic Apps and Dynamics 365 for Finance and Operations, go to the following links:

- **Logic Apps documentation:** https://docs.microsoft.com/en-us/azure/logic-apps/.
- **Finance and Operations Connector:** https://docs.microsoft.com/en-us/dynamics365/unified-operations/dev-itpro/data-entities/fin-ops-connector.

Power Automate

Power Automate (previously known as Microsoft Flow) is an online workflow service that automates actions across the most common apps and services. Power Automate is built on top of Logic Apps and has the same workflow designer and connector experience. Power Automate is designed for superusers or analysts to perform simple integrations or design a simple document workflow without going through developers or IT.

Power Automate directly integrates with many Microsoft cloud and business productivity tools such as SharePoint Online and One Drive for Business, as well as other Office 365 products, which make it perfect for common business processes and workflows. For example, the product information manager can use SharePoint online to maintain the price list and then use Power Automate to get approval and update this in Finance and Operations. In another example, the sales manager, who is using business events, can create a workflow in Power Automate so that they're notified when a new priority sales order is created but the inventory isn't available so that they can take the appropriate action promptly.

To find out about what you can do with Power Automate, go to `https://docs.microsoft.com/en-us/flow/getting-started`.

Event Hub, Event Grid, and Service Bus

Azure offers three services that assist with delivering event messages throughout a solution. These services are Event Hub, Event Grid, and Service Bus. Dynamics 365 for Finance and Operations business events and data feeds publish events and data to all these messaging services out of the box.

The following table compares these three services, explains their purpose, and suggests when to use which service:

Service	Purpose	Type	When to use
Event Grid	Enables event-driven, reactive programming. Publishers emit events but have no expectation about which events are handled. Subscribers decide which events they want to handle.	Event distribution (discrete)	React to status changes
Event Hubs	Azure Event Hubs is a big data pipeline. It facilitates the capture, retention, and replay of telemetry and event stream data.	Event streaming (series)	Telemetry and distributed data streaming
Service Bus	Service Bus is intended for traditional enterprise applications. These enterprise applications require transactions, ordering, duplicate detection, and instantaneous consistency.	Message	Order processing and financial transactions

For more details about these services, please go to their Azure documentation pages:

- **Event Grid**: `https://docs.microsoft.com/en-us/azure/event-grid/`
- **Event Hub:** `https://docs.microsoft.com/en-us/azure/event-hubs/`
- **Service Bus**: `https://docs.microsoft.com/en-us/azure/service-bus-messaging/`

Azure Storage/Azure Data Lake

Azure Data Lake Storage Gen2 makes Azure storage the foundation for building enterprise Data Lakes on Azure. If you want to build analytics and reporting on top of the business events or data feeds data, you can configure a business events endpoint in Finance and Operations to emit data events to Azure storage or Data Lakes.

Dynamics 365 for Finance and Operations Data Lake integration also uses Azure Data Lake Gen 2 to stage master and transaction data in the CDM folder format. We will discuss this more in `Chapter 10`, *Analytics, Business Intelligence, and Reporting*.

The CDM folder is a folder in a Data Lake that conforms to specific, well-defined, and standardized metadata structures and self-describing data. These folders facilitate metadata discovery and interoperability between data producers and data consumers.

Recurring integrations scheduler

The recurring integrations scheduler, also known as **QuartzAX**, is a solution that can be used in on-premise, file-based integration scenarios for Dynamics 365 for Finance and Operations. This is a free open source, community-driven sample app available on the GitHub.

The following diagram has been taken directly from the tools' wiki page and explains the conceptual architecture of the tool:

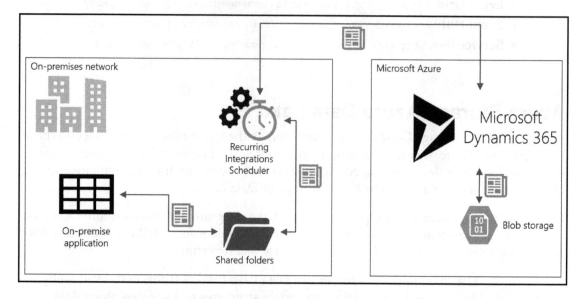

The recurring integration scheduler uses Finance and Operations batch data APIs to enable recurring data import and export scenarios. This tool can be a good implementation accelerator to use during the implementation phase of the project for data migration, ad hoc file integration needs, and as a proof of concept integration solution.

Integration planning and having a good strategy are key to a successful integration solution and the overall success of an implementation project. The next phase after you completed the integration strategy and planning is integration design and development.

Integration design and development

Once you have all the detailed integration requirements, the integration specialist works with business analysts, developers, and system administrators to create a detailed design. In this section, we'll explain the process of designing an integration solution.

Developing a high-level conceptual design

Developing a high-level conceptual design is important to explain the different integration points and directions. Let's have a look at the following diagram:

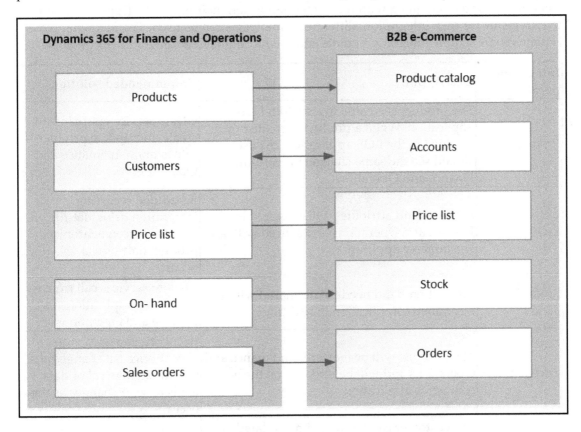

The preceding diagram represents an example of a conceptual integration design between Dynamics 365 for Finance and Operations and B2B e-commerce applications.

Selecting the right integration technology

It is important to select the best-suited integration technology for each of the identified integration requirements. The previous section described the different integration technologies and tools, along with recommendations on their use cases. Depending on the requirements for each integration, different technologies can be used. The following table explains some sample integration points and the recommended integration technologies:

Integration point	Description	Recommended solution
Product	The product is created in a custom LOB application. When a product is created or changed in the LOB application, the user should see the same change, in real-time, in Finance and Operations.	OData service endpoints to create and update product information in Finance and Operations.
Product	Products and attributes will be stored in Finance and Operations and synced with an e-commerce application.	Scheduled recurring integration using flat-file or data feeds to synchronize product data as changes occur.
Product on-hand	Product on-hand needs to be shared with the e-commerce application in real-time.	Custom services call from e-commerce applications to Finance and Operations.
Price list	The price list will be mastered in Finance and Operations and will be updated on the e-commerce application.	Recurring integration to export price list changes at a scheduled interval or data feeds to send changes as they occur.
Customers	The customer can be created or updated either on the Dynamics 365 for Sales (such as address) or updated in Finance and Operations (such as credit limit) and synced in both the systems.	Dual-write.
Sales orders	Orders will be created in the Custom LOB application and created or updated to Finance and Operations. Sales order status updates such as shipment confirmation, invoices, and payment applications need to be synced to the custom application.	Batch data APIs to create or update sales orders in Finance and Operations. Business events to provide near real-time status updates of the orders.

Sales orders	A self-hosted customer portal where customers can check the status of their orders. Order status information is maintained in Finance and Operations.	OData service endpoints to read order status information from Finance and Operations.

Defining field mapping

Defining a field-level mapping for each integration point includes providing data types, field lengths, applicable values, and validation logic for each field. This mapping helps you identify the mapping requirements between the system so that you can address any data type, field length, and restrictions. The following table shows customer integration between Finance and Operations and an e-commerce application:

Finance and Operations Field name	Data type	Requirement	Default value	E-commerce field	Description
CustTable.AccountNum	NVARCHAR(20)	Mandatory	Number sequence	Account.Id	Unique identifier for the customer record
CustTable.CustGroup	NVARCHAR(10)	Mandatory	Web	NA	Defines customer group
DirPartyPostalAddress.PostalAddress	NVARCHAR(250)	Optional		Account. PostalAddress	Stores the customer's address

Developing, configuring, and testing

The next step is to develop, configure, and test the integration. The following are some helpful tips for developing an integration solution:

- Utilize the existing code and functionalities for integration; extend as needed.
- Keep the message format generic as far as possible so that the same integration point can be used with other applications if needed. Use the XSLT transformation or other transformation tools to transform the messages into an appropriate system schema.
- Build an error handling and notification mechanism to monitor the failure. Keep a closed loop; there should be a mechanism to notify other applications of the success or failure of message processing.
- Develop the test data and a unit test scenario; perform unit testing before end-to-end integration testing.

- Develop a test simulation, if possible, for system testing. This can save a lot of time during the end-to-end testing process.
- Perform load testing by generating a large set of data. Often, the integration solution fails on the production load as the development or test environment does not have sufficient data to simulate the production load.
- Prepare a test plan that includes positive and negative scenarios. Test all exceptions and boundary scenarios. Also, test the end-to-end business process on integration data to avoid any fallback impact in the production environment.
- Develop a security and deployment plan for integration solutions and test deployment and security in the test environment before moving to production.

Finally, let's explore some of the best practices and recommendations related to integration solutions.

Best practices and recommendations

Here are a few considerations to keep in mind while designing your integration solution for Dynamics 365 for Finance and Operations:

- Simplify the overall architecture and try to reduce the number of integrations between applications wherever possible. It is one of the areas that causes recurring issues in production.
- Clearly define the master system for each data element, even though you may have it stored in multiple places. In some cases, this may have to be defined at the field level. For example, a customer master is stored in CRM and Finance and Operations as well. CRM might be the master for all the customer information except the credit limit.
- Ideally, you should avoid duplicating data across multiple systems, although in some cases you cannot avoid it for business reasons or for systems to work. For example, customer records are required in both the CRM system and operations. However, you can opt not to integrate the CRM-centric customer information that may not be needed in Finance and Operations.

- Understand and document business SLAs for each integration; think through the impact in extreme situations. One of our customers had their inventory being refreshed into their e-commerce system every 2 minutes. This was fine until the Black Friday weekend. During that 2-minute window, they oversold a product that was being sold below its cost (they only wanted to get rid of the on-hand stock). However, the customer ended up buying more to fulfill the additional orders that were received due to the delays in inventory updates. It is important to understand SLAs and business impacts while designing integrations.

With this section, we have come to the end of this chapter. Now, let's summarize what we have learned!

Summary

In this chapter, we learned about the tools and techniques for integration planning and design. We started with the integration architecture and learned how integration architecture for Dynamics 365 for Finance and Operations support multiple integration technologies. Data entities are at the center of the integration architecture and support RESTful OData services and batch data APIs for integrations. Business events and data feeds enable event-driven architecture using Azure messaging services such as Azure Event Grid, Azure Service Bus, Logic Apps, and so on.

We learned about various modern basic integration concepts, such as RESTful, SOAP, JSON, OData, OAuth, and the event-driven architecture, and how these concepts are utilized within Dynamics 365 for Finance and Operations, as well as how they can be utilized for various integration scenarios. Microsoft Dynamics 365 applications are intelligent applications that work smarter together, and we learned how these applications can be connected using dual-write with the Common Data Service. Subsequently, we learned how important integration planning is in an ERP implementation project, and how to approach integration design and development with real-life integration examples. Finally, we learned about the common industry best practices and recommendations related to integration planning.

In the next chapter, we will cover another important phase of the ERP project development. We will learn how Dynamics 365 for Finance and Operations can be customized and extended for specific business scenarios, including common recommendations and best practices.

Customization and Extension

9

Any application is released with certain standard features. In most cases, these standard features only fit 80% of the practical business scenarios, but there is the other 20% that are unique to each business/client and that do not fit the standard application offerings. The majority of customers have intentions to implement the ERP system without any customization. However, when a project team starts gathering the requirements and performing fit-gap analysis, the project team needs to decide if customization is needed or whether the gap can be covered with a business process change.

Dynamics 365 for Finance and Operations provides a broad variety of technologies and toolsets for developers to use in order to build additional solutions and functionalities. These tools not only enable the customer and the partners to customize the end product in order to meet the business requirements in a specific project, but also help **independent software vendors** (**ISVs**) build industry-specific vertical solutions for a larger ecosystem. In this chapter, we will learn about the development process and tools in Dynamics 365 for Finance and Operations.

We will cover the following topics in this chapter:

- Architecture and concepts
- Development environment
- Development planning
- Development process
- Build and continuous updates
- Guidelines and best practices

In this chapter, we will explore the things that you need to know about before starting development, for example, the development environment, tools, technical concepts, and build and versioning strategies. In development planning, you will learn about setting up the basic rules and guidelines before the development process starts. In the development process, we will walk you through the development process, frameworks, and best practices. In the *Build and continuous updates* section, we will explore the automated build and deployment processes. In the end, we will discuss some common best practices and guidelines that can be applied in the development phase.

Understanding solution architecture and development concepts

We learned about the architecture of Dynamics 365 for Finance and Operations in `Chapter 4`, *Architecture, Deployment, and Environments.* It is really important to understand the system architecture before you can architect the solution for a Dynamics 365 for Finance and Operations implementation project. In this section, we will explore development concepts in detail.

Programming language

Like earlier versions, the X++ language remains the main programming language for developing application code for Dynamics 365 for Finance and Operations. For those who don't know what X++ is, it is a native programming language used in the development of Dynamics 365 for Finance and Operations since the beginning of Axapta.

X++ is an object-oriented language with similarities to C# and provides SQL-like constructs for data selection and manipulation. In Microsoft Dynamics 365 for Finance and Operations, the X++ programming language has been modernized to achieve the following:

- Better consistency with other managed languages, such as C#
- Better integration with the managed stack (CIL)
- Some cleanup – fewer quirks and badly defined areas

Let's understand the changes in the X++ programming language.

Compiling exclusively in .NET CIL

In Microsoft Dynamics 365 for Finance and Operations, X++ is a first-class citizen in the .NET world. The X++ compiler is rewritten and compiles the source code exclusively as .NET CIL. There are important benefits to X++ code running exclusively as .NET CIL, as follows:

- CIL runs much faster in most scenarios. You can expect significant performance improvements in cases where complex algorithms are executed.
- Developers can now easily write application logic in other .NET languages, such as C#.
- AX **.NET Business Connector** or managed proxies are no longer needed; you can simply add assembly references in X++ code.
- CIL can be operated on by the many .NET tools.

Language enhancements

Along with making X++ completely compile in CIL, several language enhancements and constructs have been added to get X++ closer to C#. The following code summarizes some of the new enhancements in X++:

```
//using keyword for referencing - just like C#
using coll = System.Collections;
using System.CodeDom;
class MyMainClass
{
  // Declare variables and instantiate them in the class declaration
  // granular field access mark them public, private or protected.
  //static, constant and read only member variables
  static int loop;
  private const int constValue = 4;
  public readonly str readOnlyValue = "ReadOnly";
  CodeComment comment = new CodeComment("Print something");
  // static constructor using TypeNew keyword
  static void TypeNew()
  {
    loop = 4;
  }
  public static void main(Args _args)
  {
    MyMainClass mainClass = new MyMainClass();
    mainClass.myMethod();
  }
public void myMethod()
```

```
    {
        coll.ArrayList arrayList = new coll.ArrayList();
        // Const or readonly variables change- generate compile error
        // constValue = 5;
        //readOnlyValue = "I want to change this but i cant";
        try
        {
          info(comment.Text);
          //use var keyword
          for (var i = 1; i <= loop; i++)
          {
            arrayList.Add(i);
            if (i == 3)
            {
              throw error("Catch me.");
            }
          }
        }
        catch
        {
          error("something happened in try.");
        }
        // Finaly keyword
        finally
        {
          info(strFmt("Error happened at %1", arrayList.Count));
        }
    }
    /*Output
    Print something
    Catch me.
    something happen in try.
    Error happened at 3
    */
}
```

The preceding code highlights the following new concepts and keywords in the X++ programming language:

- The using keyword: Similar to C#, now, you can use the using keyword to reference assemblies. The preceding code shows two different ways of how you can use the using keyword.
- **Instantiate variables in the class declaration**: As shown in the preceding code, you can now instantiate variables in the class declaration.

- **Static constructor and member fields**: You can now declare member fields as static ones and create static constructors using the `TypeNew` keyword. In the example code, an earlier static constructor is used to initialize the value of the `loop` variable.

- **Const and read-only member fields**: Now, you can declare member fields as `const` or `readonly`. Attempting to change these fields throws compile errors. Similar to C#, `const` is static by default and must have a value at compilation time. The `readOnly` field must have a set value by the time constructor is evaluated and the instance is created.

- **Granular field access**: Now, a field can be explicitly marked as private/protected/public. The default is protected.

- **The var keyword**: Similar to C#, you can now use the `var` keyword in X++. The code example earlier shows `i` in the `for` loop being declared using the `var` keyword.

- **Declare anywhere/smaller scope**: Now, X++ allows you to declare variables in a smaller scope. The preceding code demonstrates this concept, where the variable `i` is declared in the scope of the `for` loop.

- **The `finally` keyword:** You can now use the `finally` keyword along with `try...catch` statements; the `finally` block is always executed.

> To learn more about these additions, check out the following link:
> `https://docs.microsoft.com/en-us/dynamics365/operations/dev-`
> `itpro/dev-tools/programming-language-support`.

Unit of compilation

Another important change you will notice in X++ is about the unit of compilation. In Dynamics 365 for Finance and Operations, the X++ compilation unit is now the same as for other .NET languages, such as C#. If any method in a model element (class, form, query, and so on) fails to compile, the whole compilation fails.

Integrated development environment (IDE)

The **integrated development environment** (IDE) is the tool that you use to develop/manage application code and metadata in Dynamics 365 for Finance and Operations. Dynamics 365 for Finance and Operations has improved upon the tools it first provided to developers to help them with better development experience. With Dynamics 365 for Finance and Operations joining the .NET family, it has expanded the number of tools available to developers so that they can do their job more efficiently. In this section, we will learn about the IDE tool provided by Dynamics 365 for Finance and Operations.

Development IDE in Dynamics 365 for Finance and Operations

Visual Studio is the exclusive integrated development environment that provides modern tooling through .NET components. The X++ language is fully integrated into the Visual Studio environment. You can use the code editor in Microsoft Visual Studio to write the X++ code for your applications. As you write your X++ code, you will see the familiar features of the Visual Studio code editor; for example, IntelliSense is displayed to help you write the code. You can also navigate to methods and classes in the code editor by using the navigation drop-down menus at the top of the code editor window. Other features, such as collapsible sections, are also available. The design experience, such as designing a UI element, is also integrated with Visual Studio. You can open the element designer that corresponds to the current X++ source code by right-clicking in the code editor and then selecting **Open Designer**.

Visual Studio is the exclusive development environment for Dynamics 365 for Finance and Operations.

The following screenshot shows the operations development environment in Visual Studio:

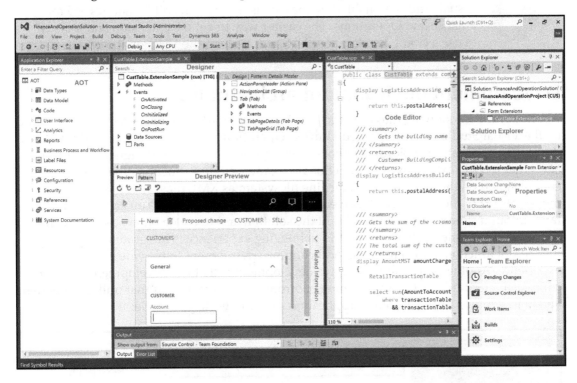

 The preceding user interface shows a combination of views to show various relevant interfaces together on one screen. Normally, a code editor or designer is present in the middle section, and the right section has a **Solution Explorer** or **Team Explorer** view.

As shown in the preceding screenshot, Visual Studio provides a user-friendly experience of designing and writing code within the Visual Studio environment. On the left, a familiar application object tree displays the application elements. The form designer can be used to design the form element, which also includes real-time design preview control to display how the control will appear on the page, as shown in the middle. On the right is the code editor to write the business logic. On the far right, you can see the standard sections to manage the solution, properties, and Team Explorer. Debugging the X++ code, displaying a form, or running a report is integrated with the Visual Studio debug (*F5, Ctrl + F5*) experience. All the other development tools, such as cross reference, best practices checks, and so on, are replaced with .NET-based tooling and are available under Dynamics 365 at the top of the toolbar.

It is important to note that the Dynamics 365 development environment in Visual Studio is enabled by the extension of Microsoft Dynamics 365 for Finance and Operations. The easiest way to get the extension and tools is to use a cloud development VM or download the VHD on the premises.

Development environment architecture

As shown in the following diagram, the development environment architecture is powered by the Visual Studio extension called **Unified Operations**. This extension provides the developer, application explorer, X++ code editor, project system, UI designer, debugger, and other tools to extend existing functionalities and add new functionalities. The source code is stored on the development machine filesystem as XML files and is used by the metadata API of the Visual Studio extension for editing and design. You can use the familiar build process developer to build the solution and to create binary assembly files and other deployment artifacts. The X++ debugging experience is integrated with the *F5/Run* function, which uses the local runtime environment to provide a debug experience. Another important change in development is that the development tools are completely decoupled from any running environment, which means that unlike the earlier versions, you don't need an active application server to write your code:

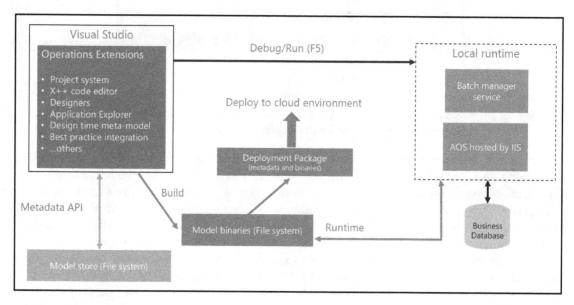

A new development environment changes the way customization and development is done in earlier versions. The following are the key advantages of using Visual Studio as the development environment for operations:

- Visual Studio is the most popular IDE and the Finance and Operations development tooling can reap benefits for continuous investment and innovations.
- X++ becomes a managed language within Visual Studio; the programming language X++ gets closer to C#, incorporating more and more familiar syntax from C#.
- It's easier than ever to onboard the .NET resources to customize and extend Dynamics 365 for Finance and Operations with familiar tooling, programming concepts, and increased interoperability with managed languages.

Programming concepts

To understand the Dynamics 365 for Finance and Operations development platform, you need to understand the key terms that are frequently used in the development process.

Models

A **model** is a group of elements, such as metadata and source files, that typically constitute the solution. A model is a design-time concept and typically represents a solution area, for example, the general ledger model and project model. A model always belongs to a package.

Packages

Packages in Finance and Operations are essentially the deployment and compilation units of one or more models. On disk, a package is a set of folders, consisting of XML files representing objects. From the compilation and deployment point, a package as a whole translates 1:1 as an assembly (DLL). Packages can have references to other packages, just like .NET assemblies can reference each other. One or more packages can be combined into a deployable package, that is, a unit of deployment.

Packages and models on disk

Packages and models are stored as a set of folders on the Microsoft Dynamics 365 for Finance and Operations application server. The following image represents the folder structure:

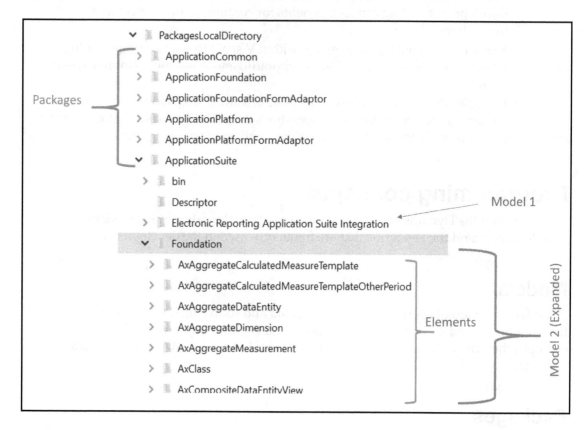

As shown in the preceding screenshot, `PackagesLocalDirectory` (called **model store**) is the root folder and contains the individual packages, for example, `ApplicationCommon`, `ApplicationFoundation`, `ApplicationSuite`, and so on. Each package can contain one or more models; for example, the `ApplicationSuite` package contains multiple models, that is, `Electronic Reporting Application Suite Integration` and `Foundation`. Each model contains folders containing metadata elements and code.

Models and packages in Visual Studio

In Visual Studio, models and packages are represented in the **Application Explorer**. You can switch to the model view by right-clicking on the main **AOT** ode and selecting **Model view**. The following screenshot shows the model view of the **Application Explorer**. As we can see, all the models are represented as tree structures in the model view. Package names are displayed in the parenthesis for each model:

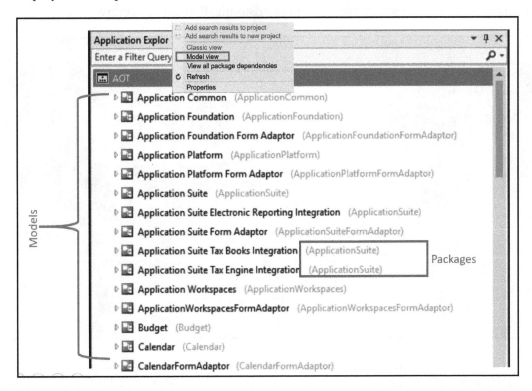

As highlighted in the preceding screenshot, **Application Suite Tax Books Integration**, and **Application Suite Tax Engine Integration** are two model parts of the ApplicationSuite package.

Overlayering

Microsoft has deprecated the overlayering concept, starting with Microsoft Dynamics 365 Finance and Operations version 8.0. We will only explain the overlayering concept in brief, as it's not in use anymore.

In Microsoft Dynamics 365 for Finance and Operations, you can only override an element in the same package where it was originally created. You also have to use a higher layer than the original layer of the element. For example, if you want to override an element created by Microsoft in the `ApplicationSuite` package, which is in the **SYS** layer, you have to create a model in the `ApplicationSuite` package and select a higher layer such as **CUS** or **USR** to override the elements.

The following diagram shows the concept of customization using overlayering:

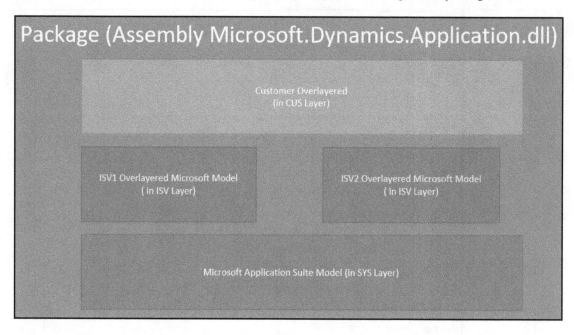

As shown in the preceding diagram, the `ApplicationSuite` model is overlayered by ISV1 and ISV2 in the ISV layer and then the customer is overlayered in the CUS layer. All these models will compile into a single assembly. If the same object is changed by the ISV layer and the customer, the CUS layer customization wins.

Extensions

Extensions are a new concept that you can use for customization in Dynamics 365 for Finance and Operations. An extension allows you to add functionality to the existing code. The extension development approach is the best practice approach as it puts your customizations in a separate assembly that does not touch the standard application at all.

Extension models have several advantages, including the following:

- **Application Lifecycle Management** (**ALM**): Extension models simplify and improve the performance of deployments, builds, test automation, and delivery to customers.
- **Design time performance**: Building your model or project doesn't require you to recompile the entire application.
- **Servicing**: In the cloud, Microsoft can install, patch, upgrade, and change internal APIs without affecting your customizations.
- **Upgrades**: Unlike overlayering, extensions reduce the cost of upgrading to a new version as this approach eliminates costly code and metadata conflicts.

The following diagram shows customization through extension:

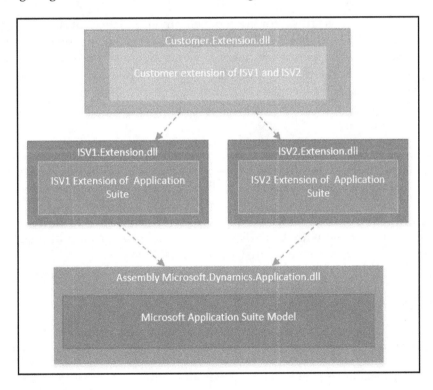

Now that we've learned about different aspects of the tools provided before developing the system, next, we will learn about development environments and how to manage them.

Understanding the development environment

Now that you understand the architecture and technical concept behind the development environment in Dynamics 365 for Finance and Operations, it is time to build a solution as per your requirements. Before the development phase of the project starts, you need to set up the development environment, version control strategy, and a few ground rules, such as coding standards, the naming convention to be followed, and the code review process. In this section, we will walk through these topics, in brief, to understand what they mean.

Version control

Keeping track of the code is critical for good development practices. Azure DevOps (formally known as VSTS, **Visual Studio Online**, or **VSO**) is the version control system supported for Finance and Operations. Azure DevOps includes source control, work item tracking, build, release and reporting services. Azure DevOps build pipelines can be used to build releases from specific elements stored in its source control system. Visual Studio's code analysis, test tools, and code coverage elements can be used to validate a build before it is deemed fit for release.

Azure DevOps is tightly integrated with LCS and can be used throughout the life cycle of the project. For example, all requirement gaps created in the LCS BPM library can be converted into work items in Azure DevOps. The build environment also uses Azure DevOps to create a deployable package. The LCS code upgrade tool utilizes Azure DevOps integration to perform automated source code management. Post-production support tools are integrated with Azure DevOps as well, where a support request created by a user can automatically create Azure DevOps work items.

Branching strategies

Before starting development, the solution architect should also decide on the right branching strategy for Azure DevOps, which can be useful in the following scenarios:

- When a stable version is needed for testing while the development work continues in other areas.

- When multiple development teams are working on a set of features that are independent, but each team also depends on the features that have been developed by the other teams. You need to isolate the risk of the changes made by each team, but you will need to merge all the features together into one product.
- When the implementation is being carried out in multiple phases, one phase that is in production may need continuous support, but the team may be working on the next phase.

The following are some popular branching strategies typically used in operations projects:

- **The main only strategy**: This is the simplest and most basic branching methodology, where one branch is created and all the developers check in the changes to the main branch. The build machine can be used to create a build-out of the **Main** branch to be released for testing and, later, for the production environment. The following screenshot shows only the **Main** branching strategy:

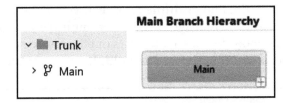

- **The development and main branching strategy**: The development and main branching strategy introduces one or more development branches from the main branch, which enables the concurrent development of the next release, multiple projects running in parallel, experimentation, or bug fixes in an isolated development branch. The following screenshot shows the **Main** and **Dev** branching strategy:

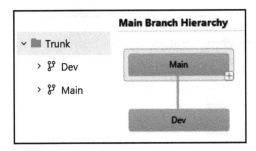

- **Development, main, and release**: If you expect to be performing emergency break fixes outside of your normal release schedule, create a release branch. The release branch represents the code that exists in production. The following screenshot shows the branching strategy with release:

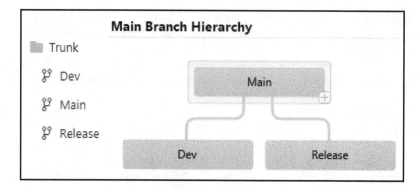

- **Development, main, and multiple release**: If you are an ISV, developing vertical solutions, and want to manage and support multiple versions of your solutions, you can create multiple release branches of the service-specific product version. The following screenshot shows the multiple-release strategy:

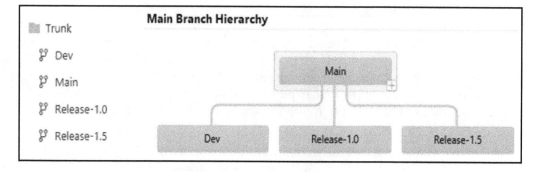

Keep the branching strategy simple! Start small, expand later.

Development machines

In Dynamics 365 for Finance and Operations, development is done on preconfigured one-box VMs. These VMs have Visual Studio, Dynamics, and SQL Server preinstalled and are integrated to ease development.

For development, you will need one development machine for each developer. Depending on the scope and complexity of your project and the number of developers working on it, you may need multiple development VMs. Along with machines for developers, you will need one build machine to build a solution and create deployable packages. Build machines can also execute best practice checks, unit tests, and automated regression tests as part of the build process.

The following diagram shows a typical development topology:

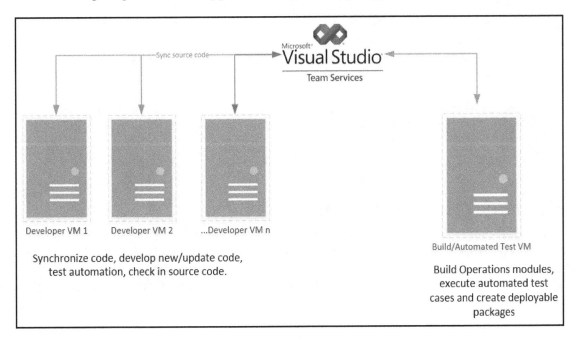

As shown in the preceding diagram, multiple developer VMs can be used by a developer to synchronize the source code, create/update code, create automated test cases, and check in the code. A build VM is used to compile source code, execute automated test cases, and create deployable packages. Cloud-based Azure DevOps links developer VMs for source control and builds automation functions.

There are two options for deploying VMs: cloud VMs and on-premises VMs, both of which are available via a downloadable VHD. Depending on your situation, you can use a combination of on-premises VMs and cloud VMs for development.

Here, we will point out some obvious scenarios of when to use on-premises and cloud:

- On-premises dev VMs are cost-effective if you already have the hardware, IT infrastructure, and Windows Server licenses to support it.
- Use cloud VMs to scale out when projects require additional resources for a limited period of time. It is more cost-effective than planning for worst-case capacity on-premises.
- Connect all VMs (on-premises and cloud VMs) to Azure DevOps for version control.

 Microsoft is also working on developer tools as installable components. This feature, when available, allows developers to install the Finance and Operations dev tools within Visual Studio.

Cloud development environment

Before you can deploy developer topology using LCS, you need to link your LCS project with an Azure DevOps profile. When you deploy dev/test topology, you can select one or more developer VMs and one build VM. In this deployment, the **Developer** VM is configured with workspace mapping to develop against an Azure DevOps project.

The build VM is auto-configured with the build agent/controller so that you can build modules for the Azure DevOps project and execute automated tests with an external endpoint for validation. The following screenshot shows a simple workflow for deploying DEV and building machines using LCS:

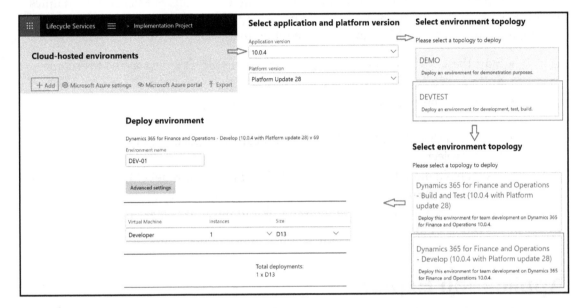

When deploying a development environment, you will have the option to choose an application/platform version. You will also choose if the environment you are deploying is a development environment or a build environment. If you have already deployed a build environment, then you don't need to deploy another build environment.

Once an environment has been deployed, it will be available 24/7, but, at the same time, you have the option to stop/start an environment when it's not in use. This way, you can stop an environment when it's not being used, so you don't have to pay for it.

Local development environment

To use the development environment on-premises, you can download the VHD file and then create a virtual machine using virtualization software such as Hyper-V or VMWare. These VMs are similar to cloud VMs and contain complete installs of Microsoft Dynamics 365 for Finance and Operations, Visual Studio, and SQL Server. To get started with development using these VMs, simply do the following:

- Start these VMs and log in using `builtin\Administrator` as the username and `pass@word1` as the password.
- Provision the admin user within Operations using the `AdminUserProvisioning` tool.
- Sign in to Visual Studio and map your local workspace to develop against the VSTS project.
- If you have more than one downloaded VM to perform development, you must rename them so that they can work with Azure DevOps.
- Optionally, you can use manual steps to add these VMs into your domain and also connect to LCS.

Application Explorer

Application Explorer is the main entry point for browsing and interacting with the elements in the model store that define the applications. Application Explorer corresponds to the AOT. To open the Application Explorer in Finance and Operations Developer VMs, in Visual Studio, click on the **View** menu and then click **Application Explorer**. Application Explorer is used to view elements, view code, find references to a selected element, and add elements to a project. To create, design, edit, and build model elements, you must use a project.

Application Explorer views

There are two views in the **Application Explorer**. The first view, called **classic** view, displays all the elements from all the models grouped according to type, while the second view, called **model view**, displays each model separately. When you expand a particular model, it displays elements from that model grouped according to type.

The following image shows the classic and model views of the application explorer in Visual Studio. To switch between these views, you can right-click on **AOT** and switch between them:

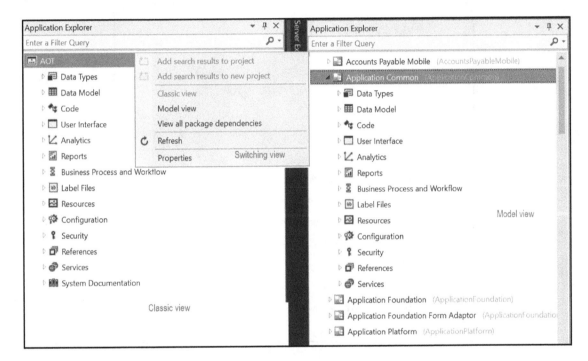

Filtering the Application Explorer

The Application Explorer allows us to filter the application elements based on various criteria and queries. This makes it easier to find specific elements you are looking to explore or modify. To do a simple search, just type the text that you want to filter by and hit *Enter*. For example, if you want to filter by `custTable`, simply type `custTable` in the search bar and hit *Enter*.

It will filter and show all the elements where the element names contain `custTable`, as shown in the following screenshot:

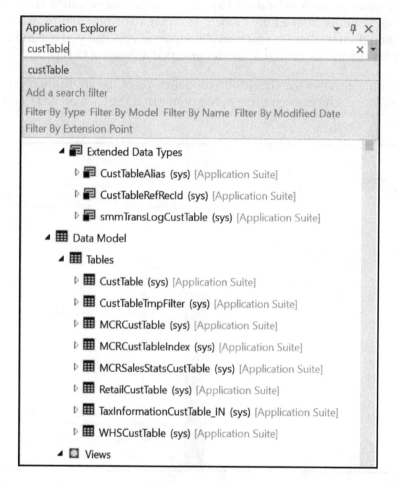

As shown in the preceding screenshot, there are various other filter options that you can add to your filter criteria to refine the search result. To get to those options, click the drop-down arrow at the end of the search bar. If you click this arrow, you will see a list of filter options that you can use to refine the filter:

- Filter by type
- Filter by model
- Filter by name
- Filter by modified date
- Filter by the extension point

After filtering the elements, you can add them to the current project or create a new project and add them. To clear the filter, you can click on the clear button (**x**) at the end of the search bar. To learn more about Application Explorer, please refer to `https://docs.` `microsoft.com/en-us/dynamics365/unified-operations/dev-itpro/dev-tools/` `application-explorer`.

Working with elements

To work with specific elements in the Application Explorer, find or search for the specific element and then right-click on the selection to see the action you can perform. The following screenshot shows the action, that the available on the `CustTable` form element:

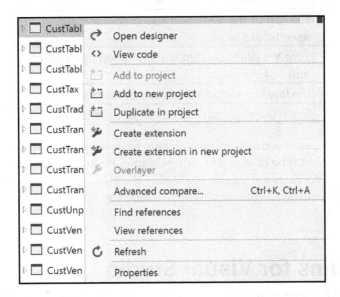

The actions that are available to perform on an element depend on the elements that you've selected. The following are some of the common actions that you can perform for elements in the Application Explorer:

Actions	Description
Open in designer	Open the element designer to view the object in element type designer. To be able to edit the object in the designer, objects must be added to the project first.
View code	Open the element in the code editor, where you can view the code.
Add to project	Add the element to the current project. You can only add an element to a project if the project belongs to the same model as the element.

Add to a new project	Create a new project and add the element to the project.
Duplicate in the project	Create a copy of the selected element and add it to the current project.
Create an extension	Create an extension for the element. A new extension model element (.extension) is added to the current project in **Solution Explorer**. This is the preferred way to work with existing elements.
Create an extension in a new project	Create an extension for the element as part of a new project. You define the new project when the **New Project** dialog box opens.
Advanced Compare	Compare the element with the different versions of the same element from a source code control repository or file on the disk.
Find references	Find all of the X++ code and other elements that reference the selected element.
View references	Create a diagram that shows the other elements that reference the selected element.
Refresh	Update the metadata of the application element that's selected.
Properties	Open the property sheet for the selected element.

Apart from these common actions, some elements have unique commands that let you perform actions for that type of element. For example, table and classes elements have a hierarchy tool that generates a diagram to display the class or table hierarchy. Table also has the **Open table browser** command, which can be used to display data in the table as a list in the program.

Tools Addins for Visual Studio

Several great tools have been added to Microsoft Visual Studio to support development. However, there will always be additional tools to meet specific requirements. To make it easier to add these additional tools, an **Addins** infrastructure has been provided for developers. The additional tools are available in two places:

- The **Addins** submenu on the Dynamics 365 menu
- The **Addins** submenu on the shortcut menu in the element designer

The following screenshot shows the **Addins** that are available in Visual Studio:

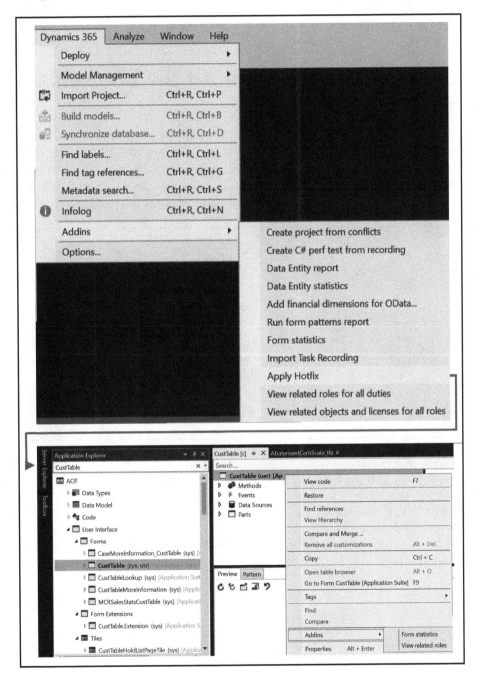

To make it easier to create your own addins, you can select the **Dynamics Developer Tools Add-in** project type when you create a new project in Visual Studio. This project type has the infrastructure that is required to implement an add-in.

Creating a new model to start the customization process

To start development in Microsoft Dynamics 365 for Finance and Operations, you need to create a model. To create a new model, open Visual Studio in the Finance and Operations development environment, click on the **Dynamics 365** menu in the toolbar, select **Model Management**, and then click on **Create model....** This opens up a wizard that you can use to create the model. The following screenshot shows the process of creating a model:

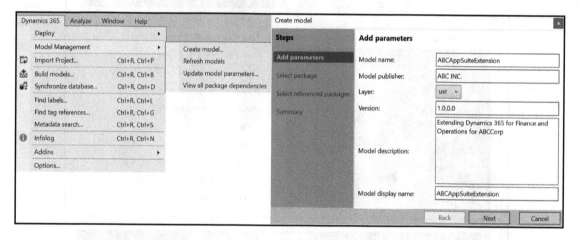

The first step in the model creation process is to provide a model name, publisher, layer, description of the model, and model display name, as shown in the preceding screenshot.

Next, you select the **Create new package** option and click **Next**. The next step will be to **Select referenced packages** and click **Next** to get to the **Summary** page. On the **Summary** page, validate the information and click **Finish** to create the model that is shown in the following screenshot:

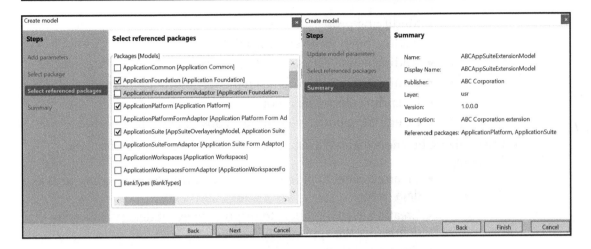

To learn more about creating a new model, please refer to `https://docs.microsoft.com/` `en-us/dynamics365/unified-operations/dev-itpro/dev-tools/create-data-model-` `elements`.

> You can update the model description, display name and package references later using the **Dynamics 365** | **Model Management** | **Update model parameters...** navigation option.

Extension capabilities

Extensions are the way to customize Dynamics 365 for Finance and Operations. Microsoft is committed and working on scenarios where customers, partners, and ISV solutions will need extension capabilities. All platform and application updates are delivering new extension capabilities, as requested by customers.

Extensions provide the following capabilities:

- Creating new model elements.
- Extending existing model elements:
    - Adding a new enum value to existing enums
    - Modifying an existing extended data type
    - Modifying existing fields or adding a new field to existing tables
    - Adding an index to existing tables
    - Adding relations to existing tables

- Modifying properties of existing tables
- Adding methods to existing tables
- Adding a new data source to the form
- Adding form captions and changing control properties
- Extending electronic reports
- Extending reports by creating a copy of existing reports

- Customizing business logic. Ways to customize business logic include the following:

    - Creating event handlers to respond to framework events, such as data events
    - Creating event handlers to respond to event delegates that are defined by the application
    - Creating new plugins
    - Using method wrapping and chains of commands

 For the latest updates and extension capabilities, check out the extensibility home page on the documentation's site: `https://docs.microsoft.com/en-us/dynamics365/unified-operations/dev-itpro/extensibility/extensibility-home-page`.

Project

When you create customization in Dynamics 365 for Finance and Operation, similar to other application development in Visual Studio, you start with a project. The project helps you organize and manage the elements that you're working with. A Finance and Operations project in Visual Studio can contain elements of only one model. If you are working with multiple models, you must create multiple projects.

Creating a new project

There are several ways to create a new project for Finance and Operations. The following are the two most common methods:

1. Using the Visual Studio **File**| **New** | **Project...** menu and selecting the **Dynamics 365** template from **Installed** | **Templates** | **Dynamics 365** | **Unified Operations**.
2. Selecting an element in the **Application Explorer** and clicking **Add to new project** or **Create extension in new project**.

Similar to other application projects in Visual Studio, enter the name and location of the project and select whether you want to create a new solution or add the project to an existing solution, as shown in the following screenshot:

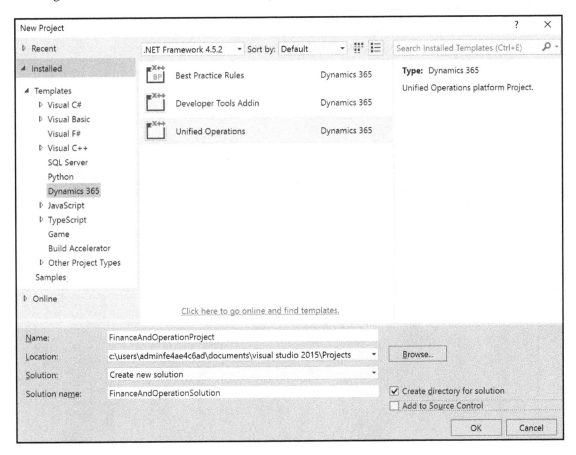

There are several important properties of the Finance and Operations project. To see and change these properties, select the project node, right-click it, and then select **Properties** to open the project's **Property Pages**. The following screenshot shows the properties for the Finance and Operations project:

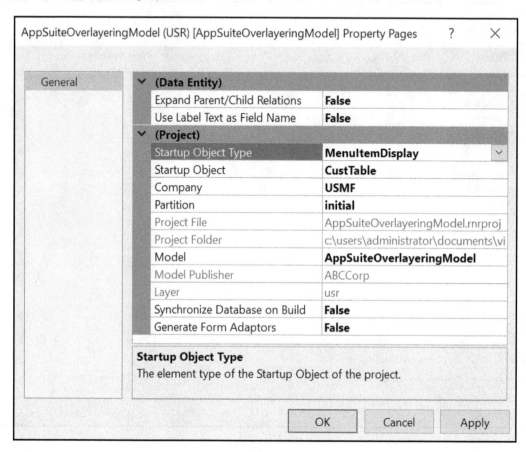

The following table describes some important properties:

Property	Description
Start Object type	This defines the type of object that will be used as the startup object when the project is run. Form, Class, and MenuItems are available options to select.
Startup Object	Based on the object type, you can select an object from the project that will be invoked when the project is run.

Company and Partition	Company and partition is used to display data when the project is run.
Project File and Project Folder	Location of the project file and folder on disk.
Model	The model that the project is associated with. All the elements in the project must be in the selected model. You can change the model if there are no elements in the project.
Synchronize database on build	A value that indicates whether the synchronize operation for tables will be performed when the build action is performed for the project.

Adding new or existing elements to the project

To add a new element to the project, right-click on the **Project**, click **Add**, and then select **New item....** This will open Dynamics 365 items from the template, as shown in the following screenshot:

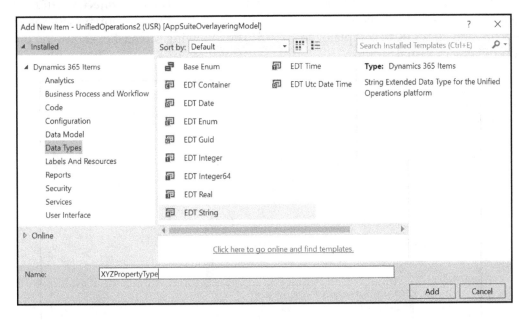

You can select the type of object you want to add, enter the name of the object, and then click the **Add** button to add elements to the project.

To add an existing element, you can search for the element in the Application Explorer and then click **Add to Project**, drag and drop the element to the project (the element must belong to the same model as the project), or click **Create extension** (the create extension element in the current project).

Import/export project

To transfer elements from one development environment to a different development environment, you can use a project package file. Project package files have the `.axpp` file name extension. A project package contains all the elements from the project. To export a project, select the project to export, right-click it, and select the **Export Project** option. This will open up a dialog where you can enter the file name and folder and export it.

When you import a `.axpp` file into another development environment, the elements from the project package file will be imported into the same model that they were exported from. If that model doesn't exist in the installation, it will be created during the import process. To import the `.axpp` file, select the **Dynamics 365 | Import Project...** menu. This opens the import dialog, where you can locate the file, select the appropriate settings, select elements, and click **OK** to complete the import. The following screenshot shows the project import dialog in Visual Studio:

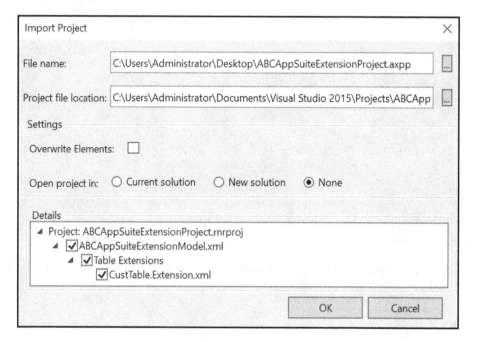

Now that we've learned about the different aspects of development tools and addins, let's look at development planning.

Development planning

The key objective of the development phase is to ensure a scalable, maintainable, and high-performing application. The next thing, after getting the development environment and the version control strategy finalized, is defining the development plan and ground rules for the development team. The following are some basic guidelines and rules that need to be established by the solution architect and the project manager before the development process.

Be agile

Irrespective of the methodology selected for overall implementation, we recommend the development phase to be executed in a CRP or agile methodology. This methodology uses a series of sprints to deliver implementation capabilities in incremental steps.

The following are some guidelines for using the CRP or agile methodology:

- For large implementation projects, create an implementation team for each functional area, for example, finance, supply chain, warehouse management, retail, and so on.
- Define the sprint cycle in full week increments. It is common to use 2 to 4-week sprints.
- Create a solution backlog containing all the customization and configuration activities and define their priority based on their business value.
- Do daily scrum meetings to discuss what each person in the team is working on and any roadblocks they may have.
- Do sprint planning sessions and select product backlog items from the backlog to work on in the next sprint to plan the activities that need to be completed.
- Use automated unit testing, functional testing, and automated build processes.
- At the end of each sprint, present the solution to stakeholders so that they can review the work and get early feedback.

Establishing the code review process

Effective code review during the development phase helps identify issues earlier and avoids rework and bug fixes during the later phases of the project. It is important for the project team to define the code review process and the guidelines for the project at the beginning of the development phase. The code review should not be limited to checking the naming conventions, indentation, and other best practices errors or warnings, which can be easily caught by best practice tools. The process should primarily be focused on achieving the following quality objectives:

- **Solution approach**: The code should be implemented in the correct way. If the existing business logic or processes have been modified, they should be modified at the appropriate level. The code should be aligned as per the technical design documents.
- **Extensibility**: The solution should be extensible and appropriate.
- **Easy to read and follow**: The code should be easy to read and follow.
- **Error handling**: The code should be able to handle errors appropriately. It's easier to catch such issues during the code review process compared to the testing phase.
- **Education for the team**: The code review process helps in educating the development team members with review feedback from more senior resources. It needs to be used as a training exercise. Set up a culture where the code reviews and feedback sharing become a learning experience rather than a blame game.

One of the common issues that we have seen in the field is that code reviews are ignored during the development phase and are considered toward the end of the development cycle, or close to going live. Most of the time, the code review feedback at such later stages is just not feasible. It is difficult to make changes to code that has already been tested and stable. The best way is to embed the code reviews as part of the development cycle. What's been learned from the previous reviews can be used by the developers to do further coding.

Development process

So far, we understand the architecture and technical concepts related to development in Dynamics 365 for Finance and Operations, Enterprise edition. Now, it's time to explore the development process itself. The key objective of the development process is to ensure a scalable, maintainable, and highly performant application.

The following diagram shows the steps that a developer goes through while developing custom solutions:

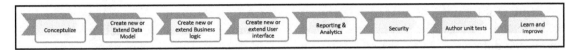

In this section, we will go through these steps and analyze how they relate to developing a custom solution in Finance and Operations, what capabilities the system offers, and the best practices to follow during each step.

Conceptualization

The first step of the development process is conceptualizing the solution. You must understand the problem that you are trying to solve. At this stage, you need to identify the where and the what – where in the standard flow you need to add your code, and what code can be reused from the standard one. Remember that Finance and Operations provides numerous application frameworks and patterns that can be reused when developing any new functionality or extending any existing functionalities. If you do not understand the existing application pattern and frameworks, you may create functionality that is necessary or one that already exists in the application.

While working with the customization requests, there are typically two kinds of scenarios presented to the developers. The first scenario is a standalone functionality, where new forms, tables, and business logic need to be developed and later integrated into the core modules. In the second scenario, the existing processes within the application need to be extended to support the requirement. In both cases, it's important for the developers to understand how the business logic for the core module and its functionalities is implemented in the application. Understanding the implementation of the core functionalities and the framework is extremely important for the developers so that they can efficiently utilize, reuse, or extend these functionalities in their custom solution. In any case, customizations need to be added on a temporary basis. The customizations should be easy to isolate and remove when they are not needed anymore, or when the required functionality is added to the product in a later release.

Create or extend the data model

The data model is the process of analyzing and defining the data structures as per your solution requirement. Similar to earlier versions of AX, in Dynamics 365 for Finance and Operations, Enterprise edition, you can create or extend existing data models using extended data types, base enums, tables, views, and data entities. Data entities are new artifacts that have been introduced in operations. Data entities provide abstraction from the physical implementation of database tables and hide the relational model by flattening out the schema. Either you are ISV building a vertical solution or you're a customer or partner developing a custom solution, creating appropriate data entities to cover your custom data model. Simply creating data entities enables the following possibilities by default:

- Ability to use data entities for configuration and data migration
- Use data entities as OData services and recurring integration
- Office integration
- Analytics and Power BI

If you need to extend the existing data models, many extensibility features are supported on data models elements, for example, extending base enums, changing properties, adding relations, creating a new field in tables, views, and so on.

Create or extend business logic

The business logic is a part of a program or code that encodes the real-world business scenarios. In Dynamics 365 for Finance and Operations, Enterprise edition, the business logic can be written at multiple levels, such as the form UI, table method, classes, SSRS reports, and so on. The following headings describe the best practices when you customize the business logic in operations:

- **Reusing the code**: As we explained earlier, Dynamics 365 for Finance and Operations provides numerous application frameworks. When developing the custom features, you should be able to extend the existing frameworks or reuse the code for your customization. The suggestion is to try not to reinvent the wheel, but investigate and utilize what is already available in the system.

- **Use extensions**: Dynamics 365 for Finance and Operations added several enhancements to improve the extensibility of business logic and continues to add features that come with continuous service updates. With extensions, you can make use of available event handlers on tables, forms, form data sources, form controls, and others, plugin classes, and extend any object available in the system. With extensions, you can write business logic that's as simple as adding a new field or writing a whole new module without disturbing the core structure of the system.

- **Customizing the code**: When the base layer code needs to be replicated or used in other places, it is always better to extend the existing classes and modify the derived class for the change in behavior, rather than creating completely new classes and then copying the entire code from the base class. Extending the standard business logic by extending the class will make it easier to upgrade the code. If you have created an extension, only the modified code must be restructured. Create classes and methods so that the same piece of code can be reused in multiple places. Avoid creating long methods. They make the code difficult to read, hard to debug, and extremely difficult to upgrade and maintain.

- **Where to add the custom code**: Create the customizations at the appropriate location. Create code for reuse as much as possible, but create it at the lowest appropriate location. For example, if something is required only in a form, do not put it at the table level.

- **Using .NET projects and assemblies**: Last but not least, business logic can be implemented in .NET programming languages much easier than in X++. Now, you can easily build extended business logic in C# or any other programming language and use it with an operations project as a reference.

Create or extend the user interface

The client in Dynamics 365 for Finance and Operations is an HTML web client that runs in major browsers such as Microsoft Edge, Safari, and Chrome. The move to a web client has created the following changes for client forms and controls:

- Form controls are split into logical and physical parts. The physical presentation of forms and controls is now HTML, JavaScript, and CSS that runs within the browser. The X++ logical API and related state run on the server.

- The logical and physical parts are kept in sync through service calls that communicate changes from each side.

- The server tier keeps the form state in memory while the form is open.

While a lot has changed regarding how forms and controls run, for developers, creating a new user interface or form is similar to Dynamics 365 for Finance and Operations. You continue to create forms, menu items, and menus to build a user interface. The form metadata continues to be used to define controls and application logic.

You create a form, add data sources, and design form layout by adding controls and add business logic by overriding the methods. A new extensible control framework has been added that lets you add additional controls.

 The operations documentation provides comprehensive technical details related to the user interface and can be found at https://docs. microsoft.com/en-us/dynamics365/operations/dev-itpro/user-interface/user-interface-development-home-page.

The following section talks about some of these user interface development concepts for operations.

Form patterns

Form patterns provide form structure, based on a particular style (including required and optional controls), and also provide many default control properties. Form patterns need to be specified when designing a form element. The reason why it is mandatory is because form patterns help guarantee that forms have a responsive layout. Finally, patterns also help guarantee better compatibility with upgrades. If your user interface design does not correspond to a given form pattern, you can select a custom form pattern; however, this means that you should test the form for a responsive layout on different devices, browsers, and form factors.

There are several form patterns and sub-patterns to choose from. Visit the following web page to find out more about form patterns and sub-patterns: https://docs.microsoft. com/en-us/dynamics365/operations/dev-itpro/user-interface/user-interface-development-home-page.

User interface extensibility

Many times, you get requirements to add additional fields, validations, or change the layout of existing forms. Most of these requirements can be achieved by metadata extensions. Business logic on the forms can be extended by subscribing to standard events at a form, data source, or control level.

 For details around user interface extensibility, go to `https://docs.microsoft.com/en-us/dynamics365/operations/dev-itpro/extensibility/extensibility-home-page`.

Control extensibility

In Dynamics 365 for Finance and Operations, typically, you use existing control to design the user interface. However, developers using modern tools such as HTML5, CSS3, and jQuery can also define entirely new controls to provide specific visualizations for business data.

 For more details, visit Microsoft's documentation on creating new controls: `https://docs.microsoft.com/en-us/dynamics365/operations/dev-itpro/user-interface/control-extensibility`.

Some sample code is also available on GitHub so that you can learn how to create extensible controls: `https://github.com/Microsoft/Dynamics-AX-Extensible-Control-Samples`.

Reporting and analytics

Reporting and analytics is a major area of customization for organizations implementing ERP solutions. Dynamics 365 for Finance and Operations provides a collection of reporting solutions to address the various reporting needs of an ERP solution. From the development and tooling perspective, the following tools are used for reporting and analytics.

We will learn more about this in `Chapter 10`, *Analytics, Business Intelligence, and Reporting*.

SQL Server Reporting Services (SRSS)

SSRS continues to be the platform for producing advanced operational and business document reports in Dynamics 365 for Finance and Operations. The process of developing a report in the current version of Dynamics 365 for Finance and Operations is easier as you can create and validate a reporting solution entirely in Visual Studio. In Finance and Operations, the administration of SSRS is also simplified by hosting the services on the Microsoft Azure compute service. The SSRS framework also provides document printing and distribution services for producing precision documents that are intended for email, printing, archive, and bulk distribution. If you have a requirement to change the existing reports, extending the SSRS report is not possible. The best practice is to leave the out of the box report as is and create a copy of it to modify as per your requirements as a new custom report. Menu item extensions can be used to redirect the business logic to run the custom report instead of the standard report.

Power BI

Power BI is used to create interactive visualizations and self-service reports for Microsoft Dynamics 365 for Finance and Operations. Power BI can connect to multiple data sources, both on-premises and in the cloud, to create combined reports and dashboards. Developer or power users can use Power BI desktop to author stunning Power BI visualizations and distribute them within the organization. Once these reports are published to `https://powerbi.microsoft.com/en-us/`, they can be pinned to the Dynamics 365 for Finance and Operations, Enterprise edition client to provide interactive visuals that are related to business processes. You can also write X++ extensions for embedded reporting scenarios that require the following:

- Drill-down navigation into detailed pages in response to user interactions
- Report filters based on user and session context information, such as company or date range
- Ability to navigate directly into a specific tab within a Power BI report via menu items

Several new concepts have been introduced in Dynamics 365 for Finance and Operations, Enterprise edition to enable aggregate data for analytics and BI perspective. Developers need to understand these concepts and constructs to extend or enable analytical data for their custom solutions. The following are some key concepts related to business analytics:

- **Aggregate measurement and dimension**: Aggregate measurement is a model that contains a collection of measures, along with their corresponding dimensions. As a developer, you can model these measures and dimensions using Visual Studio.
- **Aggregate data entities**: Aggregate data entities are read-only data entities that are used for reporting purposes. You can create aggregate data entities by directly referencing aggregate measurements and aggregate dimensions. You can use/consume information from an aggregate data entity.
- **KPIs**: A developer can model a KPI definition in Microsoft Visual Studio. After a KPI has been defined, users can customize it at runtime.
- **Entity store**: Entity store is a database dedicated to reporting and analytical purposes. In Finance and Operations, you can set up batch jobs to synchronize data entities and aggregate entities to an entity store database. Every Finance and Operations installation comes with a default entity store DB. Entity store can be used to write Power BI and any other analytical and reporting needs.

 More details about other reporting and analytics capabilities will be given in the next chapter. You can also follow the developer documentation page to learn more about reporting options and tools: `https://docs.` `microsoft.com/en-us/dynamics365/operations/dev-itpro/dev-tools/` `developer-home-page#analytics.`

Security

Microsoft Dynamics 365 for Finance and Operations' security definition is a development task, and the groundwork for the supporting security definition of the custom objects should be done as part of the development process.

In Dynamics 365 for Finance and Operations, role-based security is based on the following key concepts:

- **Security roles**: The security roles that are assigned to a user determine the duties that the user can perform and the parts of the user interface that the user can view. All users must be assigned to at least one security role in order to access Microsoft Dynamics 365 for Finance and Operations, Enterprise edition.

- **Duties**: Duties correspond to the parts of a business process. The administrator assigns duties to security roles. A duty can be assigned to more than one role.
- **Privilege**: In the security model of Microsoft Dynamics 365 for Finance and Operations, Enterprise edition, a privilege specifies the level of access that is required to perform a job, solve a problem, or complete an assignment. Privileges can be assigned directly to roles. However, for easier maintenance, it is recommended that you assign the privileges to duties and duties to roles.
- **Permissions**: Each function in Microsoft Dynamics 365 for Finance and Operations, Enterprise edition, such as a form or a service, is accessed through an entry point. The menu items, web content items, and service operations are collectively referred to as entry points. In the security model for Microsoft Dynamics 365 for Finance and Operations, Enterprise edition, permissions group the securable objects and the access levels that are required to run a function. This includes any tables, fields, forms, or server-side methods that are accessed through the entry point.
- **Policies** (**Data Security Policy or XDS**): These are used to restrict the data that a user can see in a form or a report. With this feature, you can create a query with restrictions. Then, you can create a security policy that can be applied to a security role. For example, if you wanted to limit your accounts-payable clerks from seeing the retail vendors, you could create a query on the vendor group table with a range that limits the retail vendors. You would then create a policy that includes this query and the security role.

Microsoft provides various addins in Visual Studio for developers where they can get details about specific objects used in any particular role, duty, and so on, which helps them research any security issues.

Security for custom objects

While the administrators can maintain the security role assignment for individual users, most of the work of creating the security objects needs to be done by the developer. The following security-related tasks need to be created by the developers:

- The developers should create the appropriate privileges and add entry points to associate the functionality.
- Custom duties and roles should be created for custom functions before they can be assigned to users.

- The security policy nodes should be created by the developers so that they can use the XDS security models in Microsoft Dynamics 365 for Finance and Operations, Enterprise edition.
- You can extend existing roles and duties using the metadata extension model.

Roles, duties, and privileges can also be created via the client UI and exported and imported to other environments. There are various data entities for exporting/importing them.

Acceptance test library (ATL) resources

The **Acceptance test library** (**ATL**) is an X++ test library that offers the following benefits:

- It lets you create consistent test data.
- It increases the readability of the test code.
- It provides improved discoverability of the methods that are used to create test data.
- It hides the complexity of setting up prerequisites.
- It supports high-performance test cases.

The structure and names of the classes and methods in ATL are quite rigid. This rigidity helps improve discoverability and also makes it easier to write tests, even in domains that you're unfamiliar with.

The classes are grouped into the following concepts:

- **Navigation**: Discover entities and test data methods in a familiar hierarchy (https://docs.microsoft.com/en-gb/dynamics365/fin-ops-core/dev-itpro/perf-test/concepts-navigation).
- **Test data methods**: These methods are used to set up test data (https://docs.microsoft.com/en-gb/dynamics365/fin-ops-core/dev-itpro/perf-test/test-data-methods).
- **Entities**: Entities represent data and associated behavior that is perceived as a single unit (https://docs.microsoft.com/en-gb/dynamics365/fin-ops-core/dev-itpro/perf-test/concepts-entities).
- **Creators**: Creators let you create specific test data (https://docs.microsoft.com/en-gb/dynamics365/fin-ops-core/dev-itpro/perf-test/concepts-creators).

- **Commands**: Commands run business operations (`https://docs.microsoft.com/en-gb/dynamics365/fin-ops-core/dev-itpro/perf-test/concepts-commands`).
- **Queries**: Queries find entities (`https://docs.microsoft.com/en-gb/dynamics365/fin-ops-core/dev-itpro/perf-test/concepts-queries`).
- **Specifications**: Specifications describe expected entities at the end of the test (`https://docs.microsoft.com/en-gb/dynamics365/fin-ops-core/dev-itpro/perf-test/concepts-specifications`).

To learn more about ATL, please refer to `https://docs.microsoft.com/en-gb/dynamics365/unified-operations/dev-itpro/perf-test/acceptance-test-library#example-of-a-test-that-is-written-in-atl`.

Learn and improve

ERP customization is a big investment, and bad customization can cause stability issues and business disruption. Solution architects and developers should apply best practices and do a code review to catch any such code and improve upon it. In this section, we will learn about some best practices to be followed during the development cycle:

- **Best practice check**: Run your code through the X++ best practices process, evaluate all the best practices errors and warnings, and take the appropriate action.
- **Naming variables and objects**: Use consistent metadata, variable, and method names throughout the application. Follow standard code patterns. Use meaningful and self-explanatory variable names; for example, `SalesTable salesTable` and not `SalesTable table1`.
- **Commenting the code**: Code comments enhance the readability of the code and are very useful for those involved in modifying or maintaining the code. Comments should be used to elaborate on the intent, algorithmic overview, and logical flow. Add XML documentation for classes, class methods, and table methods.
- **Labels and text**: Use labels for all text, such as labels, form caption, info-log, and so on and provide code comments.
- **Database**: The following list provides the best practices guidelines related to the database:
    - Avoid using direct SQL calls from the X++ code.
    - Direct SQL statements do not respect application security.

- Consider specifying a field list in select statements to increase performance.
- Use or create appropriate index bases on select statements and queries.
- Use `firstonly` where applicable to increase performance.
- Use aggregates in the selection criteria rather than letting the code do the aggregation.
- Use table joins in place of `while` loops.
- Use `Update_Recordset`, `insert_recordset`, and `delete_recordset` wherever applicable.

- **Exception handling**: Use appropriate exception handling when dealing with transaction processing.

Build and continuous updates

As the development phase of your project starts, you need to build your final solution, including customization (creating a deployable package), and deploy to a test environment for validation and testing. Building solutions manually every time is time-consuming and is not worth it, especially when there is a simple and easy way to automate this. In large implementation projects, when you have multiple teams working on multiple features, this build automation becomes more critical. In this section, we will go through the automated build and testing process of Dynamics 365 for Finance and Operations.

Automated build

Dynamics 365 for Finance and Operations standardizes the development application life cycle by providing build automation out the box using Azure DevOps. Irrespective of cloud VMs or downloaded VMs for on-premises development environments, you can use the build machine in the cloud Build VM to automate the build and deployment process.

When a Build VM is deployed in developer topology through LCS, it is preconfigured and ready to start a build. You can change the default configuration at any time from the Visual Studio IDE or the Azure DevOps interface. The build machine is also auto-configured with default settings for the build agent, build controller, build process template, and build definition. Tests that are integrated with the build definition are executed after the build is successful. Technically, you can turn your downloaded on-premises VM into a build machine but you have to do all the setup manually.

The following screenshot shows a build definition and configuration that's been deployed on an Azure DevOps account after deploying the build machine:

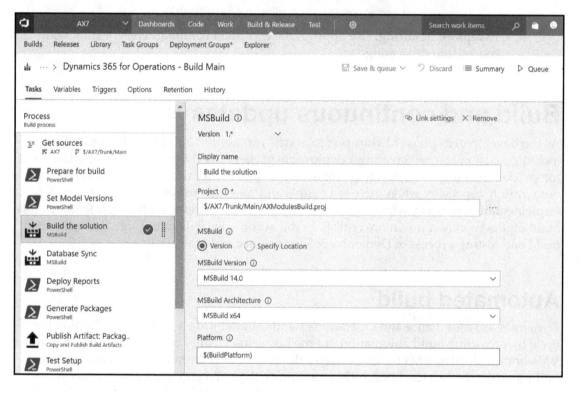

As shown in the preceding screenshot, the default build definition contains all the standard steps that you need to build solutions, including generating deployable packages. You can use this standard build definition to create builds right away or customize them as per your specific needs. Automated build definitions can also discover and execute all unit tests and automated UI tests if you have them.

If you are a customer and using an ISV solution for your implementation project, your ISV will provide their solution model. You can simply add their source code in Azure DevOps source control and the build process will pick up those models and build the final deployable package.

 One build VM can support multiple build definitions for multiple branches, as long as the version of Dynamics 365 for Finance and Operations, Enterprise edition match.

Continuous updates

One of the primary focuses of Microsoft with the release of Dynamics 365 for Finance and Operations is to enable customers to easily uptake the enhancements and fixes Microsoft has done in the product. Customers will now be able to take up to eight service updates per year and are required to take a minimum of two service updates per year. We will learn more about service updates in Chapter 13, *One Version Service Updates*.

Guidelines and best practices

The following are some common guidelines and recommendations for the development process:

- First and foremost, use the extensions model of customization, even if it is possible to overlayer some of the models in the version you are doing your development on. If you have to overlay because extensions are not possible, overlay just to add hooks and keep your business logic in extension classes.
- If you are part of the FastTrack, work with the Microsoft FastTrack team member that has been assigned to your project to raise any bugs or extension points as soon as possible.
- Build a plan to uptake the latest binary and X++ releases in your development cycle.
- Use version control and appropriate branching strategies for the development process.
- Implement a code review process to manage check-ins, and control what needs to be released to the test environment.

- Implement comments during code checking by providing a brief description of the code, the linking feature, or defects to track the changes appropriately.
- Implement the formal release process (cadence of releases, manager approval, and so on) to avoid destabilizing the test environment due to frequent releases.
- Consider scheduled builds, continuous integration, gated check-in, and so on.
- Use automated unit testing and functional testing.

Summary

In this chapter, we started by understanding the architecture and new development concepts. Microsoft is adding more and more features in the IDE to help developers write better and efficient code. X++ has become managed language and fully compiled into CIL, just like C#. Extensions are how you should do any customization. Development is now done in pre-configured VMs, where you can deploy a development environment in the cloud or download a VHD and do development on-premises. Azure DevOps is used for source control and automated builds.

We learned about the development process in operations, starting with conceptualizing the solution, understanding the importance of effective data design, implementing business logic, user interface development, analytics, and reporting. Then, we learned about the common best practices and recommendations for coding in X++. Finally, we learned how to build automation that can be used in the development life cycle, along with the common guidelines and best practices.

In the next chapter, we will learn about analytics, business intelligence, and reporting. We will cover various tools that can be used for analytics and reporting.

10
Analytics, Business Intelligence, and Reporting

In the previous chapter, you learned about customization and extensions in Dynamics 365 for Finance and Operations. In this chapter, we will be covering reporting and analytics in Finance and Operations.

Usually, reporting and **business intelligence** (**BI**) is considered as an afterthought in ERP implementations. However, this is one of the most important outcomes of the project.

Oftentimes, the business asks, *where is my report?*, and the answer that they get is, *data is there...* That's not enough; you need to deliver reports or information in a form that the business can use. It's not uncommon for business leaders to complain, *we are flying blind*, due to the lack of reports or the accuracy of the reports. For a customer, it is important to have real-time visibility of the business for the respective business owners to be able to react quickly in the changing business environment.

Out of the box, the Finance and Operations platform provides multiple reporting solutions to address the various information access needs of an ERP solution. In this chapter, we will be covering the following topics related to reporting and analytics solutions in Dynamics 365 for Finance and Operations:

- Gathering BI and reporting requirements
- BI and reporting scenarios and tools
- Analytics data strategy and integrations
- Moving from relational databases to Azure Data Lake
- Best practices in analytics, business intelligence, and reporting

Gathering reporting and analytics requirements

It is important to start working on reports and the BI stream early on, along with the rest of the functional areas. Most of the time, reporting requirements are not addressed as part of the requirement analysis phase. However, one of the most important goals of a new ERP implementation is to get good real-time visibility into the business.

To start this process, work with the business to compile a list of reports – dashboards, KPIs, and operational reports – that are currently used to run the business. Document their use and the actions that are driven by those reports. Also, spend time learning about the vision of the business leaders and the information that they would like to see, which they don't have currently. A combination of the current and future states will help you define the BI/reporting road map. When gathering and documenting reporting requirements, make sure you ask the business users the following questions so that you can evaluate the needs and be prepared to offer alternative solutions:

- Who's using the report?
    - Be mindful of your customer's needs.
    - Focus on the end user experience. The audience will drive your delivery methods.
- What information is needed?
    - Avoid information overload
    - Find the right balance
- How is this report data used?
    - Categorize reports as operational, business documents, regulatory reports, financial reports, or analytical reports
- What actions are driven by this report?
    - Are you going to explore the data to gain insights?
    - How will the results be shared with others?
    - Is there a fixed document structure for the target output?
- Is this report even necessary in the new system?
- Can we consolidate multiple reports?

As part of the requirement gathering process, collect report samples that are used in the current system, as well as manually generated reports. This will help in mapping out of the box reports and identifying the gaps. All the reports that are identified should be documented and categorized with the report name, the type of report, whether the report is internal or an externally used report, and how the report will be supported in Finance and Operations.

Remember, *no longer needed with the new system* is viable and, often, the preferred solution!

Pay extra attention to mapping each column and formatting external-facing reports, such as invoice templates and customer statement extracts going to banks. Invoice templates may show different information based on the product lines, customers, and so on.

The next step after gathering the reporting requirements is learning how to address these reporting requirements within the Finance and Operations application. In the next section of this chapter, we will deep dive into various reporting scenarios and tools that are available within Finance and Operations that can be used to address various reporting requirements.

Reporting scenarios and tools

Reporting is the process of collecting and summarizing business information to allow users to generate meaningful insights and actions from the data. One of the key premises of the ERP solution is to provide easy access to such information across the module.

In a typical business, the reporting needs of an organization can be categorized in the following categories:

- Operational reporting
- Business/commercial documents
- Regulatory and tax reporting
- Financial reporting
- Analytical reporting

Finance and Operations supports a broad spectrum of reporting and information access tools. Let's dig deeper into these reporting scenarios and discuss reporting and analytics tools within Finance and Operation to support the aforementioned reporting scenarios.

Operational reporting

Operational reporting is basically to gather data from specific products, programs, or services to identify current and immediate operational needs. Typically, operational reports use short-term and near real-time data. In different departments, operational reports serve a different purpose. For example, the finance department uses operations reports to monitor specific financial data, process inefficiencies, and make decisions for the present or immediate future. In manufacturing, operational reports help manufacturing companies to improve production. In retail, operational reports help monitor store efficiency, improve inventory, and monitor employee productivity.

Microsoft Dynamics 365 for Finance and Operations has various ways to get to the operational reporting data. Let's explore some of these tools for operational reporting in Finance and Operations.

Operational workspace

Dynamics 365 for Finance and Operations has introduced a concept called **Workspace**, which is part of the primary navigation mechanism for a targeted persona to support business activities. The operational workspace combines all the relevant information related to the particular business activity in one place and also allows simple tasks to be completed directly in the workspace.

We will see the **Manage customer credit and collections** workspace in Finance and Operations, which is designed for collecting agent persona. This workspace shows various information related to collecting agent personas all in one place. This is comprised of the following:

1. **Tiles**: Tiles in the workspace show important data counters relevant to personas. For example, the **Open cases** tile in the following screenshot shows six open cases related to the collection in the USMF legal entity. To find out the details of the chases, the collection agent can simply click the tile to open the detail form behind it.

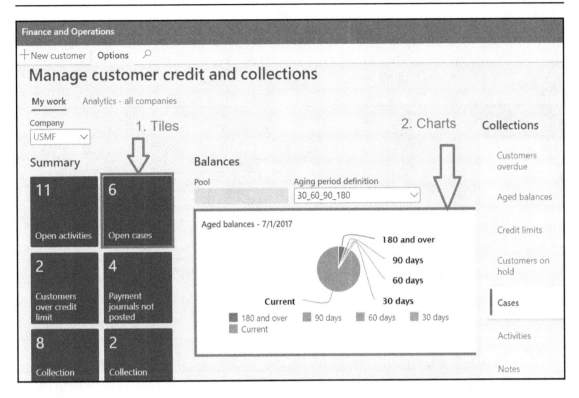

2. **Charts**: The workspace can include charts, as seen in the preceding screenshot, to display snapshots of business activity. As in this case, the preceding screenshot highlights **Aged balances** for the customer.

3. **List**: The list section of the workspace usually shows the important data for the persona to work on in the data grid. As highlighted in the following screenshot, the user can see details of all of the open cases in the list view. There could be multiple lists tabbed vertically in a single workspace:

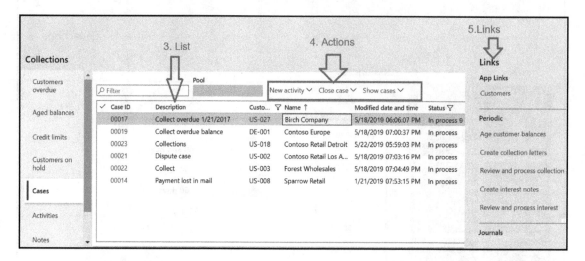

4. **Actions**: A workspace list could provide actionable controls that help maximize efficiency for common user actions directly from the workspace. As shown in the preceding screenshot, the user can take action such as close the case directly from the workspace.

5. **Links**: As highlighted in the preceding screenshot, the workspace can include common forms and reports of direct links related to functionality.

Overall, operational workspaces are built to increase operational efficiency by showing important information related to a business process in one place and provide logical presentations of data to help the user discover patterns, highlight anomalies, and act on the most important tasks. Operational workspaces are not only helpful in providing operational insight but also allow users to take actions to complete their task.

The best part of the workspace is that it can be personalized to a large extent so that it meets the unique requirements of the business process. Using the personalization feature, you can modify existing or create a new workspace, or add tiles, list pages, and links, as per requirements. You can also add Power BI reports and dashboards directly in the workspaces.

You could argue that operational workspaces are more built for operational activities than reporting. However, usually, the next step after getting operational reports is to take action. Operational workspaces combine both operational reporting and actions to make the user more productive.

To summarize, the following are the key advantages and limitations of using operational workspaces:

- The advantages are as follows:
  - Personalization
  - All information in one place
  - Take action directly from the workspace
- The limitations are as follows:
  - Not printer-friendly
  - No automated delivery

Now, we will learn how inquiry pages can be used for operational reporting in Finance and Operations.

Inquiry pages and exporting to Excel

Inquiry pages or list pages are very common and widely used to gather operational reporting data in Finance and Operations. An inquiry page in Finance and Operation presents a set of data on a user interface and lets users search, filter, and sort that data. For further analysis, the user can export the data into Microsoft Excel.

Excel has always been the ultimate choice for viewing data easily and quickly, converting it into information using charts and pivots, making informed decisions, and sharing those decisions with the other stakeholders.

Using the following steps, the user can export list page data to Excel:

1. **Navigate to page**: The user navigates to inquiry pages using the navigation pane or uses the search button at the top to open the form. In the following screenshot, you are seeing this and the next step in Finance and Operations to export inquiry page data to Excel:

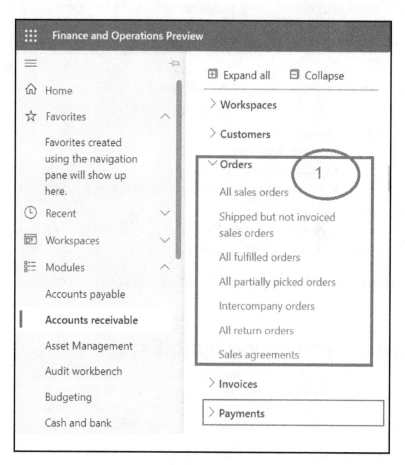

2. **Filter data**: Then, as shown in the preceding screenshot, the user can use the filter pane on the list page to apply the required filters. Let's have a look at the following screenshot:

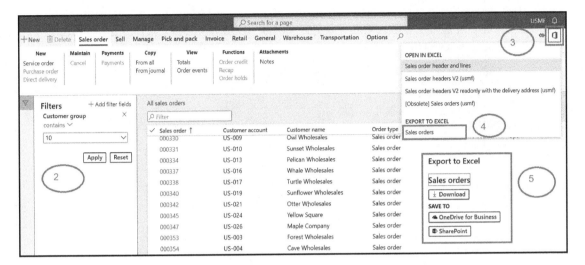

3. **Click on Office icon**: The user then clicks the Office icon.
4. **Export to Excel**: The user selects the entity to export list page data to Excel, as seen in the preceding screenshot.
5. **Download**: After exporting, the user downloads the data to a local machine or exports the data directly to OneDrive for Business or SharePoint Online.

> After platform update 22 (Jan 2019), the **Export to Excel** feature allows users to export up to 1 million rows from a grid in Finance and Operations.

Throughout Finance and Operations, there are many purpose-built inquiry pages in every module covering various operational reporting scenarios. Users can further personalize these pages by rearranging them and adding new or hiding fields.

Using the **Saved view** feature in Finance and Operations, users can create and save multiple optimized views of a page so that it suits the needs of performing a particular business task or operational report.

The following screenshot shows the **Saved view** feature in Finance and Operations, through the use of which a user can create multiple optimized views (**1**) and use them in different business scenarios:

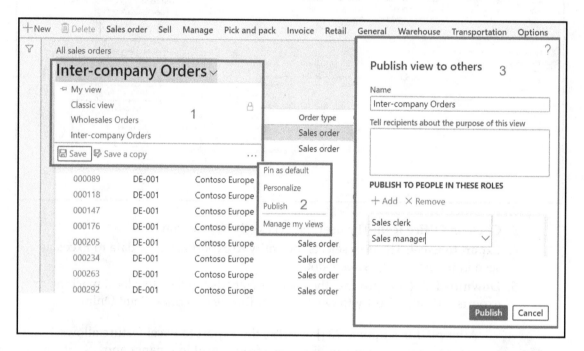

Saved views that have been created by users can also include user-added filters or sorts, which allows users to quickly return to commonly filtered datasets. Further saved views can be published (**2**) to security roles (**3**) to allow access to all the users who have security roles assigned to them.

At the time of writing this book, the **Saved view** feature was in public preview. For the latest details on this feature, make sure that you follow the documentation page at `https://docs.microsoft.com/en-us/ dynamics365/unified-operations/fin-and-ops/get-started/saved- views`.

To summarize inquiry pages for operational reporting, inquiry pages provide easy personalization, filtering, and sorting capabilities, and have the following highlights and limitations:

- Their highlights are as follows:
    - Personalization
    - Easy filtering and sorting
    - Can export to Excel
- Their limitations are as follows:
    - Not printer-friendly
    - No automated delivery
    - No calculations

Now, let's take a look at the printer-friendly **SQL Server Reporting Services** (**SSRS**) reporting option in Dynamics 365 for Finance and Operations.

Operational SSRS reports

The need for reporting in predefined formats and taking document printouts and transactional details is never expected to go out of demand.

Dynamics 365 for Finance and Operations utilizes **SSRS** to deliver many out-of-the-box operational and business document reports.

The following screenshot shows an example SSRS report, **On-hand inventory**, in Finance and Operations:

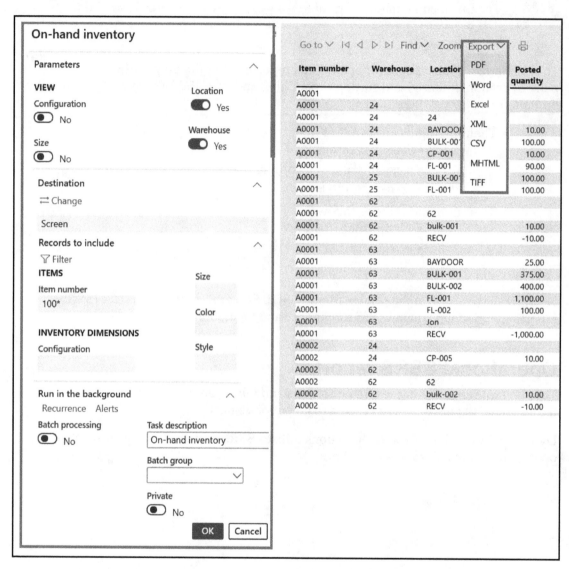

As shown on the left-hand side of the preceding screenshot, SSRS reports have parameterization, filters, and the ability to run in the background using batch processing. On the right-hand side, you can see various output formats that this report can be exported to, including **PDF**, **Excel**, **Word**, **XML**, and many others.

Similar to inquiry pages, there are hundreds of purpose-built operational SSRS reports in each and every module of Finance and Operations. The SSRS reporting framework in Finance and Operations allows users to develop complex calculation logic using the **Document Processing** (**DP**) classes. To summarize, the following are the key advantages and limitations of SSRS reports in Finance and Operations:

- The advantages are as follows:
    - Supports multiple export formats such as PDF, Excel, XML, and TIFF
    - Schedules execution via batch processing and email delivery
    - It can support parameters, filters, and complex calculations
    - Print-friendly precision design
- The limitations are as follows:
    - No personalization support

Now, let's take a look at another reporting medium, Power BI, for Dynamics 365 for Finance and Operations operational reporting.

Analytical workspaces for operational reporting

Dynamics 365 for Finance and Operations delivers interactive reports that are built using Power BI out of the box. These reports are embedded in application workspaces and are called **analytical workspaces**.

Users can interact with data by clicking or touching visuals on the page. They can see cause and effect, and perform simple what-if operations without leaving the workspace.

The following screenshot shows the **Vendor payments** analytical workspace available out of the box in Finance and Operations in the Account payable module:

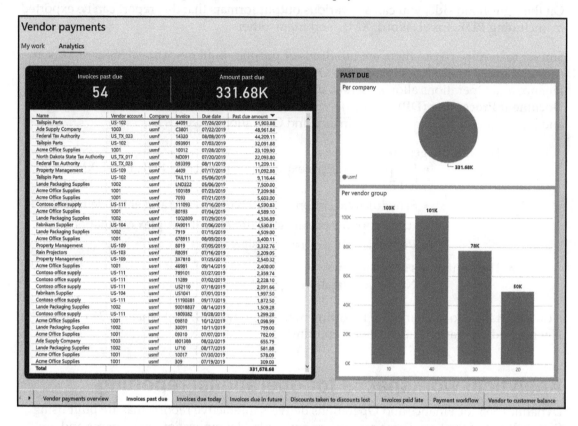

Analytical workspaces such as **Vendor payments**, in this case, provide directly embedded Power BI reports in Finance and Operations. Business users can use stunning, interactive visuals to explore data and discover hidden trends. As shown in the preceding screenshot, the second tab, **Invoices past due**, under the **Vendor payments** workspace, highlights key summary details, such as the total number of invoices and the amount past due. Further tabs such as **Invoices due today** and **Invoices due in future** are providing further detailed analysis on each topic as a separate page.

To summarize, the following are the key advantages and limitations of using analytical workspaces for operational reporting:

- The advantages are as follows:
  - Modern interactive analytical reports
  - Easy to customize by the power user
  - Reports are aware of user contexts such as company, security roles, and many others
  - Ability to drill down to Finance and Operations Forms/List pages from Report visuals
- The limitations are as follows:
  - Not printer-friendly

Power BI is a revolutionary, modern reporting and BI tool that is suitable for day-to-day operational reporting as well as high-level analytical reporting. Dynamics 365 for Finance and Operations' analytical workspaces feature brings the full power of Power BI to users without leaving the Finance and Operations user interface, which is amazing.

In summary, most of the operational reporting needs in Finance and Operations can be satisfied with operational workspaces, inquiry pages, SSRS reports, and analytical workspaces. The choice is based on business requirements and user preferences. Now, let's change our focus from operational reporting to the next reporting need: **regulatory and tax reporting** out of an ERP system.

Regulatory and tax reporting

In every country and industry, businesses have to produce many regulatory and tax reporting documents to serve the local government. Many of these reports are dependent on data from the Operational and Financial data in your ERP system. These reports have a pre-defined layout and format defined by the government agencies and must be delivered in paper or electronic format.

In Microsoft Dynamics 365 for Finance and Operations, such reporting requirements can be handled through a tool called **Electronic Reporting**, also known as **ER**. Using the ER, you can configure document formats for both incoming and outgoing electronic documents in accordance with the legal requirements of various countries/regions. Microsoft delivers and supports hundreds of such electronic documents, all of which are applicable to various countries out of the box. Microsoft also maintains and ships updated configurations as regulations and requirements change from government agencies.

A customer or partner can use ER tools to override any existing electronic documents or can create a completely new configuration. ER tools provide extensive functionality to manage the complete life cycle, including designing, versioning, and publishing an electronic document. The great thing about the ER is that its all configuration instead of code and that makes the processes of creating and adjusting formats for electronic documents faster and easier.

Let's now explore the ER tool in more detail.

Exploring ER

ER is a tool that's used to configure electronic document formats in accordance with the legal requirements of various countries/regions. This engine supports statutory/country-specific electronic documents, enabling you to manage these formats during their life cycle.

ER has the following salient features:

- It is a good tool for producing Excel, CSV, TXT, XML, and Open XML worksheet formats.
- It is designed for business users familiar with Excel-based formulas.
- It easily adheres to changes in regulatory requirements.
- Versioning is available to manage the definition life cycle.

Other applications of electronic reporting include the following:

- Financial auditing
- Tax reporting/GST/VAT
- Electronic invoicing

The following is a summarized list of ER configurations that are available in Microsoft Dynamics 365 for Finance and Operations:

- **Government compliance**: XBRL reporting and others
- **Tax authorities**: Tax reporting, revenue/turnover, and more
- **Banks**: Payments, receipts, trade reporting, and more
- **Localization through Global Tax Engine** (**GTE**): Delivered via a taxable document model, which is a key input to the tax engine and leverages various taxable document types and tax documents

For the latest information on the various offerings of ER, we recommend that you go to https://docs.microsoft.com/en-us/dynamics365/ operations/dev-itpro/analytics/general-electronic-reporting. This capability is sometimes referred to as **Global Electronic Reporting (GER)**.

In summary, the ER tool solved many country-specific incoming and outgoing electronic documents needs out of the box. As the regulations change, Microsoft delivers updated configuration through **Lifecycle Services** (**LCS**), which can be downloaded in the Finance and Operations application and used. Customers and partners can extend the existing configuration and build new configurations to support customer/project unique requirements. ER reporting is configuration-based, which makes it super easy for the power user or business analyst to create new configurations without any code development. The configuration that's created by customers and partners can be uploaded to the LCS asset library and can be used in Finance and Operations applications.

Next, let's look at operational reporting business and commercial documents. Business documents are the most critical reports for any ERP implementation projects as these go out to external parties.

Business/commercial documents

Commercial documents or business documents are written records of commercial transactions, describing various aspects of those transactions. Examples include purchase order confirmation, sales quotes, sales orders confirmations, sales invoices, commercial invoices, shipping documents, transport papers, and certificates of origin. These documents typically need to have the precision layout and must contain certain information for legal and compliance perspectives.

Dynamics 365 Finance and Operations allows the user to generate many such business/commercial documents out of the box through various such tools within the system. Let's explore some of the most common tools that are used to generate business commercial documents in Finance and Operations.

SSRS business documents

Throughout the system, Finance and Operations has many documents available out of the box; for example, Purchase order confirmation, Sales order confirmation, Sales order packing slip, Sales invoice, Intrastat and vendor checks, and many more. These business documents are developed as precision design SSRS reports and optimized for printing on paper as well as in files to ensure high-quality standards.

The following screenshot shows the sales order invoice document that was generated for a sales order in Dynamics 365 Finance and Operations:

Contoso Entertainment System USA
123 Coffee Street
Suite 300
Redmond, WA 98052
USA

Telephone		123-456-1234
Fax		456-444-1234

Contoso Europe
Bahnhofstrasse 5
79539 Berlin
DEU

Giro
Tax registration number   1234123400

Invoice

Number	CIV-000117
Invoice date	5/16/2015
Page	1 of 1
Date and time	11/15/2019 12:57 PM
Sales order	000118
Requisition	
Your reference	
Our reference	
Payment	Net 10 days
Invoice account	DE-001
Payment reference	

Contact

Packing duty license number

Item number	Description	Quantity	Unit	Unit price	Discount percent	Discount	Amount	Print code
D0001	Mid-Range Speaker	143.00	ea	330.00	0	0.00	47,190.00	
L0001	Mid-Range Speaker 2	114.00	ea	308.00	0	0.00	35,112.00	
P0001	Acoustic Foam panel	2,377.00	ea	27.50	0	0.00	65,367.50	
D0003	Standard Speaker	133.00	ea	198.00	0	0.00	26,334.00	
D0004	High End Speaker	114.00	ea	1,210.00	0	0.00	137,940.00	

This text is from the Sales Order Invoice form notes

Sales subtotal amount	Total discount	Total charges	Net amount	Sales tax	Round-off	Total
311,943.50	0.00	0.00	311,943.50	0.00	0.00	311,943.50 USD

Due date   5/26/2015

As shown in the preceding screenshot, the sales order invoice report has a nice layout with a configurable company logo and shows all the information for an invoice document, such as paying attention to address and contact, invoice number, invoice date, payment terms, due date, and line items.

In Finance and Operations, these business documents are tightly integrated with the business processes and print management feature. Utilizing the print management features, you can configure the automatic delivery of these documents to a local printer or send it directly to the business contact via email. As an example, when the sales order invoicing process is executed for a sales order in Finance and Operations, the sales order invoice document can be printed automatically to a local printer or emailed to the customer contact directly.

Similar to any other SSRS reports in Finance and Operations, customers and partners can extend these business document reports to fit their unique requirements by adding additional information or changes in the layout.

Even though business documents delivered out of the box contain comprehensive information and functionality, most of the customers implementing Finance and Operations go through the development process to change the layout of these reports so that they match their corporate standard. To reduce the need for these expensive customizations, in October 2019, Microsoft introduced a new feature called **business document management**. The business document management feature changes the customization of business documents configuration rather than a code change. Now let's learn more about business document management.

Business document management

Business document management is a feature of Finance and Operations that combines the **Electronic Reporting** (ER) framework, Microsoft Office document templates, and print management features to deliver an end-to-end business document customization experience. Business document management enables business users to customize business documents, such as purchase order, and customer invoices, within Finance and Operation applications.

Similar to other ER configurations, Microsoft provides all business document mapping configurations and templates via the LCS. Customers and partners can download base configurations and templates from LCS and use them with print management. Business users can also customize the configuration and layout using Microsoft Office 365 and ER configurations tools.

The **Business document management** feature has a dedicated workspace that's used to manage the life cycle of the business document templates. The following screenshot shows the business document management workspace in action:

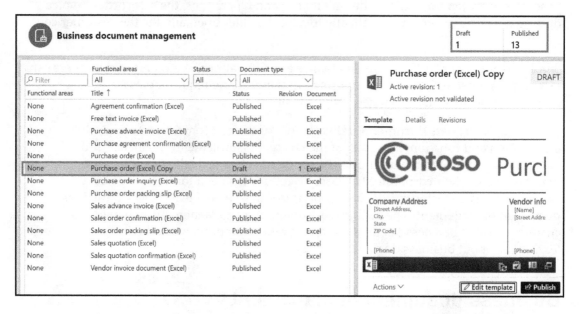

As highlighted in the preceding screenshot, the business user can use the business document management workspace to create a copy of the purchase order template and edit the template directly in Finance and Operations. The following screenshot shows the Office 365 template editing experience within Finance and Operations:

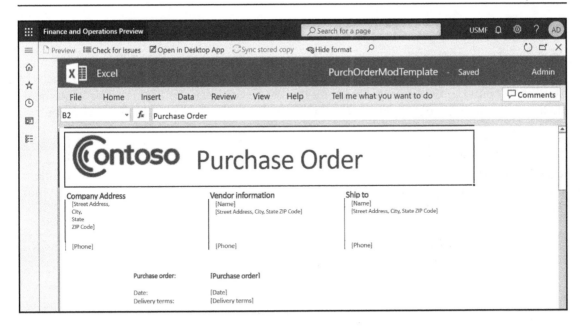

As shown in the preceding screenshot, document template editing is done in a Microsoft Office 365 system such as Excel within Finance and Operations. Using Excel, you can easily swap the logo, change the layout, change the font, color, and much more, and then save the template. Once the template has been finalized, you can publish and configure print management to use it.

In conclusion, we can see that business document management is a powerful feature that can be used to customize business documents without any coding effort.

At the time of writing this book, the business document management feature was newly released and there are tons of enhancements planned for future releases to enable end-to-end business document customization and delivery.

To learn about the latest details and capabilities of this feature, follow the documentation page at https://docs.microsoft.com/en-us/ dynamics365-release-plan/2019wave2/finance-operations-crossapp- capabilities/configurable-business-documents-reporting-word- excel.

So far, we've learned about various options for business/commercial documents in Finance and Operations. Now, let's turn our attention to another reporting need from ERP systems: financial reporting.

Financial reporting

Financial reporting is the financial results of an organization that are released to investors, creditors, or the public. Financial reports provide insights into an organization's financial state at any point in time or at the end of defined financial periods. The financial statement includes a balance sheet, income statement, profit and loss account, cash flow statement, and many other aspects.

Dynamics 365 for Finance and Operations' financial reporting feature can be used to generate a financial report. To jumpstart financial reporting, Microsoft provides multiple default financial reports, which can be modified to suit the business needs of any customer. These modifications are made in a report designer-client:

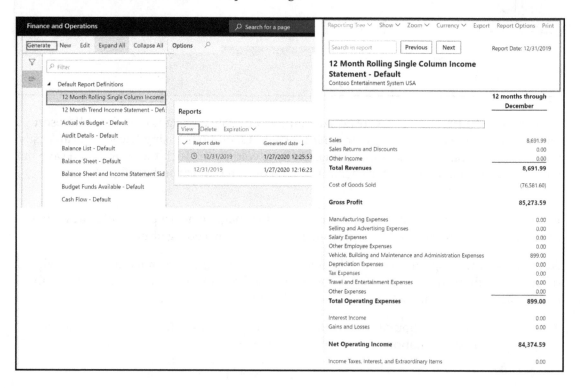

The preceding screenshot is an all-in-one visual showing the **Financial reports** listing on the left, and the actual report output on the right.

The following are the building blocks of financial reporting:

- Row definition
- Column definition
- Reporting tree definition
- Report definition

Let's explore them further.

Row definition

A row definition in the financial reports defines the descriptive lines such as Sales, Income, Cost of Goods Sold, and various expenses, as shown in the following screenshot:

As shown in the preceding screenshot, in the row definition, you can create row codes and descriptions, define calculations and formulas, and suggest the link to Dynamics 365 for Finance and Operations in the outer-most column, on the right. This is similar to creating rows in Excel.

Column definition

As the name suggests, the column definition defines columns in the financial reports. Column definitions are mapped with the financial period to display monthly, quarterly, or yearly data trends. The column definition also allows the user to define column formatting and calculations:

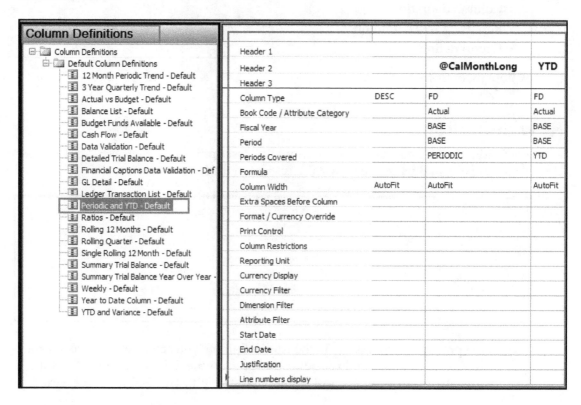

As shown in the preceding screenshot, in the column definition, you can create a number of columns, just like you can in Excel, and suggest the type and date criteria, along with other attributes.

Reporting tree definition

A reporting tree definition helps you create an organizational structure and hierarchy for financial reporting. Each box in the organizational hierarchy is represented as a unit in a reporting tree definition. Each unit can be mapped to the individual departments in Finance and Operations and you can create a summary unit to roll up multiple reporting units. You can create an unlimited number of reporting trees and use them in the report definition.

There are two ways of creating a reporting tree:

- Create one directly in the Report Designer.
- Leverage a read-only organization hierarchy from Dynamics 356 for Finance and Operations:

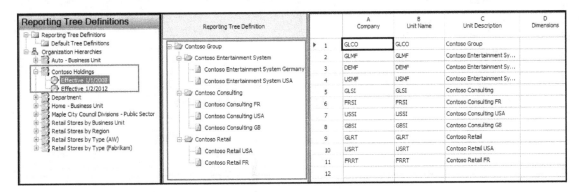

The preceding screenshot shows a reporting tree, wherein you can create a hierarchical listing of companies and units so that you can use them for slicing and dicing your financial information.

Report definition

A report definition is the final building block for financial reporting features in Finance and Operations. You use other building blocks, such as a row definition, a column definition, and a reporting tree definition to build a report definition. It also provides additional options for output and distribution, as well as other settings for defining the headers and footers of the report:

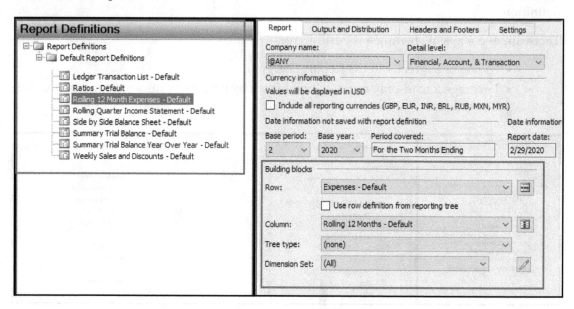

As shown in the preceding screenshot, the report definition is the binder of all the building blocks, bringing together the row definition, column definition, reporting tree, and the various run attributes of your financial information.

We recommend that every initiative involving financial reporting in Microsoft Dynamics 365 for Finance and Operations should leverage the financial reports application available out of the box. These financial reports are closely and natively integrated with Microsoft Dynamics 365 for Finance and Operations. This tool is highly flexible, supports interactive viewing and drill-down capabilities, and is also extremely user-friendly.

 To learn more about all the capabilities of financial reports, please go to
`https://docs.microsoft.com/en-us/dynamics365/finance/general-ledger/financial-reporting-getting-started`.

This covers our topic of operational reporting options in Finance and Operations. Now, let's learn about what's available in Finance and Operations for analytical reporting.

Analytical reporting

Now that we have understood how Finance and Operations accomplishes an organization's various operational, financial, and regulatory reporting scenarios, let's learn about analytical reports.

Analytical reporting is the process of analyzing historical and external data sources to gain insights into the business. It provides information about trends, predictions about future performance, and recommendations. Finance and Operations solves analytical reporting with analytical workspaces and Power BI reports within the application.

We'll discuss analytical Power BI reports next.

Analytical Power BI reports

As we discussed in the *Operational reporting* section, Finance and Operations delivers out-of-the-box interactive reports that are built using Power BI. Many of these reports include historical data and are designed to show historical trends and the overall performance of the department.

The following screenshot shows one of the pages of the CFO Overview Power BI report that's available out of the box in the General ledger module:

There are many such analytical Power BI reports available out of the box in Finance and Operations throughout the modules.

 To get complete list of Power BI reports, please go to `https://docs.microsoft.com/en-us/dynamics365/fin-ops-core/dev-itpro/analytics/power-bi-home-page`.

The best thing about these embedded Power BI reports is that they can be further customized by Power users without leaving Finance and Operations by using the **Edit Analytics** option available on the analytical workspace. Power users can change visualizations, add/remove filters, change the formatting, and add/remove pages or create a completely new report page using existing data. Once the modifications have been made and saved, they are immediately available for other users to consume.

As shown in the following screenshot, by using the **Edit** button under **Options | Power BI**, these out-of-the-box Power BI reports can be edited by Power users to address custom requirements. In addition, if you have developed and deployed reports on the Power BI service, you can replace out-of-the-box reports with your custom reports using the **Select Analytics** option:

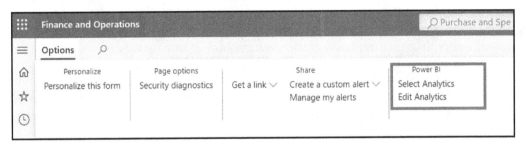

As you can see, Power BI reports within Finance and Operations have powerful edit and replace features that make it easier to modify the out-of-the-box reports so that they suit a customer's specific reporting requirements.

 The Power BI report edit experience in Finance and Operations provides the same edit experience that's available in the Power BI service.

In addition to customizing the existing Power BI reports in analytical workspaces, power users can replace the out-of-the-box reports with custom reports that you have developed and deployed on the Power BI service and shared with members of the organization. This can be useful for enterprise customers who already use Power BI service and have developed reports with a data mashup of Finance and Operations and other systems.

 To learn more about how to select reports that have been published on your own Power BI service, follow the Microsoft documentation at https://docs.microsoft.com/en-us/dynamics365/fin-ops-core/dev-itpro/analytics/select-analytical-workspace.

The Microsoft product team delivers several out-of-the-box analytical workspaces with Power BI reports applications for various business function areas. Customers and partners can further extend these reports or create new ones through code extensions.

For a list of all the available Power BI reports in Finance and Operations, please visit the Microsoft documentation at `https://docs.microsoft.com/en-us/dynamics365/unified-operations/dev-itpro/analytics/analytical-workspaces`.

So far, we've understood various organizations, reporting scenarios and how Finance and Operations deliver on these scenarios. However, often, for many organizations, these reporting scenarios have to combine Finance and Operations data with other external data to show the complete picture. In such scenarios, organizations usually adapt to data warehouse and datamart concepts. In this model, data from various source systems is ingested into a central database or data warehouse and then specialized datamart models are created to serve the final data for presentation and consumption. In the next section, we'll learn how Finance and Operations enables data integration to support datamart and data warehouse concepts.

Analytics data strategy and data integrations

For many customers, all the data that is needed for analytical and operational reporting often comes from multiple systems. Furthermore, data from various source systems needs to be mashed up before reporting and insights can be generated out of it. To enable such scenarios, customers can export Finance and Operations data and then utilize the full Azure Data Platform to unlock advanced analytical scenarios.

In this section, we are going to look at various data integration options within Finance and Operations that meet analytical and reporting requirements.

Using the Entity store

The Entity store is a feature in Finance and Operations that lets an administrator stage aggregate measurement (star schema modeled in Finance and Operations metadata) in a dedicated data store for reporting and analytics. Out of the box, the Power BI reports and analytical workspaces that are available in Finance and Operations use the Entity store.

The following diagram shows the high-level architecture of the Entity store data integration process within Finance and Operations:

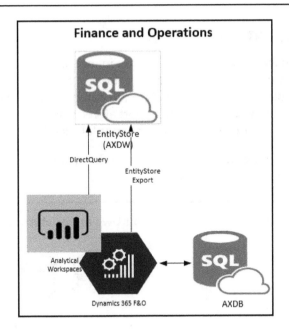

As shown in the preceding diagram, when the administrator configures the Entity store, the data gets loaded into an Azure SQL database commonly known as **AXDW**. The AXDW database is provisioned within a Microsoft subscription. The **EntityStore** database is optimized for analytics by taking advantage of the in-memory, **non-clustered column store index** (**NCCI**) technology. Power BI reports in Finance and Operations use **DirectQuery**, which means the Power BI service does not cache data; instead, it directly pulls data from the Entity store.

Despite some advantages that an Azure SQL database provides for Power BI reports, there are some disadvantages of this Entity Store, as follows:

- The Entity store database is only accessible through Power BI reports, which means you cannot bring any external data into it.
- Data exports to an Entity store SQL database only support full export mode, which can take a long time to export for large datasets.

As we mentioned earlier, for many customers, ERP data is not enough, and they must merge data from other sources before they can generate Operational and Analytical reporting. Also, many enterprise customers already use data warehousing and datamart solutions and they must bring Finance and Operations data into their existing data warehouse. In such scenarios, the Finance and Operations b**ring your own database** (**BYOD**) feature is a more suitable option than the Entity store. Let's take a look at the BYOD feature in detail.

Bring your own database

Bring your own database (BYOD) is a feature in Finance and Operations that lets administrators configure their own Azure SQL database, and then export one or more data entities that are available in the application into the database. The BYOD feature uses the **Data Import/Export Framework** (DIXF) to export all records (**full push**) or only those records that have changed or been deleted (**incremental push**).

The following diagram shows this concept at a high level and how BYOD can be used in enterprise-grade data warehouse scenarios:

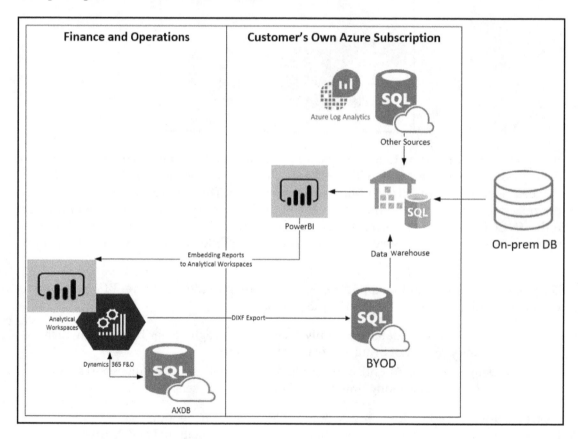

As shown in the preceding diagram, the BYOD feature lets you export incremental data in your own Azure SQL database. Customers can further integrate BYOD data into their own enterprise data warehouse solution, along with other data sources, including on-premise data, and then build Power BI reports. These Power BI reports can be deployed to the Power BI service and then embedded back into Finance and Operations analytical workspaces or consumed directly using the Power BI service.

The important thing to note here is that the Entity store stage aggregates measurements, and with BYOD, you can export data entities. There are thousands of data entities out of the box in Finance and Operations that you can use to perform exports. In many scenarios, out of the box, data entities do not cover every reporting and analytical scenario, so you may have to develop custom data entities to fill the gaps.

 To learn more about the BYOD, go to the official Microsoft documentation at `https://docs.microsoft.com/en-us/dynamics365/fin-ops-core/dev-itpro/analytics/export-entities-to-your-own-database`.

For large enterprise customers, the BYOD feature solves many key scenarios, some of which are as follows:

- Scheduled incremental data exported to your own Azure SQL database.
- You can bring external data into the BYOD database and use it for BI and reporting.
- BYOD data can also be used for third-party integration or integration with your existing data warehouse system.

Despite these advantages, the following are some key challenges with BYOD:

- BYOD uses the Finance and Operations batch framework for schedule and export data and when you have lots of data entities to export, this puts an extra load on your transactional system.
- You have to manage and monitor BYOD export jobs.
- You have to pay for the Azure SQL database in order to have storage and compute. This can become expensive as the size of the database grows. In addition, if you're exporting high-volume transactional tables on a frequent basis, you might have to provide a higher compute database tier.

So, what are the alternatives? In the next section, we'll explore how Microsoft is moving the relational databases on the Entity store and BYOD to Azure Data Lake.

Moving from relational databases to Azure Data Lake

Relational databases such as the Azure SQL database are designed for transactional workloads and optimized for **Online transactional processing** (**OLTP**) workloads, while data warehouse or **Online Analytical Processing** (**OLAP**) systems are optimized for reporting and analytics. Data in the data warehouse is cleaned, enriched, and transformed so that it can act as a **single source of truth** that users can trust. A modern data warehouse architecture suggests bringing all your structured and unstructured data into a Data Lake and cleansing, enriching, and transforming data before loading it into your data warehouse.

 The following documentation, from the Microsoft documentation site, provides details about the modern data warehouse architecture: `https://azure.microsoft.com/en-us/solutions/architecture/modern-data-warehouse/`.

The Dynamics 365 product team is working toward enabling this modern data warehouse concept for Finance and Operations application by integrating Finance and Operations data in Azure Data Lake. But before we start discovering Finance and Operations integration with Data Lake, let's learn about some basic technologies in Azure data that are used to support end-to-end scenarios.

Learning about fundamental Azure data technologies

In the last several years, Microsoft has invested a lot in building and improving Azure technologies to enable a modern data warehouse architecture in the Azure cloud. Let's learn about some of these technologies to understand the overall picture.

Azure Data Lake Storage Gen2 (ADLS)

Azure Data Lake Storage Gen2 or **ADLS** is an object storage unit that provides the foundation for building enterprise Data Lake on Azure. ADLS is designed to store massive amounts of data for a very low cost and optimized for copy or data transformations to handle analytical workloads. The following screenshot shows Azure Data Lake Storage Gen2 in the Azure portal:

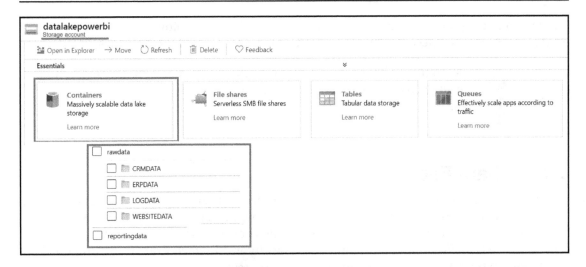

As highlighted in the preceding screenshot, ADLS is a storage account where data can be organized into containers, folders, and files. To learn about the key capabilities of ADLS, follow the Microsoft documentation page at `https://docs.microsoft.com/en-us/azure/storage/blobs/data-lake-storage-introduction`.

Common data model folder (CDM folder)

A common data model folder or CDM folder is a folder in a Data Lake that contains a `model.json` file. This `model.json` file describes the schema and location of the data. Since the `model.json` file follows a well-defined schema, it facilitates metadata discovery and interoperability across applications.

The following screenshot shows an example CDM folder stored in Azure Data Lake Storage:

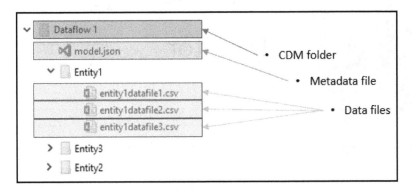

As shown in the preceding screenshot, **Dataflow 1** is the CDM folder as it contains a `model.json` file that describes the shape/schema and location of the data files.

 To learn more about the CDM folder, follow the Microsoft documentation page at `https://docs.microsoft.com/en-us/common-data-model/data-lake`.

Azure Data Factory

Azure Data Factory is a cloud data integration service that can be used to construct code-free ETL pipelines using its intuitive visual environment. Azure Data Factory has pre-built connectors that are used to ingest data from various on-premises and cloud data sources. Using Azure Data Factory, you can build complex hybrid **Extract, Transform, and Load** (**ETL**) and **Extract, Load, and Transform** (**ELT**) processes.

The following diagram summarizes the high-level capabilities of Azure Data Factory:

Ingest	• Multi-cloud copy data • On-premises copy data • Serverless and autoscale
Control Flow	• Code-free data pipelines • Loops, branches, conditional execution
Data Flow	• Code-free data execution in Spark • Designer for data engineer and data analyst
Schedule	• Build and maintain operational schedule • Wall clock, event-based, tumbling windows
Monitor	• View active executions and history • Setup alerts

To learn more about this, follow the Azure Data Factory documentation page at `https://docs.microsoft.com/en-us/azure/data-factory/introduction`.

Azure Synapse analytics and SQL On-Demand

Formally known as SQL DW, Azure Synapse Analytics brings together enterprise data warehousing and big data analytics. Azure synapse analytics combines data integration, machine learning, and Power BI into one suite to provide a complete end-to-end analytics experience.

The following diagram shows the Azure Synapse Analytics service at a high level:

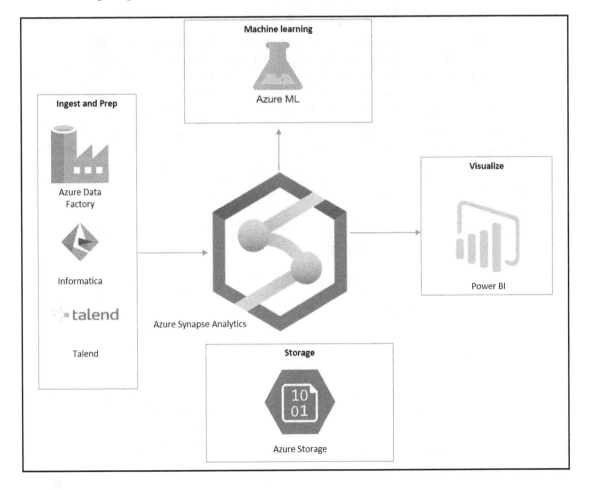

SQL On-Demand is a serverless capability within Azure Synapse Analytics that provides analytics directly over the Data Lake without creating a copy or duplicating the data. You can simply use the familiar T-SQL query data stored in Azure Data Lake.

To learn more about Azure Synapse Analytics, follow the official documentation page at `https://docs.microsoft.com/en-us/azure/sql-data-warehouse/sql-data-warehouse-overview-what-is`.

Now that we have learned the basics of Azure Data technologies, let's turn our attention back on Finance and Operations and discover how these technologies can be used with Finance and Operations.

Entity store in Azure Data Lake

To bring the Finance and Operations data to the modern data warehouse architecture, Finance and Operations has introduced a new feature that allows us to move the Entity store that was previously in the Azure SQL database to a customer's own Azure Data Lake. Setting up Entity store integration with Azure Data Lake is a simple one-time setup that can be done under **System parameters**, as shown in the following screenshot:

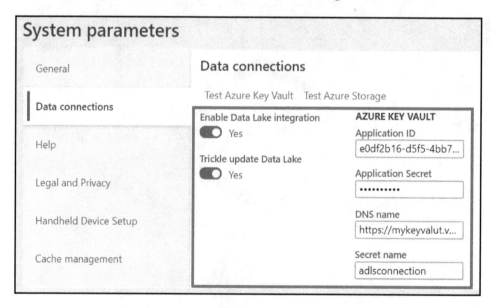

Once this feature has been enabled, aggregate measurements are staged in Azure Data Lake in CDM folder format. The Azure Data Lake integration feature also supports incremental exports, which means data in Azure Data Lake can be frequently updated.

As shown in the following diagram, you can use the Azure Factory to bring other external data sources into Azure Data Lake, perform cleansing, transformation, and machine learning, and load data into Azure Synapse Analytics. From there on, you can build Power BI reports and embed them back into Finance and Operations analytical workspaces or consume them using the Power BI service:

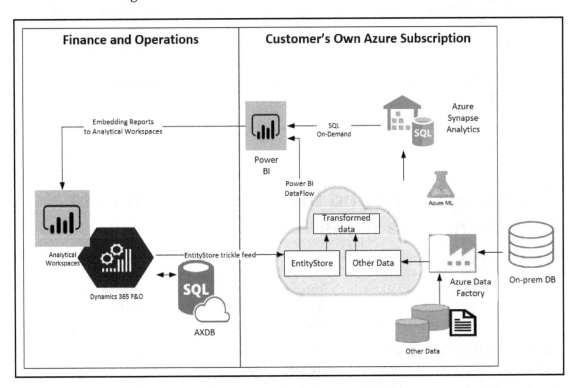

For customers who do not have the need to use the full stack of Azure Synapse Analytics, they can simply use Power BI Dataflow to connect to the Entity store CDM folder or use the SQL On-Demand feature to build Power BI reports.

At the time of writing this book, the Entity store in Azure Data Lake and Azure Synapse SQL On-Demand features were both in public preview. For the latest information, please follow the Microsoft documentation page at `https://docs.microsoft.com/en-us/dynamics365/fin-ops-core/dev-itpro/data-entities/entity-store-data-lake`.

The Entity store in Azure Data Lake is a good model; however, it still has the following shortcomings:

- The Entity Store feature only exports aggregate measurement data in Azure Data Lake.
- Creating and modifying aggregate measurements or start schemas is a development effort in Finance and Operation.
- To integrate data entities with a data warehouse, BYOD technology has to be used.

Now let's deep dive into a part of the future roadmap (at the time of writing) that Microsoft has announced.

Replacing BYOD and the Entity store in Data Lake using data feeds

To fully leverage the continuous investment of Microsoft Azure data technologies and to enable a modern data warehouse architecture, Microsoft plans to replace the BYOD and Entity store in Azure Data Lake with a feature called data feeds. The data feeds feature allows administrators to configure Finance and Operations tables so that they can be published in an Azure Data Lake in the CDM folder format.

As shown in the following diagram, the data feeds service keeps the Finance and Operations table data in sync in the Azure Data Lake. Further data entities and aggregate measurements can be modeled within the Azure Data Lake. This model will eliminate the need for exporting the BYOD database and the Entity store and will provide greater flexibility for customers to define complete enterprise data warehouses and big data analytics using Azure Data Factory, Azure ML, and Azure Synapse Analytics:

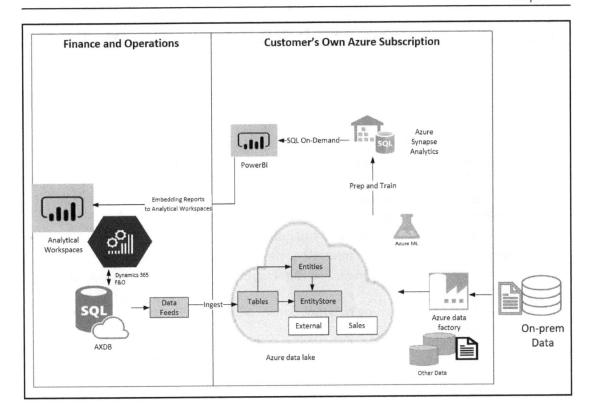

The Dynamics 365 Customer engagement application is also publishing their entities data into Azure Data Lake, which enables not only customers but Microsoft and ISV partners to build advanced analytics solutions on top of Azure Data Lake to unlock complete insights from sales, product supply chains, and finance in one place.

The data feeds service provides data in Azure Data Lake and has the ability to query the data using SQL On-Demand. This not only enables reporting and analytics, but also enables additional scenarios such as third-party integration directly using data from Azure Data Lake.

 At the time of writing, the data feeds and entities and the Entity store in Azure Data Lake were under development and have been planned to be put into public preview in April 2020. For the latest details, follow the Microsoft documentation links that have been provided throughout this chapter.

To conclude this chapter, let's look at some best practices related to analytics and information insights.

Best practices in analytics and information insights

Based on our experience, we would like to share the following best practices in this area:

- Analytics is a journey and not a destination. You have to keep on optimizing and evolving the existing methods of seeking, consuming, and acting upon data.
- It's going to be rare to find just one solution to all your information needs. Therefore, you must choose from the best-of-breed choices.
- Leverage financial reporting or management reporting for all kinds of financial insights for an enterprise.
- Leverage Excel for all one-time and quick end user-based reporting.
- Leverage Power BI for all interactive visualizations and dashboards.
- Leverage SSRS for printing all your documents and for day-to-day operational needs.
- Leverage Azure Machine Learning for all information actions and predictions using algorithms.

The world of analytics is fascinating, with a number of choices and reasons that may confuse you. Hence, due diligence in selecting the right platform, tool, and fitment is crucial when it comes to informed decision making.

Summary

In this chapter, we started by understanding the basics of gathering the BI and reporting requirements. We explored various reporting scenarios and features, such as operational reporting, financial reporting, and regulatory and tax reporting. We discovered various tools that are available out of the box in Dynamics 365 for Finance and Operations to solve these reporting scenarios. With additional capabilities delivered from modern reports, ER, and financial or management reporting, it becomes a full-suite analytics tool to make information available on time and in the medium of your choice.

We learned how Finance and Operations enables Power BI integration with the Entity store and BYOD as well as future investments from Microsoft to enable enterprise data warehouse and big data analytics integration with Azure Data Lake. With the data feeds service, Finance and Operations will be able to push raw table data into Azure Data Lake that can then be cleansed, enriched, and transformed using the Microsoft Azure Data platform for reporting using Power BI.

Analytics, as a subject, is evolving much faster than any other area; hence, we recommend that you always leverage tools and services offered by Microsoft rather than building them as this increases their agility and accuracy.

In the next chapter, we will focus on another important topic in ERP: go-live and post go-live.

11
Testing and Training

Quality, budget, and scope are the fundamental constraints on every **enterprise resource planning (ERP)**/critical initiative. Most of the time, when the scope is increased and the budget stays the same, the quality is compromised. One of the biggest mistakes that people end up making is that they reduce the testing and training budget when there is budget pressure.

In many post-release, postmortem meetings, you hear, *If I was to do this again, I would spend a hundred thousand dollars more on testing.* You have the opportunity to do it right and not regret it later.

In this chapter, we will cover the following areas of testing, in order to learn and leverage it effectively:

- The importance of testing
- Types of testing
- Automated testing strategies
- Test planning guidelines and recommendations
- Training
- Planning and execution training
- Change management

Similar to testing, training is another key aspect for the successful implementation of an ERP system. Ensuring that the users are comfortable with the new platform, and that they understand the new business processes and their role in the organization, is essential for attaining a good working platform. Many times in ERP implementation, users are not only dealing with system change, but also with a process change. Training needs to be delivered to support this cultural shift.

The process of unlearning old practices and learning new ways of doing things may take several iterations. Hence, training and the evaluation of adopting the learning from that training are very essential. We will discuss the following important aspects of training in this chapter:

- The importance of training
- Training and the help system in Finance and Operations
- Planning and executing training

While discussing this topic of testing and training, our focus will *not* be on generic areas; we will talk about them at a higher level, and focus on **Microsoft Dynamics 365 for Finance and Operations**.

The importance of testing

Testing is the process of validating the system and processes in order to meet business requirements. It includes testing the custom as well as the standard features, along with the migrated data, integrations, reports, and security aspects of the solution. It is an area that is most often underestimated and, as a result, hampers the success of your project.

A very common misconception is that testing starts after the development phase is over. The primary goal of testing is to provide feedback on the product as soon as possible. Identifying any issues in the requirements phase prevents them from becoming a part of the design. Similarly, identifying any issues in the design phase prevents them from being coded. The cost of fixing a defect depends on the phase where it has been detected; the cost of fixing a defect in the early phases of the **Software Development Life Cycle** (**SDLC**) is much lower than in the later phases. The farther you go with the backlog of testing/validation, the more debt you carry in the project. Mostly, such a debt gets unmanageable, and it becomes difficult to predict/commit to the schedule.

The majority of the ERP implementation projects fail because of improper test planning and testing. To understand the importance of ERP testing, it is important to understand the different types of testing that are typically performed in ERP implementation projects.

Types of testing

ERP implementation projects require different types of testing during the testing phase of the project. Each type represents a different objective, scope, and depth of testing.

The following diagram highlights the different types of testing in a typical implementation project:

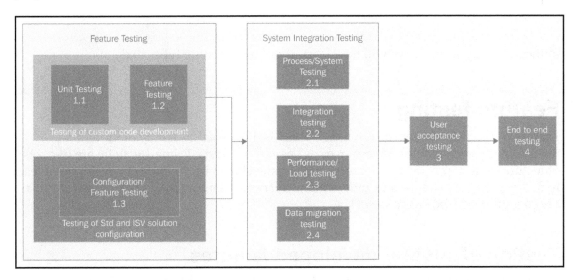

As shown in the diagram, we can categorize testing into four main categories: **Feature Testing**, **System Integration Testing**, **User acceptance testing**, and **End to end testing** (or cut-over testing).

For different types of testing, you may need different kinds of environments. Here are some of the various environment options:

Environment type	Tier	Testing options
Build	1	**Regression Suite Automation Tool** (**RSAT**) and automated system test
Test	2 or 3	Functional testing, training, **system integration test** (**SIT**), **user acceptance test** (**UAT**)
Production	Subscription provided	-
Development	1	Unit testing
Pre-production	1 or 2	Data migration/golden configuration
Performance testing	4 or 5	High-end volume, load and performance test

For more details visit the following documentation page at `https://docs.` `microsoft.com/en-us/dynamics365/fin-ops-core/fin-ops/imp-` `lifecycle/environment-planning`.

In the following sections, we will now learn about these testing types in detail.

Feature testing

Feature testing, also known as function testing, is the *standalone testing* of individual features performed by the QA resources or business analysts. Primarily, there are two sets of features to test here: custom features that are developed by the project development team to fill the gaps, and standard or **independent software vendor** (**ISV**) solution features that are configured by the business analyst.

Testing of custom-developed features

Testing of custom features by the project team involves unit testing, which is standalone testing of code artifacts, and is usually performed by the developers in order to ensure that individual code elements are working as expected. In software engineering terms, unit testing typically refers to automated testing. It provides many benefits, including finding bugs earlier, providing a safety net of tests for changes that are made later, and improving design. In the long term, unit testing improves customer satisfaction and developer productivity.

Along with the unit testing, individual custom features need to be configured and tested in order to ensure that these custom features work according to requirements.

Testing of standard and ISV solution features

While the development team is carrying out custom feature development, business analysts are usually busy working on collecting configuration and master data, and setting up the standard solution, as per the requirements. The second part of feature testing is about testing the standard and ISV product features. This includes configuration such as parameters, reference data, workflows, security, and master data, and then testing transactions such as sales orders, purchase orders, production orders, and journal entries.

System integration testing

After feature testing, the next part is to test the various subprocesses and processes together. By this time, the core configuration has already been done, some level of data migration has also been done, key custom features have been developed, and various systems and solutions are integrated. There are various parts of **SIT**, and they usually get tested in parallel. The subsequent sections are dedicated to the testing categories that typically fall under system integration testing.

Process/system testing

Process, or system testing, involves testing subprocesses and processes. In this phase, typically all major processes are tested with system configuration and master data. Depending on the implementation scope and requirements, the testing team will test processes such as record to report, order to cash, procure to pay, and plan to produce. The objective of this testing cycle is to identify the correct configuration of parameters, missing master or reference data, and any additional bugs or potential gaps.

For a simple business process example, consider the testing of the *order-to-cash*, process beginning with a single order transacted through its entire cycle. The process starts with the creation of a sales order, picking and shipping the product, and then invoicing the order. Along the way, the system updates the inventory and accounting. Finally, payment is collected from the customer, the payments are applied, and the customer balance is updated within the accounts receivable module.

As you can see, the complete cycle for a major business process may include many steps and touch various modules. During this testing, you will discover missing configurations and setups, as well as code issues.

Data migration testing

Whether you are replacing the old legacy system, or upgrading from the previous version, the business will need legacy data to be migrated to the new system. Data migration testing is basically testing the data integrity and data quality. No matter how you decided to migrate the data, the testing team needs to analyze the migrated data, and then perform validation and transactions at the end of the data migration to ensure that the migrated data is complete and accurate, in order to carry out future transactions. For example, if open sales orders are migrated from the legacy system, you need to ensure that you are able to ship and invoice these orders and ultimately, collect the cash.

You also need to ensure that numbers such as order count, account balance, and inventory levels match between the legacy system and new system in order to make the migration complete and accurate. A solid data migration strategy should also define the parameters for the success of data migration testing.

Integration testing

Testing the integrations with other systems that have been developed is just as important as the features and functional testing of the product itself. Integration testing is performed across applications in order to verify the seamless flow of information. All individual applications must be tested independently and made ready for integration testing. You will need an integrated environment across applications to perform this testing. For example, Finance and Operations requires integration with the CRM system; in this testing process, you will probably create customers in the CRM system, and you will expect them to flow to Finance and Operations.

Next, you will probably test the creation and inventory of products in Finance and Operations, and ensure that it flows back into the CRM system, so that the salespeople can sell it to the customers. Finally, you will create quotes in the CRM system and you will expect to get sales order created, shipped, invoiced, and payment collected in **Microsoft Dynamics 365 for Finance and Operations** (**D365FO**).

Performance/load testing

Performance testing or load testing is a process of identifying performance issues and then solving them. It is important to conduct performance and load testing and tuning before going live, in order to eliminate the issues that can negatively impact the business. It does not matter whether you have high volumes or not; you still need performance testing. At this stage of the project, the development of custom features is complete, and functional testing is in progress. This is the time to validate the overall performance of your Finance and Operations system. The primary goal is to ensure that the solution will accept peak load without any major issues.

The key objective of this exercise is to establish a baseline for the key business scenarios, and to test and execute performance tuning and optimization to achieve the following:

- Creating a baseline of your core business scenarios.
- Simulating users and transactions in terms of concurrency and volume, and determining the load that the system can handle
- Executing performance tuning and optimization

In the end, we have to validate all the preceding considerations and ensure that the system is ready for production. It is imperative to try to accurately identify the volume of transactions, as they relate to the new system. Use the legacy system as a base starting point, and estimate the transactions in the new system by taking into consideration how transactions are generated on the new platform.

User acceptance testing

UAT usually starts when the system integration testing is almost complete, and a minimal amount of viable product is ready. The goal of UAT is to engage the users across business groups, using the new system to run the business. This is also an opportunity to provide them with hands-on experience for learning the new system. The more testing that the users perform, the more comfortable they will be with using the new system. Unlike other types of testing that are done by experienced application consultants and testing teams, UAT is done by actual business users, and hence, planning and execution of UAT is very critical. The *Test-planning guidelines and recommendations* section of this chapter covers UAT planning and execution in detail.

End-to-end testing

In addition to UAT, you will need another round of testing to verify the end-to-end execution of a business process; this is called end-to-end testing. The key difference between UAT and end-to-end testing is that UAT is more focused on validating individual business processes, while end-to-end is focused on validating all of them together, once each of them has been stabilized and tested.

Continuous update testing

In addition to various other tests, due to the monthly cadence of updates coming from Microsoft in One Version; it is recommended that organizations have an update validation test plan and resources to execute before an update every month. Microsoft provides tools such as **RSAT** to facilitate in conducting these release validations in an automated way.

In the next section, we will cover automated testing in detail, including the use of RSAT.

Automated testing strategies

ERP systems are complex, and it is not always easy to test these systems. In order to conduct robust testing, you need the testing staff to not only know the system, but also to know the business process. Manual ERP testing consumes a lot of implementation time and budget. Test automation helps to improve the quality of the product, and reduces the cost and time spent on the process.

Here are the advantages of ERP test automation:

- First and foremost, the main advantage of an automated testing tool is reduced testing time, and as you all know, *time is money*.
- Automation removes human error from the equation, which means more reliability and accuracy of test results.
- Automated testing makes it easier to uptake future updates, bug fixes, and enhancements, as you can test and be confident that your core business processes will not break with the new enhancements in the product.

Going through the advantages, you will say that automation is best; so why do you even need manual testing? But, it is not as rosy as it sounds. Testing automation, especially for an ERP system, is not an easy task. It is complex and requires experienced staff, time, and hence, money to write an automation script. You will also need to carry out continuous maintenance of test scripts as and when changes are introduced to the features.

Automated testing has clear benefits, but it is important to find the right balance as to what processes or features you should automate, and what is not important. It is also important to consider the type of framework that your ERP system has available for test automation, and how easy it is to write these automation scripts.

Test automation features in Finance and Operations

Compared to the earlier version of Dynamics AX, Microsoft Dynamics 365 for Finance and Operations has taken a major leap in providing several automated test capabilities as part of the product.

The following diagram shows two concepts that are related to automated testing: various test cycles, targets, and the corresponding tools that are available in Finance and Operations for automation; and the reduction of automation test counts as you move up the pyramid:

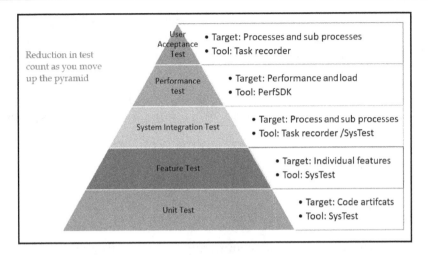

As illustrated, different testing phases (left-hand side) have different targets and tools for automation testing (right-hand side). Overall, the following are the key tools/concepts:

- **RSAT**
- **Acceptance Test Library (ATL)**
- **Data task automation (DTA)**
- SysTest framework
- Task recorder-based testing
- PerfSDK

Let's look at these tools and concepts in detail as we go further.

RSAT

Microsoft Dynamics 365 for Finance and Operations is covered by Microsoft's Modern Lifecycle Policy, which covers products and services that are serviced and supported continuously.

Microsoft will continually update the Platform and Financial Reporting components with the option to postpone up to two consecutive service updates.

With continuous, touchless service updates in **D365FO**, it maintains backward compatibility, which means there is no need to *merge your code*. However, the need to test all extensions, as well as out-of-the-box existing and new functionality, is critical in order to continuously evolve your cloud ERP.

After an update is completed in a particular environment, you need to run all business processes to test and validate the update. Hence, the need for continuous testing, and to support this effort, a no-code automation test tool for business process testing is available – RSAT.

RSAT allows us to record business tasks using the D365FO task recorder and convert them into a suite of automated tests. All this can be done without writing any code. RSAT is available for use from PU15, and beyond.

RSAT prerequisites

This section covers the installation and configuration of the RSAT tool in order to achieve touchless continuous service updates of your D365FO One Version.

The following steps share insights into configuring RSAT and its related components in order for it to be used for continuous testing:

1. Ensure the right project template is chosen in the **Lifecycle Services** (**LCS**) project, which comes from your DevOps project:

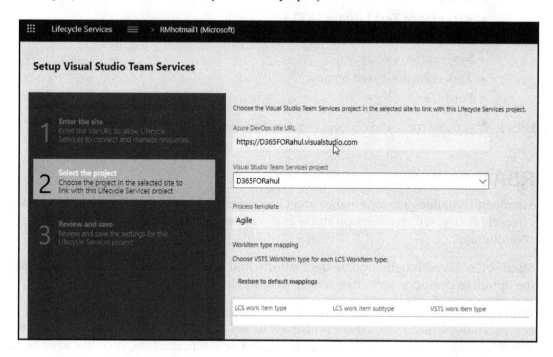

2. Ensure that your LCS project has the **Business Process Modeler** (**BPM**) library, and that it is in sync with **Visual Studio Team System** (VSTS).

3. Next, we use the D365FO task recorder and generate an AXTR file.

4. Next, we either need to save directly to the BPM library from your D365FO task recorder, or manually upload:

    1. In LCS, in your project, on the BPM business process libraries page, select the library to upload the task that you are recording to.

    2. Click **Author** and edit in the lines, and then locate and select the process to upload the task recording to. In the right pane, click **Upload**:

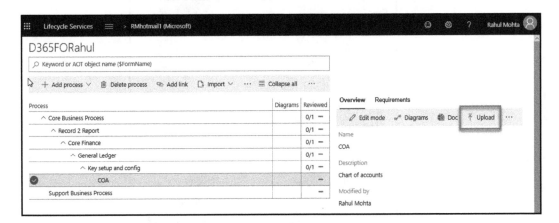

 Note: Ensure that there is at least one validation in your test.

5. When this step is complete, your task recordings will become test cases in Azure DevOps and a link will appear under the **Requirements** tab:

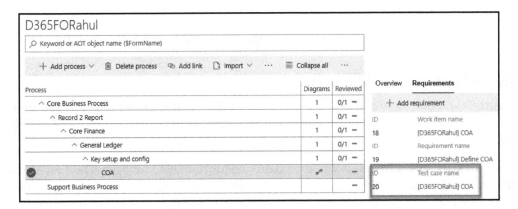

6. Synchronize your BPM library with your Azure DevOps project:

- On the **Business process libraries** page, on the tile for the library that you want to synchronize, select the ellipsis button (…), and then select **Azure DevOps sync**:

 Ensure first that the VSTS sync is enabled, and then sync up the test cases as well.

This covers the setup that is needed in LCS BPM, and ensures that test cases using task recorder are created.

In the next section, we will cover the DevOps Test Manager and RSAT configuration.

Azure DevOps Test Manager

Azure Test Manager is one of the initial prerequisites that we need to get us started on the RSAT tool, which can be done by enabling test features in your in Azure DevOps/VSTS project.

You can start with a free trial, or buy a paid one for the Test Manager. The Test Manager tool is free, but you do need Azure DevOps Test Manager subscription licenses – one per user – to be able to use it.

One of the ways that we are looking at in this chapter is to get a trial license for 30 days to start testing from the DevOps marketplace. For this, you need to sign in to your DevOps account.

 Follow this link to find and get the Test Manager: `https://marketplace.visualstudio.com/azuredevops`.

As shown in the visual here, select the **Test Manager** tool in order to install it:

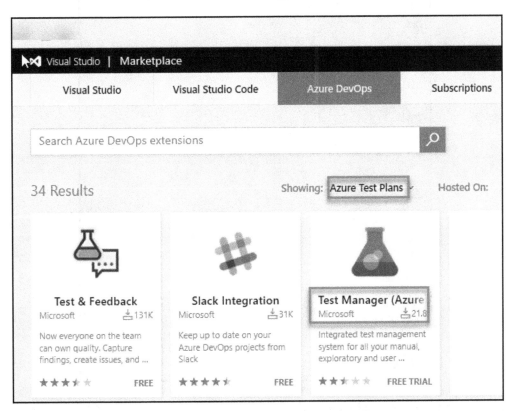

Once the tool has been added to your subscription, configure it using the following instructions:

1. Select your organization to install this extension.
2. After your extension finishes installing, go to your organization to use your extension.

Refer to the following link for more information: `https://docs.`
`microsoft.com/en-us/azure/devops/organizations/billing/try-`
`additional-features-vs?view=azure-devops`

Verify that the following test options are seen, which means that your DevOps project now has test features enabled:

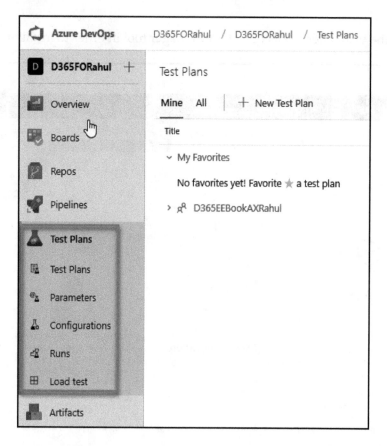

Next, we need to create a test suite in Azure DevOps and add your test cases from the LCS BPM library.

Create a test plan and test suite in Azure DevOps by following these steps:

1. On the toolbar, select **Test | Test Plans**.
2. In the left pane, select **+**, and then select the **Static** suite.

3. Enter a name for the suite and click on **Add existing**:

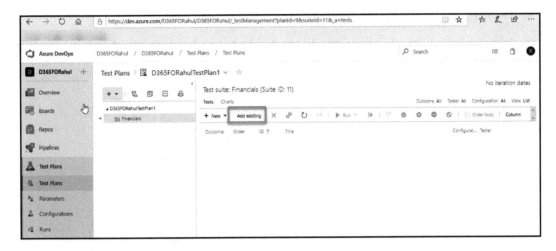

4. Click **Add existing** and query the **LCS:TestCases** tag:

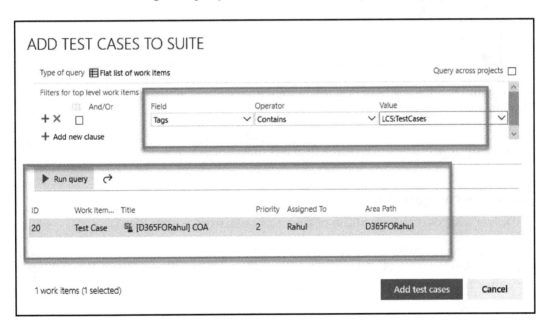

5. Select the test case in order to view the details and the attached XML file.

Here are the test case details from DevOps with steps:

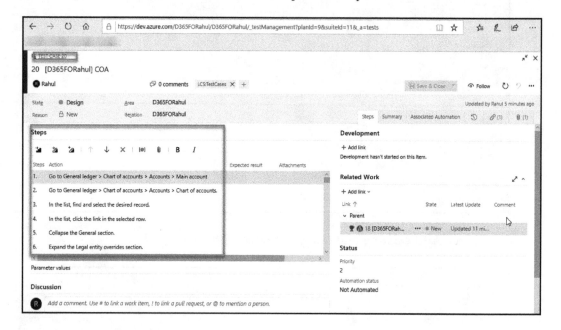

Once your DevOps test plan and test suite with test cases are ready, it is now time to download, install, and configure RSAT.

Provide your DevOps URL, access token, test plan, hostname (D365FO URL), hostname SOAP URL and admin user (O365), and test the connection.

Windows configuration

Now, we will cover the execution of such test cases from within RSAT.

We need to leverage the user manual for RSAT in order to complete RSAT installation and configuration, which includes installing a certificate, getting a thumbprint, installing Selenium for your type of browser, and many others:

1. Download latest RSAT from `https://www.microsoft.com/en-us/download/details.aspx?id=57357`. At the time of writing, the latest version is 1.200.42264.6.

RSAT has to execute as a local admin on the client machine (by design) where RSAT is installed, typically on the AOS box if multi-tiered, and in a single tier on the common box.

It is a requirement of the security model that is used for authentication.

2. Get the Windows 10 SDK from `https://developer.microsoft.com/en-US/windows/downloads/windows-10-sdk`. Install the following components:
   - Windows SDK Signing Tools for Desktop Apps.
   - Windows SDK for UWP Managed Apps.

   The following visual shows two features that you need to select to be able to install the necessary tools from the Windows 10 SDK:

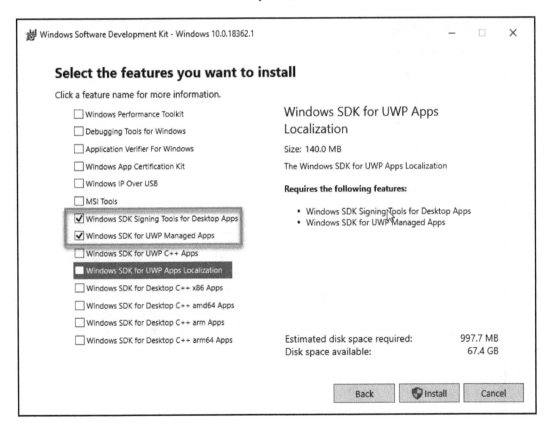

It is important to have a certificate generated on the same computer that the test tool is running on.

3. Generate a certificate file, open a command-line window as the administrator, and run the following command from the command window. When you are prompted to enter a private key password, enter None. Create a C:\Temp folder if it does not already exist on your computer:

```
C:\Program Files (x86)\Windows
Kits\10\bin\10.0.18362.0\x64\makecert.exe -n "CN=127.0.0.1" -ss My
-sr LocalMachine -a sha256 -len 2048 -cy end -r -eku
1.3.6.1.5.5.7.3.1 c:\temp\authCert.cer
```

The following screenshot shows the prompt to import the certificate:

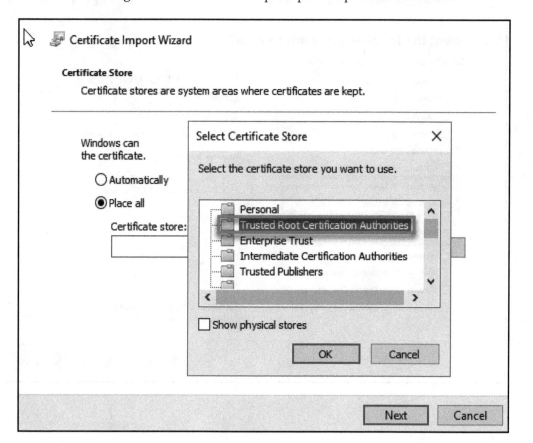

After the certificate has been successfully installed, in the **Details** tab, copy the thumbprint and take out the special characters.

4. Add **Thumbprint** to your WIF configuration file with only one command (using the open source tool or manually).

    As shown in the following visual, the **Thumbprint** information is in the **authCert** file:

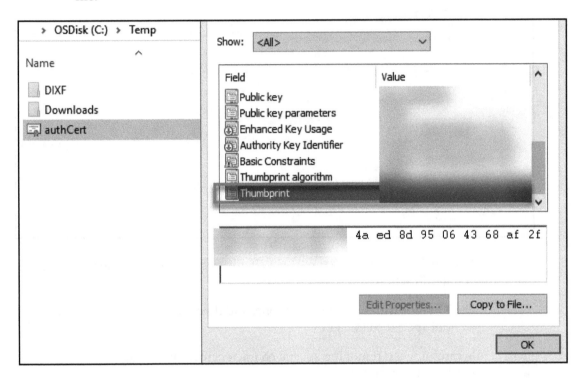

The link to download tool is `https://github.com/d365collaborative/d365fo.tools/blob/development/docs/Initialize-D365RsatCertificate.md`.

5. Next, we will make changes to the AOS configuration settings. Ensure that the `wif.config` in the AOS service in the **Internet Information Server** (IIS) looks like this:

```
wif.config
   1    <?xml version="1.0"?>
   2    <system.identityModel>
   3      <identityConfiguration>
   4        <securityTokenHandlers>
   5          <securityTokenHandlerConfiguration>
   6            <audienceUris>
   7              <!-- WARNING: MUST be first element; updated at web role instance startup -->
   8              <add value="                                        " />
   9            </audienceUris>
  10            <issuerNameRegistry type="Microsoft.Dynamics.AX.Security.SharedUtility.AxIssuerNameRegistry, Microsoft.Dynamics.AX.Security.SharedUtility">
  11              <authority name="CN=127.0.0.1">
  12                <keys>
  13                  <add thumbprint="                              " />
  14                </keys>
  15                <validIssuers>
  16                  <add name="CN=127.0.0.1" />
  17                </validIssuers>
  18              </authority>
  19              <authority name="CN=CsuClient">
  20                <keys>
  21                  <add thumbprint="                            " />
  22                </keys>
  23                <validIssuers>
  24                  <add name="CN=CsuClient" />
  25                </validIssuers>
  26              </authority>
  27              <authority name="CN=DaxRunnerTokenUser">
  28                <keys>
  29                  <add thumbprint="                            " />
  30                </keys>
  31                <validIssuers>
  32                  <add name="CN=DaxRunnerTokenUser" />
  33                </validIssuers>
  34              </authority>
  35              <authority name="CN=LocatorServiceClient">
```

After making changes to the AOS WIF file, restart IIS to be able to see the updates in action.

The **Thumbprint** is an important one, and if needed, type it in manually without special characters.

Be careful when removing special characters including spaces and then copying the thumbprint.

RSAT and Selenium

Ensure that Selenium is installed and configured as per the manuals provided in RSAT:

1. Download Selenium 3.13.1 (`http://docs.seleniumhq.org/download/`) | **Previous Releases** (the top-left corner) | **3.13** and then download the `selenium-dotnet-strongnamed-3.13.1.zip` ZIP file.

2. Install the Selenium libraries with the following steps:
    1. Unzip the downloaded file.
    2. Unpack the
       `dist\Selenium.WebDriver.StrongNamed.3.13.1.nupkg` file (to
       unpack this file, add the `.zip` suffix to the file and unzip it).
    3. Copy the contents of the
       `Selenium.WebDriver.StrongNamed.3.13.1.nupkg\lib` folder to
       `C:\Program Files (x86)\Regression Suite Automation`
       `Tool\Common\External\Selenium`.
    4. Download the Internet Explorer driver version 3.4.0, go back into the
       browser, open the `3.4` folder, and download
       `IEDriverServer_x64_3.4.0.zip`.
    5. You will get an error on execution if this file is not copied during the
       running/execution of RSAT:

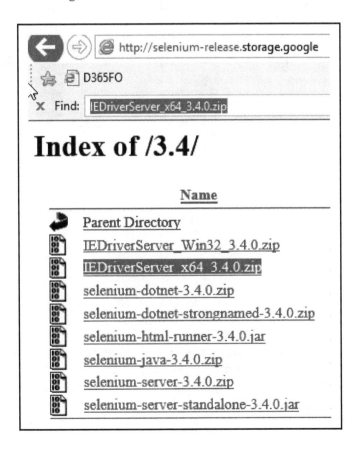

3. Unzip the downloaded file and move the `IEDriverServer` file to `C:\Program Files (x86)\Regression Suite Automation Tool\Common\External\Selenium`.

RSAT configuration

Follow these steps to configure RSAT to connect to your D365FO environment:

1. Provide an admin username – this needs to be the email address of the admin user who deployed D365FO on LCS, and thereby is admin in D365FO, as well.

   Here is a visual of RSAT configured with your LCS project, DevOps, and D365FO instance:

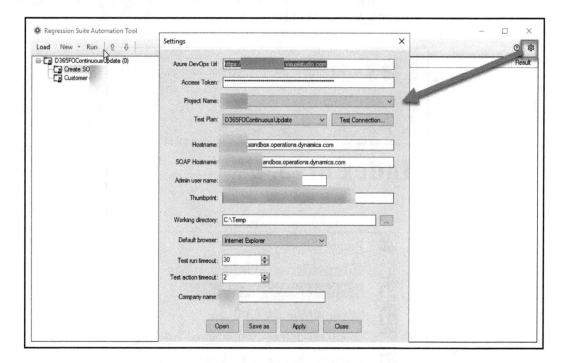

2. Provide your DevOps URL, **Access Token**, **Test Plan**, **Hostname** (D365FO URL), hostname SOAP URL, admin user (O365), and test connection.
3. Note that the files are generated when the **New** button is clicked with option – execution, and parameters:

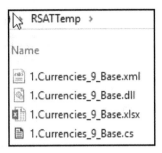

RSAT test case execution

Once the parameters and execution files are ready, you can run/execute the test. Use the **Run** button in the RSAT tool to initiate an execution. Here is a visual of a configured RSAT tool that is ready to initiate a test run:

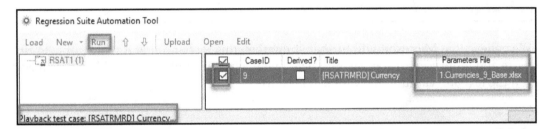

Upon the running of the test, RSAT will initiate a new **Internet Explorer** (**IE**) browser session, and using Selenium, would carry out the test as per the steps in the task recorder and the values in the parameter file:

Note the test result as **Passed** or **Failed** in RSAT:

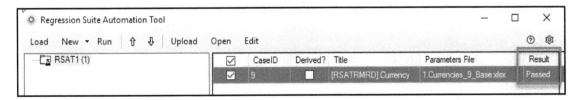

Also, you can see the test execution details in DevOps as follows:

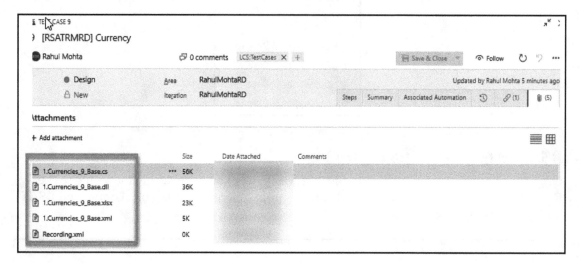

We believe that Microsoft will further strengthen this tool and that it will be able to run more and more scenarios in an automated way, with the ability to provide a data feed to run the text and capture the results in DevOps.

Acceptance Test Library

Acceptance Test Library (ATL) is used for validation testing in Microsoft Dynamics 365 Finance and Operations One version. It has been available since May 2019 in PU26, application version 10.0.2.

So, are you wondering how to leverage classes that are used internally by Microsoft to test the code? This is it. You can skip UI and directly debug the code – ATL is the tool. ATL is suggested to be best used for data setup testing, as well as for validation testing of integration and components. In some scenarios, it could be used for unit tests.

Let's now explore what this library offers us, and how we benefit:

- It lets you create consistent test data.
- It increases the readability of test code.
- It provides improved discoverability of the methods that are used to create test data.
- It hides the complexity of setting up prerequisites.
- It supports the high performance of test cases.

The internal mechanics need to be decoded in order to break the classes that are used:

- Navigation: Discover entities and test data methods in a familiar hierarchy.
- Test data methods: These methods are used to set up test data.
- Entities: Represent data and associated behavior that is perceived as a single unit.
- Creators: Allow you to create specific test data by providing fluent **application programming interfaces** (**APIs**).
- Commands: Run business operations.
- Queries: Find entities.
- Specifications: Describe the entities that are expected at the end of the test.

So, if you are keen to make a test repeatable without going through several regressions, then ATL is the way to go.

Here is a list of references you can refer to:

- `https://docs.microsoft.com/en-gb/dynamics365/unified-operations/dev-itpro/perf-test/acceptance-test-library`
- `https://community.dynamics.com/365/financeandoperations/b/mfp/archive/2019/04/10/acceptance-test-library-the-introduction`

Data task automation

Data task automation (**DTA**) in Microsoft Dynamics 365 for Finance and Operations lets you easily repeat many types of data tasks, and then validate the outcome of each task.

Data task automation is very useful for projects in the implementation phase, in order to automate the creation and configuration of data projects.

We can configure and trigger the execution of import/export operations, such as the setup of demo data and golden configuration data, and other tasks that are related to data migration.

It can also create automated testing of data entities by using task outcome validation.

 For further reference, you can visit the documentation at `https://docs.microsoft.com/en-us/dynamics365/unified-operations/dev-itpro/data-entities/data-task-automation`

SysTest framework

SysTest framework is the unit test framework in Microsoft Dynamics 365 for Finance and Operations. SysTest framework was available in the earlier version as well, and it provides developers with the ability to write unit test code for the business logic. The following improvements have been made to SysTest framework in D365FO:

- Integration with the Visual Studio Test Explorer to discover, schedule, execute test cases, and analyze test results.
- Automatic data rollback for SysTest tests, and the use of SQL savepoint transaction.
- Capturing exceptions properly (for asserts), regardless of the transaction scope.
- Ability to integrate an automated test with version control and build processes.
- Simplified scope of testing when using the extension programming model, as your business logic is separated.
- Ability to discover the existing tests for an object in your project; discovery uses cross-reference data and displays the result in the test explorer.

 The automated testing integration with build is of utmost importance, especially in large enterprise engagements.

The next screenshot shows a sample test class with two test methods that are related to business logic in Finance and Operations:

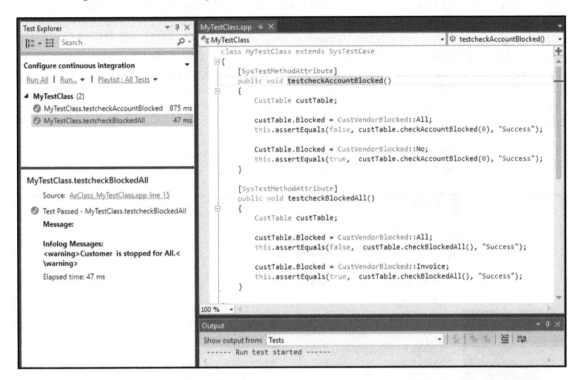

As shown, the right-hand side shows the test class and test scripts. To create a test class, you simply add a class object, extend the `SysTestCase` class, and add test cases by creating a method and decorating it with `[SysTestMethodAttribute]`. To the left, you can see Visual Studio Test Explorer, which discovers the test cases automatically. You can select one test case to run, or run them all.

Task recorder-based (Coded UI) testing

Task recorder-based test automation is new in Microsoft Dynamics 365 for Finance and Operations. This is basically coded UI testing. Using task recorder, you can record a business process as you perform it, using the browser client. After the recording is complete, you can play it back, create a Word document, or download and attach it to your BPM library as a task guide. You can also download a developer recording and import the recording file (.xml) into Visual Studio in order to create an X++ test. The task recorder import tool translates any recording gestures, validations, or tasks into the appropriate test code.

The following screenshot shows how developers can import task recording into Visual Studio and generate automated test code:

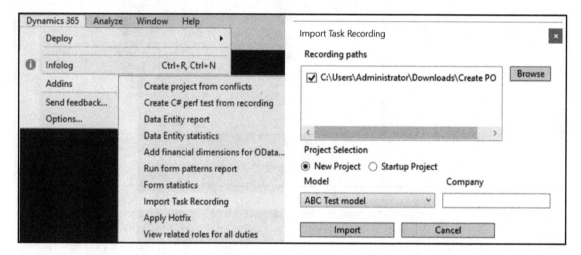

As shown, the **Import Task Recording** menu is available under **Dynamics 365 | Addins | Import Task Recording**. In the **Import Task Recording** dialog, browse to the task recorder file, select your test model, and click on **Import** to create the automated test code.

The following screenshot shows the test code that is created by the import utility, after a task recording has been imported in order to create a purchase order in Finance and Operations:

```
Create_PO.xpp*  ╨  ×
  Create_PO                                                                                                        ▼
    [SysTestCaseDataDependencyAttribute("USMF"),SysCodeGenAttribute()]
    class Create_PO extends SysTestCase
  ={  protected PurchTableFormAdaptor PurchTableForm;
       protected PurchCreateOrderFormAdaptor PurchCreateOrderForm;
       protected FormAdaptor PurchTable_OrderAccount_LookupForm;
       protected str PurchCreateOrder_groupDeliveryAddress_DeliveryName;

       [SysCodeGenAttribute(),SysTestMethodAttribute()]
       public void testMethod()
       {
           using (var c = ClientContext::create())
           {
               using (var c1 = c.navigate(menuItemDisplayStr(purchtablelistpage),formStr(PurchTable),Microsoft.Dynamics.TestTools.Dispatcher.MenuItemType::Display))
               { PurchTableForm = c1.form();
                   using (var c2 = c1.action("SystemDefinedNewButton_Click"))
                   {
                       PurchTableForm.systemDefinedNewButton().click();//Click New.
                       using (var c3 = c2.attach(formStr(PurchCreateOrder)))
                       {
                           PurchCreateOrderForm = c3.form();
                           using (var c4 = c3.action("PurchTable_OrderAccount_RequestPopup"))
                           {
                               PurchCreateOrderForm.PurchTable_OrderAccount().openLookup();//In the Vendor account field, enter or select a value.
                               using (var c5 = c4.attachPrivate(""))
                               {
                                   PurchTable_OrderAccount_LookupForm = c5.form();
                                   PurchTable_OrderAccount_LookupForm.close();
                               }
                               PurchCreateOrderForm.PurchTable_OrderAccount().openLookup();//In the Vendor account field, enter or select a value.
                               using (var c6 = c4.attachPrivate(""))
                               {
                                   PurchTable_OrderAccount_LookupForm1 = c6.form();
                                   PurchTable_OrderAccount_LookupForm1.getGrid("Grid").selectRecord();//In the list, click the link in the selected row.
                               }
                           }
                           //Validate that the value for Delivery name is 'Contoso Entertainment System USA'.
                           this.assertEquals(PurchCreateOrder_groupDeliveryAddress_DeliveryName,PurchCreateOrderForm.groupDeliveryAddress_DeliveryName().getValue(),
                               "Assertion failed for control groupDeliveryAddress_DeliveryName on form PurchCreateOrder");
                           PurchCreateOrderForm.OK().click();//Click OK.
                       }
                   }
               }
           }
       }
    }
```

As illustrated, the code that is generated by the import utility utilizes X++, providers, and the SysTest unit test framework. The automated code generated by the task guides basically uses the same SysTest framework unit test for data setup, validation, and assertion. In many cases, the automated test script that is generated by task guide is sufficient; however, developers can add more complex logic, such as random data generation, to automate advanced test requirements.

 For more details and a step-by-step guide on how to import a task guide, follow the documentation on the Finance and Operations official documentation page at https://docs.microsoft.com/en-us/dynamics365/operations/dev-itpro/perf-test/testing-validation.

Though SysTest framework is good, it's development and maintenance is more focused on the technical side of code achieving the desired functionality. With the availability of RSAT, we consider it to be a powerful tool in comparison to technical test tools (SysTest/PerfSDK), and is best suited to large implementations.

Let's now learn about other technical test tool, that is, PerfSDK.

PerfSDK

PerfSDK is the performance or load testing tool for Microsoft Dynamics 365 for Finance and Operations. It lets you test and validate all critical business processes for performance in a single user or multiuser test run. You can utilize PerfSDK in your project by adding a new, or modifying the existing, business scenario and simulating load testing. Now, let's get to the key highlights of PerfSDK:

- The PerfSDK toolkit and sample codes are available on the developer VM under `C:\PerfSDK` or `J:\PerfSDK`.
- It uses Visual Studio and Visual Studio Team Services to run load testing.
- Sample code is available to test key scenarios such as distribution, financials, and inventory replenishment and warehousing.
- You can create a task guide for additional scenarios and import task guides in order to create a C# script for performance testing.

For detailed steps on how to set up and run load testing using PerfSDK, follow the tutorial at `https://docs.microsoft.com/en-us/dynamics365/operations/dev-itpro/perf-test/perfsdk-tutorial`.

You will need a Visual Studio Enterprise edition license to run load testing in Visual Studio.

Integrating a test with a build process

After unit tests and the coded UI are developed and checked into source control, you can integrate these tests with an automated build process, so that every time a build runs, these test cases are executed automatically.

The following screenshot shows test automation steps under the default build definition for Microsoft Dynamics 365 for Finance and Operations:

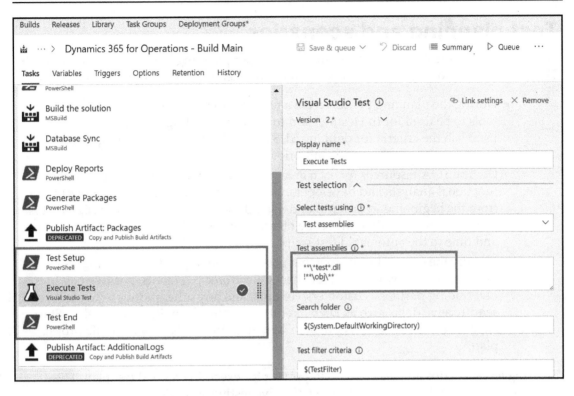

As shown, the build process will find any assemblies that contain the test word and then execute them.

Test-planning guidelines and recommendations

Testing is a big topic, and each testing type requires a special focus in order to achieve the right objective of the test cycle. To achieve success and get the desired result during the testing phase, it's very critical to plan. No matter how good the tools or testing method that you use are, if there is no planning, you will not be able to achieve and measure objectives. In this section, we will cover various test planning guidelines and recommendations during the testing cycle.

Test planning and scenarios

To conduct proper testing, it is important to do proper planning before the test cycle starts. The following are some guidelines to keep in mind when planning for the testing phase:

- During the planning phase, create a test plan to define the scope, resources, and tools to be used for the testing, and to identify how bugs will be tracked. Establish the criteria for defining S1/S2 and P1/P2 bugs, depending on the business criticality (severity and priorities).
- Dedicate QA resources for each area in a way similar to what we do for the functional analysts and developers. You need them to start on the project right from the beginning in order to understand the requirements and design that is being put in place. Plan the scope of automation testing, and dedicate resources and time to the automated test script.
- Identify the external resources that need to be engaged during testing. For example, testing with banks for checks/electronic payments, positive pay files, EDI trading partners, customers/vendors, and any other parties to whom you send/receive data, such as D&B (credit) and third-party invoice printing. Start engaging them as early as possible, and align their schedules into the project plan.

Building test scenarios and test cases is important for executing a good test plan. The following tips will help you in developing effective testing scenarios:

- Prepare test scenarios and test cases that are parallel to the design and development phase of the project. Review test cases with the business analysts and the business SMEs, as applicable.
- The goal should be to identify and document each scenario in detail in the form of test cases, rather than stay at a very high level. If you don't document the test cases, there is a high chance of missing them during the execution.
- Maintain a traceability matrix with the number of requirements, function specifications, technical specifications, test scenarios, and test-case IDs.
- Identify the test data to be used, and the specific deviations in the data, in order to maximize the coverage of your testing. Say, for example, if a company has four product lines and all are sold differently, you will need to have scenarios that address each product line.

User acceptance test (UAT)

There is quite a bit of planning required to perform a successful UAT. Just throwing the business users into a room with computers and test scripts will not get you the results of an effective UAT. Let's look at what goes on during UAT planning and execution under the following headings.

Planning

As we stated earlier, planning is critical to perform successful UAT. During the planning, you are not only required to identify what test cases to execute, but also to list the correct resources and the required training and logistics – such as the UAT environment – to perform testing. The following details should be considered when planning for UAT:

- Providing training to business users before the UAT. Untrained business users will take more time to test, which can result in low confidence in the new system.
- Ensure that the UAT/sandbox environment is ready for the UAT. Data migration should be completed, and the required configuration done and tested. Ensure that business users have the appropriate security roles assigned.
- Plan multiple rounds of testing, scheduled a few weeks apart, to fix issues. It is not uncommon to find a few pieces missing once the business starts looking at the solution. The goal should be to fix everything in between both the cycles so that the business does not experience the same issues, and the test cases are not blocked due to those issues.
- Ensure proper sequencing in the test cases. For example, you start with the data migration validation and then move on to customer/product creation, then to order processing, shipping, invoicing, processing returns, commission reports, financial postings and financial statements, tax reporting, inventory value reports, and so on.
- The people who run the business should be engaged to verify the system; the team should have cross-functional knowledge and knowledge of case scenarios. For example, your top-performing, most brilliant sales talent pool needs to be involved in testing the order entry system. They will know all the different scenarios and *gotchas* from the current system, and they can help you to break the system.

- Avoid relying on the temporary staff for testing; you need **Full-time equivalents** (**FTEs**) to review your new world. Engage the temporary staff in backfilling the FTE jobs to run the day-to-day business tasks, not in reviewing the future of the company.

- Encourage the business to bring in as many real examples as possible. For example, the AP can bring in a day's worth of a stack of invoices for processing, running a check on both the migrated open AP and newly created AP invoices to review the results, and on the real customer orders for order entry. This will help verify credit limits, customers/products, on-hand inventory migration, and the related scenarios.

- Define the process for logging the bugs (record using the task guide or screenshot, provide a reference to the test case, the step that failed, description of the issue being reported, any input file used for uploads, business impact, and so on, for every issue that is being submitted by the users). Users need to be educated on bug-tracking tools and the overall triage process. The more information you have, the less time will be required for the development team to analyze and fix the issues.

- Use a separate environment for UAT testing, rather than the regular testing environment. Limit the number of people having access to this environment; you don't want users creating random transactions and messing up the UAT test scenarios.

UAT kickoff

It is important to set the expectations of testing before starting the UAT. The key messages that should be put across during the UAT kickoff are as follows:

- Finding bugs is the goal of performing UAT. If you find them in UAT, it's a great thing. Don't get frustrated because you've found issues, get stuck in testing.

- Focus on first verifying all the critical business scenarios before getting into exceptional scenarios that won't happen frequently. Follow the 80/20 rule to define focus. This is also a good time to remind everybody about the goals for the project.

- Review the reports from the previous testing and communicate any open areas:
  - Communicate the schedule for testing and retesting.
  - Cover the tools/processes to be used for logging bugs, triage, and communication after fixing the bugs.

- Set the sign-off and exit criteria (communicate upfront that they need to sign off at the end of it). Set the client expectations with regard to the types of bugs that are expected to be fixed versus deferred. If this is not clear, you might struggle to obtain sign off with low-severity bugs open. Usually, severity 1 and 2 bugs must be closed for sign off, while severity 3 and 4 bugs can be postponed or handled post sign-off.

Execution

To achieve results from a good plan, you need to execute the plan well. As explained earlier, you might have to do multiple rounds of UAT testing with the same group in order to ensure that business users are comfortable with the new system, and that any issue found during the testing is addressed. To do so, you have to ensure progress of the UAT execution and that the identified issues are tracked. During the execution of UAT, consider the following points:

- Track the testing progress along with the test cases that passed/failed. Publish reports on progress, bugs reported, and resolved bugs (for retesting).
- Actively manage blocking issues. You need to stay on top of the issues that are blocking the testing of certain areas; try to be creative in finding workarounds to continue testing.
- Issue a triage and managing issue list. Have multiple reviews with the team every day for issue statuses and resolutions. Set daily meetings with the business leaders to discuss issues and provide updates on the progress made. You need to hear their first-hand feedback on the issues that are being experienced.
- Ensure that the formal release process is defined and validations are performed to verify that the release has not broken the environment. This will ensure that precious testing time is not lost due to a broken UAT environment.
- Track dependencies between test cases. You may have a dependency between test cases that will need coordination among the different business groups for testing. For example, when a sales order is created, you need to verify with the warehouse for it to be shipped, and then the AR can see the invoice and collect against it.
- On larger projects with a multilocation roll out, it is a good idea to execute testing at a central location. However, you should also perform some testing locally, especially features that require local resources, such as local printing.

- Poor analysis and design for complex areas will get exposed in UAT and will cause a lot of rework/continuous break-fixing. Identify such critical areas and allocate dedicated resources in order to get extra focus on such critical path items.
- In one of our implementation experiences, a focus team was defined for testing and fixing the revenue recognition and deferral scenarios. It was one of the most complex parts of the project, and was dependent on many other processes, such as correct product and customer setup, order entry with different combinations of products and the way in which the billing frequency was chosen by the customer, order entry and CRM integrations, and invoice distribution and rounding of totals. Every time a scenario was fixed, another was broken in deferrals; issues in the upstream processes, such as order entry, impacted the testing of the deferrals' functionality. The focus group helped to track this subproject with additional visibility, which helped to fix the issues faster.

Sign-off

A successful UAT is one where the business can show that they are comfortable with the application features, and thorough testing has been done with good involvement of the business users across areas. The key deliverable of UAT is the business sign-off on the UAT and test results. There may be cases where items do fail, but the team agrees to a conditional sign-off. Track any bugs that are critical for going live as a part of this conditional sign-off. Most importantly, all areas should have been tested by now. There is a difference between knowing the open issues, and being unable to test specific areas due to open issues.

End-to-end test planning and execution

You need to complete the testing of individual features and all the areas need to be stable to truly start end-to-end testing. In reality, you end up making some exceptions sometimes, but this is not ideal. Pick a selected core group for end-to-end testing. Everyone involved needs to know the end-to-end business flow. Usually, the finance team has a bigger role to play here, as they have a visibility into all the parts of the organization.

Plan for at least two rounds of end-to-end testing, with some time in between to fix the bugs. Define the exit and success criteria prior to getting into end-to-end testing (such as 100 percent test execution, more than a 95 percent pass rate, and no more than five critical bugs open).

Execution and real-life examples

The goal of end-to-end testing is to simulate real business, from data migration to new product and customer creation; using this data for placing orders, fulfillment, invoicing, receiving cash, reverse logistics, transactions using migrated data, to verify reporting, and so on.

Similar to UAT, you need to publish reports on the test results and follow a triage process. Areas that are blocked during testing need to be unblocked and tested again. Assess whether you have met the exit criteria and review it with the executives.

The project team should come up with all the key business scenarios that should be tested. The following are a few examples of the areas on which you should focus during end-to-end testing:

- **Customer invoicing**: The timing and accuracy of invoicing customers is such a critical business function because it has a direct impact on both the customer and on the cash flow of the company. On the other hand, invoicing is a downstream function – you have a dependency on products, customers, tax, fulfillment processes, and so on – which must work correctly before you can produce the invoices.
- **Commission reporting**: As commission reporting has an impact on the paychecks of the sales floor, you need to verify the accuracy of the commission reports with migrated orders and invoices. It should be a top priority, as you want the sales team to trust the system and focus on selling (rather than tracking) their orders on spreadsheets for an expected commission, or worrying whether they'll be paid. Commission reporting can be even trickier for orders shipped in the previous system, and you may have to pay a commission upon receiving customer payments.
- **Inventory costing and valuation**: Each customer has a different way of using a weighted average, **FIFO** (short for **First-In, First-Out**), and other inventory-costing methods. It impacts the profit and loss statement, their bottom line, how executives are compensated, the inventory value on the balance sheet, and so on. Efforts need to be put in during UAT and end-to-end testing in order to validate that the inventory costing is done according to the needs of the company, and that it is understood by the financial controllers and the rest of the stakeholders.

- **General ledger postings**: You need to verify the posting for each type of transaction, and run month-end reconciliation reports (to verify that the general ledger and sub-ledger are in balance).
- **Key reports**: Identify the key reports that are important to run the business, and validate the data based on the transactions that were processed in end-to-end testing.

Engage domain experts during end-to-end testing, such as tax auditors for tax integration testing. They will be able to put together a great test plan and execute it through unique scenarios in order to ensure that you have configured the system correctly.

Once testing areas are well planned, it is highly important to impart sufficient training to users as their daily work life is going to change with the new system. In the next section, we will cover the details of training, tools, preparation, execution, and environment planning.

Training

Training drives the successful adoption of the new system and processes. The learning capacity of the audience and the amount of changes being introduced to them dictate the amount of time you need to spend on training and retraining. The more people you have up to speed on the new processes and system, the smaller are the chances of them making mistakes, and the volume of support calls will be highly reduced. Ultimately, this results in a smoother adoption of the new system.

The ERP project is an opportunity for organizations to get people up to speed on end-to-end processes, and to train them on cross-functional areas. If you have a great system designed but people are not able to use it, can you call it a success?

Training and the help system

The help system in Microsoft Dynamics 365 for Finance and Operations has improved significantly. It is easier to train users on how to use Microsoft Dynamics 365 for Finance and Operations than ever before. Significant investment gone into designing an aesthetic user interface, navigation concepts, and tooling that is related to the help and training system. In this section, we will discover how these concepts and tools help during training.

Modern clients and navigation concepts

Browser-based user interfaces are easier to use when compared to desktop applications. Microsoft Dynamics 365 for Finance and Operations provides a modern browser-based HTML5 client and a mobile application to allow access to application functionality and data.

Listed here are some advantages of browser-based applications, as compared to desktop applications:

- You do not need a client application to be deployed to every user. Users can simply bookmark the application URL and access it at any time.
- Browser-based applications are platform-independent, which means they can be accessed from any device and platform.
- Application usability is rated higher with the browser-based client, as compared to desktop applications.

On the new browser-based client, Microsoft Dynamics 365 for Finance and Operations introduced many new modern navigation concepts that focused on the productivity and usability of the system. The following bullets represent new navigation concepts in Microsoft Dynamics 365 for Finance and Operations:

- **Dashboard**: The dashboard is a new concept, and is the first page that users see when they access the client. The dashboard contains tiles that show workspaces that a user has access to. This removes the clutter, and users do not have to remember the navigation paths for regular activities and can simply click on the dashboard tiles, open the workspace, and start their work.

The following screenshot shows the dashboard for a user with an account role that shows the workspaces that they have access to:

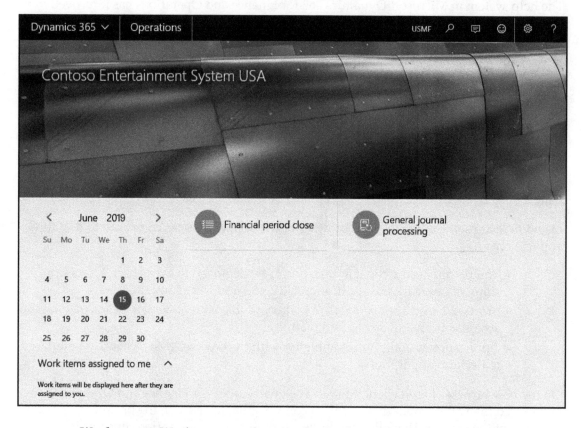

- **Workspaces**: Workspaces represent a business activity or logical group of tasks that a particular business user performs daily. Workspaces are designed for efficiency and productivity. With workspaces, business users do not have to remember different navigation paths in order to perform their tasks. For most users, they can simply be on one workspace and do all their daily work. Workspaces have the following primary goals:
    - To reduce the need for navigation
    - To enable the user to understand the current state of their activities on one screen

- To perform light tasks in the workspaces, and to avoid round trips to deeper pages

- **Form and action search**: Another great new feature added in Finance and Operations, which business users are very happy about, is the search field to find forms, and even the feature of searching for the action buttons on the form. Users simply type the keyword and all the forms containing that keyword will be displayed as a dropdown, from which the user can select the form that they want to open.

  As illustrated in the following screenshot, the search field is available right after the company selection button. For example, users simply type Ledger, and the system displays all the menu options that have **Ledger** in it:

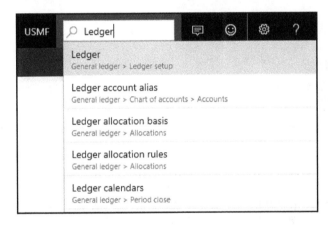

Not only can a user search the menus and open the form, they can also search for the **Action** button on the form if there are too many buttons. Users do not have to remember which tab that button is on; if they simply remember the keyword, they can type it under the **Search** button on the form, and the system will show all the buttons on the form with the keyword.

As shown in the following screenshot, if a user wants to find the **View activities** button on the vendor form, which is under **GENERAL** | Activities | **View activities**, they can simply type the keyword in the search box and get to the button without navigating to tabs and then clicking on the button:

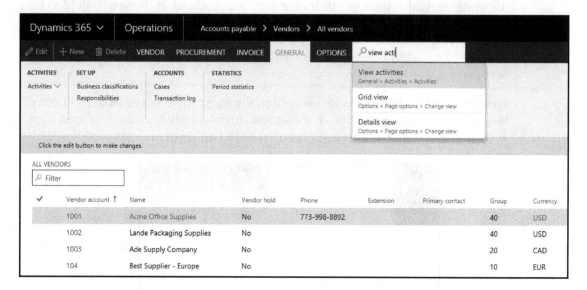

In-product help

Another key feature that will help training go more smoothly is the in-product help system, which is built for new users who are learning the system. The in-product help system pulls articles from the Microsoft Dynamics 365 for Finance and Operations site on `https://docs.microsoft.com`, as well as from task guides that are stored in the **BPM** in **LCS**.

The following screenshot shows the in-product **Help** button that is available on the right corner of the page. A user simply clicks on the **Help** button to access the task guides from the LCS – and articles from the public site – in the context of the user language and the form they are trying to get help on:

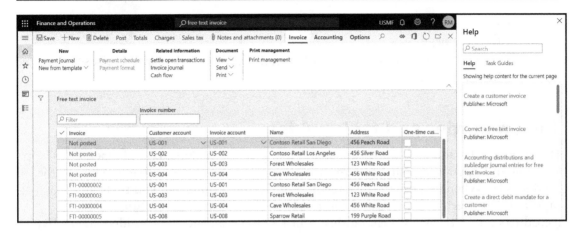

As shown in the screenshot, if the user is new and does not know how to create a free text invoice, they can simply open the free text invoices form and click on **Help**. This will bring up the **Help** pane and show **Task Guides** and **wiki** articles, all of which are related to free text invoices. Users can simply select the task guide that they need to be guided through, or access the knowledge article from the wiki page.

Business process modeler (BPM)

In the LCS, you can use the BPM to create, view, and modify the business-process libraries and flowcharts for Microsoft Dynamics 365 for Finance and Operations. The BPM helps you to align your Finance and Operations processes with industry-standard processes, as described by the **American Productivity and Quality Center** (**APQC**). There are more than 1,000 business processes that are available, and you can tweak them as per your needs. As referenced in the earlier chapters, the BPM can be used right from the Gap/Fit analysis phase of the project to track all customizations, and to add a Visio process diagram, task recording, Word documents, or external links.

The BPM library makes training easier in the following ways:

- Linking one or more BPM libraries in the LCS to your Finance and Operations environment.
- Central repository for business- and system-process documentation.
- Business-process documentation and links can be attached to BPM libraries that are available in the **Help** page.

- Associate task recording and guides with business processes that are available on the help page.
- Convert BPM process flows to Microsoft Word documents, and for use as printed training material.

Task recorder and task guides

The task recorder and task guides are an integral piece of the Finance and Operations help and training experience. Using task recorder, you can record actions that you take in the product's UI. When you use the task recorder, all of the actions that you perform are captured. The specific UI fields and controls that are used are also captured. Task recordings can be played as **task guides**. A task guide is a controlled, guided, interactive experience through the steps of a business process. The user is instructed to complete each step by means of a pop-up prompt (*bubble*), which will move across the UI and point to the UI element that the user should interact with. The bubble also provides information about how to interact with the element, such as **Click here** or **In this field, enter a value**. A task guide runs against the user's current dataset and the data that is entered is saved in the user's environment.

This screenshot shows a user running the task guide to create a free text invoice:

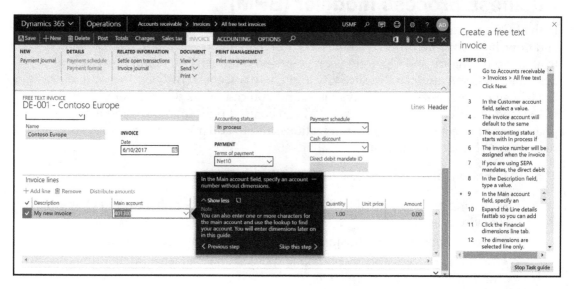

Documentation website

Another enhancement that Microsoft did, which will make training users much easier, is a brand new website for all its standard features. The following are some key highlights for the new documentation site:

- Microsoft documentation now focuses on business processes as well, rather than just explaining what the form does. Business users can really go through this, and understand how they can use the particular business function.
- Microsoft documentation is integrated into the product, and provides users with contextual help on what it means if a business user is learning how to create a free text invoice; they get the help for free text invoices right there in the product.
- Help is personalized based on the user language in the system; for users who are set up with the Japanese language, when they access help, Japanese documentation is presented.
- With the new model of help maintained in GitHub, a customer can copy Microsoft help content, and create their own help repository and link it to the product; this way, you are accessing your custom help, which is relevant to your business processes, and not a generic one.

Planning and executing training

In the earlier section, we learned all of the great tools and enhancements that Finance and Operations brings for training users. Along with great tools, you need a good plan in order to conduct successful and effective training. In this section, we will go through some of the essential training planning and execution guidelines, to ensure that you get effective and proper training when using these great tools.

Training plan

Training planning is an essential part of ERP implementation. It is more important because you are training business users who are used to a different process or system, and are completely new to this new system and processes.

Put together a training plan that covers the following points:

- **Understanding the audience**: How quickly are your users likely to catch up with the changes? The training plan needs to be defined accordingly to support their transition.
- **Train the trainers**: Consultants train the trainers, who are the business superusers or internal business analysts. The idea is to train superusers through multiple rounds of CRP sessions – training and testing to get them up to speed on the system in order for them to be trainers. The trainer approach will ensure that the business SMEs or internal business analysts have gotten up to speed well enough. It will reduce the dependency on the consulting team post go-live, and internal resources can be your tier-one support.
- **Scope of training/areas to be trained**: You need to account for both system and process changes. There are three usual cycles of the training process: UAT training, end user training, and post go-live (training for areas that are struggling).
- **Logistics**: This includes factors such as meeting rooms/travel, centralized versus location-specific, and much more.
- **Training schedule and timing**: Timing is key. In some areas, you may need to train the users multiple times to ensure that they are comfortable. On the other hand, areas that have not changed much may only need light training close to going live, to ensure that the users don't forget.
- **Training assessment**: This pertains to the ways and methods that you will use to get feedback on the training process.
- **Training material and user manuals**: Reviewed with the business SMEs, they may come in different forms, for example, checklists, Visio for business processes, documents with screenshots, recorded videos, mapping between the old and new world, and/or a combination of multiple methods. The development of the training materials should be agreed on at the beginning of the project – in the planning phase – so that appropriate time and resources are built into the plan.
- **Signing off**: Define the sign-off process and the criteria for training sign-off. It is one of the major considerations for go-live.
- **Handling change:** The usual human psychology is to resist change. ERP implementations are not only system changes but, often, process changes as well. These changes may shift jobs or workloads from one department to another. It is important to factor this resistance into the planning. Training is a good opportunity to help prepare people for the change. The more training you provide, the higher the confidence that the users will have in embracing the change, and you will receive less pushback.

Training preparation

A lot of preparation goes into executing smooth and effective training. This preparation includes validating system readiness, verifying the roles, putting together multiple forms of training materials, creating and maintaining a stable training environment with valid data, and so on.

Ensure that the system is ready and stable enough (testing complete) prior to training a larger audience. You also need to gauge the business's readiness for training and help them prepare; the following are some tips to do so:

- If a smaller group is being trained prior to UAT, the expectations may be different, as the system has not been tested as yet, and you may want to communicate the known open issues. However, when training larger groups, try to do it post-UAT, when the system is stable enough and the processes have been finalized.
- Create a forum for the users to participate in, and get more hands-on experience from, training through go-live. Arrange a *Lunch 'n' Learn* or other such team activities that will encourage more practice. From my experience, business leaders who encourage their teams to do extra practice after training, and take the initiative to drive it, will have fewer issues to deal with, post-release.
- Have a process to capture and respond to bugs/queries that are raised in the training. Most likely, you will find some critical items that were not known before.
- Let every user be configured with their to-be production security role. Avoid the use of the system admin role during training. Of course, roles should be tested prior to doing this.
- Use the business process flows at the beginning of every session. Give a 10-thousand-feet-high walkthrough of the overall business process, and of the piece that you plan to show, before getting into the application and the details.

Training environment

Having a stable training environment is important for successful training. A lot of time will be wasted in training if the training environment is not in good working order. Take a look at the following tips, which should be kept in mind when managing your training environment:

- You need to treat it like production; many people will be using it at the same time, and you want it to be stable while the training is going on, or when the users are practicing after training.
- Keep it updated with the latest code and data. Have a communication plan for any downtimes for deployment, to ensure that the users are aware.
- Have it available for the users to practice after training.
- It should share an integrated environment with other applications. For example, if you plan to use Dynamics CRM in production for order entry and integrate it with Finance and Operations for the fulfillment, ensure that you have the training instance of the CRM connected to the Finance and Operations training environment. This will ensure an end-to-end training experience for the users.

Even once training and testing areas are planned, they are incomplete without planning for change. Hence, change management is key in such an important initiative, and many organizations start preparing for it even before the project starts. Let us get into the details of change management in next section.

Change management

In every phase of the project, you are dealing with actual users who will use the system and are the folks who'll be experiencing the most change. The usual human psychology is to resist change, be it a new process or a new system. As part of an implementation project team, you may find that many of the issues that are raised by the users are not completely aligned to the scope of the project, the signed requirement, or the solution design specs, and the success of your project is dependent on how these changes are managed.

For a CRP lead/project manager, it is very important to review and highlight any such change, and take it through the change management process, as any change may impact the system design, timeline, budget, risk, goals, and many other factors. These changes must be addressed carefully, as the implementation of any change, without proper analysis, can potentially derail the project effort.

Training is a good opportunity to help prepare people for the change. The more training that is provided, the higher is the confidence of the users in embracing the change and the system, resulting in less pushback. Let's explore the various options for managing change with users of the system, as follows:

- **Empathy**: Listen carefully to what the end users are asking and trying to achieve. They may be going through nervousness, apprehension, and fear, and hence there is a need for you to stay calm and show empathy; many of the concerns can be sought out with effective communication.
- **Signed scope**: Always be on top of signed scope, whether you are an advisor/partner/customer implementation team member, and treat any unresolved request as a new candidate for change, which must then go through the change management process.
- **Impact:** Once the change is identified, it must be adequately documented, added to the **Requirements Traceability Matrix** (**RTM**), and analyzed with the right stakeholders.
- **Workarounds**: Once the change is analyzed and identified to be included in the scope, the project manager should re-baseline the project, while the implementation team should look out for various solution options.
  Similar to the original requirements' analysis, the change must also be analyzed for suitability in the original solution; also, where it's a system gap, always look for suitable workarounds to try and have minimum impact, to agree to solution specs, and yet be able to address the change.
- **Pushback:** If a change is identified as not critical, not system-related, not urgent, or not factual, the change management team, CRP lead, advisor, and project manager must try to push the change back to the business and the end user.

> Change management may shift jobs or workload from one department to another, and hence, it is an important topic in any transformation initiative.

A popular methodology is **Organization Change Management** (**OCM**), which is used in training plans to ensure that the project stakeholders know what to do when a change is reported or adapted by the users of the system. In large projects, we have seen a dedicated team for OCM, who report directly to the steering committee, possess solid business knowledge and system backgrounds, and are efficient in soft skills. When there is no dedicated OCM team, there should be a designated person who owns this OCM effort, known as the change management lead.

The CRP lead, change management lead, and the project manager must utilize a lot of political power to fight battles where the change that is requested from end users is not something that is a *must-have*, is out of original scope, and the impact to the business is not high and is not needed immediately. This is possible when changes are properly logged, analyzed, and approved before any effort is spent on implementing the change.

Summary

In this chapter, we have reviewed the importance of the testing and training phase of the project, and how to execute successful testing and training through effective planning and execution using the available tools. The ERP system goes through different testing phases, such as feature testing, system integration testing, UAT, and end-to-end testing, in order to ensure the overall quality of the configuration and custom features.

Testing the ERP system can be costly, and automation testing can mitigate that. Many improvements and new features have been added to Microsoft Dynamics 365 for Finance and Operations to enhance the automated testability of the product. The unit test framework has been improved and integrated with Visual Studio to author unit tests for code artifacts, and to integrate with the build process. Task recorder-based test automation lets developers create a test script, by simply importing the task recorder recording in Visual Studio.

In the end, we have learned about the importance of test planning and guidelines for how to conduct successful testing. We discussed the ways to make UAT and end-to-end testing most effective, by uncovering issues prior to going live.

In the training section, we discussed the importance of training and the different enhancement and tools that are available in Finance and Operations for effective training. A new **In-Product** help pane integrates with LCS and Microsoft documentation to provide context-based help to users. In the end, we discussed the importance of training planning, execution, and best practices.

In the next chapter, we will learn about the final phase of the project – go-live. Go-live is the final milestone of the project, and it's important to plan and execute in order to avoid any business disruption. In the next chapter, we will cover go-live planning, execution, and tooling concepts in detail.

12
Managing Go-Live and Post Go-Live

Go-live is what the whole implementation project team works for. During the whole implementation project, you will hear the term go-live again and again. Its literal meaning is when something becomes live. In the **enterprise resource planning** (**ERP**) world, it means that the production environment is available to end users so that they can perform day-to-day business processes.

Go-live is one of the last events that need to be executed as part of the ERP implementation project. It is the end result of the ERP implementation project. It is exciting; however, it is also the most hectic and intense period in the entire ERP project and deserves a fair amount of planning and attention to go smoother. So far, the project implementation team has been working extremely hard designing, developing, testing, and training, and a lot of time and money has been put into the project. A successful go-live can make all that hard work and investment worth it and smoothen the adoption of the new ERP system.

In this chapter, we will cover the following topics:

- Learning about the production environment and responsibilities
- Understanding go-live activities
- Exploring the organization's readiness to go live
- Understanding go-live planning and execution
- Learning about post go-live support

By the end of this chapter, you will have learned how to plan for go-live and make a successful go-live. You will have also learned how you can support a production environment, since taking a project to the go-live state is a major milestone. Keeping it up and running is equally important.

Learning about the production environment and responsibilities

Before diving deep into the go-live planning and related activities, it is important to understand its production environment. Dynamics 365 for Finance and Operations offers two distinct deployment options – cloud and on-premises. We will learn about these two deployment options in the following sections.

All the deployment options use the same application code base and tooling. However, the process, roles, and responsibilities of managing these production environments are different.

In this section, we will walk through the difference in processes and understand the roles and responsibilities that you can use to manage the production infrastructure and deployments.

Understanding cloud deployment

In the cloud deployment model, the ERP service is fully managed by Microsoft, and Microsoft is responsible for actively monitoring the health of the production environment. Microsoft is also jointly responsible for sizing any application and for infrastructure updates.

The customer and the partner will not have direct access to the production servers but will be able to monitor their performance and activities through the **Microsoft Dynamics Lifecycle Services** (**LCS**) environment's monitoring and telemetry tools. From deploying any new code to the production environment to any issue in the production environment, the Microsoft team finishes the job.

The Microsoft team will investigate the issue and work with the customers and partners to find a resolution. For application updates such as deploying a code update to Dynamics 365 for Finance and Operations, the customer typically deploys and tests the changes in the sandbox environment and then creates a service request to schedule the production deployment.

The Microsoft service engineering team works on applying the deployment in the scheduled deployment window. Finally, the customer validates and provides sign-off to close the release. The following diagram shows the production environment life cycle and lists out the roles and responsibilities of Microsoft, customers, and partners in this process:

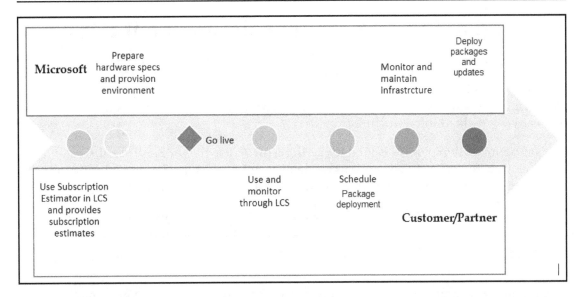

As shown in the preceding diagram, production environment provisioning starts with the customers and partners collecting the subscription estimation data and uploading it into the LCS subscription estimator tool.

In the subscription estimation, you typically describe your implementation project, for example, the number of legal entities, countries, languages, users, master data, and transactions, including the batch and integration volume. This data helps the Microsoft team create the appropriate hardware specifications for the production environment.

Once the production environment has been provisioned and all the development, testing, and training activities have been completed and signed off, the project team works with Microsoft to deploy the final code, configuration, and master data. The customers or partners then perform additional setups for data migration, configuration, and integration, each as part of the go-live activities.

 Please refer to the following link to find out more about the cloud deployment option: `https://docs.microsoft.com/en-us/dynamics365/fin-ops-core/dev-itpro/deployment/cloud-deployment-overview?toc=/dynamics365/commerce/toc.json`.

Once the customers start using the production environment, they can monitor the performance and activities through LCS and schedule updates for their deployment through a regular servicing model.

Now, let's look at the on-premises deployment option.

Looking at the on-premises deployment option

Unlike in the cloud deployment model, where Microsoft manages the production environment and controls deployment and servicing, in the on-premises model, all the responsibilities lie with the customers and partners. On-premises deployment means deploying Dynamics 365 for Finance and Operation on the customer's own data centers or with any other cloud infrastructure provider.

The on-premises deployment option uses **Microsoft Azure Server Service Fabric** stand-alone clusters to deploy the operations on the local infrastructure. Service Fabric stand-alone clusters can be deployed on any computer that runs the Windows Server.

 Service Fabric is a next-generation Microsoft middleware platform for building and managing enterprise-class, high-scale applications.

The following diagram shows the timeline for local business data deployment mode:

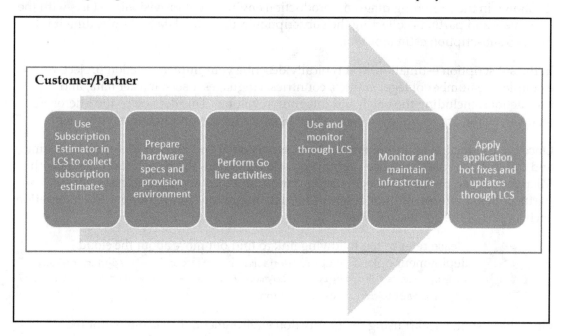

As shown in the preceding diagram, the process of managing the production environment is similar to what we have in the cloud deployment model. However, just like any other on-premises application deployment, the customers or partners are responsible for the infrastructure.

As a customer or partner, you are responsible for defining the environment specifications and the provisions of the environment. LCS tooling is provided by Microsoft so that you can plan, provision, and deploy the changes to the production environment. As shown in the preceding diagram, you still start by filling out the subscription estimator to help you figure out the hardware specifications that you need for your implementation.

> Please refer to the following link to find out more about the on-premises deployment option: https://docs.microsoft.com/en-us/dynamics365/ fin-ops-core/dev-itpro/deployment/on-premises-deployment- landing-page.

Once the production environment has been provisioned and all the other project activities have been completed and signed off, you will perform the final go-live activities to deploy the final code and data and start using the system. LCS monitoring and telemetry tools can still be used to monitor the production environment performance and activities.

You can also use LCS to deploy any changes to the production environment. In addition, your IT team can monitor and manage the production infrastructure, such as applying critical patching, infrastructure updates, and so on.

> Please refer to Chapter 1, *Introduction to Dynamics 365 Finance and Operations*, for more about the Dynamics 365 for Finance and Operations deployment options, as well as a comparison of them.

As a customer, you will be working with partners and Microsoft to identify which deployment options fit the best for your business needs. There are many factors that you need to look at before deciding. In most cases, customers go for cloud deployment options because, here, Microsoft is taking care of all your hardware needs and making sure that your system is up and running all the time.

Understanding go-live activities

Now that we understand the production environment and the roles and responsibilities involved, let's focus on the go-live activities, that is, what needs to be done as part of go-live. Depending on the size of the project and the scope of go-live, there can be hundreds of activities that need to be performed during go-live.

At a high level, the following list represents the various key activities performed during go-live:

- **Final code deployment**: You need to deploy the final signed-off application, including all your customizations, ISV solutions, and so on. For cloud deployment, you have to submit a service request to deploy the final build on the production environment before go-live.
- **Dependent application changes**: As part of your implementation project, you may have some new or existing application changes that integrate with or support Dynamics 365 for Finance and Operations, Enterprise edition; for example, changes to your front office applications, application code for integration, and so on.
- **Golden configuration and master data**: As part of the project, you must be maintaining a golden configuration and master data environment that has already been tested. You need to bring this golden configuration to your production environment. This golden configuration can also include your initial data migration if you have built-in incremental data migration.
  For cloud deployments, you can bring the database backup of your golden configuration environment, apply it to the production environment before go-live, and then update any additional final configurations and settings on top of it.
- **Additional setup and integrations**: After the golden configuration and master data has been loaded, you may need to set up some additional configurations, such as integration settings, batch jobs, and so on. An ideal scenario would be to have most of the configurations as part of the golden configuration, but there could still be some configurations that need to be updated or created for the production environment.
- **Final data migration and cut-over**: Once you have your golden configuration and the initial data migration in the production environment, you may have to run the final data migration to catch up on any new transactions that were generated in your legacy system for the final cut-over. You will probably be doing this with a system downtime so that no new transactions are generated in the legacy system.
- **Validation and sign-off**: Once the final data migration is done, it is time for business users to run validation and create some staged end-to-end transactions to make sure that the system is ready for production use.

Running multiple rounds of simulation or mock releases before the final go-live will help you identify any gaps or issues in the release steps. It is recommended to execute two or three mock go-lives to prepare for go-live.

Understanding the go-live activities and following them will ensure you have a smooth go-live. The core team needs to keep track of these activities and keep all the stakeholders informed of their progress. In the next section, we will talk about go-live readiness.

Exploring the organization's readiness to go-live

There is always a tremendous amount of pressure to meet the go-live date. However, the readiness of the organization for a new system needs to be evaluated carefully prior to flipping the switch. Readiness for go-live is based on the fact that all the prior activities are completed, as per the satisfaction of the key business users and stakeholders, and that they are confident enough to flip the switch and are ready to use the new system.

Let's look at how we can ensure that we have a successful go-live.

Sign-offs

One of the most important criteria to determine an organization's readiness to go-live is whether your key end users and stakeholders are comfortable and are signed off on the new ERP system. The following list covers a few important considerations and criteria that you can use to evaluate whether you are ready to go-live:

- **UAT sign-off**: It is very critical that **user acceptance testing** (**UAT**) has been performed. Make sure that the business users have tested the system using real business scenarios, including integrations, reporting, data migration, and so on. All the business leaders should have signed off the testing for their areas. Any open issue needs to be documented. Review any critical issues that are open, and identify their impact on go-live and whether there are any possible workarounds.

- **Training sign-off**: The business teams should be comfortable with the training that they've received and should have access to the training documents. People play a key role in your ERP success, and the end users across all areas need to be comfortable with using a new system and the business process changes. All the business leaders should have signed off on the training for their teams.

- **Go-live plan**: This is a step-by-step, hour-by-hour plan that is reviewed by all the IT/business teams involved in the release, including the rollback plan and an overall timing to fit within the downtime window. The go-live plan should include the validation scenarios and processes that have been defined by the business. Use the go-live plan in the previous iterations of the release simulations (including UAT and data validations). Make sure that the go-live plan has been signed off by the business and IT stakeholders.

- **Support plan**: The support plan includes the support resources per area, their location and schedule, the issue communication process (templates for providing issue description, screenshots, business impact, severity, and the information and tools for tracking or logging issues), triage, and loop back with the business teams. You need to ensure that an adequate budget has been approved for support (prior to going live). You don't want to be in a situation where you have to discuss dollars with the customer/business leaders while the business is impacted due to system issues. Also, you need to have a budget so that you don't lose the resources that would be required to fix these issues. Review the support plan with all the stakeholders and users to ensure that the process for logging the issues and communication is clear. Set up business and IT war rooms at different locations; the handover process between support teams can help with better communication.

- **Operations team's readiness**: The IT operations team needs to have enough knowledge to support the new system. The team should be comfortable with the monitoring of services/processes within the application and in LCS. It is important to get a sign-off from the IT operations team.

- **External sign-offs and communication**: External sign-off as applicable for the business is a must, for example, sign-off from the bank for check/electronic payments testing, **Electronic Data Interchange** (**EDI**) customers, vendors testing, and auditors. Get sign-offs from the involved parties and make sure everyone is aware of the activities they need to perform.

Any sign-off exceptions need to be documented and presented to the business team and management when making decisions. Discounting any of these areas could result in an unquiet environment post go-live and negatively impact the business.

Sign-offs will help the team work toward a common goal and help make the go-live decision.

The decision to go live

The decision to go live or not to go live is one of the most important decisions in the project lifecycle, and it should not be taken lightly. Wrong decisions can jeopardize the success of the entire project. The decision to go live is highly dependent on the quality of end-to-end testing, user/organizational readiness, and sign-offs from business stakeholders.

The implications and costs of a failed or unstable go live are often far worse than a minor delay in the schedule. Most of the time, the project manager and the delivery team can be under pressure to deliver the project on time. However, if there is any doubt, it is important to take a step back and delay go-live rather than risking the project's success.

The following are a few instances we have encountered in this area:

- Imagine that you are in a room full of executives, making a decision about pulling the trigger on a new system. Everyone is under pressure from the CEO to say *we are ready*. However, most of them are not ready. They do not have enough time to go through the testing phase due to lack of staff, but everyone says yes (there is a fear of getting fired, considering this is way back in 2009 when the economy wasn't doing well). You fail to push back as well. Any guesses as to what happens next? The customer goes live, and it is very painful to stabilize the system, but a lesson has been learned!
- A similar situation occurs again, a couple of years later. Of course, you are smarter this time. The CIO calls for a meeting to check the readiness of the project. Everyone says they are ready (the CIO is driving the dates very hard, and again there is a fear of getting fired). It is your turn – you bravely stand up and say no, and hand over a list of areas you are not comfortable with and that need more testing. The CIO calls for another meeting to better understand what is needed to finish those areas and decides not to go-live. Your team ends up extending the schedule by six weeks based on what is on the list. The CIO thanks you (and still continues to) for standing up and challenging the decision to go-live based on the bugs that were reported/fixed in those six weeks.
- On another project, you are involved in the capacity of an executive reviewer; you challenge their readiness, but the CEO doesn't want to listen. You tell them that it is their call and that we are supporting the release if they sign a liability waiver as your team is not comfortable with them going live (due to a lack of testing from the business team). When you give them a piece of paper to sign, the CEO chooses to reconsider his decision. The customer ends up delaying the release by four weeks. The CEO is not very happy when he receives the pushback but now feels thankful to your team for *watching his back*.

There are more instances like these that we can share. The point is to think about the impact on business. As a consultant/project manager, you are their advocate, and you need to protect the customer from hurting themselves (even though it's not what they want to hear, you are doing it in their best interests). This is the time to utilize the relationships and respect you have earned from the customer to protect them. Don't be shy.

It is even trickier when you have to stand up for someone else's deliverables. For example, say the customer owns certain deliverables internally, which are not production-ready. You need to request the delay due to their internal deliverables as you don't want the project to fail due to specific areas.

Saying that you need more testing is easy. The tough part is to decide how much more time you need. You won't get such an opportunity again. Thorough planning needs to be done to identify all the pieces that are incomplete and to put a plan together so that you can come up with a realistic date. Many project managers fail in this exercise; just hitting the snooze button and delaying this by a few weeks without identifying the action item won't help the project.

Picking realistic dates that will work for the business is important. You don't want to perform an ERP go-live right before or during the peak periods of the business. Challenges from go-live will have a severe impact on the business. There are many examples of companies going out of business due to an ERP go-live during or just before the busy holiday season.

Business contingency planning

Part of your go-live planning must address business contingency planning. Conduct a premortem session to brainstorm areas that may go wrong and to find ways in which the team can reduce the likelihood or mitigate the business impact if the issue occurs. Review the critical business functions that are important for the organization and develop contingency plans in order to run the business if you don't have the computer systems in place momentarily.

The goal of this contingency planning is to plan for the unknowns that may come your way. The following are a few examples that will help with the brainstorming process:

- **Additional workforce considerations**: Look at adding temporary staff or approving overtime for areas that have changed the most or processes that would need more hand-holding. Suppose the warehouse area has the most processes that have been changed. Here, it would be advisable to add more staff to the warehouse so that they can do extra work during go-live.

- **Additional technology resources to support go-live**: You may have a lot of things being uncovered during go-live. It is like having an insurance policy – it's good to have it, but it's better if you don't have to use it.

- **Third-party considerations**: You have SLAs for next-day deliveries to customers; work with your shipping carriers and have them stand by to schedule a delayed pickup in case you need it.

- **Inventory levels**: You have a great dependency on planning and the stock levels; consider increasing your inventory prior to go-live.

- **Communication team**: Have them stand by in case you need to communicate with the outside parties (customers and vendors) or even internally. You may not want to let the customers know ahead of time about the ERP release as they would see it as an upcoming glitch and go somewhere else.

- **Cash flows**: You need to plan for additional cash flow as it may take a little longer to get paid for a few weeks (or months) after go-live due to system or training issues. You need to have an additional line of credit available in case you need it.

- **Key processes and proactive planning**: Identify the key processes and their first occurrence to provide some hand-holding and validation. For example, after processing the checks for the first time, ensure that you can validate the printed checks against the checks that have passed during the testing process. The first time you are ready to start invoicing, try to invoice a few orders first manually and verify the results before you use the batch process to invoice orders automatically in the hundreds. In the case of files that are supposed to be sent out (such as EDI or positive pay files for the bank), verify the ones that were sent and were accepted faultlessly at the receiving end.

- **Going back to the previous system after a few days or few hours into using the new system**: Once you move to the new ERP system, it may not be possible to go back to the previous system. It is not easy to perform a reverse migration from a new platform to legacy. Make sure that everyone understands that once you are live, there is no going back. Everybody is in it together and issues need to be resolved on the new system. This helps in avoiding unproductive discussions of going back to the previous system after going live.

- **Running parallel**: This means that you are running your legacy system/ERP in parallel with Dynamics 365 for finance and operations. It seems like an easy solution for business contingency planning. However, it may not be practical, unless you are highly staffed and the transaction volume isn't very high. Running in parallel usually adds more burdens and stress on your staff while they are trying to deal with the new system. In general, it will cause issues/noise (as users may make more mistakes under stress) more than helping. If you had to go for running both the systems in parallel, the amount of time to run in parallel should be kept to a minimum.

  Quite often, running in parallel is looked at as a replacement for inadequate testing; you think you are better off not doing testing in production (and hoping everything will be fine). There is sometimes a belief that running in parallel helps validate the new processes against the legacy system processes. This is a fallacy as part of the point of implementing a new system is to improve the processes that may fundamentally change the way you do business. So, it is like trying to compare apples with oranges.

- **Release validation**: As we mentioned earlier, going back to the previous system or running in parallel is not easy. How can you verify that there are no critical issues as part of the release itself? It is ideal if you can hold certain transactions from the previous day; for example, let the AP team enter real vendor invoices, perform a check run based on what's due, enter orders that were received from the customers during system downtime, enter the incoming EDI transactions, and so on. The goal is to have good samples and real transactions to verify system behavior.

These are some ideas based on my past experiences. You need to review these with the business leaders and determine what is applicable to your business in order to make appropriate arrangements.

So far, we've learned about the go-live readiness and go-live activities that, as a customer, you need to understand. However, at the same time, it is equally important to execute these activities for a successful go-live. In the next section, we'll talk about the planning and execution of these activities.

Understanding go-live planning and execution

Putting together a detailed plan that can be used for multiple simulations prior to go-live is important. It gives you the opportunity to get the go-live plan validated and address any bugs/issues due to missed steps in the release plan. It also allows you to make changes to the plan, gives you more time to review with multiple groups and identify the missing elements, and helps educate the team about the dependencies and the big picture.

Let's discuss how you can plan and execute these go-live activities.

Planning

As part of the release, you may be performing hundreds of tasks, so it is important to track their progress, dependencies, and corrective actions. Go-live planning involves the following:

- Putting together all the steps in the plan
- Defining the sequence and dependencies between the steps
- Determining the time needed for each step
- Defining the owners and ensuring that all the concerned parties have a clear understanding of what is required

Multiple reviews with the IT and business teams can ensure that you have identified every task that needs to be performed as part of the cut-over and that everyone involved understands the big picture of all the tasks involved in the release.

Using such a plan for UAT, end-to-end testing, and pilot releases can help you identify any gaps in the plan as you practice the overall release execution process. This includes the communication required across groups, such as turning off certain integrations of the legacy system, setting up a new system, data migration, data validation, release testing, or a rollback process.

All these steps need to be documented in the go-live plan and should contain any relevant information, as described in the following table:

Column	Description
Task type	The type of tasks you are dealing with.
Description	This is the task's description.

Owner(s)	This defines the owners of the tasks.
Start date/time	This is the planned start time for the task. It is important to keep track of the timing of tasks that are on a critical path. Any delays in critical path items will impact the overall schedule of the release.
Time needed	This is the time that's needed to execute the task.
Comments	These are the comments and/or additional information.
Detail steps	These are the detailed steps that are needed in order to execute the overall task, if applicable. Attach or link the detailed document if required.
Status tracking—Status, actual start time, finish time	Keep track of the actuals in the release simulation cycles to adjust your plan, and work with the technical teams to reduce the time taken by the critical path items. During the production release, keep track of the actual timings for each task.

The following are some typical task types you will be putting in your go-live plan:

- **Pre-release**: Identify all the tasks that can be completed prior to getting into the system's downtime window for release. For example, communication for the upcoming changes, setting up the future production environments, moving the golden configuration and master data, and any dependent application code or configuration that has no hard dependency. Also, add the tasks for tracking all the necessary sign-offs.

- **Release**: Identify the tasks to be completed during the system's downtime window for release, such as taking the systems down, ensuring that all the transactions are completed, and so on. Also, identify that your source for data migration has the latest information, runs the extraction and migration tasks, communicates at specific intervals during the release, takes backups during the release, and identifies good checkpoints when backups should be taken (in case you have to go back to the previous state). For example, you do this before you start posting transactions as you can't un-post them easily if you find an issue.

- **Validation**: These are the tasks for validation, such as IT validation and business validation (verify the vendors and addresses, open balances, the validation of processes or functionalities that were identified in the release validation, and so on).

- **Decisions (Go-No-Go)**: Identify multiple checkpoints when you need to make Go-No-Go decisions with the executive or project team.
- **Post-release**: These are the tasks to be performed after the final decision has been made to go-live. These tasks may go on for multiple days into using the new system, for example, communication for release, turning on automated processes, verifying the acceptance of outgoing EDI files by customers, verifying the acceptance of positive pay files by each of the banks, and so on.
- **Rollback:** You may have to roll back to a state prior to the release in unfortunate events such as when something goes wrong during the release when critical issues are identified, or when external, uncontrolled dependencies have caused issues. In any case, you need to have rollback steps defined and practiced in the release simulation phase in order to have an uninterrupted availability of the systems to the business. The time needed for the rollback procedure needs to be considered in the release process and the Go-No-Go decisions must be made in a timely manner to allow the rollback procedure to be completed.

The following are some guidelines for putting together your go-live plan:

- A smaller number of manual steps and more automation is ideal to ensure that you don't have too many steps to perform and track.
- Minimize the dependencies; if activities can be completed in the production environment, mention them as a pre-release item. For example, if an integration solution requires the creation of a new database, and if it can be done prior to the release, mention it as a pre-release item.
- You may be implementing ISV solutions or integrations with third-party systems, or integrating with an application being managed by a different team in the same organization. Coordinate with the different teams to understand the dependencies and activities needed to deploy their solution. There should be one single deployment plan for all the components that need to be deployed as part of the release.
- Keep the overall deployment plan simple. Add additional attachments or links for the detailed steps that need to be performed.
- Create a repository to collect the artifacts and documentation required for completing individual tasks, including release notes, validation plan documents, configuration checklist, code artifacts, and so on.
- Put together a visual summary of the detailed plan. This helps in communicating with the stakeholders.

- Every step (including logistics such as booking hotel rooms and ordering pizza) should be put on the plan with their owners.
- Ensure that you have not exhausted your key resources with the release. Spread out the tasks in a way that allows for some downtime for the key resources. The real journey starts after putting the system into production, and you need everyone to stay energized for those first few weeks of transition.

Once you have made the go-live plan, it's time to execute it. Without a great execution, the plan is of no use, so, as a project team, you will be working on executing the plan you have put together.

Executing a release

More simulations, prior to going live, will make the final execution easy. It also helps prepare the team regarding what to expect at the time of going live. No matter how much preparation goes into planning a release, there may still be a few last-minute new discoveries. It is important to make sure that you record these new discoveries and address these as needed. Consider the following while executing a release:

- Track the tasks as per the go-live plan and their dependencies.
- Send communications to multiple numbers at a time (on track, ahead, or behind) during the release window (communicate the frequency to all the stakeholders).
- Schedule conference calls with the leadership team to provide updates (you need to be giving them proactive updates rather than having them on your back, asking for updates), as well as the Go-No-Go decisions, at specific intervals.
- Engage the IT **small-to-medium enterprises** (**SMEs**) and business SMEs for data validation. You need to record these tests (reports from the previous system and the new system) and save the test results. You will need them for your audit.
- Run through the release validation tests to verify that the functionality is working as expected. If you can hold a good sample of transactions from the previous working day, try to process them in the system and take them from end to end.
  You can hold half a day's worth of orders from a day prior to going live, enter them manually in the new system, and try to take them all the way through invoicing. Verify the reverse logistics as well. Verify access to reports and integrations across multiple systems.
- Stay alert for upcoming surprises and handle them sooner.

The following diagram shows an example of the go-live's execution plan, as well as the communication plan:

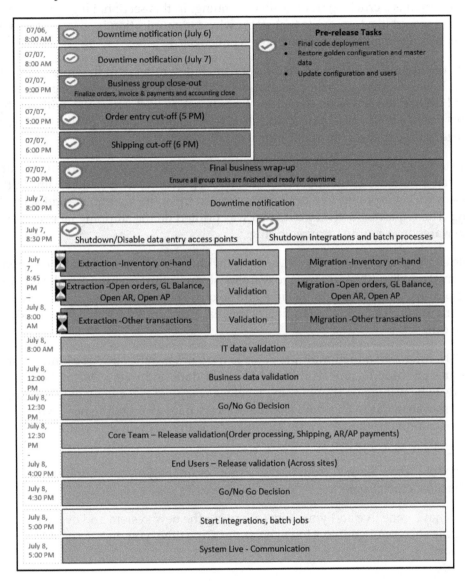

As shown in the preceding diagram, you can use this kind of format to track the execution of the go-live plan, as well as to communicate the progress of its execution with the stakeholders.

The importance of communication

Communication is a crucial part of go-live planning. In this section, I'll go over one of the references I would like to provide that states why communication is so important when avoiding turning smaller issues into bigger challenges.

In one of the upgrade projects, we had a very small downtime window to perform the upgrade. It was shortened further, as updates in the data warehouse were going to take time, and we had to keep aside some time for rollback as well. However, with multiple iterations (thanks to the great project technical team that was on the project), we were able to squeeze in time to meet our requirements.

The core technical team worked hard and was up the whole night performing the upgrade in the given timeframe so that people could start using the system as they came in the next morning. It was almost bug-free until users showed up at the warehouse and started shipping. The requested delivery date that was printed on the shipping labels was the same day; the warehouse couldn't start shipping.

Multiple emails and phone calls were received with messages stating that the warehouse was having trouble with shipping (the warehouse can't ship, we need to call FedEx for delayed pickup, should we stop picking, and so on). The messages went on for two hours. It was hard to get a clear understanding of the real issue until we reduced the audience and got on to call.

In **AX 2009**, Microsoft added multiple dates to the sales orders, such as estimated shipping date, requested shipping date, confirmed shipping date, and so on. One of these custom date fields to be printed on the shipping label was mapped incorrectly to the default value (that is, the system date). This date was the delivery date given to the post, which, obviously, couldn't be the same date. It was just one line of code change for the developer, once the real issue was explained.

Based on what we've learned from past experiences, managing communications after go-live is the most crucial aspect.

Now, you have gone live and your users are using the new system and everyone is enjoying the successful go-live. However, at the same time, you need to plan for post go-live support.

Learning about post go-live support

In the previous sections, we learned about going live, cutover activities, and how best to manage those activities.

In this section, we will cover post go-live activities spanning support, issue identification, tracking, resolutions, and the whole 360-degree issue life cycle.

Support in the cloud world is expected to be quick and one-touch-enabled, and have as small an impact on daily business operations as possible. However, you need to be able to know about and leverage various tools in order to seek support.

To provide context from Dynamics 365, you may have successfully gone live, but it takes a significant effort to ensure smooth operations post go-live.

In this section, you'll explore various options for seeking support, tools that are used in support, an end to the support life cycle, and best practices in support. We will go over the following:

- Resources for support
- Support tools and LCS
- Issue or support life cycle
- Production environment support with Microsoft
- Support analytics using monitoring and diagnostics
- Best practices in post go-live or support

Glancing on resources for support

With a lot of choices comes a lot of decision-making; hence, we would like to empower you with various helpful resources that will allow you to maintain your Dynamics 365 solution.

You can find out more about the issue at hand using a number of options, as follows:

- **Issue search** (**LCS**): Always search with keywords in LCS for the issue or situation to see whether it's a known issue and for possible solutions or workarounds. Here, you search not only for an issue but also its triage history, fixes, and solution information for resolution. The following screenshot shows the icon tile for issue search:

- **Microsoft help documentation** (**wiki**): This is a single place for all help content for Dynamics 365 for Finance and Operations, Enterprise edition (the link to the documentation is `https://docs.microsoft.com/en-us/dynamics365/operations`).

- **Forums and blogs**: Always search for whether the issue or situation you are facing was ever faced by someone and whether a potential analysis and solution is available in these forums. These forums include but are not limited to the following:
  - Microsoft Dynamics Community (the link to the forum is `https://community.dynamics.com/365/financeandoperations/b`)
  - MSDynamicsWorld (the link to the forum is `https://msdynamicsworld.com`)
  - D365 User Group (D365UG) (the link to the forum is `https://www.D365ug.com/`)

- **Google or Bing search**: If nothing can be found, just try searching the entire web using a good search engine to find a solution to your situation.

- **Advisor, MVP, and experts**: When a solution has been identified and you are unsure whether to go with it or not, or a solution hasn't been found, it is best to approach an expert from that area.

- **Dynamics Learning Portal** (**DLP**): DLP has evolved a lot and is a great knowledge repository for partners to leverage detailed documentation from Microsoft about its product and features. This portal is available to Microsoft Dynamics partners only.

- **Roadmap**: We are all curious about the future and what may come next, so visiting the roadmap site is going to help you plan your future solution growth. For further information, please go to `https://dynamics.microsoft.com/en-us/roadmap/finance/` and `https://dynamics.microsoft.com/en-us/roadmap/supply-chain-management/`.

- **Feedback**: If you want to help Microsoft when it comes to improving Dynamics 365 and its family of products and solutions, you can go to `https://experience.dynamics.com/ideas/` and share ideas, suggestions, and feedback.

- **Portals**: There are two portals, namely, for customers and partners. To go to these portals, go to the following links:
  - For customers: `https://mbs.microsoft.com/customersource`
  - For partners: `https://mbs.microsoft.com/partnersource`

Please verify whether your team or partner has evaluated all the preceding options before logging a support incident with Microsoft.

Now, let's explore various support tools that are available in LCS that are recommended for your implementation journey.

Understanding support tools and LCS

LCS has a number of tools that can empower users and implementation teams so that they can collaborate on issues, resolutions, and quick turnarounds for closure.

Let's see how we can create an issue in LCS using the following options:

- Directly from within Dynamics 365 for Finance and Operations:
    - Cloud deployment of Finance and Operations provides users and administrators with the ability to search for any ongoing issue using a browser client. **Issue search** in the client provides the same search functionality as an available **Issue search** tool in LCS. If any hotfix is available based on the searched-for context, the user can submit a request for the hotfix. This step creates a hotfix request within the LCS project's **Support** page for further investigation and analysis.
    - Users can also create and submit issues from the client. Issues that are created by the client are available in the LCS under the **Support** tile. Issues that are created through the Finance and Operations client contain metadata about the Dynamics 365 Finance and Operations environment. When these issues are selected in the issue grid, the **Troubleshoot** button becomes available.
    - When you click on **Troubleshoot**, the event monitoring page opens. This will give you access to events and logs that are related to the issue. On this page, you can also view activities, error messages, and other information that has occurred in the last two hours since the issue was reported.

- Directly from within LCS:
  - When a support option is clicked on in LCS, you will be taken to the **Work items** screen.
  - The **Work items** screen is comprised of four areas, as shown in the following screenshot:

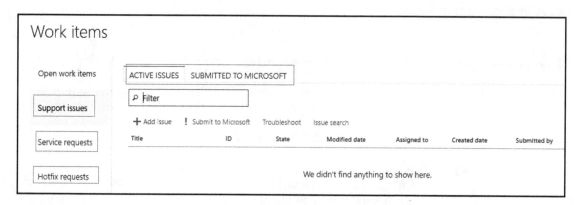

Now, let's explore the preceding **Work items** options and their use case scenarios:

- **Open work items**:
  - Based on the LCS project settings to map different work items in VSTS, this is the only place where information flows from VSTS to LCS for visibility purposes.
  - Work items that are of the bug type or tasks that have been created within VSTS are available in LCS.

- **Support issues**:
  - Issues that are created directly in LCS or via Dynamics 365 for Finance and Operations are seen on the list, as shown in the preceding screenshot under the **Support issues** tab.
  - These issues could be product issues that have been escalated to Microsoft via a support ticket or could be implementation or solution issues that your advisor or partner can help in resolving.
  - Once the issue has been logged, its status can be tracked through LCS.

- **Service requests**: There are three kinds of service requests available that can be leveraged:

  - **Database point-in-time restore request**: This is for database backup restoration for your production environment.
  - **Database refresh request**: This is used to restore a copy of production data in the Sandbox environment.
  - **Other requests**: These are generic requests that do not belong to the preceding two requests.

- **Hotfix requests**: For an application X++ hotfix, apply the package in a development environment. After resolving any conflicts, generate a deployable package from Visual Studio and upload the package to the asset library software deployable package.

The following screenshot shows an application X++ hotfix search screen and how to click and select one or many hotfixes so that you can download the package:

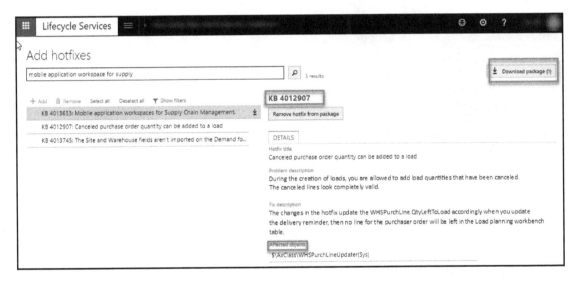

 In Chapter 3, *Lifecycle Services (LCS) and Tools*, we looked at LCS and the various tooling it offers. We recommended that you get conversant with all the key LCS tools for your implementation and post-implementation activities.

Sometimes, you can fix an issue while working with a partner or an internal IT team, but in some cases, you will have to contact Microsoft.

Learning about production environment support with Microsoft

If you are using the cloud-only version of Dynamics 365 for Finance and Operations, then, to perform any activity on the production environment, you need to work with Microsoft as they are the owner of the environment and only Microsoft can perform environment maintenance-related activities.

Any interaction with the production environment can be done with a Microsoft service engineer. Hence, any communication with a **Dynamics Service Engineer** (**DSE**) needs to be tracked, organized, and user-friendly. Thus, you need to make a service request so that the customer, partners, advisors, and implementation teams can raise a request for any service needs in the production environment.

The following screenshot shows the three types of request that can be initiated in LCS as a service request:

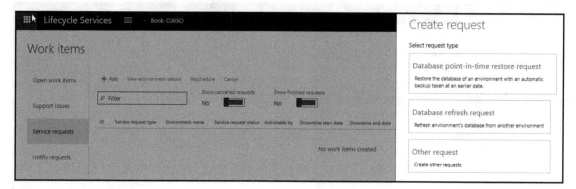

The preceding screenshot shows the fly-out when a user clicks on the **Add** button in the **Work items** screen under the **Service requests** section.

For any solution issues, you should use the **Support issues** capability, while for any production environment-related request, you need to use **Service requests**.

With ongoing support and a lot of moving parts and issues, it is important to gain insightful information. Hence, support analytics plays a significant role in decision-making and also proactive support.

Integrating support analytics with monitoring and diagnostics

In the cloud world, advisors, partners, and customer implementation teams need to leverage all the available data in LCS to monitor and diagnose an environment. Telemetry data is the basis of monitoring and diagnostics in LCS.

Support analytics comprises three information tenets – monitoring, diagnostics, and analytics. Let's take a look at these now:

- **Monitoring**: Microsoft supports two types of monitoring to view the health of an environment through LCS via availability and health monitoring. These are as follows:
  - **Availability monitoring**: This type of monitoring performs a check against the environment to make sure that it's available at all times. If the check fails, the Microsoft service engineering team is immediately notified:

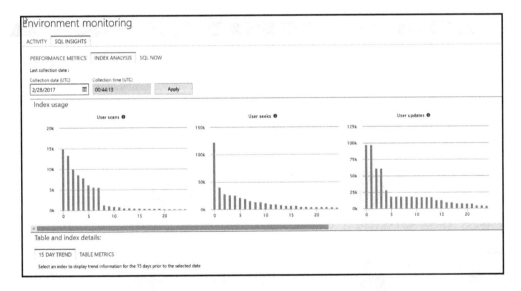

The various charts in the preceding screenshot are for index analysis on SQL Azure for a production environment. The **Index usage** view shows the most expensive indices on the environment based on seeks versus scans, along with tables with the highest row count. Also, you can gather information about the state and run on SQL Azure, as well as performance metrics.

The **SQL NOW** feature allows us to troubleshoot SQL Azure issues in real time by looking into which queries are blocked and which queries are blocking them. It also provides a view of tables that have locks on them.

- **Health monitoring**: In addition to availability checks, some basic health checks must be performed. These basic health checks include CPU level, memory consumption of the **virtual machines** (**VMs**), and the total number of deadlocks in a five minute period. Microsoft Telemetry Infrastructure collects health metrics from the environments, and if a metric crosses a threshold value, the Microsoft service engineering team is alerted so that the issue can be investigated.

- **Diagnostics:** Telemetry data helps build a storyboard view that shows what that user and other users were doing when the issue was reported. In addition to user activity tracking, a rich set of SQL data is also available for performance troubleshooting using **SQL NOW**:

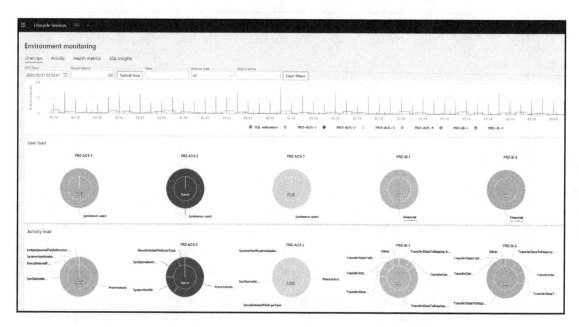

As shown in the preceding screenshot, **Environment monitoring** gives you information about the state spanning user load, activity load, SQL, server utilization, and so on that's been spread across a configurable time scale.

> Please refer to `Chapter 3`, *Life Cycle Services (LCS) and Tools*, for more on system diagnostics and its usage, which also plays a significant role in proactive monitoring.

- **Analytics:** Analytics is another critical use case for the telemetry data that is collected. Currently, only Microsoft can perform analytics so that it can gauge and understand feature usage and performance through Microsoft Power BI.

For Dynamics 365 for Finance and Operations, Enterprise edition, Microsoft is responsible for actively monitoring the health of production environments at all times as it is a managed cloud service.

> The customer, however, is responsible for monitoring and troubleshooting the health of non-production environments.

As you continue to work on your production environment, it is important to keep in mind that your ERP system is always a work in progress, which means you are always doing something new in the system. Therefore, it's important to keep best practices in mind when making any changes to the production environment.

Best practices in post go-live support

We recommend the following best practices while managing support or issues in Dynamics 365 for Finance and Operations, Enterprise edition:

- Always use VSTS sync with LCS BPM. This ensures end-to-end traceability.
- Leverage Dynamics 365 for Finance and Operations or LCS to raise any support issues.
- The issue should always be supported with information regarding its impact, symptoms, and task guides, along with steps and developer recording.
- Issue management should be done in VSTS until its closure and an issue should only be closed by the originator.

- Issue tracking should cover ownership assignments and artifacts linking with requirements, test cases, and other issues or bugs.
- Ensure a rigorous release and test process to ensure there's a minimal impact on working solutions.
- Always use telemetric data in the form of monitoring and diagnosis so that you're proactive when managing your Dynamics 365 for Finance and Operations production instance.

Summary

We started this chapter by learning about one of the final phases of the implementation project, go-live. Go-live is exciting but is also the most hectic and intense period of the project. The cloud has changed the way a production environment is managed and updated. Roles and responsibilities have changed. We started by understanding how a production environment's responsibilities vary based on the deployment model you selected for your project. We discussed go-live activities to understand what goes on during the go-live phase of the project. The decision of going live or not is not easy and needs many considerations. We went through everything you need to understand to make that decision, the different sign-offs you need, how it can be difficult for project managers and stakeholders to make a decision to not go live if things are not good, and the importance of planning business contingency. In the end, we discussed how you can put together a plan and mitigate the risks through multiple simulations and reviews. This was followed by tips for the execution of a go-live plan and the importance of managing communication.

Later, we learned about post-go-live activities, support planning, issue management, and the tools to use throughout the life cycle of an issue. We covered capabilities in LCS, such as Issue Search, Work items, Support, and various other kinds of services requests. We also touched upon hotfixes and the three types – binary, X++ application, and metadata – which will be covered in the next chapter in detail. We also covered the steps of submitting product-related issues to Microsoft using support tooling in LCS, as well as how to raise various kinds of service requests related to your production environment on Azure when managed by Microsoft. We also covered various options regarding how to manage your environment, such as monitoring, diagnostics, and analytics. The resources that were shared in the first section of this chapter are your knowledge repositories for any support situation and your continuous learning.

In the next chapter, we will look at the One Version update process of Dynamics 365 for Finance and Operations.

13
One Version Service Updates

In the previous chapter, you learned about go-live and post-go-live activities, support, and best practices to keep the ERP value momentum going. The post-go-live phase is an interesting phase, as it is never static. Its dynamic nature calls for continuous improvement of your business platform, keeping up to date with the latest features, and having a healthy system to fuel your organization's growth.

Once your project is live on Finance and Operations, you need to make sure that your instance is updated and supported as per the Microsoft Product Lifecycle. Before **One Version**, customers used to go through the upgrade process but with One Version, it will only be updated. Let's first understand the difference between update and upgrade:

- **Update**: We will use the term update to refer to the process of keeping your **Dynamics 365 for Finance and Operations** (**D365FO**) up to date with the latest releases. With new concepts, such as models and new programming model extensions, it is easier than ever for organizations to adopt continuous innovation from Microsoft.
- **Upgrade**: The term upgrade is used when upgrading to D365FO from an earlier version of Dynamics AX 2012. In this scenario, Microsoft supports the direct upgrade path by providing the toolset for code and data upgrades.

In this chapter, we will deep dive into the update process and how One Version makes it more exciting to implement D365FO. We will learn about the Finance and Operations product lifecycle and support policy and how you can prepare for it. We will be sharing knowledge using the following topics:

- Exploring One Version:
  - Update availability
  - Update early adoption
  - Service updates
  - Quality update
  - Service update FAQ
- Feature management

Exploring One Version

Every software product—either its on-premises or cloud version—is usually backed by a life cycle and support policy, which defines how frequently the product will be updated and for how long it will be supported. All Dynamics 365 products including Finance and Operations follow the Microsoft Modern Lifecycle Policy. Product and services under this policy are serviced and supported continuously. The Finance and Operations product life cycle and support policy are called **One Version**.

In a typical ERP implementation, the common strategy used to be once you had implemented a particular version of the ERP product, then in few years, you would have to go through the upgrade process to get on to the latest version. For example, if you are on Microsoft Dynamics AX 2012 and are trying to implement D365FO, then you would have to go through the upgrade process. This upgrade process is not simple and requires a lot of effort. With the previous versions, the customer had to go through the painful upgrade process every few years to be on the latest version.

Microsoft has learned a lot through customer/partner feedback and has been working on a better solution to provide an easier path for customers to move to the latest updates with as little effort as possible. Microsoft has now achieved that goal with One Version.

The *core idea* behind One Version is to never go through the upgrade process. With One Version, Microsoft's aim is to provide a predictable and continuous update to the Finance and Operations application. Now that we understand what One Version is, let's deep-dive and explore how it is achieved in the subsequent sections.

Principles of One Version

What are the core principles behind the One Version service update? Let's explore them here:

- **All customers on the latest product version**: The first and foremost principle of One Version is to get all of the customers using Finance and Operations on the latest product version. This helps customers to continuously make use of new features at the same time. This way Microsoft can have better support for all the customers and, at the same time, customers know what to expect and never have to worry about upgrades.
- **Backward compatible:** Service updates come with backward compatibility, which means service updates can be applied to an environment with existing customization from a partner or an environment with an **independent software vendor** (ISV) solution that hasn't been updated yet.
- **Ring-based validation and release**: One of the most important steps in any new feature release is to make sure it goes through an extensive testing and validation process. Ring-based testing is used before the update is released for general use, as follows:
  - **Ring 0**: Testing starts with the feature team.
  - **Ring 1**: The Dynamics Finance and Operations team and the retail team test the new update.
  - **Ring 2**: Customers, partners, and ISV who have joined the **Preview Early Access Program** (PEAP) for targeted release test the update; in this phase, the update cannot be applied to the production environment.
  - **Ring 3**: This is similar to **Ring 2** but in this case, once the customer is satisfied, then they can apply the update to the production environment.
  - **Ring 4**: The update is ready for general public use.

Let's see this in a graphical presentation:

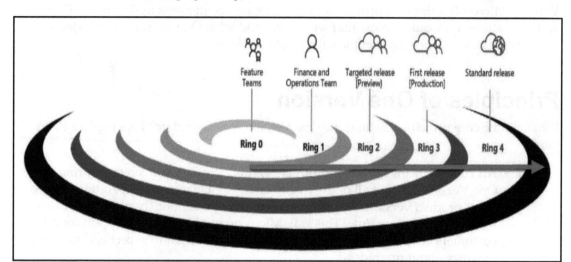

- **Automated testing**: Using the RSAT tool, customers can automate the testing and reduce the testing and deployment time significantly. Users can create the test scripts using the task recorder and then feed it to the RSAT tool for automated testing.
- **Reduced downtime window**: As a customer, if you are planning to update your ERP system continuously throughout the year, one of the most critical aspects is to plan for system downtime. One thing we have seen in a typical ERP upgrade project is that you need a significant downtime window to execute the final upgrade process and this downtime can be several hours to days depending on your data size and the complexity of the upgrade. With One Version, Microsoft aims to reduce the downtime required to uptake service updates to zero. Currently, zero downtime is applicable to Microsoft Package deployment only.
- **Customer in control**: Customers can choose and decide when to get the new service update. Service updates are released eight times a year, and the customer can either choose to get all eight of these or skip some but they need to get at least two service updates, which are required in a year.

Update availability

Microsoft has been focusing on making D365FO more and more user friendly to apply new updates. Microsoft has put out a release cadence process that provides customers/partners with much-needed advance notice to prepare for new updates.

Service updates are continuous, automatic updates that provide new features and functionality. They maintain backward compatibility, which means there is no need to *merge your code.*

The customer/partner is in control to decide when to get these updates. You are in control and manage how your organization receives these updates.

The Microsoft Dynamics team will release eight service updates each year, and the customer may choose to get all eight service updates or would have to get at least two service updates per year. **Lifecycle Services** (**LCS**) will be used to apply these updates to test, production, and other environments. Customers can pause updating up to three consecutive updates, but after that, customers would have to update. If the customer doesn't get the update after three consecutive updates, then Microsoft would automatically apply the updates to the environments through LCS. The following screenshot shows when the updates will be released:

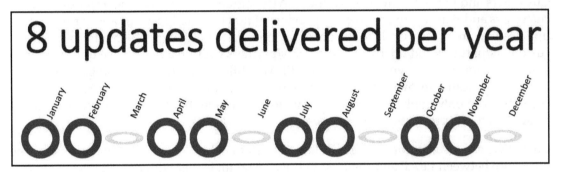

The customer gets the opportunity to apply the update to the sandbox at least seven days before it's applied to the production environment. This gives customers enough time to test the new update and features that come with it. The **Regression Suite Automation Tool** (**RSAT**) can be used to test the system once the updates are installed to make sure that the system is working as expected.

> There are detailed steps to pause a service update at `https://docs.`
> `microsoft.com/en-us/dynamics365/fin-ops-core/dev-itpro/`
> `lifecycle-services/pause-service-updates.`

Update early adoption

When the Microsoft Dynamics team develops a new feature or module, it goes through a very thorough testing process. It is tested in its entirety and in conjunction with other existing features/modules to make sure it's working as expected and not breaking anything. During this time, customers can also join the **Release Validation Program**. This program allows the customer to share their code base and database with Microsoft, using the provided artifacts for benchmarking and automated testing to prove that it would work with the customer's data/code as well.

Use the following form to join the Release Validation Program, at `https:/` `/forms.office.com/Pages/ResponsePage.aspx?id=` `v4j5cvGGr0GRqy180BHbR56j81Zs0FdAvwT75_` `WNFyxUQVdKVkVORjVDNloxTEkwS1JUSUxWN1pSWi4u.`

Customers and partners can also join the **PEAP** program. PEAP gives the opportunity to customers and partners to get an early preview of newly added features and service updates that are not available to the general public yet. This program benefits both customers/partners and Microsoft; customers/partners get to see the service update sooner than the people who haven't signed up for PEAP while, in return, Microsoft gets early feedback and can improve the product if there are any shortcomings. With PEAP, customers can only apply the service update to development or test environments; it cannot be applied to the production environment.

Customers can also opt for the **First Release Program**, which is open for all customers. The difference between PEAP and the First Release Program is that with the latter, customers can deploy the service update to the production environment as well. Customers who join the First Release Program will also have the benefit of a dedicated Microsoft engineer who would monitor the production environment once the service update has been applied for any issues.

Use the following link to join PEAP or the First Release Program: `https://experience.dynamics.com/SignIn?ReturnUrl=%2Fins` `ider%2F.`

Service updates

In this section, we will talk about the steps you need to take to apply a service update:

1. **Configure**: This is the step where you can configure when you want to take the service update. As explained in an earlier section, updates would be applied to the UAT environment first so that customer has time to validate and test the updates before it's applied to the production environment. You can define the maintenance window on LCS. It is under the **PRODUCTION ENVIRONMENT UPDATE CADENCE** section on the **Update settings** tab of the **Project settings** page, as shown here:

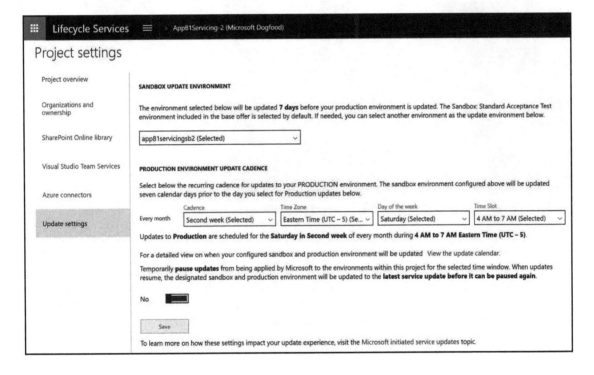

2. **Notice**: Microsoft is making every effort to provide advance notice to the customers to get ready for new updates. Notifications will start showing up on LCS 5 before the scheduled update. So, when you log in to LCS, you would see the notification. A notification email is also sent to the LCS project owners, notifying the team about the scheduled update. The following screenshot shows an example of a notification on LCS:

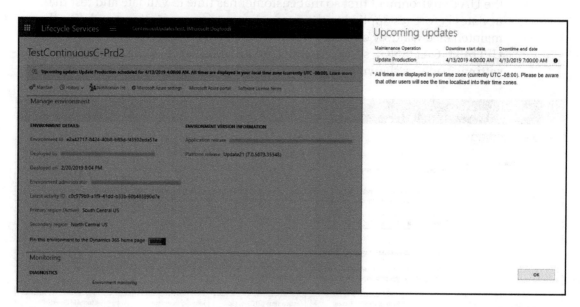

3. **Update**: This is the step where the actual update is applied to an environment. This update is applied automatically during the maintenance window set in the configure step. Once the update is completed, an automatic email notification is sent to the project owners about the status of the update. If the customer doesn't want the automatic update, then they can still apply the update manually using LCS. Our recommendation is to have Microsoft take care of the update and have it applied automatically. The following screenshot shows how the customer can go for self-update using LCS:

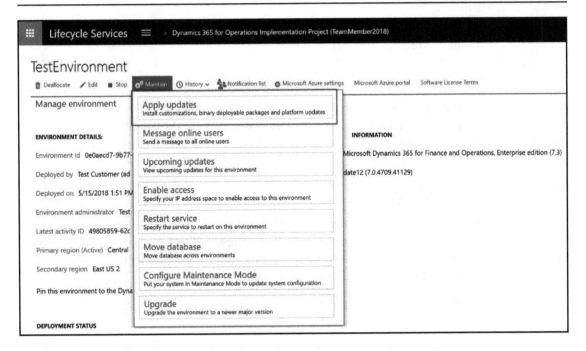

4. **Validate**: This is the last step in the service update process. In this step, the customer would validate the newly applied update. This step should be done in the UAT environment before applying the update to the production environment. Customers can use the RSAT tool as discussed earlier to automate the testing process to save time, as shown in the following screenshot:

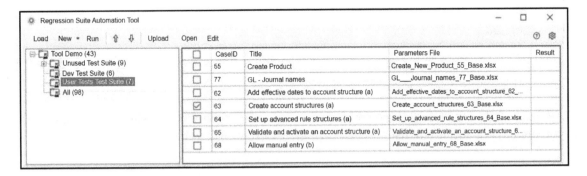

There is a useful link with details about creating test cases and testing them with RSAT (`https://docs.microsoft.com/en-us/dynamics365/ fin-ops-core/dev-itpro/lifecycle-services/using-task-guides-and- bpm-to-create-user-acceptance-tests`).

We learned about service updates, which are continuous updates, but what if you need an urgent fix that can't wait for a service update? Then you can get the quality update as explained in the next section.

Quality updates

Mircosoft has introduced the concept of the **quality update** to adopt any fixes coming in between any two service updates. These intermittent fixes will be available through LCS. You should be looking at getting these quality updates only if you are facing any issue and you are not able to run the business due to these issues.

To check for a quality update, log in to LCS and go to the environment page and click on the **View update** button:

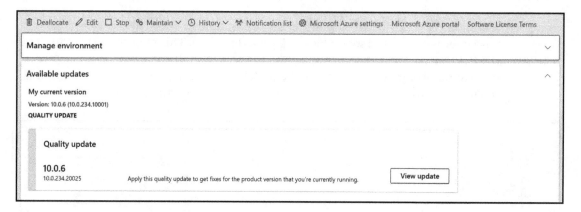

As illustrated in the following screenshot, you can search for a hotfix related to the issue you are having and it will list all of the available hotfixes for you:

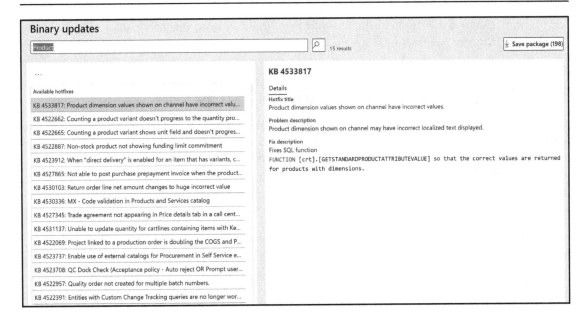

Once you have identified the hotfix you need to get, you can save it as a package in the asset library, as shown in the following screenshot:

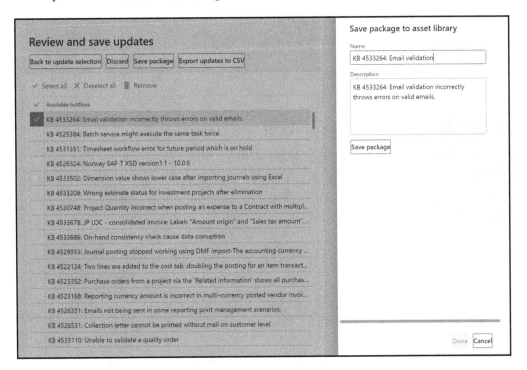

Once the package is available in the asset library, then you can use this package and deploy it to an environment as needed.

One Version service update FAQs

One Version and continuous service updates are a new concept and customers/partners are getting used to it. There are still a lot of questions. Microsoft has put together an FAQ page that answers some of the very commonly asked questions. Here, you will find the link to this page, which you can read at your convenience and get some of the answers you might be looking for, at `https://docs.microsoft.com/en-us/dynamics365/fin-ops-core/fin-ops/get-started/one-version?toc=/dynamics365/commerce/toc.json`.

One of the many benefits of the One Version service update is new features. Each service update has some new features added to D365FO. Microsoft has added a new functionality, **feature management**, which gives customers the power to choose which feature to use as needed for the business.

Understanding feature management

Feature management is a new workspace that was recently added to D365FO. Any newly released features are added to this workspace. By default, any newly released feature is turned off and this workspace allows the customer to turn on a feature that they want to start using. Let's look at this new workspace in detail.

The feature management workspace

The feature management workspace provides a list of all available features that are supported by feature management.

You can look at the details about a feature that you would like to enable before turning it on to learn more about this new feature.

Access to feature management can be controlled using the feature manager and feature viewer roles.

The following screenshot illustrates the feature management workspace:

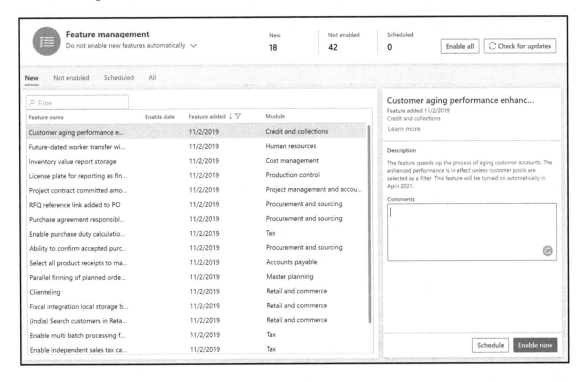

The feature management workspace seen here contains the following details:

- Name: This is under **Feature name**.
- Status: This shows whether this feature is enabled or not. As we can see in the preceding screenshot, none of the features are enabled and hence we can see the **Enable now** button on the screen on selecting the first feature.
- **Enable date**: This shows on which date the feature was enabled. As seen in the preceding screenshot, the **Enable date** column is empty for the reason stated in the preceding point here.
- **Feature added**: This shows on which date the feature was added.
- **Module**: This is the module that is affected by this feature.

Turning on a feature

Use the **Enable now** button to turn on a feature. If a feature is not turned on, then the **Enable now** button will appear. Click on the **Enable now** button to turn on the desired feature. You can also schedule a feature to be turned on by a certain date. Rescheduling can also be done for an already scheduled feature.

The following screenshot illustrates how you can use the **Enable all** and **Schedule** features:

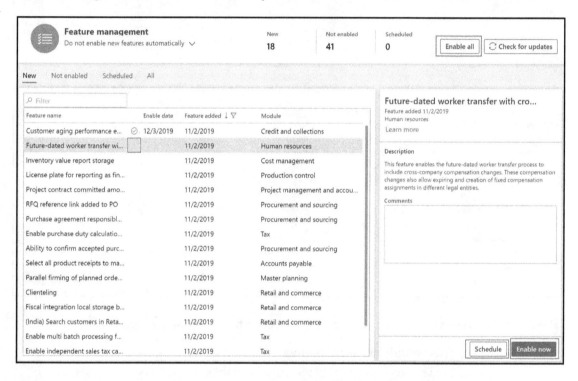

Here are some options you can use to turn on a feature or all of the features:

- **Enable all**: You can use this button to enable all of the features.
- **Turn on features automatically**: You can use this feature to enable the new features automatically.

- **Turn on message**: Depending on features you are trying to turn on, you might see certain messages when you try to turn on the feature, as in these examples:
  - Some features cannot be turned off once they are turned on.
  - Some features need additional information that you need to provide before turning them on.
  - Some features need some prerequisite actions before you turn them on.

Turning off a feature

Use the **Disable** button to turn off a feature. If a feature is turned on and it can be turned off, then the **Disable** button would appear. The following screenshot illustrates how you can use the **Disable** button:

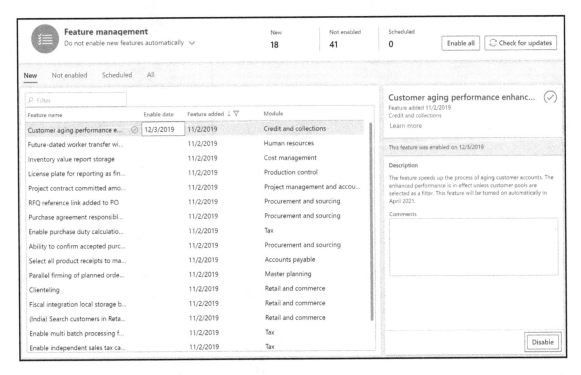

If a feature cannot be turned off, for such features, the **Disable** button would not appear.

Check for updates

With every service update, new features are added to D365FO. These new features are continuously added to the feature management workspace. Users can also use the **Check for updates** button to manually check for updates and new features. The following screenshot illustrates how you can use the **Check for updates** button to get the latest features:

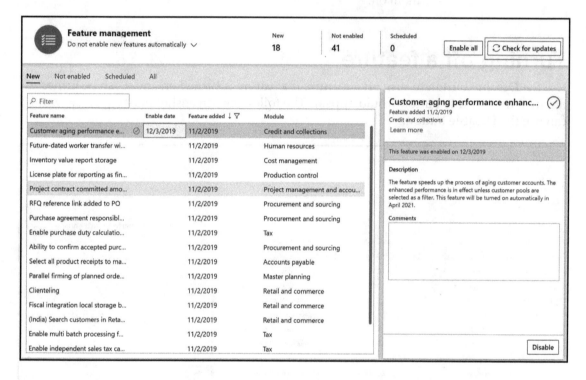

Feature management is a great tool to manage the available features and enable them, which is important to your business. Microsoft is giving more and more power to end users so users can be self-sufficient and they don't have to rely on the IT team for such simple tasks.

Summary

In this chapter, you learned about the concepts behind One Version and how it is a game-changer for D365FO and has eliminated the tedious and painful task of upgrading the version every few years.

You also learned about service updates. Continuous service updates will keep your system up to date and provide you with the latest and greatest features available in D365FO products.

In this chapter, we also shared insight into the feature management workspace and how it can empower customers to **enable/disable** features based on business needs. Never before has something like this been available; with feature management, you can control the features available to your users.

Although Microsoft is making it easier and easier for users to apply service updates, nothing can replace a good testing/validation process. It doesn't matter how foolproof a service update is—it is up to you to make sure that service update is good for your business by doing thorough testing.

Microsoft is making improvements every day to all of its products and Dynamics 365 is no exception. Microsoft is very committed to the Dynamics 365 product suite. The Dynamics team at Microsoft is taking feedback from customers, partners, and ISVs to make D365FO more flexible and user friendly.

In this book, we have covered many topics related to D365FO, and a quick recap gives a chapter-wise snapshot of the topics covered in each chapter. We believe you should know these covered topics before implementing D365FO.

This being the last chapter of this book, let's try memorizing all that we have learned so far! We started off by introducing Microsoft Dynamics 365 and describing different apps and tools under Microsoft Dynamics 365. We learned about different implementation methodologies for your project as well as **LCS** and its features on offer. We tried to understand various application components and architectures of Dynamics. With the help of tips, tricks, and best practices, we learned different strategies for managing configurations and data migrations.

We explored different development tools and processes in Dynamics that will help you to build customized solutions. We also discussed analytics and financial reporting options such as Power BI. Toward the end, we learned about the importance of testing and discussed various automated testing strategies. We ended with the go-live process and post-go-live support in D365FO and learned about how to use service updates to your advantage.

We hope this will help you with the digital transformation of your business by implementing D365FO!!

Other Books You May Enjoy

If you enjoyed this book, you may be interested in these other books by Packt:

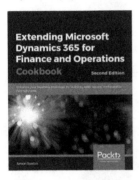

Extending Microsoft Dynamics 365 for Finance and Operations Cookbook - Second Edition
Simon Buxton

ISBN: 978-1-83864-381-2

- Understand the importance of using patterns and frameworks for creating unique solutions
- Write code that can make your solution extendable
- Leverage new frameworks that allow your solution to adapt as your business grows
- Write and perform unit tests to automate the testing process
- Design your security model and policies to provide code access privileges
- Design the UI and business logic to fit standard patterns

Mastering Microsoft Dynamics 365 Business Central

Stefano Demiliani, Duilio Tacconi

ISBN: 978-1-78995-125-7

- Create a sandbox environment with Dynamics 365 Business Central
- Handle source control management when developing solutions
- Explore extension testing, debugging, and deployment
- Create real-world business processes using Business Central and different Azure services
- Integrate Business Central with external applications
- Apply DevOps and CI/CD to development projects
- Move existing solutions to the new extension-based architecture

Leave a review - let other readers know what you think

Please share your thoughts on this book with others by leaving a review on the site that you bought it from. If you purchased the book from Amazon, please leave us an honest review on this book's Amazon page. This is vital so that other potential readers can see and use your unbiased opinion to make purchasing decisions, we can understand what our customers think about our products, and our authors can see your feedback on the title that they have worked with Packt to create. It will only take a few minutes of your time, but is valuable to other potential customers, our authors, and Packt. Thank you!

Index